150 GREAT BOOKS

SYNOPSES, QUIZZES, & TESTS
FOR INDEPENDENT READING

BONNIE A. HELMS

J. Weston Walch, Publisher
Portland, Maine

2   3   4   5   6   7   8   9   10

ISBN 0–8251–0117–4

01-1635

Copyright 1986
J. Weston Walch, Publisher
P.O. Box 658 • Portland, Maine 04104-0658

Printed in the United States of America

Notes of Appreciation

To Deborah Locke for her help in suggesting titles and obtaining library materials.

To Margaret Hughes and Susan Julavits for assistance in field-testing sample pages with their classes.

To Maurice and Mary Jane Stone for their support, love and encouragement while this book was in process.

Contents

Letter indication before each title refers to the reading level: Easy, Medium, or Difficult. Answer keys for the tests in each section appear at the end of that section.

TO THE TEACHER *xi*

UNIT 1

Soldiers, Pirates, and Knights—Tales of Adventure and Survival

SYNOPSES   3-7

QUIZZES AND TESTS

E	*Born Free*	Joy Adamson	8
M	*The Red Badge of Courage*	Stephen Crane	10
M	*The African Queen*	C.S. Forester	12
D	*Green Dolphin Street*	Elizabeth Goudge	14
E	*The Call of the Wild*	Jack London	16
M	*Day of Infamy*	Walter Lord	18
E	*A Night to Remember*	Walter Lord	20
D	*Moby Dick*	Herman Melville	22
E	*Never Cry Wolf*	Farley Mowat	24
M	*All Quiet on the Western Front*	Erich Maria Remarque	26
D	*Rabble in Arms*	Kenneth Roberts	28
M	*Ivanhoe*	Sir Walter Scott	30
E	*Treasure Island*	Robert Louis Stevenson	32
D	*The Once and Future King*	T.H. White	34
M	*The Virginian*	Owen Wister	36
	ANSWER KEYS		39

UNIT 2

Coming of Age—The Maturation of Self

SYNOPSES   47-52

QUIZZES AND TESTS

M	*When the Legends Die*	Hal Borland	53
M	*Jane Eyre*	Charlotte Brontë	55
M	*Great Expectations*	Charles Dickens	57
E	*The Summer of My German Soldier*	Bette Greene	59
E	*Tex*	S.E. Hinton	61
D	*The Metamorphosis*	Franz Kafka	63
E	*A Separate Peace*	John Knowles	65
M	*Christy*	Catherine Marshall	67
M	*The Heart is a Lonely Hunter*	Carson McCullers	69
M	*The Member of the Wedding*	Carson McCullers	71
M	*The Chosen*	Chaim Potok	73
M	*The Catcher in the Rye*	J.D. Salinger	75
E	*Shane*	Jack Schaefer	77
E	*The Odd Couple*	Neil Simon	79
D	*Rabbit, Run*	John Updike	81
M	*Macho*	Edmund Villasenor	83
	ANSWER KEYS		85

UNIT 3

The Imagined Past—History in Fiction

SYNOPSES   95-100

QUIZZES AND TESTS

M	*Elizabeth the Queen*	Maxwell Anderson	101
M	*Becket*	Jean Anouilh	103
D	*A Tale of Two Cities*	Charles Dickens	105
E	*April Morning*	Howard Fast	107
M	*Cimarron*	Edna Ferber	109
M	*The Great Gatsby*	F. Scott Fitzgerald	111
E	*Johnny Tremain*	Esther Forbes	113
M	*The Lion in Winter*	James Goldman	115
D	*The House of the Seven Gables*	Nathaniel Hawthorne	117
D	*The Scarlet Letter*	Nathaniel Hawthorne	119
M	*The Country of the Pointed Firs*	Sarah Orne Jewett	121
D	*Doctor Zhivago*	Boris Pasternak	123
D	*The Winthrop Woman*	Anya Seton	125
D	*Exodus*	Leon Uris	127
E	*The Friendly Persuasion*	Jessamyn West	129
M	*The Caine Mutiny Court-Martial*	Herman Wouk	131
	ANSWER KEYS		133

UNIT 4

Other Worlds and Future Times—Tales of Fantasy and Science Fiction

SYNOPSES   143-146

QUIZZES AND TESTS

E	*The Fantastic Voyage*	Isaac Asimov	147
M	*Fahrenheit 451*	Ray Bradbury	149
E	*Harvey*	Mary Chase	151
M	*2001: A Space Odyssey*	Arthur C. Clarke	153
E	*Blithe Spirit*	Noel Coward	155
M	*Alas, Babylon*	Pat Frank	157
D	*Stranger in a Strange Land*	Robert Heinlein	159
E	*Lost Horizon*	James Hilton	161
M	*Brave New World*	Aldous Huxley	163
E	*The Lion, the Witch, and the Wardrobe*	C.S. Lewis	165
D	*A Canticle for Leibowitz*	Walter Miller	167
M	*The Hobbit*	J.R.R. Tolkien	169
	ANSWER KEYS		171

UNIT 5

In Search of Conscience—The Literature of Social Issues

SYNOPSES   179-184

QUIZZES AND TESTS

E	*To Sir With Love*	E.R. Braithwaite	185
M	*The Good Earth*	Pearl Buck	187
E	*The Chocolate War*	Robert Cormier	189
M	*I Am the Cheese*	Robert Cormier	191
E	*The Autobiography of Miss Jane Pittman*	Ernest J. Gaines	193
M	*Black Like Me*	John Howard Griffin	195
M	*A Raisin in the Sun*	Lorraine Hansbury	197
M	*The Little Foxes*	Lillian Hellman	199
E	*Inherit the Wind*	Jerome Lawrence and Robert E. Lee	201
M	*To Kill a Mockingbird*	Harper Lee	203
M	*Main Street*	Sinclair Lewis	205
M	*The Crucible*	Arthur Miller	207
E	*Animal Farm*	George Orwell	209
M	*Cry, the Beloved Country*	Alan Paton	211
M	*Twelve Angry Men*	Reginald Rose	213
M	*A Majority of One*	Leonard Spigelgass	215
E	*The Hiding Place*	Corrie Ten Boom	217
D	*Native Son*	Richard Wright	219
	ANSWER KEYS		221

UNIT 6

The Triumph of the Spirit—Overcoming Handicaps

SYNOPSES   233-239

QUIZZES AND TESTS

E	*Strong at the Broken Places*	Max Cleland	240
E	*I Heard the Owl Call My Name*	Margaret Craven	242
E	*Ice Castles*	Leonore Fleischer	244
M	*The Miracle Worker*	William Gibson	246
M	*I Never Promised You a Rose Garden*	Joanne Greenberg	248
M	*Ordinary People*	Judith Guest	250
M	*Death Be Not Proud*	John Gunther	252
M	*Susan's Story*	Susan Hampshire	254
E	*The Old Man and the Sea*	Ernest Hemingway	256
M	*Flowers for Algernon*	Daniel Keyes	258
M	*Eric*	Doris Lund	260
E	*Requiem for a Heavyweight*	Rod Serling	262
E	*One Day in the Life of Ivan Denisovich*	Alexander Solzhenitsyn	264
M	*Cannery Row*	John Steinbeck	266
E	*The Pearl*	John Steinbeck	268
E	*On Golden Pond*	Ernest Thompson	270
M	*The Other Side of the Mountain*	E.G. Valens	272
E	*The Bridge of San Luis Rey*	Thornton Wilder	274
M	*The Skin of Our Teeth*	Thornton Wilder	276
	ANSWER KEYS		279

UNIT 7

The Top of the Ladder—Stories of Professional Success and Achievement

SYNOPSES   291-298

QUIZZES AND TESTS

M	*Life and Death in a Coral Sea*	Jacques-Yves Cousteau	299
M	*Babe: the Legend Comes to Life*	Robert W. Creamer	301
M	*Citizen Tom Paine*	Howard Fast	303
E	*I Always Wanted to Be Somebody*	Althea Gibson	305
M	*All Creatures Great and Small*	James Herriot	307
M	*Teacher: Anne Sullivan Macy*	Helen Keller	309
M	*Joseph*	Joyce Landorf	311
M	*Auntie Mame*	Jerome Lawrence and Robert E. Lee	313
E	*The Contender*	Robert Lipsyte	315
D	*My Life*	Golda Meir	317
M	*Death of a Salesman*	Arthur Miller	319
M	*The Greatest Story Ever Told*	Fulton Oursler	321
E	*The Teahouse of the August Moon*	John Patrick	323
M	*The Paper Lion*	George Plimpton	325
D	*My Name is Asher Lev*	Chaim Potok	327
M	*The Camera Never Blinks*	Dan Rather with Mickey Herskowitz	329
E	*Go Up for Glory*	Bill Russell	331
E	*Anchorwoman*	Jessica Savitch	333
E	*Babe Didrikson: The World's Greatest Woman Athlete*	Gene Schoor	335
M	*Pygmalion*	George Bernard Shaw	337
E	*The Prime of Miss Jean Brodie*	Muriel Spark	339
M	*The Playboy of the Western World*	John M. Synge	341
D	*The House of Mirth*	Edith Wharton	343
	ANSWER KEYS		345

UNIT 8

Who Done It???—Tales of the Dark and Mysterious

SYNOPSES   357-360

QUIZZES AND TESTS

M	*The Innocents*	William Archibald	361
M	*The Chalk Garden*	Enid Bagnold	363
E	*Where Are the Children?*	Mary Higgins Clark	365
E	*And Then There Were None*	Agatha Christie	367
M	*The Mousetrap*	Agatha Christie	369
E	*Jamaica Inn*	Daphne Du Maurier	371
M	*Rebecca*	Daphne Du Maurier	373
M	*Angel Street (Gas Light)*	Patrick Hamilton	375
M	*Arsenic and Old Lace*	Joseph Kesselring	377
M	*Cloud of Witness*	Dorothy L. Sayers	379
E	*Nine Coaches Waiting*	Mary Stewart	381
	ANSWER KEYS		383

UNIT 9

Relived Memories—Childhood Remembered

SYNOPSES   391-394

QUIZZES AND TESTS

D	*A Death in the Family*	James Agee	395
M	*Little Women*	Louisa May Alcott	397
E	*I Know Why the Caged Bird Sings*	Maya Angelou	399
M	*My Antonia*	Willa Cather	401
E	*Cheaper by the Dozen*	Frank Gilbreth Jr. and Ernestine Gilbreth Carey	403
E	*Life With Father*	Howard Lindsay and Russel Crouse	405
D	*How Green Was My Valley*	Richard Llewellyn	407
M	*The Learning Tree*	Gordon Parks	409
E	*A Day No Pigs Would Die*	Robert Newton Peck	411
M	*Our Town*	Thornton Wilder	413
M	*The Glass Menagerie*	Tennessee Williams	415
M	*The Effect of Gamma Rays on Man-in-the-Moon Marigolds*	Paul Zindel	417
	ANSWER KEYS		419

UNIT 10

Moonlight and Roses—Tales of Love and Romance

SYNOPSES   427-429

QUIZZES AND TESTS

D	*Pride and Prejudice*	Jane Austen	430
D	*Wuthering Heights*	Emily Brontë	432
M	*Madame Bovary*	Gustave Flaubert	434
M	*The Peacock Spring*	Rumer Godden	436
D	*The Return of the Native*	Thomas Hardy	438
E	*Mistress of Mellyn*	Victoria Holt	440
E	*The Beloved Invader*	Eugenia Price	442
M	*Ethan Frome*	Edith Wharton	444
	ANSWER KEYS		447
	SUPPLEMENTAL BIBLIOGRAPHY		451

TO THE TEACHER

Reading good literature should open wide the windows of the world. A body of materials which will link the student in grades seven though twelve with the general experience of mankind is provided in **150 Great Books.** Contact with the plots, themes, and imagery of various authors will begin to launch the mind of the student into the currents of human motivation for people in all times and places. The young reader will become aware that the same great questions have provided themes for writers of all historical ages, as the soul of man has always reached out for answers. The meaning of life, the inevitability of death, the quest for faith, the spirit of adventure, and the process of maturation into adulthood were of concern to the ancient Egyptian as they are to the man of the space age. A book that is worth reading is a book which considers one or more of these great human universals. While reading, the student should find in the novel, biography, or drama a piece of his or her own experience, a mirror for the mind. In his essay, ''A Platform and a Passion or Two,'' the American dramatist Thornton Wilder said that reading literature assumes meaningful human dimensions only when the reader can say, ''This is the way things are. I have always known it without being fully aware that I knew it. Now in the presence of this play or novel or poem or picture or piece of music, I know that I know it.'' (*Adventures in American Literature,* Harcourt, Brace, Jovanovich, p. 744.)

This collection of **150 Great Books** is designed to motivate student exploration and is divided into ten units presenting experiences common to people in all times and societies. Particular works have been selected to provide as wide a scope of these experiences as possible. No single volume could include every writer whose work has great value. Many omitted selections would be as meaningful for the students as the chosen selections. In addition to tests on one hundred fifty titles, an additional bibliography of thirty-five titles appears at the end of the text. By beginning the reading program with the selections included, students can then go on, with the guidance of teacher and librarian, to explore in depth the subject areas which appeal to their individual reading tastes. All of the titles in this collection will not be suitable for all students, but something will interest each individual reader.

Each test in this volume contains three types of questions: (1) A set of objective questions will measure the student's understanding of the reading content. Has the reader grasped the basics of plot, characterization, and setting which the author has presented? (2) Five short-answer questions require more inferential responses. What are the larger ideas that the author wishes the reader to grasp? Answering these questions will also help to develop the student's writing skills, as the directions require the responses to be written in complete sentences. (3) The challenge essay requires a more mature level of thinking. The reader is asked to relate the material in a specific book to wider areas of thought. How is this book related to other books on the same subject? The first two sets of questions are basically factual. The challenge essay asks the student to express observations on the work that has been read, to support those observations with information gained from reading, and to link those observations with wider human experience.

Through the use of these challenge questions, the student may use the readings as raw material for learning the basics of expository writing forms. The books begin to answer one perpetual question that the beginning writer asks: ''What in the world do I write about?'' Reading the book should be only the beginning of the thinking and reacting process. More subjective writing assignments could also be based on the student's outside reading. As the students mentally put themselves into the protagonist's situation, they may begin to link these characters with their own experiences. Writing assignments would consider these links. How would they survive on a kibbutz in Palestine? Could they make a choice between love and political ambition? Would they have the courage to fight for emotional survival if crippled in a skiing accident, or suddenly told that someone close to them has inoperable cancer? When the students begin to ask some of these meaningful questions, real learning is beginning to take place. The titles in this collection have been chosen to provide some sparks for the beginning or continued growth of this reading, writing, and thinking experience.

If an entire class has read a particular title, the test in this collection may well be used for a closed-book evaluation. If the teacher does choose to use a particular test with the entire class, not all questions may be suitable for all students or groups of students. For example, in a heterogeneous classroom, the slower students might answer only the twenty objective questions. The more advanced students could exercise inferential reading skills by answering the short-answer and the essays. In an honors group or a writing class, the students might write only the challenge essay. The majority of these tests are designed to serve as open-book evaluations and to stimulate the student's independent reading program. Tests used in this manner may serve as alternatives to the more traditional book reports.

The table of contents of **150 Great Books** has been divided into ten topical units. To guide the student in selecting books within the appropriate interest and ability range, the titles have been graded with three different designations: (E) indicates easy-reading for students who may really be reluctant to read anything at all; (M) indicates medium or average-level titles which will present no problem for the student who is reading on grade level; (D) indicates longer or more difficult titles. These books provide the real challenge for the mature reader. Even though the reading may take more time and the student may consequently complete fewer titles, these (D) titles will be well worth the capable student's effort.

Many titles in this collection could fit into two or three different units. Sir Walter Scott's *Ivanhoe* is a tale of adventure and also a novel which reflects the historical and social realities of the Middle Ages. Charlotte Brontë's *Jane Eyre* chronicles a young woman's personal maturation, and also tells a wonderful love story. In seeking material on a particular subject, the student, teacher, and librarian should look through the collection's entire table of contents. The table of contents in **150 Great Books** may be reproduced to provide a bibliography for the student. Topical relationships not presented in these ten unit divisions may also emerge as the student reads and writes: How was the experience of being female different for Flaubert's Emma Bovary, for Lewis' Carol Kennicott, or for Golda Meir?

Each unit section of tests is followed by answer keys for the titles that appear in that section. Brief suggested answers are provided for the short-answer questions and the challenge essays. Teachers should allow the students some latitude in their short-answer and essay responses, since several possible answers may be equally correct. If the teacher questions a student's response, the teacher may require the student to prove his statement by reference to the book.

The most obvious uses for **150 Great Books** will be in the English or Language Arts classroom. A copy would also be a valuable reference tool in the school library. The test materials could be used for evaluation of outside readings in social studies classes. Students can learn much by comparing the fictional treatment of historical subject matter with the presentation given in the history text. Information which may seem rather dull on the textbook page comes to life in the hands of a skilled craftsman. The beginning of the American Revolution comes to life in the rapid maturation of Adam Cooper in Howard Fast's *April Morning*. Unit 3 of this test collection would be helpful in this area.

Since students and *parents* place such great importance on grades, methods of point evaluation must be developed for the use of these tests. These evaluation methods will vary widely. At the beginning of the year or of the semester, the teacher and the students may establish a point system for the evaluation of the outside reading. The student will receive points for the number of books that he reads and for the number of test questions that he answers correctly. More difficult books should have greater point value. Challenge-essay answers should also have more point value. At the end of the grading period, the number of reading and writing points received would be included as a portion of the student's total grade average. During the quarter, the student may place each finished piece of work in a folder, which the teacher will evaluate every two or three weeks. Conference time should also be provided when the student can discuss the readings with the teacher. The importance of this independent reading program will be greatly emphasized if class time is set aside for reading, and if the teacher reads with the students. The teacher must remain flexible and must fit both the reading procedure and the evaluation techniques to the individual or to the class.

An effective teacher becomes a salesperson who encourages the students to read. As each student moves beyond the limits of this particular collection of titles to read books by the same authors or books by other authors on the same subjects, native curiosity will take over. The student readers will launch out on their own. Minimum requirements may be necessary as the reading program is begun, for example two books per ranking period. However, when each student begins to exceed the minimum, then the learning experience really begins.

Each student brings two basic ingredients to a teacher's classroom: the native thinking equipment that the student possesses, and the student's personal experience, those lessons which his life has already taught him. The function of the teacher is twofold: to train and polish the mind by helping the student develop skills so he may become independent of his teacher, and to show the student how his personal experience relates to the experience of others. Great teachers feel most satisfied when their pupils reach the learning level where the teacher is no longer necessary. Anne Sullivan Macy taught Helen Keller so Helen could think and act on her own. Miss Jean Brodie, on the other hand, manipulated minds by filling her students' heads with her own ideas. Independent thinking became an act of betrayal.

An introduction to the philosophies of the world's great writers is the beginning of a student's mental independence. Educators are being very unfair to their students if the only books that the student ever reads are those titles assigned to a class, and if the only ideas that the student gains from the books are the thoughts which come from the teacher's lecture notes. Turn the student loose in the library. Provide a road map for growth, but don't try to build a fence around his or her mind. The individual must be free to question. Is this author right in his or her view of human nature? Does experience prove the themes of this book true?

World literature is a giant smorgasbord. Many different writing styles and conflicting philosophies will appeal to many varied student interests. Not everyone will appreciate everything that is offered, but many special treats await each one that can be motivated to sample the feast. The teacher and the student will gain a surface measure of the personal growth which comes from a varied independent reading program. As the student learns of the universal truths which are the common denominators of life, he matures in understanding himself and others. This mental growth moves the reader from narrow thinking, bigotry, and prejudice toward the understanding that other men, though very different from himself, may be equally and wonderfully human.

The teacher provides the spark for the growth process. To simply correct a student's test and give him a grade shows that the teacher is indifferent to the learning that really matters. An instructor must listen with an open mind as the student desires to share what he or she has learned. The question, "What have you been reading this week, Bill?" may be the beginning of a learning experience for the teacher also. A teacher will in turn be taught much by the students, and *150 Great Books* offers a beginning. May the titles included in this volume generate new excitement about reading for student and teacher alike.

UNIT 1

Soldiers, Pirates and Knights —
Tales of ADVENTURE and SURVIVAL

SYNOPSES

Born Free
by Joy Adamson

Can a lion cub raised as a pet survive when she is returned to the wild? While working as a game warden in central Kenya, George Adamson and his wife Joy rescue the cub, whose mother has been killed. The Adamsons then experience mixed joys and tribulations as the playful Elsa grows to adulthood. The lioness makes life exciting by knocking over furniture, frightening visitors, and causing herds of pack animals to stampede. However, the Adamsons know that Elsa must be returned to the free life for which she had been born. *Born Free* describes that return. The reader can feel Mrs. Adamson's personal conflict as she struggles between her emotional attachment for her pet and her knowledge that Elsa must be free to feed and mate as nature intended. Elsa's story will be a special treat for all animal lovers, especially students who have seen the film or the television series "Born Free."

The Red Badge of Courage
by Stephen Crane

This realistic American novel is a classic study of the feelings and behavior of men in combat. After Henry Fleming's romantic fantasies are shattered by the brutal wartime experiences of marching, endless waiting, and bone-chilling cold, the young recruit is haunted by one question: "Will I run?" The novel really has two settings: the outer landscape of the battle and the inner landscape of Henry's mind. Henry meets death in the persons of the "tattered man" and the "tall soldier," and eventually receives his own "red badge of courage." Cowardice becomes courage as Henry and his friend Wilson lead the troops and capture the flag. Henry finally passes to manhood. Although the novel is set during the American Civil War, the characters in *The Red Badge of Courage* could be any men in any conflict.

The African Queen
by C.S. Forester

Forester's tale is set in central Africa during World War I. Rose Sayer, an English missionary whose brother has just died, and Charlie Allnutt, a diamond-in-the-rough mining engineer, join forces in a supreme effort to navigate the Ulanga River on the aging river boat the *African Queen*. Rose and Allnutt escape enemy fire, run the river's rapids, become entangled in a morass of weeds, and attempt to blow up a German patrol boat. The real focus of the novel, however, is the love relationship which gradually develops between two people from totally different backgrounds. The bond between Rose and Charlie grows through shared experience. Forester's setting and characters come to life as the reader becomes involved in Rose and Charlie's struggles. Suspense, comedy, and romance make *The African Queen* excellent reading.

Green Dolphin Street
by Elizabeth Goudge

This is the epic nineteenth-century adventure of one man, William Ozanne, and the story of his relationship with two sisters, Marianne and Marguerite La Patourel. The story begins as William and his physician father return to the English Channel Islands in the 1830s. The adventure unfolds as William falls under the spells of both sisters: he admires Marianne's determined personality, but he loves Marguerite. After joining the British navy, William is drugged and robbed in Hong Kong. Finally arriving in New Zealand, William sends home for his bride. However, in his mental confusion, he sends for the wrong woman. Marianne's strength enables William to build an empire, but his heart belongs to Marguerite. Years of spine-tingling adventures follow as the characters survive shipwrecks, earthquakes, and native uprisings. This tale of a lifetime climaxes when Marianne learns William's secret and is finally reconciled with her sister. An exciting saga of pioneer settlement and personal survival, *Green Dolphin Street* makes excellent reading.

The Call of the Wild
by Jack London

The Call of the Wild is the tale of Buck the Husky, who is kidnapped from his soft life in sunny California and sold to become a sled dog. As he encounters the hardships of life during the Alaskan gold rush of the 1890s, Buck learns to adapt as he survives by his strength and his wits. He defeats all rivals and becomes the leader of his team. Buck's life changes again as the dog develops a special love for a special man. Buck is saved from drowning by John Thornton. The novel's developing conflict is between Buck's love for Thornton and the dog's desire to follow his wild nature and run with his wolf-brothers, to respond to "the call of the wild." Buck becomes "human" as Jack London gives his animal protagonist the ability to reason and to feel love and anger.

Day of Infamy
by Walter Lord

December 7, 1941, began as a quiet Sunday for American naval troops stationed at Pearl Harbor, Hawaii. But history was changed and the peace was shattered as Japanese bombers swooped down on the unprepared fleet. Walter H. Lord presents an hour-by-hour account of this attack, which caused America's entry into World War II. The events are seen from both sides. The author's thorough research has provided both Japanese and American viewpoints. Many ordinary people behaved very heroically. Cooks and bakers manned anti-aircraft guns. Military wives kept their children calm and tried to rescue precious family possessions. *Day of Infamy* would be useful in a social studies class because the author places history on a very human level.

A Night to Remember
by Walter Lord

A Night to Remember tells the story of the *Titanic.* The luxury ship of the White Star Line struck an iceberg and sank in the North Atlantic in April 1912. In describing the behavior of the *Titanic's* passengers and crew during the ship's final hours, the author presents both the noble and the base aspects of human behavior. One man disguised as a woman tried to jump into a departing lifeboat. Mr. and Mrs. Isidor Straus chose to go down with the ship rather than to be parted after sixty years of marriage. The book places the reader on the scene of the significant maritime catastrophe which helped to change forever the safety regulations for passenger shipping.

Moby Dick
by Herman Melville

This is the American classic of nineteenth-century whaling. The novel's narrator is Ishmael, a common seaman on the *Pequod.* The protagonist is the mad Captain Ahab, who will sacrifice his ship and his crew to get revenge on Moby Dick, the white whale which took off Ahab's leg. The plot climaxes in a three-day chase in which man is pitted against the brute force of nature. Melville's novel also profoundly questions man's place in the universe. Does life have sense and meaning, or is there only the endless rolling of the ever-present sea? *Moby Dick* pictures the world of whaling and asks stirring questions about the ultimate meaning of life.

Never Cry Wolf
by Farley Mowat

Never Cry Wolf is the humorous account of a scientist employed by the Canadian government to conduct Project Lupine—a study of wolves. Camping in the Yukon, Mowat becomes involved in the lives of his animal subjects, whom he names George, Evangeline, and Uncle Albert. After studying the wolves' living and hunting habits, Mowat concludes that man, not the wolf, is the greatest danger to the northland's environment. The wolves often display far more common sense than do the men who hunt them. Mowat is never sure if he is observing the wolves or if the wolves are observing him. *Never Cry Wolf* is based on the author's firsthand observations and provides a very different view of animals which were thought to be vicious and destructive.

All Quiet on the Western Front
by Erich Maria Remarque

All Quiet on the Western Front chronicles the experiences of young German soldiers caught in the hell of World War I. This novel could well be compared with *The Red Badge of Courage*. Remarque's use of detail is very realistic as he describes Paul, a poetic young recruit who must struggle to survive in the trenches. A moment of comic relief is provided when Paul and his comrades are the sole conquerors of a small village. Paul is forced to face himself; the face of a man that he kills becomes Paul's own face. The Russian prisoners become reflections of the young Germans themselves. The hero is everyman, the young soldier who experiences combat and will never be the same again.

Rabble in Arms
by Kenneth Roberts

Peter Merrill and his brother Nathaniel leave their farm in Arundel, Maine in 1775 to follow General Benedict Arnold on a march against the British occupying forces in Canada. The men's worst enemies become heat, disease, lack of supplies and poor leadership. However, the men respect Arnold so much they will follow the general anywhere. This rabble army manages to build a fleet on Lake Champlain and ultimately defeat the British at the Battle of Saratoga. Against the backdrop of battle, Peter falls in love with Ellen Phipps. The novel has its comic moments when Peter and his men, disguised as Indians, slip through the British lines to rejoin the American troops. *Rabble in Arms* would make excellent related reading for a history class studying the American Revolution.

Ivanhoe
by Sir Walter Scott

Medieval England is presented in a glorious romance of fair ladies and bold knights. The native Saxons have been subjugated by Prince John and his evil Norman nobility—Front-de-Boeuf, de Bracey, and Brian de Bois-Guilbert. Ivanhoe, the young Saxon who has been disinherited by his father Cedric, must return to lead the Saxon cause and to reclaim his lady Rowena. Ivanhoe is injured in a tournament and is nursed by the beautiful Jewess Rebecca, daughter of Isaac of York. Evil seems to have triumphed when the Saxon nobles and the wounded Ivanhoe are imprisoned in Torquilstone Castle. After the forces of evil are defeated by the mysterious Black Knight, Ivanhoe acts as Rebecca's champion and saves her from the charge of witchcraft. *Ivanhoe* is a well-written tale of chivalric romance. Reading this novel may interest the student in one of Scott's many other tales of the Middle Ages.

Treasure Island
by Robert Louis Stevenson

Treasure Island is the adventure of young Jim Hawkins. Having discovered a map indicating the location of Captain Flint's buried treasure, Jim and his friends Dr. Livesey and Squire Trelawney set off to find the island. Captured by pirate Long John Silver and Silver's mutinous crew, Jim and his friends are finally led to the treasure by Ben Gunn, a strange man who had been abandoned on the island by Flint's crew. Stevenson's colorful characters and fast-moving plot make *Treasure Island* a classic to be enjoyed.

The Once and Future King
by T.H. White

The Once and Future King is the modern retelling of the medieval King Arthur legends. Young Arthur is tutored by Merlin, who educates the lad by transforming him into various animals. Finding his destiny, Arthur marries the beautiful Guinevere and establishes the Round Table, where might will be used for right. After Arthur has unified his kingdom, the greatest danger to the ideals of chivalry comes when Queen Guinevere falls in love with Lancelot, the bravest of Arthur's knights. Their love is discovered by Modred, Arthur's illegitimate son who seeks to destroy everything that Arthur has built. Numerous subplots enrich the story and bring the Middle Ages to life in a brilliant mixture of myth and mystery. Students reading *The Once and Future King* may wish to compare the book with the musical *Camelot*.

The Virginian
by Owen Wister

The Virginian is a cowboy adventure of the nineteenth-century American West. The narrator is an eastern "tenderfoot" who has come west to Judge Henry's ranch to hunt. He meets an exceptional cowboy gentleman, known only as "The Virginian." Love enters the Virginian's life in the person of Miss Molly Stark Wood, the new school teacher from Bennington, Vermont. The Virginian must also prove himself worthy of the Judge's confidence by defeating his adversary, Trampas, and by breaking up a rustling ring. Molly and the Virginian face a crisis in their relationship: she must learn to understand the unwritten legal code of the range, and he must come to terms with the death of his friend Steve. The hero and the villain then meet in a final confrontation. Owen Wister has presented a portrait of the men whose moral backbone and refusal to compromise helped to build the American West.

NAME _____ DATE _____

Born Free by Joy Adamson

Place a (+) before each statement that is true and a (0) before each statement that is false.

_____ 1. Elsa's mother was killed by another lion.

_____ 2. Part of George Adamson's job was to protect the wild animals of Kenya from poachers.

_____ 3. Elsa was the largest and strongest of the three lion cubs that the Adamsons found.

_____ 4. Elsa's two sisters were sold to a European zoo.

_____ 5. On the safari to Lake Rudolphe, Elsa and the donkeys got along very peacefully.

_____ 6. Elsa loved the water and was an excellent swimmer.

_____ 7. Elsa was the only wild animal that the Adamsons ever domesticated as a pet.

_____ 8. Elephants posed the greatest single danger to Elsa when she was a cub.

_____ 9. When the group went on safari into the mountains, Elsa adapted well to the colder climate.

_____ 10. Whenever she was nervous or upset, Elsa would lick Mrs. Adamson's hands.

_____ 11. When the Adamsons released her for the first time, Elsa was able to adapt easily to life in the wilds.

_____ 12. Whenever she traveled with the Adamsons, Elsa usually rode on top of their truck.

_____ 13. When Mrs. Adamson returned to Kenya from England, Elsa did not recognize her.

_____ 14. The Adamsons left Elsa alone in the wilds when they were satisfied that she could kill to feed herself.

_____ 15. Elsa liked to have her picture taken.

_____ 16. Elsa was the first lion raised in captivity who ever survived a return to the wilds.

_____ 17. Elsa was generally more friendly toward the African natives than she was toward Europeans.

_____ 18. When George went to visit Elsa, he knew that the lion was coming by the noise that the birds made.

_____ 19. Elsa's return to the wild was complete when she gave birth to cubs.

_____ 20. When the book was written, Elsa had been living in the wilds for three years.

NAME _____ DATE _____

Born Free by Joy Adamson

Answer each of the following questions in two or three complete sentences.

1. Under what circumstances did the Adamsons adopt the three lion cubs?

_____

_____

_____

_____

2. How did Elsa's size and weight become a problem for her human family?

_____

_____

_____

_____

3. Why were the African natives so afraid of the lions?

_____

_____

_____

_____

4. Why did the first attempt to release Elsa fail?

_____

_____

_____

_____

5. What conflicting emotions did Joy Adamson experience as she and George tried to teach Elsa to live free?

_____

_____

_____

_____

CHALLENGE

Describe the conflict that Elsa faced between her affection for her human "family" and her own instincts as a wild lion.

150 Great Books

NAME _____ DATE _____

The Red Badge of Courage by Stephen Crane

Correctly complete each sentence with information from the novel.

1. The nickname given to Jim Conklin is _____.

2. Henry Fleming enlisted in the army because _____.

3. Most of Henry's ideas about war came from _____.

4. During the first weeks, the regiment's military maneuvers consisted mainly of ___

   _____.

5. During his first battle, Henry _____.

6. Internal plot means that much of the story's action takes place _____.

7. Before the battle, Wilson gives Henry _____.

8. When Crane calls war "the great blood-swollen god," he is using a figure of speech

   called _____.

9. After he is helped back to his regiment, Henry is cared for by _____.

10. The death of _____ is Henry's first real encounter with the
    brutality of war.

11. The tattered man kept asking Henry, "_____?"

12. The colors of Nature in the novel are _____.

13. "The side looked as if it had been chewed by wolves," describes _____.

14. The generals refer to Henry's regiment as _____.

15. Henry is wounded when _____.

16. The phrase "a red badge of courage" means _____.

17. When Henry's regiment charges the enemy, the men fail because _____.

18. Henry and Wilson become heroes in the second battle when _____.

19. The capture of the enemy flag represents _____.

20. When the battle is over, Henry's feelings may be described as _____.

   _____.

NAME _____ DATE _____

The Red Badge of Courage by Stephen Crane

Answer each of the following questions in two or three sentences.

1. How does the actual battle differ from the ideas that Henry had about fighting?

    _____

    _____

    _____

    _____

2. What question does Henry keep asking himself?

    _____

    _____

    _____

    _____

3. Why does Crane use names like, "the youth, the loud soldier, and the tall soldier?"

    _____

    _____

    _____

    _____

4. What does this novel have to say about the effect of combat on fighting men?

    _____

    _____

    _____

    _____

CHALLENGE
What does *The Red Badge of Courage* show about the importance of human brotherhood?

NAME _____ DATE _____

The African Queen by C.S. Forester

Correctly complete each sentence with information from the novel.

1. Allnutt had worked for _____.

2. Rose leaves the mission after the death of _____.

3. The German commander for central Africa was _____.

4. Rose's job on the *African Queen* is mainly _____.

5. Rose gets rid of Allnutt's liquor by _____.

6. The *African Queen* is in greatest danger from the Germans when she passes _____

    _____.

7. The river they navigate is named the _____.

8. The most exciting part of their journey was _____.

9. Rose and Allnutt constantly had to go on shore for supplies of _____.

10. Allnutt's biggest accomplishment was being able to repair _____.

11. Rose wanted to blow up the German ship because _____.

12. The most difficult part of the journey was pulling the boat through _____.

13. Both Rose and Allnutt became ill with _____.

14. They first saw the *Konigen Luise* when the ship _____.

15. Allnutt made the torpedoes from _____.

16. Instead of hanging Allnutt and Rose, the Germans _____.

17. The *African Queen's* attack fails when _____.

18. The *Konigen Luise* is destroyed by _____.

19. The English commander intends to send Rose _____.

20. At the end of the novel, Rose and Allnutt _____.

NAME _____ DATE _____

The African Queen by C.S. Forester

Answer the following questions in two or three complete sentences.

1. How had the arrival of the Germans destroyed the work at the mission?

   _____

   _____

   _____

   _____

2. How does Rose come to life as she begins the voyage on the *African Queen?*

   _____

   _____

   _____

3. Why does Allnutt follow Rose's leadership so willingly?

   _____

   _____

   _____

   _____

4. For what two reasons is Rose so determined to complete the voyage down the river?

   _____

   _____

   _____

5. Why is the trip below the rapids so much more difficult than the run through the rapids?

   _____

   _____

   _____

   _____

CHALLENGE

Write an essay describing the character development of Rose Sayer. How does her experience on the river totally change her personality?

150 Great Books

NAME _____ DATE _____

Green Dolphin Street by Elizabeth Goudge

Select the letter of the word or phrase which correctly completes each statement.

_____ 1. The story opens (A) on Marguerite's birthday (B) on Sophie's wedding day (C) on the day William and his father arrive on the island (D) on the day of the military review.

_____ 2. Edmond Ozanne (A) is a doctor (B) works mainly among the poor (C) was once in love with Sophie (D) all of the above.

_____ 3. The money for William's navy career came from (A) the government (B) his mother (C) his father (D) Octavius.

_____ 4. As a child, Marianne's characteristics included all of the following except: (A) determination (B) sewing skill (C) submissiveness (D) intelligence.

_____ 5. Marguerite first visits the convent on the rocks (A) to make a contribution to charity (B) to seek spiritual advice (C) to escape from the rising tide (D) to tour the old buildings.

_____ 6. William's talk with Marguerite on the *Orion* is interrupted by (A) Marguerite's father (B) Marianne's meddling (C) news of William's father's death (D) news of war.

_____ 7. William gets separated from his ship (A) in Shanghai (B) in Hong Kong (C) in Australia (D) in Liverpool.

_____ 8. William's first wealth in New Zealand comes from (A) sheep (B) lumber (C) coal (D) furs.

_____ 9. William asks for the wrong bride because (A) he has been drinking (B) he is interrupted while he is writing (C) he feels obligated to Marianne for her help (D) he cannot remember which girl he loves.

_____ 10. The time span between William's departure from England and his sending for a wife is about (A) ten years (B) five years (C) two years (D) six months.

_____ 11. Tai Haruru was (A) William's partner (B) an Englishman who had lived with the natives (C) Timothy Haslam (D) all of the above.

_____ 12. When the *Green Dolphin* was wrecked, all were saved except (A) Nat (B) Old Nick (C) Captain O'Hara (D) the first mate.

_____ 13. The Ozannes made money in all of the following except (A) lumber (B) sheep herding (C) railroading (D) gold mining.

_____ 14. The strongest link between Marguerite and William was (A) the letter (B) Veronique (C) the necklace (D) the small wooden mouse.

_____ 15. The Ozannes escape being murdered by (A) the arrival of the British soldiers (B) disguising themselves as natives (C) the rescue attempts of Kelley (D) the arrival of the *Green Dolphin*.

_____ 16. Marguerite returns to the island when (A) her father dies (B) her mother dies (C) she becomes Superior of the convent (D) she first takes her vows as a nun.

_____ 17. The best example of total unselfishness is provided by (A) Samuel and Suzanna Kelley (B) Veronique (C) John Ogilvie (D) William.

_____ 18. Marianne finds out the truth about William's feelings for Marguerite (A) at the convent (B) on the sheep ranch (C) on the *Green Dolphin* (D) after their return to the island.

_____ 19. Marianne's feelings for William throughout the entire story may best be described as (A) love (B) pity (C) adoration (D) possessiveness.

_____ 20. The novel's plot spans about (A) fifteen years (B) twenty years (C) thirty years (D) fifty years.

NAME _____ DATE _____

Green Dolphin Street by Elizabeth Goudge

Answer each of the following questions in two or three complete sentences.

1. How does Marianne's visit to the *Green Dolphin* when she is a girl completely change her life?

   _____

   _____

   _____

   _____

2. Under what circumstances does William first arrive in New Zealand?

   _____

   _____

   _____

3. How does Marguerite show great strength after William's marriage to Marianne?

   _____

   _____

   _____

   _____

4. In what ways is Veronique more like her father than she is like her mother?

   _____

   _____

   _____

5. How are Marguerite and Marianne finally reconciled?

   _____

   _____

   _____

   _____

CHALLENGE

Throughout the entire novel, Marianne shows great stubbornness and determination. Write an essay describing how this attitude is both an asset and a liability. How does this determination help her to survive? How does this attitude also become a source of pain, both to herself and to others?

NAME _____ DATE _____

The Call of the Wild by Jack London

Place a (+) before each statement that is true and a (0) before each statement that is false.

_____ 1. Buck was part St. Bernard and part Alaskan Husky.

_____ 2. Buck was stolen from his owner and sent north to be a sled dog.

_____ 3. The man with the red sweater taught Buck how to pull evenly in the sled harness.

_____ 4. Perrault and Francois carried mail and documents for the Canadian government.

_____ 5. Buck had to battle Dave to establish his leadership in the team.

_____ 6. Sol-leks was a dog who was blind in one eye.

_____ 7. Perrault and Francois abused their sled dogs.

_____ 8. The sled dogs were fed a diet of basically fish.

_____ 9. Hal and Charles were very experienced in the handling of dog teams.

_____ 10. Buck and his mates were sold cheaply because all the dogs were exhausted from too much work and too little rest.

_____ 11. Dave was shot by his owners because he refused to stay in harness.

_____ 12. Charles and Hal died with their team when the sled fell through the ice.

_____ 13. Buck was the only dog of the original team who survived.

_____ 14. Buck loved John Thornton in the same way that he had loved the Judge in California.

_____ 15. Buck saved Thornton's life twice.

_____ 16. Thornton won his bet that Buck could pull a sled loaded with five hundred pounds of flour.

_____ 17. Buck expressed his love for Thornton by nuzzling Thornton's neck.

_____ 18. Buck began to respond more and more to the call of his own primitive nature.

_____ 19. Thornton and his partners were killed by other miners who wanted to steal their claim.

_____ 20. Buck never returned to the spot where Thornton had died.

NAME _____ DATE _____

The Call of the Wild by Jack London

Answer each of the following questions in two or three complete sentences.

1. How did Buck's treatment on the ranch contrast with the treatment that he received from his new masters?

    _____

    _____

    _____

    _____

2. In what ways did Buck adapt quickly to his new life?

    _____

    _____

    _____

3. How did Buck finally win the leadership of the team?

    _____

    _____

    _____

    _____

4. In what ways did Buck show his love for Thornton?

    _____

    _____

    _____

    _____

5. Why did Buck totally revert to the wildness of his ancestry?

    _____

    _____

    _____

    _____

CHALLENGE

Write an essay describing how Jack London uses personification, giving human characteristics to an animal, in developing the character of Buck.

NAME _____ DATE _____

Day of Infamy by Walter Lord

Place a (+) before each statement that is true and a (0) before each statement that is false.

_____ 1. All of the Pacific Fleet's battleships were in port when the Japanese attack came.

_____ 2. The Japanese attackers were helped by many Japanese residents of Hawaii.

_____ 3. When the Japanese fleet left port, every man on board knew where the ships were headed.

_____ 4. Sunday was selected for the attack because military alertness was greatly relaxed on weekends.

_____ 5. Pearl's wide-open harbor made the use of torpedoes easy.

_____ 6. The author chronicles the heroism of both the American and Japanese fighting forces.

_____ 7. The most total loss was the *Arizona*, on which one thousand men were killed instantly.

_____ 8. After the first wave of Japanese bombers hit, the United States planes were able to retaliate quickly.

_____ 9. After the attack itself, the greatest single danger was from fire and fuel explosions.

_____ 10. All military personnel were on or near their ships when the attack came.

_____ 11. The Japanese mini-subs were the least effective phase of the attack.

_____ 12. Admiral Nugumo decided to regroup his forces for a second wave of attacks.

_____ 13. The response of the people of Pearl Harbor during and after the attack showed a typical mixture of the good and bad in human nature.

_____ 14. Many military wives did not know for a day or two if their husbands were dead or alive.

_____ 15. Only military personnel were injured by the Japanese attackers.

_____ 16. Very few service men at Pearl Harbor had their families with them.

_____ 17. After the attack, news and communication were clear and accurate.

_____ 18. The nearby army and air force installations were unharmed by the Japanese assault.

_____ 19. Public opinion in the United States favored immediate retaliation against Japan.

_____ 20. Lack of preparedness was a clearly contributing factor in the effectiveness of the surprise attack.

NAME _____ DATE _____

Day of Infamy by Walter Lord

Answer each of the following in two or three complete sentences.

1. How were the weekend activities around Pearl Harbor on December 6, 1941 typical of the average military base?

   _____

   _____

   _____

   _____

2. What advance reconnaissance had been done by the Japanese intelligence?

   _____

   _____

   _____

   _____

3. What is meant by "fifth column espionage"? Why was this so feared?

   _____

   _____

   _____

   _____

4. How did many of the military dependents show great courage?

   _____

   _____

   _____

   _____

5. Why did the Japanese decide to withdraw?

   _____

   _____

   _____

   _____

CHALLENGE

Write an essay describing some of the ways that ordinary people showed extraordinary courage during the assault on Pearl Harbor.

NAME _____ DATE _____

A Night to Remember by Walter Lord

Place a (+) before each statement that is true and a (0) before each statement that is false.

_____ 1. The *Titanic* sank as she crossed the Atlantic for the second time.

_____ 2. The ship belonged to the White Star Line.

_____ 3. The *Titanic* was able to stay afloat for three days after she was struck by the iceberg.

_____ 4. Many wealthy society people were on the *Titanic*'s passenger list.

_____ 5. The iceberg struck directly on the bow of the ship.

_____ 6. Immediately after the ship was damaged, the captain ordered that all of the engines be turned off.

_____ 7. When the accident occurred, the *Carpathia* was about ten miles away from the *Titanic*.

_____ 8. The builder of the *Titanic* said that the ship could stay afloat even if six of her ten compartments were flooded.

_____ 9. On the day that the ship left England, lifeboat drills had been conducted for passengers on all levels.

_____ 10. Most of the *Titanic*'s cargo was saved.

_____ 11. The majority of the surviving passengers were from First Class.

_____ 12. Mrs. John Jacob Astor chose to remain with her husband and to go down with the ship.

_____ 13. All of the *Titanic*'s lifeboats were full to capacity when they were lowered into the water.

_____ 14. The investigations of the accident heard equal testimony from all of the people involved.

_____ 15. The passengers and crew of the *Carpathia* gave a great deal of help to the *Titanic*'s survivors.

_____ 16. Many confusing and contradictory accounts were given of the events surrounding the sinking.

_____ 17. The *Titanic* disaster brought about very important legislation for standards of maritime safety.

_____ 18. All of the survivors were very willing to discuss with the press the experiences of the disaster.

_____ 19. The *Californian* played an important role in the rescue operations.

_____ 20. The *Titanic* had enough lifeboats for about half of her passengers and crew.

NAME _____ DATE _____

A Night to Remember by Walter Lord

Answer each of the following questions in two or three complete sentences.

1. What kinds of special treatment did the First Class passengers receive during the evacuation operations?

    _____

    _____

    _____

    _____

2. How were Mr. and Mrs. Isidor Straus a special example of love and loyalty?

    _____

    _____

    _____

3. What permanent changes in standards of ocean travel resulted from the *Titanic* disaster?

    _____

    _____

    _____

    _____

4. How did Captain Smith show himself to be a good leader of men?

    _____

    _____

    _____

5. What warnings had the *Titanic* received which, if heeded, might have prevented the disaster?

    _____

    _____

    _____

    _____

CHALLENGE

Write an essay describing how the *Titanic* disaster showed both the nobility and the meanness of human nature. Give two examples of those whose actions showed nobility, and two examples of those who acted very selfishly.

150 Great Books

NAME _____ DATE _____

Moby Dick by Herman Melville

Select the letter of the word or phrase that correctly answers each statement.

_____ 1. The narrator of the novel is (A) an ordinary sailor (B) Ahab (C) the first mate (D) a third-person observer.

_____ 2. Ishmael comes to New Bedford (A) on business (B) because he intends to go to sea (C) to purchase household supplies (D) because he needs work.

_____ 3. The mood of *Moby Dick* may be best described as (A) optimistic (B) comic (C) gloomy and grim (D) light-hearted and adventurous.

_____ 4. Ishmael shares his lodgings at the Spouter Inn with (A) Peter Coffin (B) Starbuck (C) Queequeg (D) Father Mapple.

_____ 5. Before they leave on the whaling voyage, all of the sailors (A) buy supplies (B) go to church (C) get drunk (D) send letters to their families.

_____ 6. The preacher selects his text from (A) the book of Jonah (B) the account of St. Paul's shipwreck (C) the Sermon on the Mount (D) the story of Noah.

_____ 7. Queequeg (A) was a harpooner (B) collected shrunken heads (C) was tattooed all over (D) all of the above.

_____ 8. Elijah warns Ishmael (A) not to go to sea (B) not to sail on the *Pequod* (C) that whaling can be dangerous (D) that he may die.

_____ 9. Ahab is chasing Moby Dick (A) for revenge (B) because whale oil brings a high price (C) because Ahab likes excitement (D) because Ahab has made a bet with another sea captain.

_____ 10. Melville compares Ahab to (A) Christ (B) a man struck by lightning (C) a man burned at the stake (D) all of the above.

_____ 11. The second mate of the *Pequod* was (A) Ishmael (B) Starbuck (C) Stubb (D) Evans.

_____ 12. Who built his own coffin? (A) Queequeg (B) Ishmael (C) Ishtago (D) Ahab.

_____ 13. Who was the only survivor of the voyage? (A) Queequeg (B) Ishmael (C) Starbuck (D) Stubb.

_____ 14. Who died when he was strangled by a harpoon line? (A) Stubb (B) Starbuck (C) Ishmael (D) Ahab.

_____ 15. The man who tried to get Ahab to change his mind about chasing Moby Dick was (A) Elijah (B) Father Mapple (C) Starbuck (D) Stubb.

NAME _____ DATE _____

Moby Dick by Herman Melville

Answer each of the following questions in two or three complete sentences.

1. How does Ahab offer to reward his men for sighting Moby Dick?

   _____

   _____

   _____

   _____

2. Describe the way that the men chase the whale.

   _____

   _____

   _____

   _____

3. How is the *Pequod* destroyed?

   _____

   _____

   _____

   _____

4. How is Ishmael saved from death?

   _____

   _____

   _____

   _____

5. What is the symbolism of the sea in *Moby Dick*?

   _____

   _____

   _____

   _____

CHALLENGE

One critic has called Melville, "a man with grim November in his soul." Explain how you feel that *Moby Dick* proves or disproves this evaluation.

NAME _____ DATE _____

Never Cry Wolf by Farley Mowat

Correctly complete each sentence with information from the novel.

1. Mowat was employed by the _____.

2. His study was officially named _____.

3. Mowat named the area where he lived and worked _____.

4. The total time that Mowat lived in the tundra region was _____.

5. The cabin that became Mowat's headquarters was owned by a young man named

    _____.

6. The only radio contact that Mowat had with the outside world was with a man in

    _____.

7. The Eskimo who helped Mowat understand the wolves' language was named

    _____.

8. The married pair of wolves Mowat named _____ and _____.

9. The third adult wolf in the den Mowat named _____.

10. Wolves help to keep the caribou herds strong by _____.

11. The usual food supply of the wolves consisted of _____ and _____.

12. The male wolves spent most of their nights _____.

13. One of Mowat's wolves was mated with _____.

14. The author believes that wolves kill only _____.

15. The mother wolf supplied food to her cubs by _____.

16. In addition to studying the wolves, Mowat was also supposed to _____.

17. Most arctic wolves are slaughtered by _____ or _____.

18. Most caribou slaughter that had been blamed on the wolves was really done by

    _____.

19. The only caribou stampede that Mowat ever saw was begun by _____.

20. Mowat concludes that the real enemy to the natural balance of the subarctic regions is

    _____.

NAME _____ DATE _____

Never Cry Wolf by Farley Mowat

Answer each of the following questions in two or three complete sentences.

1. What incorrect ideas, according to Mowat, do most men have about wolves?

    _____

    _____

    _____

    _____

2. What was the family structure of the wolves that Mowat observed?

    _____

    _____

    _____

    _____

3. Why did the hunting practices of the wolves make more sense than the hunting practices of men?

    _____

    _____

    _____

    _____

4. In what ways does Mowat personify the wolves as he writes about them?

    _____

    _____

    _____

    _____

5. What frightening experience did Mowat have when he tried to enter the wolves' den to take measurements?

    _____

    _____

    _____

    _____

CHALLENGE

Discuss the ways that Farley Mowat's conclusions about the lifestyle and nature of the subarctic wolves differ from the commonly accepted opinions about these animals.

NAME _____ DATE _____

All Quiet on the Western Front by Erich Maria Remarque

Place a (+) before each statement that is true and a (0) before each statement that is false.

_____ 1. The characters in the novel are French soldiers.

_____ 2. Flashbacks are used to narrate episodes in Paul's childhood and school days.

_____ 3. When Muller knows that Kemmerich is dying, Muller most wants Kemmerich's helmet and gun.

_____ 4. Katczinsky has a wonderful ability to find food for his friends.

_____ 5. Himmelstoss was a captain who abused the recruits.

_____ 6. Most of the central characters in the novel are career soldiers who are thirty or forty years of age.

_____ 7. Paul had wanted to be a poet before he joined the army.

_____ 8. The men are taken to the front at night in trucks to dig trenches.

_____ 9. After his visit home, Paul feels that he is better able to handle the experience of combat.

_____ 10. To these men, the most important objective becomes simply staying alive.

_____ 11. The men find that the English prisoners that they are asked to guard are men exactly like themselves.

_____ 12. Paul has his leg amputated when he is wounded.

_____ 13. The man that Paul kills in the trench is a mirror image of Paul himself.

_____ 14. The novel takes place during World War II.

_____ 15. At the end of the novel, the hero returns home safely.

_____ 16. There are no comic moments in the story.

_____ 17. Albert and Paul return to the front together after their stay in the hospital.

_____ 18. Paul feels that he will be able to readjust easily to civilian life.

_____ 19. Paul and his mother are not able to communicate easily.

_____ 20. Gas is a greater danger to the soldiers than bullets are.

NAME _____ DATE _____

All Quiet on the Western Front by Erich Maria Remarque

Answer each of the following questions in two or three complete sentences.

1. How did the men find the glory of warfare that had been presented to them by the teacher Kantork very different from the realities of combat?

    _____

    _____

    _____

    _____

2. How do these soldiers show that they have great skill in the art of survival?

    _____

    _____

    _____

    _____

3. Why does the account of their occupation of the village provide a comic interlude in the account of battle?

    _____

    _____

    _____

    _____

4. How does Paul's trip home show the young soldier how much he has changed?

    _____

    _____

    _____

    _____

5. Why is Kat's death the most difficult of all for Paul?

    _____

    _____

    _____

    _____

CHALLENGE

How does *All Quiet on the Western Front* illustrate the spirit of brotherhood which is created when men share the tense experiences of combat?

150 Great Books

NAME _____ DATE _____

Rabble in Arms by Kenneth Roberts

In the numbered blanks at the left, write the letter of the matching person or place.

_____ 1. Traveled under an assumed name from England with Peter and Nathaniel

_____ 2. Where Peter was captured by the Indians

_____ 3. Ellen's brother, Indian scout for the American army

_____ 4. Native of Arundel who became a British spy under an assumed French name

_____ 5. Was killed by the American sentries when the captured men attempted to return to their own lines

_____ 6. Hid in his headquarters while the battle was going on

_____ 7. Narrator of the novel

_____ 8. Innocent girl who was brutally massacred by the Indians

_____ 9. Deathpit of smallpox and fever for the retreating American army

_____ 10. Seaport home of Peter and Nathaniel

_____ 11. Had traveled as a scout on Arnold's first expedition to Quebec

_____ 12. Disloyal aide to Arnold, later became aide to General Gates

_____ 13. Where Arnold's fleet was built

_____ 14. Became an "adopted" Indian medicine man

_____ 15. Stayed in the British camp because he believed that the Americans were going to lose the war

_____ 16. General who led the evacuation of Ticonderoga

_____ 17. Loud, bragging, homespun soldier

_____ 18. Was refused promotion, and was finally removed from his command

_____ 19. Innocent courier used to carry information to the British in Canada

_____ 20. Commander of the British forces at the Battle of Saratoga

A. Marie de Sabrevois
B. Steven Nason
C. Isle aux Noix
D. Doc Means
E. Wilkinson
F. Verrieul
G. Valcour Island
H. Burgoyne
I. Ellen Phipps
J. Peter Merrill
K. Benedict Arnold
L. Lanaudiere
M. Nathaniel Merrill
N. Arundel
O. Cap Huff
P. General Gates
Q. Jennie McCrae
R. Skenesboro
S. St. Clair
T. Joseph

NAME _____ DATE _____

Rabble in Arms by Kenneth Roberts

Answer each of the following questions in two or three complete sentences.

1. What specific events prove to Peter that Marie de Sabrevois is a spy?

_____

_____

_____

_____

2. How did Benedict Arnold show himself to be a superior general?

_____

_____

_____

_____

3. How did Peter manage to return to the American lines after he had been captured by the Indians?

_____

_____

_____

_____

4. How did the members of the Continental Congress harm the efforts of the army to defeat the British?

_____

_____

_____

_____

5. What actions of Peter's show him to be stronger and more mature than his brother Nathaniel?

_____

_____

_____

_____

CHALLENGE

Write an essay describing some of the hardships encountered by Peter Merrill and his friends as they fought for America's freedom. How does author Kenneth Roberts realistically describe these hardships?

NAME _____ DATE _____

Ivanhoe by Sir Walter Scott

In the numbered blanks at the left, write the letter of the matching person or place.

_____ 1. Demanded a champion to fight for her life

_____ 2. Home of Cedric, the Saxon

_____ 3. Churchman more interested in good food and horses than in God

_____ 4. Promoted a marriage between Rowena and Athelstane to restore Saxon power to England

_____ 5. Castle where Cedric and Rowena were held prisoner

_____ 6. Skilled archer who dressed in green

_____ 7. King Richard of England

_____ 8. Chief counselor to Prince John

_____ 9. Jester who risked his life to save his master

_____ 10. Named as "Queen of Love and Beauty"

_____ 11. Moneylender to Prince John and his nobles

_____ 12. Died in the burning ruins of his castle

_____ 13. Site of Rebecca's trial and Ivanhoe's triumph

_____ 14. Templar who loved Rebecca

_____ 15. Disguise worn by Ivanhoe at the tournament

_____ 16. Was "resurrected" at his own funeral

_____ 17. Grand master of the Templars

_____ 18. Norman noble who loved Lady Rowena

_____ 19. Served as Ivanhoe's squire

_____ 20. Recovered from his injuries because of Rebecca's medical skill

A. Prior Aymer
B. Brian de Bois-Guilbert
C. Black Knight
D. Rowena
E. Ivanhoe
F. Tourquilstone
G. Rebecca
H. Athelstane
I. Gurth
J. Wamba
K. Disinherited Knight
L. Locksley
M. Isaac of York
N. Lucas Beaumanoir
O. Front-de-Boeuf
P. De Bracy
Q. Cedric
R. Waldemar Fitzurse
S. Rotherwood
T. Templestowe

NAME _____ DATE _____

Ivanhoe by Sir Walter Scott

Answer each of the following questions in two or three complete sentences.

1. What were some causes of the conflicts between the Saxons and the Normans?

_____

_____

_____

_____

2. Why had Cedric disowned his son?

_____

_____

_____

_____

3. How does Wamba, who is supposedly a fool, show a great deal of sense and courage?

_____

_____

_____

_____

4. Who is Ulrica? Why is she so willing to help destroy the Norman nobility?

_____

_____

_____

_____

5. How does Brian de Bois Guilbert try to help Rebecca and to save himself at the same time?

_____

_____

_____

_____

CHALLENGE

How does Scott make the outcast Jewess Rebecca a much more thoroughly developed character than the aristocratic heroine, Rowena?

NAME _____ DATE _____

Treasure Island by Robert Louis Stevenson

Correctly complete each sentence with information from the novel.

1. The narrator of most of the story is _____.

2. The most frequent guest at the "Admiral Benbow" is _____.

3. _____ causes the death of the Captain.

4. The most valuable find among the dead man's possessions is _____

   _____.

5. The commander of the treasure expedition is _____.

6. Long John Silver is employed by the Squire as _____.

7. Jim learns of the planned mutiny when _____.

8. _____ is the man most seriously injured when the mutineers
   attack the stockade.

9. Ben Gunn was left on Treasure Island by _____.

10. _____ is Long John Silver's parrot, who constantly repeats the phrase

    _____.

11. Jim is able to get back to the ship by _____.

12. Jim is wounded by _____.

13. The sign of death to a pirate is _____.

14. Jim is captured by the mutineers when he _____.

15. In exchange for a promise of Jim's safety, Dr. Livesey agrees to _____

    _____.

16. The key landmark in the search for the treasure is _____.

17. As they search for the treasure, the men are frightened when _____

    _____.

18. When they reach the treasure site, the mutineers find _____.

19. The treasure had been found and stored by _____.

20. At the end of the novel, Silver _____.

NAME _____ DATE _____

Treasure Island by Robert Louis Stevenson

Answer each of the following questions in two or three complete sentences.

1. Describe the personality of Jim Hawkins.

   _____

   _____

   _____

   _____

2. What actions of Long John Silver show that the man's chief goal is to save himself, even at the expense of group loyalty?

   _____

   _____

   _____

   _____

3. How does Jim justify his running away from his post at the stockade?

   _____

   _____

   _____

   _____

4. Describe some of the physical features of Treasure Island.

   _____

   _____

   _____

   _____

5. At the end of the novel, why does Jim have no desire to retrieve the rest of the buried treasure?

   _____

   _____

   _____

   _____

CHALLENGE

Sickly for most of his life, Robert Louis Stevenson had to live out his desire for adventure through his fiction. In what ways are the experiences of Jim Hawkins on Treasure Island typical of boyhood adventure fantasies?

150 Great Books

NAME _____ DATE _____

The Once and Future King by T.H. White

In the numbered blanks at the left, write the letter of the matching character.

A. Wart
B. Kay
C. Sir Ector
D. Merlyn
E. King Pellinore
F. Galahad
G. Uter Pendragon
H. Archimedes
I. Gawaine
J. Morgause
K. Nimue
L. Uncle Dap
M. Sir Turquine
N. Lancelot
O. Modred
P. Elaine
Q. Guinevere
R. Tom of Warwick
S. Chevalier Mal Fet
T. Agravaine

_____ 1. Trapped in a conflict between loyalty and love

_____ 2. Arthur's guardian

_____ 3. Arthur's sister, Modred's mother

_____ 4. Son of Elaine and Lancelot; had a vision of the Holy Grail

_____ 5. Arthur's childhood nickname

_____ 6. Wise, magic owl

_____ 7. Represents hope for a new generation

_____ 8. Was to be knighted instead of Arthur

_____ 9. Killer of a unicorn

_____ 10. Lancelot's squire and teacher

_____ 11. Arthur's teacher, who lived backwards

_____ 12. Committed suicide because of unreturned love

_____ 13. Was rescued from being burned at the stake

_____ 14. Constantly searched for the Questing Beast

_____ 15. Began a civil war to destroy the ideals of the Round Table

_____ 16. "The ill-made knight"

_____ 17. Captor of sixty-four knights, slain by Lancelot

_____ 18. Enchantress who imprisoned Merlin

_____ 19. Leader of the Orkney faction that opposed Arthur

_____ 20. Arthur's father

NAME _____ DATE _____

The Once and Future King by T.H. White

Answer each of the following questions in two or three complete sentences.

1. What were some of the concepts that Arthur learned when Merlyn changed him into various birds and animals?

_____

_____

_____

_____

2. Explain briefly the philosophy of the Round Table: "Might for Right."

_____

_____

_____

3. How were both Lancelot and Guinevere caught by a conflict of loyalties? How did Modred exploit that conflict?

_____

_____

_____

_____

4. How is King Pellinore a comic figure who offsets the dark side of the King Arthur story?

_____

_____

_____

5. What is Arthur's hope as he sends young Tom back to England away from the battle?

_____

_____

_____

_____

CHALLENGE

A round character in a work of fiction is one who has a complexity of traits, both good and bad. A flat character is either entirely good or entirely evil. Write an essay to contrast the character of Lancelot with the character of Modred. In what ways is Lancelot's character complex, while Modred's is flat?

NAME _____ DATE _____

The Virginian by Owen Wister

In the numbered blanks at the left, write the letter of the matching person or place.

_____ 1. Steve's nickname for the Virginian

_____ 2. Town nearest the ranch

_____ 3. Hen with mixed-up maternal instincts

_____ 4. Explained to Molly the necessity of the hang-ings

_____ 5. Cook and close friend of the Virginian

_____ 6. Helped Molly nurse her injured sweetheart

_____ 7. Molly's complaining older sister

_____ 8. Helped the Virginian mix up the babies at the Swindon's barbecue

_____ 9. Loved the horse, Pedro

_____ 10. Notorious abuser of animals

_____ 11. Friend turned cattle thief

_____ 12. Pompous preacher who became the object of a practical joke

_____ 13. Accidental witness to the hanging of the cattle thieves

_____ 14. Location of Judge Henry's ranch

_____ 15. Molly's Vermont suitor

_____ 16. Helped the Virginian with his choice of ring stones

_____ 17. Shot Shorty in the back

_____ 18. Molly's hometown

_____ 19. Descendant of a Revolutionary War heroine

_____ 20. Recognized the reality of Molly's love because of her own experience

A. Steve
B. Medicine Bow
C. Scipio
D. Sam Bannett
E. Molly Stark Wood
F. Lin McLean
G. Great Aunt
H. Shorty
I. Dr. McBride
J. Mrs. Taylor
K. The Tenderfoot
L. Jeff
M. Judge Henry
N. Mrs. Henry
O. Sarah
P. Bennington
Q. Sunk Creek
R. Trampas
S. Baalam
T. Emily

The Virginian by Owen Wister

Answer each of the following questions in two or three complete sentences.

1. What role does "the tenderfoot" play in the novel?

    _____

    _____

    _____

    _____

2. What episodes show the Virginian's grand sense of humor?

    _____

    _____

    _____

    _____

3. What aspects of Western life are most difficult for Molly to understand?

    _____

    _____

    _____

    _____

4. Why does Steve's death trouble the Virginian so deeply?

    _____

    _____

    _____

    _____

5. Why must the Virginian, on his wedding eve, face Trampas in a shoot-out?

    _____

    _____

    _____

    _____

CHALLENGE

Write an essay describing the character traits of the Virginian and Molly Stark Wood which show them both to be people of "quality" who are well-suited to each other.

ANSWER KEYS

Born Free by Joy Adamson

OBJECTIVE:

1. 0	6. +	11. 0	16. +
2. +	7. 0	12. +	17. 0
3. 0	8. +	13. 0	18. 0
4. +	9. 0	14. +	19. +
5. 0	10. 0	15. 0	20. 0

SHORT ANSWER:

1. Cubs' mother killed, cubs left defenseless.
2. Knocked over dishes and furniture, rough play, frightened visitors.
3. Man-eaters, slaughtered livestock.
4. Failure to adapt to climate, got sick, couldn't kill to provide food.
5. Loved Elsa, but knew that life in the wild was better than life in a cage.

CHALLENGE:

Elsa's conflict in love and caring for her "human" family opposed her animal instincts to kill and mate in the wilds.

The Red Badge of Courage by Stephen Crane

OBJECTIVE:

1. the tall soldier
2. dreams of glory
3. books
4. marching, waiting to fight
5. ran away
6. in Henry's mind
7. his papers
8. personification
9. Wilson
10. Jim Conklin
11. "Where ye hit?"
12. green, blue, yellow
13. Jim
14. mule drivers
15. hit in the head
16. wound in battle
17. they come back too soon
18. capture the flag
19. victory
20. relief, being a man again, joy in being alive

SHORT ANSWER:

1. Romantic vision of knights and heroes contrasted to tedious marching and waiting and the grim realities of death
2. Will he run when the fighting starts?
3. The men become men in any war anywhere.
4. Growth through experience from boy to man

CHALLENGE:

The ways that men help each other, the tattered man's search for company, Wilson's aid to Henry, the man with the cheery voice.

The African Queen by C.S. Forester

OBJECTIVE:

1. a Belgian mining company
2. her brother Samuel
3. von Hannelkan
4. steering
5. dumped it overboard
6. Shona
7. Ulanga
8. shooting the rapids
9. wood
10. shaft and propeller
11. she was patriotic, revenge for Samuel
12. weeds, mud, water lilies, leaches
13. malaria
14. anchored near them
15. gas cylinders
16. sent them to the English
17. sank in a storm
18. English gunfire
19. back to England
20. get married

ANSWER KEYS (continued)

The African Queen by C.S. Forester (continued)

SHORT ANSWER:

1. Men and supplies all taken by the Germans.
2. Assumes leadership, finds adventure exciting, begins to think for herself.
3. Admires her strength, has nothing else to do.
4. Revenge and patriotism.
5. Pulling through weeds, mechanical failure, illness.

CHALLENGE:

Follow Rose's character from totally passive follower to one who thinks for herself and faces danger. Her awakening to love as a woman. Questioning of pat religious beliefs.

Green Dolphin Street by Elizabeth Goudge

OBJECTIVE:

1. C	6. B	11. D	16. C
2. D	7. B	12. C	17. A
3. D	8. B	13. C	18. D
4. C	9. A	14. B	19. D
5. C	10. A	15. B	20. D

SHORT ANSWER:

1. Love for William, desire for sea adventure.
2. Drugged in Hong Kong, lost Navy ship, traveled with Cpt. O'Hara.
3. Looks after her parents, finds strength in spiritual life, heads convent.
4. Warm and giving, prefers simple life to wealth.
5. Meet on the rock footprints of the two sisters.

CHALLENGE:

Marianne's positive traits, determination survives catastrophe, builds business empire as a manager. Negative loss in meaningful human relationships as she manages and manipulates.

The Call of the Wild by Jack London

OBJECTIVE:

1. 0	6. +	11. 0	16. 0
2. +	7. 0	12. +	17. 0
3. 0	8. +	13. +	18. +
4. +	9. 0	14. 0	19. 0
5. 0	10. +	15. +	20. 0

SHORT ANSWER:

1. Soft life as a pet versus extremely harsh work and discipline.
2. Steal food, sleep in snow, pull in harness.
3. Defeated Spitz, placed in lead dog position.
4. Attacked Thornton's attacker, saved Thornton from drowning, pulled load and won the bet.
5. Following his wolf brother, returning to run with the pack.

CHALLENGE:

Buck reasons through problems, feels emotions of anger and love.

ANSWER KEYS (continued)

Day of Infamy by Walter Lord

OBJECTIVE:

1. +	6. +	11. +	16. 0
2. 0	7. +	12. 0	17. 0
3. 0	8. 0	13. +	18. 0
4. +	9. +	14. +	19. +
5. 0	10. 0	15. 0	20. +

SHORT ANSWER:

1. Dates, golf, church services, relaxed military posture.
2. Aerial photos of military bases, radio surveillance.
3. Help for the enemy from Hawaiian residents, that civilians would help the invaders.
4. Read to children, kept calm, took husbands to work, saved family possessions.
5. Low on fuel, feared American retaliation.

CHALLENGE:

Bands played under gunfire, men saved others, cooks and civilians helped man guns.

A Night to Remember by Walter Lord

OBJECTIVE:

1. 0	6. +	11. +	16. +
2. +	7. 0	12. 0	17. +
3. 0	8. 0	13. 0	18. 0
4. +	9. 0	14. 0	19. 0
5. 0	10. 0	15. +	20. +

SHORT ANSWER:

1. Help from maids and stewards, first access to life boats.
2. Refused to leave each other, went down with ship.
3. Ship must have enough life boats, boat drills, twenty-four-hour communication.
4. Kept order, saved as many as he could, went down with his ship.
5. Sightings of icebergs by various other ships.

CHALLENGE:

Brave crew stayed with the ship—radiomen and boiler workers. Passengers who helped others in lifeboats. Cowardice of the builder who left his ship, men who tried to disguise themselves as women.

Moby Dick by Herman Melville

OBJECTIVE:

1. A	6. A	11. C
2. B	7. D	12. A
3. C	8. B	13. B
4. C	9. A	14. D
5. B	10. D	15. C

SHORT ANSWER:

1. A gold piece nailed to the mast.
2. Chase in small boats, attack whales with harpoons.
3. Moby Dick charges the ship.
4. Queequeg's coffin in the wreckage.
5. Endless, formless universe.

ANSWER KEYS (continued)

Moby Dick by Herman Melville (continued)

CHALLENGE:

Life as grim—no meaning beyond man's individual actions. Heroism lies in making some gesture of defiance.

Never Cry Wolf by Farley Mowat

OBJECTIVE:

1. the Canadian government
2. the Lupine project
3. Wolf House Bay
4. six months
5. Mike
6. Peru
7. Ootek
8. George and Angeline
9. Uncle Albert
10. killing the weak animals
11. mice, fish, caribou
12. hunting
13. Mike's hunting dog Kooa
14. what they need for food
15. chewing the food, then spitting it up
16. catalogue plant life
17. traps and poison
18. hunters
19. Mowat himself
20. man

SHORT ANSWER:

1. Wolves as killers of caribou and men.
2. Monogamous mating, training of cubs, other wolves as "aunts or uncles."
3. Kill only what they needed.
4. Play, love, feel pride in their young.
5. Found wolves inside.

CHALLENGE:

Wolves are not killers, help natural balance, humans can approach them. Man is the more dangerous animal to the balance of nature.

All Quiet on the Western Front by Erich Maria Remarque

OBJECTIVE:

1. 0
2. +
3. 0
4. +
5. 0
6. 0
7. +
8. 0
9. 0
10. +
11. 0
12. 0
13. +
14. 0
15. 0
16. 0
17. 0
18. 0
19. +
20. +

SHORT ANSWER:

1. Tiresome drills, dirt, waiting, bad food.
2. Stealing food, protecting themselves from gassing, taking equipment from dead men.
3. Occupy house and beds, find food and pleasure in the middle of war.
4. Poetic ideals do not fit experience, cannot communicate with his mother, no longer fits into civilian life.
5. Close friends, shared combat experiences.

CHALLENGE:

Men provide and share food, more experienced help the younger, get revenge together on persecutors.

Rabble in Arms by Kenneth Roberts

OBJECTIVE:

1. L	6. P	11. B	16. S
2. G	7. J	12. E	17. O
3. T	8. Q	13. R	18. K
4. A	9. C	14. D	19. I
5. F	10. N	15. M	20. H

SHORT ANSWER:

1. Numbers (800) used in letters, friendship with British officers, using Ellen as a courier for messages.
2. Willingly followed by his men, willing to take aggressive action when other officers did nothing.
3. Passed off as Indians got through British lines.
4. Took away good generals, refused to send needed arms and supplies.
5. Leadership in sea battle, not fooled by Marie's act, helping persuade other men to join the colonial cause.

CHALLENGE:

Detailed description of hardships during the march. Death at Ile aux Noix, battle destruction, physical hardships of being a soldier.

Ivanhoe by Sir Walter Scott

OBJECTIVE:

1. G	6. L	11. M	16. H
2. S	7. C	12. O	17. N
3. A	8. R	13. T	18. P
4. Q	9. J	14. B	19. I
5. F	10. D	15. K	20. E

SHORT ANSWER:

1. Land rights, loyalty to Richard vs. John, right to self-rule.
2. He had left home to follow Richard to the Crusades.
3. Entered the castle and got his master out.
4. Family destroyed by Front-de-Boeuf's father.
5. Arranges for a champion, wants to take her out of the country.

CHALLENGE:

Rebecca shows caring, courage, loves Ivanhoe, but relinquishes him for another. Rowena a flat character, typical noble lady.

Treasure Island by Robert Louis Stevenson

OBJECTIVE:

1. Jim Hawkins	8. Cpt. Smollett	12. Israel Hands	16. Spyglass Hill—the tree
2. the Captain	9. pirate Captain Flint	13. black spot	17. Ben Gunn's song
3. Pue, the blind man	10. Captain Flint, "pieces of eight"	14. returns to stockade	18. treasure is gone
4. the treasure map	11. using Ben Gunn's boat	15. let the mutineers have the treasure	19. Ben Gunn
5. Trelawney			20. has run away
6. cook			
7. hiding in the apple barrel			

44

ANSWER KEYS (continued)

Treasure Island by Robert Louis Stevenson (continued)

SHORT ANSWER:
1. Courageous, curious.
2. Joins the mutiny, abandons the ship.
3. To get back the *Hispanola*.
4. Coves, inlets, swamp, small hills.
5. Haunted by memories of his experiences there.

CHALLENGE:
Boy's ideal of physical courage, hunt for treasure, battle against pirates.

The Once and Future King by T.H. White

OBJECTIVE:

1. N	6. H	11. D	16. S
2. C	7. R	12. P	17. M
3. J	8. B	13. Q	18. K
4. F	9. T	14. E	19. I
5. A	10. L	15. O	20. G

SHORT ANSWER:
1. No boundaries, how to get along with those who are different.
2. Use man's fighting instincts to fight for a good cause.
3. Love versus loyalty. Modred traps them into betraying Arthur, forces Arthur to condemn them.
4. Questing Beast search—comic blusterer, opposite of serious Galahad and Lancelot.
5. Reestablish the ideals of chivalry.

CHALLENGE:
Lancelot's conflict between desires and ideas, Arthur's hopes for a better world, Modred's desire only to destroy, various other personifications of good and evil principles.

The Virginian by Owen Wister

OBJECTIVE:

1. L	6. J	11. A	16. N
2. B	7. O	12. I	17. R
3. T	8. F	13. K	18. P
4. M	9. H	14. Q	19. E
5. C	10. S	15. D	20. G

SHORT ANSWER:
1. Outside narrator, observer, Virginian's friend.
2. Episodes with the drummer's bed and the frogs' legs.
3. Law of frontier justice, why men killed other men.
4. Close friendship, no word of farewell.
5. Could not have love without honor.

CHALLENGE:
Virginian's quality—courage, fairness, defense of the weak, trustworthy foreman. Molly—desire for a real love, need to teach courage in saving his life.

UNIT 2

Coming of Age—
The MATURATION of SELF

SYNOPSES

When the Legends Die
by Hal Borland

Tom Black Bull is a young Indian who struggles for survival in a white man's world. After his parents are forced to flee from the reservation, Tom is brought up in the wilderness and is educated in the old ways of his people. After the death of Tom's parents, the boy becomes brother to a bear cub. Although Tom is brought back by Blue Elk, a traitor to his own people, the boy refuses to adapt to the humiliation of the reservation school. A skilled rider, Tom is found by Red Dillon, who uses the boy to win money on a "fixed" rodeo circuit. After Tom breaks Red's control on his life, the young Indian becomes "Killer Tom Black," who takes out his isolation and rage on the horses that he rides. After being seriously injured in a fall, Tom returns to Bald Mountain to recover his physical strength and to find his identity as a man and as an Indian. *When Legends Die* considers whether an Indian must be assimilated into the white man's culture to survive. This novel is an important contribution to the literature of America's minority groups.

Jane Eyre
by Charlotte Brontë

Jane Eyre is a novel set in nineteenth-century England. The young heroine develops character as she struggles for love, survival, and human dignity. As a child, Jane suffers a great deal of abuse at the hands of her cruel aunt, Mrs. Reed. Sent to Lowood, a charity school for girls, Jane experiences further cruelty, but she also matures through the teaching of Miss Temple and the loving friendship of Helen Burns. Jane's desire for independence takes her to Thornfield Hall, where she is employed to teach Adele, the ward of Mr. Edward Rochester. Jane's relationship with Rochester ripens into love. Happiness, however, is shattered by the revelation of a dark secret from Rochester's past. Jane shows her strength in parting from Rochester. Her firm character also shines in her resistance to the strong personality of St. John Rivers. Jane's reunion with the man she really loves gives the novel a happy ending. *Jane Eyre* is a strong statement of the dignity of women and the rights of every individual.

Great Expectations
by Charles Dickens

Pip, a young English boy who lives in a nineteenth-century village, has been brought up by his cruel sister, Mrs. Joe Gargery. Pip's only friend is the kindly blacksmith Joe. After Pip meets the mysterious Miss Havisham and her beautiful ward, Estella, the lad becomes discontent and desires to be a gentleman. He is then told that he has "great expectations," which will be supplied by a mysterious benefactor. Dickens' masterpiece contains a host of marvelous characters: the fearful convict, the pompous Pumblechook, the lawyer Jaggers. Most of all, the novel traces the growth of Pip himself from boy to man. Filled with Gothic description and powerful social commentary, *Great Expectations* shows the reader the England of Dickens' time through Pip's eyes as the young hero learns to distinguish true values from false. A strong plot line is created by the mystery of Pip's unknown benefactor and his unrequited love for the beautiful Estella. This novel of passage is important to any student's reading experience.

The Summer of My German Soldier
by Bette Greene

Patty Bergen is a sensitive twelve-year-old Jewish girl who lives in Jenkinsville, Arkansas in the 1940s. Wanting only to be loved, Patty is cruelly rejected by a self-centered mother and an abusive father. Her only solace is Ruth, the black housekeeper. When a group of German POWs is sent to Jenkinsville to pick cotton, Patty becomes friends with one special German, Anton Reiker. When Anton tries to escape, Patty hides and protects him. After Anton's departure, Patty must hold to the belief that she is a person of value, and not the criminal that the world proclaims her to be. Patty Bergen's needs are the needs of every person—to belong and to be loved. *The Summer of My German Soldier* is simply written, but the novel contains ideas to which students of all ability levels can relate.

Tex
by S.E. Hinton

Tex is another of this author's novels of teenagers surviving without adults. Tex lives with his older brother Mace. Their mother is dead, and their father is away on the rodeo circuit for many months at a time. Tex's great loves are horses and Jamie Collins, the girl next door. The novel contains exciting scenes as Tex is involved in confrontations with an escaped convict and a drug pusher. Tex matures as he battles with his feelings for Jamie, and is forced to cope with the truth about his own parentage. *Tex* presents to the teenage reader significant problems of making choices and accepting the consequences of those choices.

The Metamorphosis
by Franz Kafka

The Metamorphosis is a dark, absurdist story in which Gregor Samsa, an average little man, is inexplicably transformed into a giant beetle. Gregor, who has been the chief support of his family, seeks their help in his dilemma. Although he is at first aided by his sister, Gregor is brutally rejected and attacked by his father. The novel's plot recounts Gregor's mental deterioration, total rejection, and death. *The Metamorphosis* is a significant work by one of modern literature's most tortured authors. Gregor's need is the need of all men—to find significance and security in personal relationships. Yet Gregor feels guilty and rejected for reasons the reader never understands. This puzzling story will provide a challenge for the mature reader.

A Separate Peace
by John Knowles

Phineas and Gene are students at Devon Preparatory School in the early years of World War II. The story is told as a flashback as Gene returns to the campus years later. Phineas is an athlete whose outrageous behavior and charismatic personality quickly make him a school leader. Gene is the scholar who follows Phineas admiringly, yet is angered by Phineas' disruption of the academic routine. When a freak accident cripples Phineas, Gene tries to atone for his guilt in causing the mishap. The ruthless Brinker and the tragic Lenny play significant roles in Gene's growth as the war moves closer to Devon. Phineas' tragic death brings the story to its climax. Gene said that he could later face the war because he had met and conquered his enemy at Devon. *A Separate Peace* is a well-written account of one boy's march toward manhood.

Christy
by Catherine Marshall

Christy is a novel loosely based on the girlhood experiences of the author's mother. In 1912, idealistic young Christy Huddleston goes to teach school in the mountain community of Cutter Gap, Tennessee. Although horrified by the primitive living conditions and the barbaric superstitions, Christy also finds much love and beauty in the hearts of the mountain people. As Christy teaches, she encounters moonshiners and an epidemic of typhoid fever. The gentle beauty of Fairlight Spencer, the strong faith of Miss Alice Henderson, the mission teacher, and the determination of Dr. Neil MacNeill all help to transform Christy from a girl to a mature young woman. The author presents beautiful natural description and details of mountain life. *Christy* is a novel of faith and belief in the triumph of the human spirit.

The Heart is a Lonely Hunter
by Carson McCullers

The Heart is a Lonely Hunter is set in a small southern town in the 1930s. Mick Kelley, a young girl struggling to grow up, lives in the "outside room" of the real world and in the "inside room" of her imagination. Mick can communicate best with Mr. Singer, a watchmaker who boards with her family. Ironically, Singer himself is mute. Other characters who visit Singer with a need to communicate are Blount, a roving handyman, Biff Brannon, a widowed cafe owner, and Dr. Copeland, a black physician with a burning need to help his people. *The Heart is a Lonely Hunter* has a loosely unified plot. By opening up to Singer, each character finds the courage to grow. Sadly, Singer has no one. The gentle irony of the author's characterizations makes this novel well worth reading.

The Member of the Wedding
by Carson McCullers

This play, set in a small southern town in the 1930s, explores the need for belonging. Frankie Addams is a lonely girl with a gift for exaggerated fantasy. Her only companions are her cousin, John Henry, and Berenice, the black cook. When her brother Jarvis and his fiancée Janice visit, Frankie decides that she will go away with the bride and groom after the wedding. Her brother and his bride will give her identity. Frankie says, "They are the *we* of me." Berenice also knows the importance of belonging and love as she remembers her special love for Ludie Freeman. Frankie's frustrations are reflected in Berenice's brother Honey, a young black man who is about to explode. Reality closes in at the end of the play, but Frankie remains unchanged. She still must create dream relationships to meet her emotional needs. *The Member of the Wedding* is a strong psychological classic of the modern American theater.

The Chosen
by Chaim Potok

The Chosen is drawn from the author's boyhood and recounts the experience of growing up as an orthodox Jew in America during the turbulent 1940s. Reuven Malter and Danny Saunders come from different Jewish backgrounds. Reuven's father believes that the Jews must work through the political process to establish a homeland. Danny's father is the leader of the Hasidim, a supremely conservative group who believe that the Jews' only salvation lies in the Torah. Danny has been chosen at birth to be the tzaddik, the leader of his people. Yet his brilliant mind craves much more knowledge than can be had in the narrow confines of his sect. Through a baseball accident, Danny and Reuven become friends. Danny and Reuven find the way to maturity amid the turmoil created in the Jewish community as the state of Israel is born. The author contrasts Danny's remote father, who brings his son up "in silence," with Reuven's father who has a loving closeness with his son. *The Chosen* presents the conflict between faith and intellect while showing a fine picture of Jewish belief and practice.

The Catcher in the Rye
by J.D. Salinger

Holden Caulfield is a prep school adolescent who seeks to shock by sensational actions and vulgar language. The real Holden hides from a reality which he cannot face. He is closest to his little sister Phoebe in a struggle to cope with his brother's death. In a world filled with "phonies," Holden becomes the most pathetic "phoney" of them all, as he struggles to protect himself from what he cannot face. Holden's weekend odyssey around New York City does not help him to mature. He hides in the museum, where things always remain the same. The journey ends at a carousel in Central Park. The author's fine use of first person point of view gives this novel a significant place in the fiction of a young man's struggles to grow up.

Shane
by Jack Schaefer

Bob Starrett and his family are struggling farmers in the western territory of the 1890s. Into their lives rides the courteous and mysterious man Shane, who owns a gun but does not wear it. When Fletcher, the neighboring large ranch owner, tries to drive the small farmers from their homes, Bob's father is forced to stand and fight for his land and his family. The final confrontation comes between Shane and Wilson, who is Fletcher's hired gunman. *Shane* presents the excitement of the West and the noble cowboy hero as seen through the eyes of a small boy.

The Odd Couple
by Neil Simon

This classic comedy pairs Oscar Madison, the slob, with Felix Unger, the neatness maniac. When Felix's poker buddies fear the distraught man will commit suicide, Oscar takes pity on Felix and asks Felix to move in. Comic chaos results as Oscar and Felix begin to influence each other. Witty dialogue and fast-moving action make this play light reading. The play comes to a climax as the two roommates compete for the attentions of the Pigeon sisters, who live upstairs. *The Odd Couple* is a fine example of modern comic technique.

Rabbit, Run
by John Updike

Harry "Rabbit" Angstrom is a forty-year-old adult who cannot cope. Having had his moment of greatness as a high school basketball star, Rabbit spends the rest of his life running away. He leaves his wife Janice and his two children and moves in with Ruth Leonard. After abandoning Ruth, he returns to Janice. Rabbit's irresponsibility increases his wife's drinking and leads to the tragic death of his daughter. Yet, at the end of the novel, Rabbit is still running. Updike's character is a likeable but pathetic man who constantly needs to prove his manhood, but cannot face the obligations that manhood represents. Containing specific descriptive passages, *Rabbit, Run* is a powerful novel of personal failure which would be suitable for more mature readers.

Macho
by Edmund Villasenor

Macho is a powerful novel of the American Chicano community. Roberto is a Mexican youth who struggles to help his family survive. Roberto is lured north by promises of great money to be made working in the United States. Juan Anguilar, an experienced *norteno* or border crosser, becomes Roberto's patron. Together they plan to cross the border *a la brava*, as illegal immigrants. After being defrauded by men who promised to issue entry papers, Juan and Roberto almost die as they attempt to cross the border in a locked van. They eventually find work in the California lettuce fields, but refuse to join the efforts of Chavez and his union. Roberto falls in love with Lydia. He must leave his love, however, to return to Mexico and uphold the family honor by settling an old score with his enemy. *Macho* presents clearly the problems faced by Chicano immigrants as the reader follows Roberto's development from a boy into a man.

NAME _____ DATE _____

When the Legends Die by Hal Borland

In the numbered blanks at the left, write the letter of the matching person or place.

_____ 1. Taught her son the crafts and customs of his people

_____ 2. Told Tom to recover from his injuries by eating, sleeping, and walking

_____ 3. Tom's roommate

_____ 4. Put Tom to work herding sheep

_____ 5. Site of the country's largest rodeo

_____ 6. Store owner who recognized the quality of Tom's work

_____ 7. Was trained to take fake falls in rodeo competition

_____ 8. Man that Tom's father killed

_____ 9. Tom's childhood home in the wilderness

_____ 10. Offered love which Tom could not accept

_____ 11. Indian who sold his people to the white man

_____ 12. Nickname given because of a rider's violence

_____ 13. Tom's tribe and language

_____ 14. Town near the reservation

_____ 15. Made huge profits by placing crooked bets on Tom's riding ability

_____ 16. Tried to help Tom learn English

_____ 17. Paid Blue Elk to bring Tom to school

_____ 18. Attempted to discipline Tom so he would learn the white man's ways

_____ 19. Name that Tom gave himself

_____ 20. Old man who had an identity with the land

A. Blue Elk
B. Ute
C. Frank No Deer
D. Bald Mountain
E. Jim Thatcher
F. Bear's Brother
G. Luther Spotted Dog
H. Rowena Ellis
I. Benny Grayback
J. Red Dillon
K. Meo
L. Albert Left Hand
M. Bessie
N. Tom
O. Killer Tom Black
P. Madison Square Garden
Q. Mary Redmond
R. Pagosa
S. Agent
T. Dr. Ferguson

NAME _____ DATE _____

When the Legends Die by Hal Borland

Answer each of the following questions in two or three complete sentences.

1. In what ways was Blue Elk a traitor to all Indians?

    _____

    _____

    _____

    _____

2. How does Tom become brother to the bear after his parents die? Why does Tom later send the bear away?

    _____

    _____

    _____

    _____

3. Why does Tom allow Red Dillon to control him? How does Tom finally break that control?

    _____

    _____

    _____

    _____

4. Why is Tom so violent as a rodeo rider?

    _____

    _____

    _____

    _____

5. Why can Tom not accept the love and companionship that Mary wants to give him?

    _____

    _____

    _____

    _____

CHALLENGE

Write an essay discussing the ways that Tom Black Bull lost his identity as an Indian, and the steps by which he again found that identity.

NAME _____ DATE _____

Jane Eyre by Charlotte Brontë

In the numbered blanks at the left, write the letter of the matching person or place.

_____	1. A mysterious servant	A. Helen Burns
_____	2. Mr. Rochester's ward	B. Adele
_____	3. Beautiful and conceited	C. Diana and Mary
_____	4. Saves Jane from death	D. Rochester
_____	5. Runs away from Thornfield	E. Blanche
_____	6. Old faithful family servant	F. Bertha
_____	7. Insane woman who dies in a fire	G. St. John Rivers
_____	8. Intelligent, concerned sisters	H. Jane
_____	9. Eventually marries Jane	I. Hannah
_____	10. Dies of tuberculosis	J. Grace Poole
_____	11. Jane's only friend at Gateshead	K. Celene
_____	12. Jane's legal guardian when she was a child	L. Mrs. Reed
_____	13. Stern, hypocritical clergyman	M. Miss Temple
_____	14. Wise, compassionate teacher	N. Mr. Brocklehurst
_____	15. Housekeeper at Thornfield	O. Eliza and Georgianna
_____	16. Jane's selfish cousins	P. Ferndean
_____	17. Place where Jane taught school	Q. Bessie
_____	18. Adele's mother	R. Morton
_____	19. Home of Jane's uncle	S. Mrs. Fairfax
	20. Where Jane lives at the end of the novel	T. Madeira

NAME _____ DATE _____

Jane Eyre by Charlotte Brontë

Answer each of the following questions in two or three complete sentences.

1. Why would Jane's first attempt to marry Rochester not have been legal?

   _____

   _____

   _____

   _____

2. What were the difficulties that Jane encountered as she fled from Thornfield?

   _____

   _____

   _____

   _____

3. What does Rivers want Jane to do? Why does she refuse?

   _____

   _____

   _____

   _____

4. What had happened to Thornfield and to Rochester during Jane's absence?

   _____

   _____

   _____

   _____

5. State in your own words two of the important themes in *Jane Eyre*.

   _____

   _____

   _____

   _____

CHALLENGE

Why has *Jane Eyre* been considered one of the first important novels to make an important statement about the equality of the sexes?

NAME _____ DATE _____

Great Expectations by Charles Dickens

In the numbered blanks at the left, write the letter of the matching person or place.

_____	1. The pub in Pip's village	A.	Miss Skiffins
_____	2. Learns to love through experiencing suffering	B.	Wemmick
_____	3. The pale young gentleman	C.	Orlick
_____	4. Attempts to kill Pip out on the marshes	D.	Satis House
_____	5. Estella's mother	E.	Jolly Bargeman
_____	6. Pip's benefactor	F.	The Forge
_____	7. Was married to Wemmick	G.	Barnard's Inn
_____	8. Is married to Joe at the end of the novel	H.	Magwitch
_____	9. Wanted to claim credit for Pip's good fortune	I.	Drummele
_____	10. Miss Havisham's deceitful half-brother	J.	Pumblechook
_____	11. Pip's lodgings in London	K.	Mrs. Joe
_____	12. Lawyer who became Pip's guardian	L.	Miss Havisham
_____	13. Lived with The Aged in his "Castle"	M.	Biddy
_____	14. Wanted to hurt others as she had been hurt	N.	Joe
_____	15. Decaying old mansion	O.	Herbert
_____	16. Deserted his bride on their wedding day	P.	Molly
_____	17. Pip's boyhood home	Q.	Jaggers
_____	18. Fine example of simple, honest goodness	R.	Estella
_____	19. Estella's first husband	S.	Compeyson
_____	20. Pip's sister	T.	Arthur

NAME _____ DATE _____

Great Expectations by Charles Dickens

Answer each of the following questions in two or three complete sentences.

1. How does Pip's childhood encounter with the convict affect him?

   _____

   _____

   _____

   _____

2. How does Joe try to help Pip when Pip is a child?

   _____

   _____

   _____

   _____

3. Why does spending time at Miss Havisham's make Pip dissatisfied with his life?

   _____

   _____

   _____

   _____

4. In what ways does Pip become spoiled and selfish after he goes to London?

   _____

   _____

   _____

   _____

5. How do Pip's experiences after the arrival of Magwitch contribute to Pip's growth and maturity?

   _____

   _____

   _____

   _____

CHALLENGE

Great Expectations is a fine character study in Pip's growth from childhood innocence to mature adulthood. Write an essay tracing the important phases in this change. Support your statements by listing some of the specific events which cause these changes to occur.

NAME _____ DATE _____

The Summer of My German Soldier by Bette Greene

In the numbered blanks at the left, write the letter of the matching person or place.

_____ 1. Known as the prettiest girl in town

_____ 2. Location of the prison camp

_____ 3. Patty's grandfather

_____ 4. Made Patty feel that she was really a person of value

_____ 5. Location of the reform school

_____ 6. Newspaper reporter who tried to help Patty

_____ 7. Had a cruel and abusive father

_____ 8. Worked in Bergen's department store

_____ 9. Tried to be the mother that Patty needed

_____ 10. Transported Patty to reform school

_____ 11. Always felt inferior to his wife's family

_____ 12. Ruth's son

_____ 13. Got Patty into trouble by throwing rocks at cars

_____ 14. Patty's neurotic, self-centered mother

_____ 15. Headmistress of the reform school

_____ 16. Richest man in Jenkinsville

_____ 17. FBI agent who questioned Patty

_____ 18. Tried to give Patty love by buying her things

_____ 19. Patty's lawyer

_____ 20. Patty's adorable younger sister

A. Jenkinsville
B. Ruth
C. Harry Bergen
D. Sharon
E. Patty
F. Anton Reiker
G. Pearl
H. J.G. Jackson
I. Samuel Fried
J. Grandma Fried
K. Sister Parker
L. Robert
M. Charlene Madlee
N. Freddy
O. Edna Louise
P. Pierce
Q. Calvin Grimes
R. Mr. Kishner
S. Bolton
T. Miss Laud

NAME _____ DATE _____

The Summer of My German Soldier by Bette Greene

Answer each of the following questions in two or three complete sentences.

1. How do Patty's interests and feelings show her to be a special, sensitive person?

   _____

   _____

   _____

   _____

2. In what ways is Patty a victim of family circumstances for which she is not responsible?

   _____

   _____

   _____

   _____

3. Why does being Jewish create problems for Patty?

   _____

   _____

   _____

   _____

4. Why is Patty's relationship with Anton so special?

   _____

   _____

   _____

   _____

5. Explain the meaning of Ruth's statement: "You've got yourself some irregular second folks, and you've been paying more 'n top dollar for them. So jest don't go a-wishing for what ain't nevah gonna be" (p. 192).

   _____

   _____

   _____

   _____

CHALLENGE

Developing characters are those who change and grow throughout the progress of a novel. Discuss the ways in which Patty's experiences have made her a stronger person. Why is she indeed, "a beginning swimmer who will make it to shore" (p. 199)?

NAME _____ DATE _____

Tex by S.E. Hinton

Place a (+) before each statement that is true and a (0) before each statement that is false.

_____ 1.   Tex is a junior in high school.

_____ 2.   Tex and Johnny Collins share a mutual love of horses.

_____ 3.   Mason had to sell the horses to get money for the brothers to live on.

_____ 4.   Mason hoped to get into college on a football scholarship.

_____ 5.   The boys have heard from their father regularly.

_____ 6.   Tex frequently has nightmares about the death of his mother.

_____ 7.   Cole Collins blames Mason for Johnny's getting drunk.

_____ 8.   Tex is arrested for shoplifting in a clothing store.

_____ 9.   Lem Peters is dealing in drugs so he can support his wife and child.

_____ 10. Mason and Tex become heroes when they single-handedly capture two escaped convicts.

_____ 11. Pop is able to buy Negrito back for Tex.

_____ 12. Tex's favorite member of the school faculty is Coach McCollough.

_____ 13. When Johnny and Tex quarrel, Jamie wants to get the boys to be friends again.

_____ 14. Pop is very angry when Mrs. Johnson calls him about Tex's school pranks.

_____ 15. Tex learns from a statement of Mason's that Pop is not his real father.

_____ 16. Lem Peters accidently shoots Tex in the chest.

_____ 17. After he is injured, Tex telephones Mason.

_____ 18. Tex had been born while Pop was in prison.

_____ 19. Jamie tells Tex at the end of the story that she is willing to marry him.

_____ 20. At the end of the novel, Mason has given up his plans for college.

NAME _____ DATE _____

Tex by S.E. Hinton

Answer each of the following questions in two or three complete sentences.

1. What does Tex mean when he says that he is a "stayer," and Mason is a "goer"?

    _____

    _____

    _____

    _____

2. Although the brothers fight frequently, how does the author show the reader that Mason and Tex love each other?

    _____

    _____

    _____

3. Why is Tex so confused about his feelings for Jamie Collins?

    _____

    _____

    _____

    _____

4. Why does Tex say that the dead convict reminds Tex of himself?

    _____

    _____

    _____

5. What happens to Tex when he runs away from the school with Lem Peters?

    _____

    _____

    _____

    _____

CHALLENGE

Write an essay discussing the choices made by the characters in *Tex*. Which characters make choices which will probably yield positive results? Which characters make choices which will probably lead to trouble?

150 Great Books

NAME _____ DATE _____

The Metamorphosis by Franz Kafka

Correctly complete each sentence with information from the novel.

1. Gregor Samsa works as _____.

2. Gregor's greatest fear about his work is that _____.

3. When he becomes an insect, Gregor's physical difficulties include _____ and _____.

4. The person that Gregor fears most is _____.

5. Gregor is finally able to open the locked door of his room by _____ _____.

6. The person who reacts most violently to the change in Gregor is _____.

7. The first time Gregor leaves his room, his father injures him by _____.

8. The family member who tries to help and feed Gregor is _____.

9. Gregor had to support his family financially after _____.

10. Gregor finds his room more comfortable when _____.

11. Physical changes which take place in Gregor over a period of time include _____ _____.

12. The kind of motion that Gregor enjoys most is _____.

13. Because Gregor cannot work, to gain income the family _____.

14. Gregor's chief contact with his family comes through _____.

15. The father attempts to kill Gregor by _____.

16. The figure of Death is represented in the story by _____.

17. Gregor is drawn from his room by the sound of _____.

18. When the lodgers see Gregor, they _____.

19. After his death, Gregor's body is disposed of by _____.

20. After Gregor's death, the rest of the family expresses freedom by _____ _____.

NAME _____ DATE _____

The Metamorphosis by Franz Kafka

Answer each of the following questions in two or three complete sentences.

1. What positive traits, as a family member and a workman, does Gregor Samsa possess?

   _____

   _____

   _____

   _____

2. Why does he fear the chief clerk?

   _____

   _____

   _____

   _____

3. Why is the reaction of others to Gregor's situation both unfair and illogical?

   _____

   _____

   _____

   _____

4. How is Gregor rejected every time he tries to communicate with the other members of his family?

   _____

   _____

   _____

   _____

5. How does Gregor deteriorate mentally from his metamorphosis until his death?

   _____

   _____

   _____

   _____

CHALLENGE

Kafka presents an absurd plot, with a very vital theme: the struggle of the individual to find meaning in life and personal relationships. Discuss the ways in which Gregor struggles for this meaning, and the reasons that he fails to find any meaning at all.

NAME _____ DATE _____

A *Separate Peace* by John Knowles

Correctly complete each sentence with information from the novel.

1. Gene begins his story when he returns to _____

   about _____ years after the main action of the novel.

2. Phineas got away with breaking rules because he had a marvelous ability to _____

   _____.

3. Phineas says that his pink shirt is a symbol of _____.

4. Membership in the Suicide Society of the Summer Session involved _____

   _____.

5. The game Phineas invented was called _____.

6. Phineas said that the war had been invented by _____.

7. Gene and Phineas skip school and spend the night _____.

8. Gene is angry because he knows that Phineas had tried to wreck _____

   _____.

9. Phineas falls out of the tree because _____.

10. Dr. Stanpole says that Phineas will _____

    but will never be able to _____.

11. When he goes to visit Phineas at home, Gene tells Phineas that _____

    _____.

12. Gene takes a job as crew manager to _____.

13. In Phineas' absence, leadership in school affairs is taken over by _____.

14. When Phineas returns, he makes Gene begin to _____.

15. To help the war effort, the Devon students _____

    and _____.

16. The first boy to enlist from Devon is _____.

17. Brinker calls a night meeting to _____.

18. The only witness to Phineas' accident was _____.

19. Phineas dies when _____.

20. Phineas had to pretend that the war did not exist because _____

    _____.

NAME _____ DATE _____

A Separate Peace by John Knowles

Answer each of the following questions in two or three complete sentences.

1. When Gene returns to his old school, what things seem different? What things seem the same?

    _____

    _____

    _____

    _____

2. Contrast the personalities of Gene and Phineas.

    _____

    _____

    _____

    _____

3. How does Gene try to relieve his guilt feelings about Phineas' accident?

    _____

    _____

    _____

    _____

4. Why is Leper a real "casualty" of the war?

    _____

    _____

    _____

    _____

5. How does Phineas respond to the accusations made against Gene?

    _____

    _____

    _____

    _____

CHALLENGE

Write an essay explaining Gene's statement (p. 255):   "My war ended before I ever put on a uniform; I was on active duty all my time at school; I killed my enemy there."

Christy by Catherine Marshall

In the numbered blanks at the left, write the letter of the matching person or place.

_____ 1. Was unsure of his calling to be a minister

_____ 2. Mailman, Christy's escort to the Cove

_____ 3. Had an idiot son

_____ 4. Had once been Bird's Eye's sweetheart

_____ 5. Christy's home town

_____ 6. Shot Tom McHone in the back

_____ 7. Had been raped by a man whom she trusted

_____ 8. Most gentle and sensitive of the mountain women

_____ 9. Housekeeper at the Mission

_____ 10. Challenged David at the "working" with a gun

_____ 11. Learned from Christy how to be a more attractive woman

_____ 12. Introduced Christy to the idea of the Danish Folk Schools

_____ 13. Hired Christy to teach in Cutter Gap

_____ 14. Was saved when Dr. MacNeill operated

_____ 15. Proud owner of a pet raccoon

_____ 16. Native of the Cove who returned to help his own people

_____ 17. Old lady who died in peace and confidence

_____ 18. Was recalled to life by the power of love

_____ 19. Miss Alice's daughter

_____ 20. Businessman who helped to supply the Mission with needed books and equipment

A. Asheville
B. Mr. Pentland
C. Dr. Ferrand
D. Miss Ida
E. Creed Allen
F. Ruby Mae
G. Hazen Smith
H. Lundy Taylor
I. Margaret MacNeill
J. Fairlight Spencer
K. Opal McHone
L. Christy
M. David Grantland
N. Aunt Polly Teague
O. Miss Alice
P. Dr. MacNeill
Q. Bird's Eye Taylor
R. Mrs. Browning
S. Little Burl Allen
T. Mrs. O'Teale

NAME _____ DATE _____

Christy by Catherine Marshall

Answer each of the following questions in two or three complete sentences.

1. What were Christy's motives for going to Cutter Gap?

    _____

    _____

    _____

    _____

2. What were some of the difficulties that Christy faced in her teaching?

    _____

    _____

    _____

    _____

3. What were some of the character traits and prejudices of the people of Cutter Gap?

    _____

    _____

    _____

    _____

4. How was the religion practiced by Miss Alice Henderson different from the religion of most of the Cove people?

    _____

    _____

    _____

    _____

5. Why did David Grantland have problems with his parishioners? Why was David unsure of his own role with these people?

    _____

    _____

    _____

    _____

CHALLENGE

What specific experiences helped Christy Huddleston grow from an immature schoolgirl into a mature young woman?

NAME _____ DATE _____

The Heart is a Lonely Hunter by Carson McCullers

Place a (+) before each statement that is true and a (0) before each statement that is false.

_____ 1. Singer did most of the cooking for Antonapoulous and himself.

_____ 2. Antonapoulous was committed to a mental institution by his cousin.

_____ 3. Mick's father had been a railroad worker before he was injured.

_____ 4. Mick took care of her two younger brothers.

_____ 5. Biff Brannon got a job as handyman with a carnival.

_____ 6. Mick was the only girl in her family.

_____ 7. Doctor Copeland's daughter worked as a waitress in Biff's restaurant.

_____ 8. Mick's greatest passion in life was music.

_____ 9. Singer rarely attempted to really talk with anyone after Antonapoulous left.

_____ 10. Portia's husband was sent to jail for knifing a man.

_____ 11. Doctor Copeland was himself seriously ill.

_____ 12. Mick's brother Ralph shot Baby Wilson with a rifle.

_____ 13. At Mick's first party, all of the boys and girls danced easily and had a good time.

_____ 14. Blount and Mick liked to spend time with Singer because Singer was such a good listener.

_____ 15. Singer received a telegram informing him that Antonapoulous had died.

_____ 16. After Mick and Harry spent the day in the woods, Harry offered to marry Mick.

_____ 17. Doctor Copeland committed suicide.

_____ 18. Mick got a job working at Woolworth's.

_____ 19. Brannon decided to close his cafe and move on to a new town.

_____ 20. Willie Copeland died in prison.

NAME _____ DATE _____

The Heart is a Lonely Hunter by Carson McCullers

Answer each of the following questions in two or three complete sentences.

1. What did Mick mean by her "inside room" and her "outside room"?

    _____

    _____

    _____

    _____

2. Why did each of the four main characters enjoy spending time with Singer?

    _____

    _____

    _____

    _____

3. How does Dr. Copeland try to help his people?

    _____

    _____

    _____

    _____

4. How does Biff change after Alice's death?

    _____

    _____

    _____

    _____

5. How has Mick Kelley grown up by the end of the novel?

    _____

    _____

    _____

    _____

CHALLENGE

Write an essay explaining how each character in the novel is a "lonely hunter." What is each one seeking? How is Singer important to each one's search?

150 Great Books

NAME_____ DATE_____

The Member of the Wedding by Carson McCullers

Select the letter of the word or phrase which correctly completes each statement.

_____ 1. Berenice is described as all of the following except: (A) blind in one eye (B) slender (C) loving and affectionate (D) the family cook.

_____ 2. Frankie's mother (A) works in a jewelry store (B) is very active socially (C) died when Frankie was born (D) doesn't want Frankie and John Henry to play together.

_____ 3. Jarvis (A) is older than Frankie (B) is engaged (C) is in the army (D) all of the above.

_____ 4. Frankie's tendency to fantasize is shown by (A) her desire to belong to a club (B) her relationship with John Henry (C) writing and acting in plays (D) her desire to be helpful to Berenice.

_____ 5. Frankie's greatest desire in life is (A) to be pretty (B) to be married (C) to be intelligent (D) to belong and to be loved.

_____ 6. Frankie's greatest source of anxiety is (A) her weight (B) her height (C) her name (D) her dirty elbows.

_____ 7. The other character whose feelings most closely resemble Frankie's feelings is (A) T.T. (B) John Henry (C) Honey (D) Uncle Charles.

_____ 8. Frankie is absolutely convinced that she will (A) marry Barney McKean (B) never amount to anything (C) be able to go with Janice and Jarvis (D) become a concert pianist.

_____ 9. Frankie's father (A) is a jeweler (B) doesn't understand Frankie (C) gives Frankie permission to go shopping by herself (D) all of the above.

_____ 10. Berenice says that all of her husbands and boyfriends (A) reminded her of Ludie (B) were small pieces of Ludie (C) were different from Ludie (D) gave her as much happiness as Ludie had given her.

_____ 11. When Frankie refers to the "we of me" she is referring to (A) Berenice and John Henry (B) Jarvis and Janis (C) her father and late mother (D) her neighborhood.

_____ 12. The clothes that Frankie buys for the wedding (A) are totally inappropriate (B) could easily be exchanged (C) were picked out by Berenice (D) were very attractive and suitable.

_____ 13. After the wedding ceremony, (A) Frankie goes with Janice and Jarvis (B) Berenice finds another job (C) Frankie has to be dragged from the car (D) Mr. Addams becomes seriously ill.

_____ 14. The death of Uncle Charles foreshadows (looks ahead to) (A) the wedding (B) the death of John Henry (C) the departure of Janice and Jarvis (D) the death of Ludie.

_____ 15. Act One ends with (A) the wedding ceremony (B) the singing of a Negro spiritual (C) John Henry's death (D) a real change in Frankie's personality.

_____ 16. At the end of the story, Honey is (A) dead (B) in a mental hospital (C) on his way to Cuba (D) in jail.

_____ 17. When she cannot go with her brother and his bride, Frankie (A) tries to run away (B) tries to kill herself (C) blames her father (D) faints.

_____ 18. At the end of the play, Frankie has transferred her fantasies to (A) Mary (B) the movies (C) the girls next door (D) John Henry.

_____ 19. In the final scene, the family (A) is going to John Henry's funeral (B) is leaving town (C) is moving to a different house (D) is planning a vacation.

_____ 20. The author's main theme in this play is (A) the importance of marriage (B) racial tensions in the South (C) the need for belonging (D) the problems of neglected children.

NAME _____ DATE _____

The Member of the Wedding by Carson McCullers

Answer each of the following questions in two or three complete sentences.

1. Explain Frankie's statement regarding Janice and Jarvis: "They are the we of me."

   _____

   _____

   _____

   _____

2. What episodes in the play most clearly show Frankie's need to belong?

   _____

   _____

   _____

   _____

3. How is Berenice a mother figure to Frankie and John Henry?

   _____

   _____

   _____

   _____

4. How does Berenice say that her feelings for T.T. differ from the feelings that she had had for Ludie?

   _____

   _____

   _____

   _____

5. What problems do Frankie and Honey have in common?

   _____

   _____

   _____

   _____

CHALLENGE

A developing character in literature is one who changes and learns from experience. A static character shows no change at all. Is Frankie Addams a developing character or a static character? Support your answer with evidence from the play.

NAME _____ DATE _____

The Chosen by Chaim Potok

In the numbered blanks at the left, write the letter of the matching person, place, or thing.

_____ 1. Danny's choice for graduate school

_____ 2. Narrator of the novel

_____ 3. Danny's younger brother

_____ 4. Jewish sacred scriptures

_____ 5. Group that supported the establishment of a Jewish political state in Israel

_____ 6. Complicated verbal quiz used by Danny's father to show off his brilliant son to his congregation

_____ 7. Rabbi or leader

_____ 8. Hebrew secondary school

_____ 9. Had a photographic memory

_____ 10. Deliverer that the Jews believed would come

_____ 11. Spoken Hebrew language of European Jews

_____ 12. Blind boy that Reuven meets in the hospital

_____ 13. Mystical orthodox Jewish sect which began in Eastern Europe

_____ 14. Where Reuven and Danny went to college together

_____ 15. Brought his son up "in silence"

_____ 16. Non-Jews

_____ 17. Complicated text for Hebrew religious and philosophical studies

_____ 18. Helped Danny select his reading material at the public library

_____ 19. Important German psychiatrist

_____ 20. Danny and Reuven's college professor of Talmud

A. Reuven Malter
B. Danny Saunders
C. Reb Malter
D. Reb Saunders
E. Talmud
F. Yeshiva
G. Billy
H. Hasidim
I. Levi
J. Zionists
K. Messiah
L. Tzaddik
M. Freud
N. Goyim
O. Torah
P. Hirsh
Q. Reb Gershenson
R. Columbia
S. Yiddish
T. Gematriya

NAME _____ DATE _____

The Chosen by Chaim Potok

Answer each of the following questions in two or three complete sentences.

1. Describe the circumstances under which Danny and Reuven become friends.

    _____

    _____

    _____

    _____

2. How is Danny's relationship with his father different from Reuven's relationship with his father?

    _____

    _____

    _____

    _____

3. In what ways is Danny Saunders a very special person? Why does he rebel against the life that his father has planned for him?

    _____

    _____

    _____

    _____

4. What is the cause of the conflict between Reb Malter and Reb Saunders when the state of Israel is established?

    _____

    _____

    _____

    _____

5. Why did Reb Saunders choose to bring up Danny "in silence"?

    _____

    _____

    _____

    _____

CHALLENGE

Reb Saunders says that Danny will be "a tzaddik to the world." Write an essay discussing what Saunders means by this statement. How have Danny's education and upbringing prepared the young man for this very special role?

NAME _____ DATE _____

The Catcher in the Rye by J.D. Salinger

In the numbered blanks at the left, write the letter of the matching person or place.

_____ 1. Boy who died by jumping from the window of his dorm room

_____ 2. Girl that Holden took to a play

_____ 3. Last school from which Holden was expelled

_____ 4. The place where everything always stayed the same

_____ 5. History teacher at Pencey Prep

_____ 6. Piano player in a Greenwich Village bar

_____ 7. Pseudonym that Phoebe used for writing stories

_____ 8. Prostitute who visited Holden in his hotel room

_____ 9. Holden's younger brother who had died of leukemia

_____ 10. Boy with bad breath and pimples

_____ 11. English teacher who destroys Holden's last illusions about adults

_____ 12. The one person that Holden is really close to

_____ 13. Girl that Holden had dated briefly one summer

_____ 14. Location of the carousel with the gold ring

_____ 15. Beats up Holden for not paying

_____ 16. A corporation lawyer

_____ 17. Used to give the younger boys lectures on sex

_____ 18. Student whose mother Holden meets on the train

_____ 19. Holden's roommate at Pencey

_____ 20. Holden's older brother who works in Hollywood

A. Sunny
B. Mr. Caulfield
C. Central Park
D. Mr. Antolini
E. Museum of Natural History
F. James Castle
G. Hazel Weatherfield
H. Carl Luce
I. Ernie
J. Phoebe
K. Ernest Morrow
L. Sally Hayes
M. Maurice
N. Stradtlater
O. Ackely
P. D.B.
Q. Allie
R. Mr. Spencer
S. Jane Gallagher
T. Pencey Prep

NAME _____ DATE _____

The Catcher in the Rye by J.D Salinger

Answer each of the following questions in two or three complete sentences.

1. Why has Holden been a misfit in every school that he has attended?

_____

_____

_____

_____

2. How is Holden's relationship with Jane Gallagher different from his relationship with Sally Hayes?

_____

_____

_____

_____

3. How do you know that Holden was deeply affected by the death of his brother?

_____

_____

_____

_____

4. Why is Holden able to be honest with his younger sister?

_____

_____

_____

_____

5. Why does Holden like the museum and the zoo?

_____

_____

_____

_____

CHALLENGE

How does Holden Caulfield, by becoming the biggest phoney of all, create a fantasy world to protect himself from a reality that he cannot face?

NAME _____ DATE _____

Shane by Jack Schaefer

In the numbered blanks at the left, write the letter of the matching person or place. You will use some letters more than once.

_____	1. Was hit on the head to prevent his being involved in a fight	A. Bob Starrett
_____	2. Rancher who intended to drive the small farmers from the valley	B. Joe Starrett
_____	3. Boy who tells the story	C. Shane
_____	4. Tried to beat Shane up by having two of his men hold Shane down	D. Grafton
_____	5. Came and offered to work for Bob's father after Shane left	E. Fletcher
_____	6. Man to whom the farmers looked for leadership	F. Ernie Wright
_____	7. Wanted the house in the West painted like a house in New England	G. Morgan
_____	8. Rode out of the valley after his job was done	H. Chris
_____	9. Gunfighter hired to drive the small farmers from their land	I. Territory
_____	10. Unorganized western land where the story takes place	J. Marian
_____	11. Farmer who saw the new gunfighter arrive in town	K. Johnson
_____	12. Had his arm broken in a fight with Shane	L. Wilson

_____ 13. Refused Fletcher's offer of a job as his foreman

_____ 14. Recognized that the family's roots had been planted deep into the soil by Shane

_____ 15. Tried to shoot Shane from a saloon balcony

_____ 16. Fletcher's foreman who was badly beaten by Shane

_____ 17. The first small farmer who was killed

_____ 18. Owner of the local store and saloon

_____ 19. Only wore his gun when he intended to use it

_____ 20. Made the best apple pies in the territory

NAME _____ DATE _____

Shane by Jack Schaefer

Answer each of the following questions in two or three complete sentences.

1. Why did Shane decide to remain with the Starretts?

_____

_____

_____

_____

2. What actions of Shane's made him seem mysterious to the family?

_____

_____

_____

_____

3. What did Shane mean when he told Bob that a gun was a tool?

_____

_____

_____

_____

4. How did Marian show her support for her husband?

_____

_____

_____

_____

5. How did Shane take care of both Wilson and Fletcher in one fight?

_____

_____

_____

_____

CHALLENGE

Write a newspaper article describing the events of the final showdown from the time that
Shane entered the saloon until he left. Explain how a third-person observer, one who was
not emotionally involved in the action, would have seen the fight.

150 Great Books

NAME _____ DATE _____

The Odd Couple by Neil Simon

Correctly complete each sentence with information from the play.

1. As the play opens, the poker players are concerned because _____

    _____.

2. By profession, Oscar Madison is _____.

3. The general condition of Oscar's apartment at the beginning of the play may best be

    described as _____.

4. Instead of a suicide note, Felix sent his wife _____.

5. Felix's feelings about himself may be best described as _____

    _____.

6. Oscar offers to let Felix _____.

7. For the poker party in Act II, Felix has prepared _____.

8. The other poker players envy Oscar and Felix because _____.

9. Felix and Oscar have spent most of their evenings _____.

10. Oscar first met the Pigeon sisters _____.

11. On the night of the dinner party, Felix is very upset because Oscar _____

    _____.

12. The elaborate dinner that Felix had planned _____.

13. Felix gets the sympathy of the Pigeon sisters by _____.

14. The girls invite Felix and Oscar _____.

15. At the end of Act II, Felix refuses _____

    _____.

16. At the beginning of Act III, Oscar deliberately _____.

17. Oscar has made a typewritten list of _____.

18. Oscar orders Felix to _____.

19. Before Felix leaves he makes Oscar _____.

20. At the end of the play, Felix _____.

150 Great Books

NAME _____ DATE _____

The Odd Couple by Neil Simon

Answer each of the following questions in two or three complete sentences.

1. Why are Felix's poker buddies very concerned about him?

    _____

    _____

    _____

    _____

2. In what ways does Oscar's personality directly contrast with Felix's?

    _____

    _____

    _____

    _____

3. How does the appearance of the set change from the opening of Act I to the opening of Act II?

    _____

    _____

    _____

    _____

4. What habits of Felix's annoy Oscar the most?

    _____

    _____

    _____

    _____

5. How does Felix win with the Pigeon sisters, while Oscar fails?

    _____

    _____

    _____

    _____

CHALLENGE

Write an essay describing the ways that Oscar and Felix change each other during the time that the two men live together. What indications are there that Felix has the stronger personality of the two?

NAME _____ DATE _____

Rabbit, Run by John Updike

Select the letter of the word or phrase which correctly completes the sentence.

_____ 1. The boys playing basketball in the opening scene of the novel remind Rabbit of (A) his son (B) his own high school greatness (C) his dead hopes for a professional sports career (D) his job selling sports equipment.

_____ 2. When the story opens, Rabbit is working (A) as a coach (B) at a gas station (C) as a used-car salesman (D) demonstrating kitchen gadgets.

_____ 3. Rabbit's age is about (A) 40 (B) 20 (C) 30 (D) 50.

_____ 4. Rabbit's wife Janice (A) is an alcoholic (B) is pregnant (C) escapes into the fantasy world of television (D) all of the above.

_____ 5. When Rabbit first begins to run away, he thinks he will head for (A) Boston (B) Europe (C) Florida (D) Philadelphia.

_____ 6. Rabbit is introduced to Ruth Leonard by (A) his sister, Mim (B) Coach Tothero (C) Reverend Eccles (D) Janice's mother.

_____ 7. Rabbit enjoys being with Ruth because (A) she makes him feel completely masculine (B) he has no responsibility for her (C) she does not demand that he marry her (D) all of the above.

_____ 8. Rabbit's first name is (A) Harry (B) Nelson (C) Jack (D) William.

_____ 9. Rabbit lives with Ruth for about (A) a year (B) two weeks (C) a month (D) six months.

_____ 10. Reverend Eccles tries to help Rabbit (A) learn to accept responsibility (B) find God (C) as a favor to Janice's family (D) because he feels sorry for Rabbit.

_____ 11. While living with Ruth, Rabbit works (A) as a janitor (B) as a gardener (C) as a cab driver (D) at nothing at all.

_____ 12. Rabbit is most totally at ease with (A) Ruth (B) his son Nelson (C) his father-in-law (D) Reverend Eccles.

_____ 13. Rabbit abandons Ruth (A) at Eccles' insistence (B) when his daughter is born (C) when Ruth throws him out (D) when he decides to leave town.

_____ 14. Tothero (A) was Rabbit's basketball coach (B) has a stroke (C) comes to offer Rabbit and Janice his sympathy (D) all of the above.

_____ 15. Reverend Eccles (A) is a basketball fan (B) has two sons (C) feels inadequate as a minister and as a person (D) has a very homely wife.

_____ 16. Janice drowns Rebecca (A) because she can't stand to hear the child's crying (B) because Janice is drunk (C) because Janice wants to hurt Rabbit (D) because Janice doesn't love the child.

_____ 17. The baby's death was seen by (A) Nelson (B) no one (C) Janice's mother (D) the next-door neighbor.

_____ 18. At his daughter's funeral, Rabbit (A) takes the responsibility for his family (B) runs away again (C) apologizes to Eccles (D) tries to commit suicide.

_____ 19. When Rabbit learns that Ruth is pregnant, he (A) offers to marry her (B) is pleased (C) is angry (D) tells her to have an abortion.

_____ 20. Rabbit's character traits include all of the following except: (A) a mean, malicious nature (B) an inability to accept responsibility (C) a need to prove his manhood (D) a love of motion.

150 Great Books

NAME _____ DATE _____

Rabbit, Run by John Updike

Answer each of the following questions in two or three complete sentences.

1. How did Rabbit get his nickname? Why does the name suit his personality?

_____

_____

_____

_____

2. In what specific ways does Jack Eccles try to help Rabbit?

_____

_____

_____

_____

3. Why does Rabbit go to Tothero's when he first leaves his wife?

_____

_____

_____

_____

4. Why does Rabbit feel trapped after he goes back to Janice?

_____

_____

_____

_____

5. In what ways is Rabbit responsible for Rebecca's death?

_____

_____

_____

_____

CHALLENGE
A static character does not grow or change through experience. Why is Harry Angstrom such a static character? Cite examples of his behavior at the end of the novel which duplicate his earlier actions.

150 Great Books

NAME _____ DATE _____

Macho by Edmund Villasenor

Place a (+) before each statement that is true and a (0) before each statement that is false.

_____ 1. Roberto was the eldest son in his family.

_____ 2. Roberto's father had been made foreman over many men who were older than he was.

_____ 3. Roberto's employer had no sympathy for Roberto's difficult family situation.

_____ 4. The Nortenos lured the village boys with stories of the great fortunes that were to be made in the United States.

_____ 5. Roberto agreed to give Juan Aguilar half of each day's pay in return for Juan's help and protection.

_____ 6. Roberto's sister is braver and more responsible than any other member of his family.

_____ 7. Pedro was a childhood friend who later became Roberto's enemy.

_____ 8. Juan Aguilar was well-liked by all of the other men in Roberto's village.

_____ 9. In Empalme, Roberto and Aguilar are able to buy work permits to allow them to enter the United States.

_____ 10. Aguilar is clever enough to make money off the other men who are waiting to immigrate.

_____ 11. "A la brava" meant illegal entry.

_____ 12. Chavez and his union were trying to persuade the American government to admit a larger Mexican working force into California.

_____ 13. Aguilar prevents Pedro from killing Roberto in a knife fight.

_____ 14. Roberto gets very sick from drinking contaminated water.

_____ 15. Luis Espinoza gets Roberto and Aguilar into California and finds work for them.

_____ 16. Little John is the driver of the truck in which the men almost die of suffocation.

_____ 17. Roberto is amazed at the amount of food provided for the farm workers.

_____ 18. Roberto and Aguilar join the forces of Chavez in a strike against the field management.

_____ 19. Roberto's family becomes very prosperous because of the money Roberto is able to send home.

_____ 20. In the final confrontation of the story, Roberto kills Pedro in a gunfight.

NAME _____ DATE _____

Macho by Edmund Villasenor

Answer each of the following questions in two or three complete sentences.

1. Describe the family circumstances which force Roberto to go north.

   _____

   _____

   _____

   _____

2. How is the ignorance of the Mexican workers exploited by the unscrupulous men in the immigration camp?

   _____

   _____

   _____

   _____

3. Describe the relationship which develops between Roberto and Aguilar.

   _____

   _____

   _____

   _____

4. How does Roberto's love for Lydia conflict with his drive for revenge against Pedro?

   _____

   _____

   _____

5. Why does Roberto leave Lydia and return to his village, even though his sister warns him not to come?

   _____

   _____

   _____

   _____

CHALLENGE

Write an essay describing Roberto's development from a boy into a man. What are some of the experiences that cause him to change?

150 Great Books

ANSWER KEYS

When the Legends Die by Hal Borland

OBJECTIVE:

1. M	6. E	11. A	16. H
2. T	7. N	12. O	17. S
3. G	8. C	13. B	18. I
4. L	9. D	14. R	19. F
5. P	10. Q	15. J	20. K

SHORT ANSWER:

1. Tricked his own people, made money by trading the Indian to the white man.
2. Cub's mother dead. Boy and cub fill each other's loneliness. Sends cub away to save bear from being killed.
3. To become a rodeo rider—total world gone, no motivation. Takes Red's money and goes off on his own.
4. Takes out his anger on the animals.
5. Cannot let himself feel love.

CHALLENGE:

Lost meaning on reservation, in school, crooked rodeo system, burning Meo's home. Found by a return to the land and confronting the bear.

Jane Eyre by Charlotte Brontë

OBJECTIVE:

1. J	6. I	11. Q	16. O
2. B	7. F	12. L	17. R
3. E	8. C	13. N	18. K
4. G	9. D	14. M	19. T
5. H	10. A	15. S	20. P

SHORT ANSWER:

1. His first wife was still alive.
2. Rain, hunger, no money, homelessness.
3. Marry him and go to India. She doesn't love him.
4. House burned, Rochester blinded.
5. Equality of all people, importance of individual integrity.

CHALLENGE:

Jane and Rochester as mental equals, her struggle for survival at Lowood against Rivers, final winning of identity.

Great Expectations by Charles Dickens

OBJECTIVE:

1. E	6. H	11. G	16. S
2. R	7. A	12. Q	17. F
3. O	8. M	13. B	18. N
4. C	9. J	14. L	19. I
5. P	10. T	15. D	20. K

ANSWER KEYS (continued)

Great Expectations by Charles Dickens (continued)

SHORT ANSWER:
1. Made him feel afraid and guilty.
2. Defended Pip from Mrs. Joe's temper, tried to give him special treats.
3. Estella made him feel crude, common, and discontented.
4. Spends too much money, cares only for Estella, selfish lifestyle.
5. Helps Magwitch instead of thinking about himself.

CHALLENGE:

Abused child, dissatisfied with life, spoiled young gentleman, rises to meet crisis, learns what real values are.

The Summer of My German Soldier by Bette Greene

OBJECTIVE:

1. O	6. M	11. C	16. H
2. A	7. E	12. L	17. P
3. I	8. K	13. N	18. J
4. F	9. B	14. G	19. R
5. S	10. Q	15. T	20. D

SHORT ANSWER:
1. Desire to be loved and to please, caring for Ruth and Anton.
2. Weak mother, violent, masochistic father.
3. Couldn't go to the summer camp, community violence when they learned that she had hidden a German.
4. He made her feel loved.
5. They will never treat her differently. She must accept things as they are.

CHALLENGE:

Learns to withstand community pressure, to see that she is really a good person, to begin to develop her own goals.

Tex by S.E. Hinton

OBJECTIVE:

1. 0	6. +	11. 0	16. 0
2. 0	7. 0	12. 0	17. 0
3. +	8. 0	13. +	18. +
4. 0	9. +	14. 0	19. 0
5. 0	10. 0	15. +	20. 0

SHORT ANSWER:
1. Tex content on farm, Mason needs to get away.
2. Tex concerned when Mace is sick, Mace caring when Tex is hurt.
3. Typical adolescent friendship confused by awakening sexual instincts.
4. Young image of Tex's own youth.
5. Shot in drug raid, taken by Collins to the hospital. He learns true meaning of his family relationships.

CHALLENGE:

Tex—constructive, reaching and growing. Mace—desire to succeed. Lem Peters moves further into the destructive world of drugs.

ANSWER KEYS (continued)

The Metamorphosis by Franz Kafka

OBJECTIVE:

1. a clerk
2. he will lose his job
3. getting out of bed, opening the door
4. chief clerk
5. taking the key in his teeth
6. his father
7. hitting him with a stick
8. his sister
9. his father went bankrupt
10. furniture is gone
11. loss of sight
12. crawling up the ceiling
13. takes lodgers
14. sights and sounds through the door
15. throwing apples
16. charwoman
17. sister's violin
18. leave
19. charwoman, like garbage
20. going on a picnic

SHORT ANSWER:

1. Faithful worker, good son, takes care of family.
2. That his job will be taken away, that he will be punished for something.
3. Find him disgusting, keep him inside.
4. Hitting him, throwing apples.
5. Becomes a total insect, lives on garbage, crawls around his room, dried up when he dies.

CHALLENGE:

No reason why this has happened, struggle to explain, no communication, response negative from his family, in death becomes garbage.

A Separate Peace by John Knowles

OBJECTIVE:

1. Devon, fifteen years
2. talk his way out of everything
3. war, liberty
4. jumping out of the tree
5. Blitzball
6. the old men
7. at the beach
8. his chances to be the top student
9. Gene bounced the limb
10. walk, play sports
11. Gene deliberately injured him
12. get rid of his guilt
13. Brinker Hadley
14. train for the Olympics
15. pick apples, shovel railroad tracks
16. Leper
17. Determine the cause of the accident
18. Leper
19. Bone marrow goes to his bloodstream
20. He couldn't be part of it

SHORT ANSWER:

1. Buildings more worn, tree seems smaller.
2. Phineas the extrovert, Gene the serious student.
3. Becoming an athlete in Phineas' place.
4. Joins the army. Can't handle the mental reality.
5. Pretending they do not exist.

CHALLENGE:

The ways that Gene deals with his fears about death in coming to terms with the death of Phineas.

ANSWER KEYS (continued)

Christy by Catherine Marshall

OBJECTIVE:

1. M	6. H	11. F	16. P
2. B	7. O	12. R	17. N
3. T	8. J	13. C	18. L
4. K	9. D	14. S	19. I
5. A	10. Q	15. E	20. G

SHORT ANSWER:

1. Wanted to do something good for others.
2. Few books, no equipment, terrible hygienic conditions, suspicion from the people.
3. Superstitious practices, primitive medicine, ancient feuds between families.
4. Religion of love rather than God of anger.
5. Cove people didn't see him as a real man, he was unsure of his own faith.

CHALLENGE:

Growing to love the children, Miss Alice, relationship with Fairlight, Dr. MacNeill, finding her own real faith.

The Heart is a Lonely Hunter by Carson McCullers

OBJECTIVE:

1. 0	6. 0	11. +	16. 0
2. +	7. 0	12. +	17. 0
3. 0	8. +	13. 0	18. +
4. +	9. +	14. +	19. 0
5. 0	10. 0	15. 0	20. 0

SHORT ANSWER:

1. World of reality—world of imagination.
2. Because Singer was such a good listener.
3. By raising the blacks' standard of living and health.
4. Becomes more outgoing, redecorates, relates to people.
5. Job of her own, away from family, dressing up.

CHALLENGE:

Each of these four seeks to find himself. Singer helps as each expresses feelings. Irony that Singer cannot respond. Mick, Biff, Blount, and Dr. Copeland each talk about what is important to him.

The Member of the Wedding by Carson McCullers

OBJECTIVE:

1. B	6. B	11. B	16. D
2. C	7. C	12. A	17. A
3. D	8. C	13. C	18. A
4. C	9. D	14. B	19. C
5. D	10. B	15. B	20. C

ANSWER KEYS (continued)

The Member of the Wedding by Carson McCullers (continued)
SHORT ANSWER:
1. She depends on them for her identity.
2. Wanting to join the club next door, desire to go away with Janice and Jarvis.
3. Listens to them, feeds them, really cares.
4. T.T. just someone to go out with. Ludie was the great love of her life.
5. Neither really belongs anywhere.

CHALLENGE:
Frankie's fantasies at the end of the play are the same as at the beginning. Go around the world with Mary. No growth or grasp of reality.

The Chosen by Chaim Potok
OBJECTIVE:

1. R	6. T	11. S	16. N
2. A	7. L	12. G	17. E
3. I	8. F	13. H	18. C
4. O	9. B	14. P	19. M
5. J	10. K	15. D	20. Q

SHORT ANSWER:
1. Danny hits Reuven with a baseball, later comes to the hospital. Reuven's father suggests that they be friends.
2. Reuven and his father very close, Danny brought up in silence.
3. Brilliant mind, desire to study psychology, not to lead small religious group.
4. Saunders—a religious state, Malter—a political state.
5. To teach Danny to look into his own heart.

CHALLENGE:
Danny will learn to help those who hurt because of the things he has learned about himself.

The Catcher in the Rye by J.D. Salinger
OBJECTIVE:

1. F	6. I	11. D	16. B
2. L	7. G	12. J	17. H
3. T	8. A	13. S	18. K
4. E	9. Q	14. C	19. N
5. R	10. O	15. M	20. P

SHORT ANSWER:
1. Totally refuses to conform to the system.
2. Sally makes him feel like a he-man, Jane he really cared about.
3. Writes about the baseball mitt, keeps dreaming about Allie.
4. He can say to her what he really feels.
5. He can stay in a child's world so he does not have to face reality.

CHALLENGE:
Hides his hurt behind "phoniness", attempt of the typical young man to grow up. Holden can still only relate to children.

90

ANSWER KEYS (continued)

Shane by Jack Schaefer

OBJECTIVE:

1. B	6. B	11. K	16. G
2. E	7. J	12. H	17. F
3. A	8. C	13. B	18. D
4. G	9. L	14. J	19. C
5. H	10. I	15. A	20. J

SHORT ANSWER:

1. Likes the peaceful farm life—Starrett needs him.
2. Doesn't wear a gun, refuses to talk about himself.
3. Must be used wisely by the man who wears it.
4. By making him realize that they cannot run.
5. Shot Wilson in the bar, Fletcher from the balcony.

CHALLENGE:

Reporter would recount action, interview those who saw the fight, describe Shane's departure.

The Odd Couple by Neil Simon

OBJECTIVE:

1. Felix is late	6. move in	11. is late	16. messes up the house
2. a sportswriter	7. fancy sandwiches	12. gets burned up	17. things Felix does to annoy him
3. a mess	8. they are free	13. telling his troubles	18. get out
4. a telegram	9. watching television	14. to come for dinner	19. feel guilty
5. self-pity	10. in the elevator	15. to go to the girls	20. moves in with the girls

SHORT ANSWER:

1. Has not shown up, has tried to kill himself.
2. Oscar—gruff and messy, Felix—neat and sensitive.
3. Act I a total mess, Act II super-neat and efficient.
4. Air freshener, constant cleaning, fancy dinners, coasters on tables.
5. Felix appeals to their emotions.

CHALLENGE:

Felix doesn't really change. He gets his way by being himself. Oscar becomes more aware of his feelings, especially with his family.

Rabbit, Run by John Updike

OBJECTIVE:

1. B	6. B	11. B	16. B
2. D	7. D	12. B	17. A
3. C	8. A	13. B	18. B
4. D	9. C	14. D	19. B
5. C	10. C	15. C	20. A

ANSWER KEYS (continued)

Rabbit, Run by John Updike (continued)

SHORT ANSWER:

1. From his basketball days. He can never stay and face responsibility.
2. To face his obligations as a family man.
3. Back to his high-school days—the only time that had meaning.
4. Shut in by the routine of family responsibility.
5. Rabbit leaves, Janice gets drunk and drowns the baby.

CHALLENGE:

Same weaknesses of character. Runs away at the beginning, from Ruth when she is pregnant, from Janice a second time. He even runs away from the cemetery.

Macho by Edmund Villasenor

OBJECTIVE:

1. +	6. +	11. +	16. 0
2. 0	7. 0	12. 0	17. +
3. 0	8. 0	13. +	18. 0
4. +	9. 0	14. 0	19. 0
5. 0	10. +	15. +	20. 0

SHORT ANSWER:

1. Father a drunk who doesn't work—no money to take care of younger children.
2. Took money for fake papers, food at high prices, men killed in illegal entry attempts.
3. He became the father Roberto did not have, Roberto was his substitute son.
4. Must revenge the insult, code of honor before love.
5. Revenge before love.

CHALLENGE:

Work responsibility on the ranch, trip north to learn the realities of life, love for Lydia, return home to responsibilities.

UNIT 3

The Imagined Past—
HISTORY in FICTION

SYNOPSES

Elizabeth the Queen
by Maxwell Anderson

Set in the court of Elizabeth I of England, this powerful historical drama presents the queen and the woman as Elizabeth is forced to choose between the man she loves, Lord Essex, and her throne. Through a plot engineered by Essex's political enemies, the ambitious noble is separated from Elizabeth and sent on a hopeless military mission to Ireland. Messages between Essex and Elizabeth never reach their intended destination. When Essex returns home, his rebellious troops seize the palace. Because Essex desires the throne, Elizabeth is forced to arrest him for treason. Until the last moment she hopes her proud lover will ask for mercy. The confrontation scenes between Elizabeth and Essex present a very human view of history. The woman who must be first the queen is left alone.

Becket
by Jean Anouilh

In eleventh-century England, King Henry II sows his wild oats with his Saxon friend, Thomas Becket. Becket tries to teach the young monarch how to be a ruler. In an attempt to break the power of the Church of England, Henry appoints Becket as Archbishop of Canterbury. The king mistakenly believes that Becket will become his tool. The new archbishop, however, has found a new purpose for his life. As Becket honors his vows to God, he becomes Henry's mortal enemy. The love-hate relationship between the two men remains until Becket is assassinated. The archbishop wins in death as the king must acknowledge the power of the Church within his realm. Yet, Henry the man still loves the friend he has lost.

A Tale of Two Cities
by Charles Dickens

This epic novel tells the story of people caught in the political and social turmoil of the French Revolution. Lucie Manette and her father, a former political prisoner in the hated Bastille, return to England to build a new life. Lucie's love for Charles Darnay is endangered because Charles is a member of the hated Evremonde family, the most ruthless branch of the French aristocracy. When the Revolution explodes in 1779, Charles is drawn back to Paris in an effort to save a faithful family servant. Charles and Lucie's lives are endangered by the vicious Madame DeFarge and the bloodthirsty mobs of Paris. Only Sidney Carton, a drunken wastrel who has loved Lucie from afar, can save Charles from certain death. Dickens' well-constructed plot and superb characters show the ways in which the larger currents of history can affect the lives of ordinary people.

April Morning
by Howard Fast

The maturation of Adam Cooper of Lexington, Massachusetts takes place in one day, April 18, 1775. When the men of the Lexington militia learn that the British are marching from Boston to seize stores of ammunition, the farmers muster to defend their homes. Adam has never felt close to his father Moses; yet love between father and son is expressed for the first time just before Moses becomes one of the first casualties of the American Revolution. Adam sees firsthand the realities of death, for both American and British soldiers alike. After his father's death, Adam must become the head of his family. He knows that the fighting must continue in order to drive the British out altogether. During the several skirmishes in which he participates in one day of combat, Adam becomes a young man who can face his new responsibilities. This novel is written very simply; however, the war becomes very real when it is seen through one boy's eyes.

Cimarron
by Edna Ferber

Yancey and Sabra Cravat come to the Oklahoma Territory during the wild land rush of the 1880s. As the years pass, the family builds a life in Osage, the small settlement that becomes a boom town. Yancey becomes a legend through his flashy dress and daring exploits. Sabra is the guiding force behind *The Wigwam*, the local newspaper. The discovery of oil in the territory changes life forever. The citizens gain more wealth than they know how to use. Yancey disappears for weeks at a time on various quixotic adventures. Sabra becomes increasingly involved in local and state politics. Frontier men have been pictured in many novels as strong, colorful figures. This narrative shows Edna Ferber's strong belief that the strength of the pioneer woman was largely responsible for the building of the American West.

The Great Gatsby
by F. Scott Fitzgerald

At the height of the Roaring Twenties, Nick Carroway, an average young man from the Midwest, comes to Long Island and moves in next door to the wealthy and mysterious Jay Gatsby. Nick becomes involved in Gatsby's swinging lifestyle. Nick learns of Gatsby's idealized love for Daisy, the wife of Tom Buchanan. Nick assists Gatsby in arranging meetings with Daisy. Contrasted with Gatsby's and Daisy's love is Tom's rather sordid relationship with Myrtle Wilson. When Myrtle is accidentally killed, her enraged husband believes that Gatsby is responsible. The final scenes of the novel show the emptiness of wealth as Gatsby's body floats face down in his swimming pool. The vision of life as a grand party is gone forever. This novel presents the same "jazz age" lifestyle which destroyed Scott and Zelda Fitzgerald. The quest for pleasure ends in nothingness when the bottom falls out.

Johnny Tremain
by Esther Forbes

Johnny Tremain is a promising young silversmith living in Boston just before the American Revolution. An accident injures Johnny's hand, ends his usefulness at the Laphams, and destroys his hopes for a career as a craftsman. After a period of wandering and bitterness, Johnny meets Rab, a young printer, and becomes involved in the exciting activities of the Sons of Liberty. Johnny also must solve a very personal mystery. His dead mother had left him a cup bearing the family crest of Mr. Lyte, a wealthy Boston merchant. When Johnny tries to establish a connection with the Lyte family, he is accused of theft. Johnny is also angered and fascinated by the beautiful Lavinia Lyte, the belle of Boston. This novel presents both the British and the Americans as men caught in the current of the times. As war with England becomes inevitable, Johnny becomes a rider and a courier. His friend Rab obtains a musket from a very ordinary British soldier, who is later shot for desertion. The climax of the novel comes in the exciting account of the Boston Tea Party. This fine historical novel presents one young man's growth and the birth of a new nation.

The Lion in Winter
by William Goldman

Aging King Henry II will soon be forced to choose an heir to his kingdom. Who will win the fight for political power? Will it be Richard, Geoffrey, or John? Henry knows that the real threat to his power is his wife, Eleanor of Aquitaine. The play takes place at Christmastime, when the queen has been released from prison to attend Christmas Court at Chinon Castle. The king and queen verbally spar with each other, taunt each other, and plot against one another. The prize is the crown of England. In spite of this feud, Henry and Eleanor still love each other because they are perfectly matched antagonists. This play presents, in the vitality of his old age, the same king who is portrayed as a young man in *Becket*.

The House of the Seven Gables
by Nathaniel Hawthorne

Set in Salem, Massachusetts in the nineteenth century, this novel shows the psychological consequences that the sins of one generation can have on the next. The Pyncheons, owners of the House of the Seven Gables, bear the curse of Matthew Maule, who was hanged so that the first Pyncheon might steal his land to build the mansion. Hepzibah Pyncheon, a withered old maid, lives in the musty house awaiting the return of her brother Clifford. Phoebe, a young country cousin, comes to share Hepzibah's home and to brighten her life. Phoebe also falls in love with Holgrave, a young artist. When Clifford returns, he and his sister try to free themselves from the threats of the present Judge Pyncheon and from the ghosts of the past. Phoebe and Holgrave also must fight the shadows of the past to secure their love. Hawthorne has presented a powerful study in the psychology of guilt and its consequences.

The Scarlet Letter
by Nathaniel Hawthorne

The Scarlet Letter is a powerful psychological novel which reveals the destructive consequences of hidden guilt. Hester Prynne, the novel's heroine, has been found guilty of adultery. Her husband, Roger Chillingworth, is determined to learn the identity of Hester's lover. The town's Puritan minister, Arthur Dimmesdale, struggles with the torments of his own soul. The novel chronicles seven years in the lives of these three. Hester faces the community alone, finding strength for survival as she cares for her child. Dimmesdale progressively deteriorates because his guilt is hidden. Chillingworth becomes a demon in human form as he relentlessly seeks revenge. *The Scarlet Letter* presents a clear study of the interior world of these characters, played against the backdrop of harsh Puritan Boston. The narrative provides a fascinating study in the depths of human personality.

The Country of the Pointed Firs
by Sarah Orne Jewett

In the mid-1850s, a young writer from the city goes to spend the summer in Dunnet Landing, an island community off the coast of Maine. Her landlady, Mrs. Almira Todd, is an herb specialist and a narrator of the community's history. The book is a collection of short narratives linked by the accounts of the young writer's encounters with the various inhabitants of Dunnet Landing. She hears the tales of Elijah Tilley, of the forsaken recluse Joanna, and of Almira's own love Nathan, who was lost at sea. The city girl also meets characters who impart local color as she visits Almira's mother, attends the Blackett family reunion, and visits with a woman who believes herself to be the twin of Queen Victoria. This fine narrative collection is a beautiful picture of life in seafaring New England during the late nineteenth century.

Dr. Zhivago
by Boris Pasternak

Against the massive background of the Russian Revolution of 1917, the reader sees the life of one man, physician Yuri Zhivago. Young Zhivago marries Tonia, the daughter of an aristocratic family. After he sends his family to the country for safety, Yuri meets the beautiful Lara. Lara, victimized as a child by the brutal Komarovsky, has married Pasha, the young idealist who eventually becomes a general of the Revolution. After a brief affair with Lara, Yuri decides that he must return to his family. The young doctor is, however, kidnapped by one of the warring revolutionary groups. Yuri experiences war in its most brutal forms. After the doctor escapes from his captors, he and Lara meet again and spend a brief time in the country village of Varykino. The two lovers live an idyllic existence in the midst of a world at war. As the wolves surround their villa, the lovers must part. This novel is a masterpiece of historical fiction, in which Nobel prize winner Pasternak shows how individuals must struggle for their humanity. Hope lies in being able to snatch a moment of love before the final separation comes.

The Winthrop Woman
by Anya Seton

This novel portrays the lives of the determined Puritans who settled New England in the 1630s. Elizabeth Winthrop, niece of Massachusetts Bay leader John Winthrop, loves John's son Jack, but is married to Harry Winthrop instead. After Harry is killed, Elizabeth immigrates with the Winthrop party to Massachusetts. Married to weak Robert Feake, Elizabeth becomes the steadying force in her family and exerts the strength of her personality. She defies the autocratic rule of her uncle John. Her support of religious heretic Anne Hutchinson and her defiance of authority cause Elizabeth to be accused of witchcraft and to be driven out of Massachusetts Bay. Elizabeth and her husband are assisted in their flight to Connecticut by sea captain Thomas Hallet. Elizabeth and Hallet fall in love. After Feake becomes totally unstable, Elizabeth seeks a civil divorce in the Dutch colony of New Amsterdam so she and Hallet can be married. *The Winthrop Woman* might be well compared with *Cimarron* (p. 96). Like Sabra Cravat, Elizabeth is a survivor. She builds a new life in a new land by the sheer force of her will and by the defiance of arbitrary authority. This novel is an excellent picture of the realities of daily life in colonial America.

Exodus
by Leon Uris

This novel of the Jewish settlement of Palestine and the establishment of the state of Israel shows determined men and women who survived the pogroms of Russia and the holocaust of Germany to build a homeland for their people. The personal histories of freedom fighters Ari and Barak Ben Canaan and Dov Landau are told in flashbacks. The main plot of the novel is a story of great courage. American nurse Kitty Fremont and German refugee Karen Hansen work with the freedom fighters. They defeat the British blockade of Palestine by running a shipload of refugee children from Cyprus to Tel Aviv. The novel contains several beautiful love stories: Barak and Sarah, Ari and Kitty, Dov and Karen. Human tenderness must be found in moments surrounded by violence and terrorism. Leon Uris gives the reader a strong sense of the past, present, and future of the Jewish people.

The Friendly Persuasion
by Jessamyn West

Jess Birdwell is a Quaker nurseryman in Pennsylvania in the 1830s–1850s. His wife Eliza is a Quaker minister. Despite their differences of temperament, Jess and Eliza love each other deeply. That love survives the loss of a child as well as many lesser family tribulations. The book's loosely-woven plot recounts various episodes in the lives of various family members. The children, Josh, young Jess, and Mattie, all gain a strength and determination inherited from their parents. Some episodes are very light in tone: the story of Samantha, the pacing goose, and Jess's purchase of Lady, a most unlikely race horse. Other episodes deal with more serious choices. Josh must choose between his family's nonviolent religious beliefs and his need to defend his family as the Civil War approaches. The novel's characters are each complete short stories which reaffirm the enormous value to be found in the lives of ordinary people.

The Caine Mutiny Court-Martial
by Herman Wouk

This dramatic adaptation of Wouk's novel considers how leaders are responsible for behaving during times of pressure in combat. Maryk, the executive officer of the minesweeper *Caine*, is being court-martialed for leading a mutiny. The defense contends that Captain Queeg was too mentally unstable to retain his command, and that Maryk acted to save the ship. The officers of the court must decide if this action was mutiny. Lieutenant Keefer, a novelist and amateur psychologist, wished to get even with Queeg. Keefer fed Maryk the information necessary to make the executive officer believe that the captain was unbalanced. Greenwald, the counsel for the defense, must prove that Queeg is mentally incompetent. The tension in the courtroom mounts as the captain is called as the chief defense witness. How much discipline was necessary on the ship? Was Queeg acting in the best interests of his crew? Were his harsh acts simply good military discipline? This play probes many aspects of the effects of wars on the men who fight them.

NAME _____   DATE _____

Elizabeth the Queen by Maxwell Anderson

Correctly complete each sentence with information from the novel.

1. The lady-in-waiting who also loves Essex is _____.

2. At court, Essex's most dangerous enemies are _____ and _____.

3. Essex angers Raleigh by making fun of _____.

4. A great military victory had been won by Essex at _____.

5. In council, Essex urges Elizabeth to _____.

6. Essex's closest friend at court is _____.

7. Raleigh tricks Essex into leading an army into _____.

8. Essex's greatest weakness is his _____.

9. Elizabeth is forced to choose between _____ and _____.

10. For his protection against her own anger, the queen gives Essex _____.

11. The queen does not receive Essex's letters because _____.

12. Upon his return to England, Essex refuses to _____.

13. A messenger tells Elizabeth that _____.

14. Essex most wants to be _____.

15. After Essex dismisses his troops, Elizabeth _____.

16. Before Essex's execution, the queen waits for _____.

17. To distract the queen, the actors present a scene from _____.

18. When Essex comes, Elizabeth offers to _____.

19. Essex says that the only thing in life he regrets leaving is _____.

20. At the end of the play, the queen is left alone with _____.

NAME _____ DATE _____

Elizabeth the Queen by Maxwell Anderson

Answer each of the following questions in two or three complete sentences.

1. In the opening scene, what schemes are being plotted by the two court factions?

    _____

    _____

    _____

    _____

2. How is Essex tricked into going to Ireland?

    _____

    _____

    _____

3. How does the queen show the disturbed state of mind that her love for Essex has created?

    _____

    _____

    _____

    _____

4. How does the play show the popularity of Essex with the common people? Why does Elizabeth fear this popularity?

    _____

    _____

    _____

5. Why does Essex refuse to allow the queen to spare his life?

    _____

    _____

    _____

    _____

CHALLENGE

Write an essay describing the internal conflict of the play between Elizabeth the Queen and Elizabeth the woman. At the end, what does Elizabeth win and what does she lose?

NAME _____ DATE _____

Becket by Jean Anouilh

In the numbered blanks at the left, write the letter of the matching person, place, or thing.

_____ 1. Becket's servant and friend

_____ 2. Saxon who collaborated with the Normans

_____ 3. Torn between a need for love and a desire for power

_____ 4. Rose up to protect Becket when he returned to England

_____ 5. Home of the young Saxon monk

_____ 6. First office given to Becket

_____ 7. Bishop of London, Becket's enemy

_____ 8. Hated Becket as "competition" for Henry's love

_____ 9. Becket's Welch mistress

_____ 10. Where Becket took refuge in France

_____ 11. Showed great humanity and understanding for the Saxon common people

_____ 12. Given by Henry in exchange for Gwendolen

_____ 13. Flogged Henry

_____ 14. Had been Becket's spiritual father

_____ 15. Took money from Henry and helped Becket at the same time

_____ 16. Was to be crowned before his father's death

_____ 17. Banishing a person from the rites of the Church

_____ 18. Negotiated the final meeting between Henry and Becket

_____ 19. Becket's killers

_____ 20. Scene of Becket's death

A. Becket's father
B. Hastings
C. Archbishop of Canterbury
D. Gwendolen
E. Folliot
F. Henry III
G. Becket
H. Louis of France
I. Chancellor
J. Young Monk
K. Abbey of St. Martin
L. Canterbury Cathedral
M. The Queen
N. Excommunication
O. Saxon common people
P. Norman barons
Q. Saxon peasant girl
R. The Pope
S. Saxon monks
T. Henry

NAME _____ DATE _____

Becket by Jean Anouilh

Answer each of the following questions in two or three complete sentences.

1. In the scene with the Saxon peasant family, how does Becket show that he is more humane than Henry is?

   _____

   _____

   _____

   _____

2. Why does Becket spare the life of the young Saxon monk?

   _____

   _____

   _____

   _____

3. How does Becket change after he becomes Archbishop of Canterbury?

   _____

   _____

   _____

   _____

4. Why does Becket decide to come out of hiding and return to his post as Archbishop?

   _____

   _____

   _____

   _____

5. How does the final meeting scene show Henry's loneliness and confusion?

   _____

   _____

   _____

   _____

CHALLENGE

A developing character is one who changes by growth and experience. Write an essay to explain which of the two is the more developing character, Henry or Becket. Support your answer with evidence from the play.

NAME _____ DATE _____

A Tale of Two Cities by Charles Dickens

In the numbered blanks at the left, write the letter of the matching person or place. You may use a letter more than once.

_____ 1. The most hated aristocratic name in France

_____ 2. London residence of the Manettes

_____ 3. Loyal employee of Tellson's bank

_____ 4. French hometown of Dr. Manette

_____ 5. The Golden Thread

_____ 6. Worked as a spy on both sides of the Revolution

_____ 7. Was acquitted on a charge of treason against the King of England

_____ 8. Secret society of the French Revolution

_____ 9. Prisoner in 105 North Tower

_____ 10. Faithful servant who cared for his former employer

_____ 11. Poorest section of Paris

_____ 12. Had been responsible for the death of Madame DeFarge's family

_____ 13. Gave his life to save the life of another

_____ 14. Was fiercely protective of her "Lady Bird"

_____ 15. Gained his legal reputation through the hard work of another

_____ 16. Kept the records of those who would be exterminated by the Revolution

_____ 17. Symbol of French oppression and injustice

_____ 18. Was hanged for the murder of an aristocrat

_____ 19. Described himself as a "fisherman"

_____ 20. Wrote to his former employer for help

A. Jarvis Lorry
B. Alexandre Manette
C. Miss Pross
D. Lucie Manette
E. Jerry Cruncher
F. Madame DeFarge
G. Gabelle
H. John Basard
I. Monsieur DeFarge
J. Evremonde
K. Monsieur Le Marquis
L. Mr. Stryver
M. Charles Darnay
N. Saint Antoine
O. Beauvais
P. Bastille
Q. Sidney Carton
R. Soho
S. Jacques

NAME _____ DATE _____

A Tale of Two Cities by Charles Dickens

Answer each of the following questions in two or three complete sentences.

1. Why does Mr. Lorry go to meet Miss Manette in Dover?

    _____

    _____

    _____

    _____

2. Why are Stryver and Carton called "the lion and the jackal"?

    _____

    _____

    _____

    _____

3. How does Charles Darnay differ from his uncle in his attitude toward wealth and class privilege?

    _____

    _____

    _____

    _____

4. Why is the term, "a man of business," an ironic contradiction to Jarvis Lorry's real character?

    _____

    _____

    _____

    _____

5. How does Sidney Carton get into LaForce, and how does he get Charles Darnay out?

    _____

    _____

    _____

    _____

CHALLENGE

Loyalty and love, even at the cost of great personal sacrifice, are major themes in *A Tale of Two Cities*. Discuss three characters, and the way that each illustrates such loyalty in his/her actions.

NAME _____ DATE _____

April Morning by Howard Fast

Correctly complete each sentence with information from the novel.

1. The events of this novel cover a period of _____.

2. Moses Cooper most loved to _____.

3. _____ was Adam's younger brother.

4. Of all his family members, Adam was closest to _____.

5. Adam officially joins the Lexington militia by _____.

6. _____ was the commander of the Lexington militia.

7. Joseph Simmons was a _____ by profession.

8. The militia appointed _____ as their spokesman to talk with the British.

9. The first Lexington man shot by the British was _____.

10. The main highway from Concord to Boston was the _____.

11. _____ found Adam in the woods, and took him to the gathering of the other militiamen.

12. The militia attacked the British army from _____.

13. _____ became a substitute father for Adam and his brother.

14. The militia was divided into two companies: men with _____, and men with _____.

15. The first dead soldier that Adam saw up close was _____.

16. For a time, the men thought Adam was dead because he _____.

17. The Lexington militia helped drive the British back to _____.

18. Adam decided to marry _____.

19. Adam's mother sent him to church with _____.

20. All of the militiamen were planning to muster for _____.

NAME _____ DATE _____

April Morning by Howard Fast

Answer each of the following questions in two or three complete sentences.

1. Why did Adam think that his father hated him?

   _____
   _____
   _____
   _____

2. On the night before the fighting began, how did Moses Cooper show his love for his son?

   _____
   _____
   _____
   _____

3. What did the Lexington men plan to do when the British came? Why did this plan fail?

   _____
   _____
   _____
   _____

4. Why did Cousin Simmons tell Adam that the fighting must continue?

   _____
   _____
   _____
   _____

5. How does Adam Cooper change in a single day?

   _____
   _____
   _____
   _____

CHALLENGE

Write an essay describing some of the things that may happen to Adam Cooper in the days and weeks that followed the Battle of Lexington.

NAME _____ DATE _____

Cimarron by Edna Ferber

Select the letter of the word or phrase which correctly completes each statement.

_____ 1. Yancey and Sabra came to Oklahoma from (A) Massachusetts (B) Kentucky (C) Mississippi (D) Kansas.

_____ 2. Yancey intended to earn his living by (A) mining (B) selling real estate (C) practicing law (D) publishing a newspaper.

_____ 3. Sabra's most valuable possession brought from her old home was (A) her china (B) Mother Briget's quilt (C) the silver (D) the family photo album.

_____ 4. Yancey did all of the following in Osage except (A) conduct a church service (B) practice law (C) write flaming editorials (D) run for public office.

_____ 5. Of greatest help to Sabra during their first years in Oklahoma was (A) Cim (B) Isaiah (C) Ruby (D) Jesse.

_____ 6. Yancey left Sabra the first time to (A) fight in World War I (B) participate in another land run (C) drill for oil (D) run for Congress.

_____ 7. When Sabra went home to visit, she (A) decided to stay (B) was bored (C) loved the life of luxury again (D) decided to divorce Yancey.

_____ 8. Yancey's most spectacular court appearance was in defense of (A) Dixie Lee (B) Pegler (C) the Kid (D) Sol Levy.

_____ 9. *The Wigwam* was a success through the efforts of (A) Yancey (B) Jesse (C) Sabra (D) the territorial government.

_____ 10. Yancey continually championed the cause of (A) the oil men (B) the original settlers (C) the Indians (D) the ranch owners.

_____ 11. Isaiah was killed by (A) outlaws (B) Indian torture (C) a tornado (D) a white posse.

_____ 12. Sabra gained influence in the community through (A) the paper (B) women's groups (C) political involvement (D) all of the above.

_____ 13. The rich man who always remained an outsider was (A) Sol Levy (B) Tracy Wyatt (C) Big Elk (D) Doctor Valliant.

_____ 14. Donna Cravat (A) was sent to finishing school (B) married a rich man (C) was a great disappointment to her mother (D) all of the above.

_____ 15. The total social revolution in Osage came with the discovery of (A) oil (B) gold (C) silver (D) copper.

_____ 16. Yancey forced Sabra to (A) shut down the paper (B) stay out of politics (C) attend her son's wedding (D) not to hire any more Indian help.

_____ 17. Sabra was elected (A) mayor (B) governor (C) Congresswoman (D) chairman of the town's political action committee.

_____ 18. The statue representing pioneer spirit was a portrait of (A) Sabra (B) Yancey (C) the Kid (D) young Cim.

_____ 19. The symbol of real power behind the growth of Oklahoma, according to Edna Ferber, was (A) the rifle (B) the covered wagon (C) the sunbonnet (D) the oil well.

_____ 20. Yancey Cravat died (A) on an oil field (B) after he had saved the lives of others (C) in the arms of his wife (D) all of the above.

NAME _____ DATE _____

Cimarron by Edna Ferber

Answer each of the following questions in two or three complete sentences.

1. Describe how Yancey lost his claim when he made his first land run.

   _____

   _____

   _____

   _____

2. What characteristics quickly made Yancey an Oklahoma legend?

   _____

   _____

   _____

   _____

3. How did Sabra keep the family together during Yancey's long absences?

   _____

   _____

   _____

   _____

4. Why were both of Sabra's children a disappointment to her?

   _____

   _____

   _____

   _____

5. How did the discovery of oil drastically change life in Oklahoma?

   _____

   _____

   _____

   _____

CHALLENGE

How were both Sabra and Yancey Cravat symbols of the pioneer spirit which developed the American West?

NAME _____ DATE _____

The Great Gatsby by F. Scott Fitzgerald
Correctly complete each sentence with information from the novel.

1. The story is told by _____.

2. Nick meets Gatsby when _____.

3. Jordan Baker's boredom with life is shown by _____.

4. Daisy believes the best thing a girl can be in this world is _____

   _____.

5. Four adjectives which would best describe Gatsby's parties are _____ ,

   _____ , _____ , and _____.

6. The area between Long Island and the city is called _____ ,

   and is presided over by _____.

7. Nick sees Gatsby staring across the water at _____.

8. Myrtle Wilson may be totally contrasted with Daisy as _____.

9. The party at Tom's city apartment ends abruptly when _____.

10. When he attends Gatsby's party, the only person Nick knows is _____.

11. Nick learns from Jordan the story of _____.

12. Daisy did not marry Gatsby because _____.

13. The big mystery about Gatsby's money was _____.

14. Nick made arrangements for a meeting between _____

    at _____.

15. When they toured Gatsby's mansion, Daisy is most emotionally affected by _____.

16. Gatsby had inherited his money from _____.

17. When the group goes to the city, Tom drives _____.

18. Myrtle is jealous when she thinks that _____ is _____.

19. Myrtle Wilson is killed by _____ , but _____ takes the blame.

20. Wilson shoots Gatsby because _____.

NAME _____ DATE _____

The Great Gatsby by F. Scott Fitzgerald

Answer each of the following questions in two or three complete sentences.

1. Nick says that Tom and Daisy were "careless people." How does the novel support this statement?

    _____

    _____

    _____

    _____

2. Why does Nick, as an outside observer, make an effective narrator?

    _____

    _____

    _____

    _____

3. How is the reality of Gatsby's past contrasted to the false image of wealth that he has presented to the world?

    _____

    _____

    _____

    _____

4. How do Tom and Gatsby present a definite study in contrast?

    _____

    _____

    _____

5. How is Gatsby's funeral scene a contrast to the party scenes presented earlier in the novel?

    _____

    _____

    _____

    _____

CHALLENGE

Write an essay citing specific scenes from *The Great Gatsby* which illustrate the lostness of the American fun-seeking generation of the 1920s.

NAME _____ DATE _____

Johnny Tremain by Esther Forbes

Select the letter of the word or phrase which correctly completes each statement.

_____ 1. Johnny had been apprenticed to Mr. Lapham at the request of (A) his father (B) Paul Revere (C) his mother (D) Mrs. Lapham.

_____ 2. Johnny bossed the other apprentices because (A) he was older (B) he was more skilled as a silversmith (C) he was bigger (D) he was related to the Laphams.

_____ 3. Johnny injured his hand while he was making a sugar bowl for (A) Lavinia Lyte (B) John Hancock (C) James Otis (D) Paul Revere.

_____ 4. Mrs. Lapham did not call a doctor when Johnny injured his hand because (A) she didn't care about Johnny (B) working on the Sabbath was illegal (C) she didn't want Mr. Lapham to know that they had been working (D) she didn't want Dove to get into any trouble.

_____ 5. Of all the Lapham girls, Johnny was closest to (A) Madge (B) Dorcas (C) Isannah (D) Cilla.

_____ 6. After he was injured, the first job that Johnny could get was (A) with a butcher (B) with Mr. Hancock (C) with the *Observer* (D) at the Lytes.

_____ 7. The Observers were (A) a secret political organization (B) a group of British sympathizers (C) a social club (D) a branch of the colonial militia.

_____ 8. The British officer who became Johnny's friend was (A) Lt. Stranger (B) Col. Smith (C) Sgt. Gale (D) Maj. Pitcairn.

_____ 9. Mr. Tweedie was finally married to (A) Madge (B) Dorcas (C) Mrs. Lapham (D) Cilla.

_____ 10. Johnny's sources of information about British activities included (A) Dove (B) wastebasket scraps (C) Lydia (D) all of the above.

_____ 11. Rab finally got his musket (A) from Sgt. Gale (B) from Pumpkin (C) by stealing it (D) from the stable at the Afric Queen.

_____ 12. Uncle Lorne's contribution to the rebellion was as a (A) printer (B) spy (C) rider and courier (D) gunsmith.

_____ 13. The greatest orator in Boston was (A) Sam Adams (B) Paul Revere (C) James Otis (D) Dr. Warren.

_____ 14. Johnny learned the truth of his relationship with the Lyte family from (A) Lavinia (B) the judge in court (C) Mr. Lyte (D) Bessie the housekeeper.

_____ 15. Johnny got out of Boston by (A) riding Goblin (B) pretending to be drunk (C) disguising himself as a British private (D) stowing away on a ship.

_____ 16. The one who died of wounds received at Lexington was (A) Rab (B) Pumpkin (C) Dr. Warren (D) Grandsire Silsbee.

_____ 17. Isannah Lapham (A) died of illness (B) went to England with Lavinia (C) went home to live with her mother (D) married Johnny.

_____ 18. The British soldiers in this novel are presented as (A) totally evil men (B) enemies of all colonials (C) ordinary men with a nasty job to do (D) men without thoughts or personalities.

_____ 19. Johnny's attitude most greatly changes toward (A) Dove (B) Cilla (C) Rab (D) Mr. Lyte.

_____ 20. Dr. Warren says that he can operate on Johnny's hand so Johnny will be able to (A) fire a gun (B) become a silversmith (C) work in a print shop (D) make bullets.

NAME _____ DATE _____

Johnny Tremain by Esther Forbes

Answer each of the following questions in two or three complete sentences.

1. How does Johnny injure his hand?

   _____

   _____

   _____

   _____

2. How does Johnny change after he is injured?

   _____

   _____

   _____

   _____

3. In what ways does Johnny become useful to the Sons of Liberty?

   _____

   _____

   _____

   _____

4. What are Johnny's connections with the Lyte family?

   _____

   _____

   _____

   _____

5. What does James Otis mean when he says that the colonials must fight "so that a man can stand up"?

   _____

   _____

   _____

   _____

CHALLENGE

What are some of the ways that Esther Forbes presents both the British and the Americans as people who are caught up in forces of conflict which are beyond their control?

NAME _____ DATE _____

The Lion in Winter by James Goldman

In the numbered blanks at the left, write the letter of the matching person or place. You may use a letter more than once.

_____ 1. Henry's eldest son who had died

_____ 2. Determined to leave his kingdom intact to only one of his sons

_____ 3. Had raised Alais as a child

_____ 4. Refused to be called any man's "boy"

_____ 5. Philip's sister, who had been promised in marriage to Richard

_____ 6. Sought Philip as an ally in a war against his father

_____ 7. Middle son with the cold, calculating mind

_____ 8. Section of France that had been Eleanor's dowry

_____ 9. Youngest, weakest, most disgusting of Henry's sons

_____ 10. Could resist almost any temptation except Henry's offer of freedom

_____ 11. Time when the main action of the play takes place

_____ 12. Setting of the play

_____ 13. Henry's friend and personal messenger

_____ 14. Eleanor's favorite son

_____ 15. Where Eleanor was imprisoned

_____ 16. Eleanor's first husband

_____ 17. Son not mentioned as a possible king

_____ 18. Wanted a divorce so he could marry and have more sons

_____ 19. Henry's mistress whom Eleanor hated

_____ 20. Land that was Alais' dowry

A. Alais Capet
B. Chinon Castle
C. Salisbury Tower
D. Prince Henry
E. Richard
F. John
G. Rosamund
H. Henry II
I. Eleanor
J. Geoffrey
K. Christmas Court
L. William Marshal
M. Aquitaine
N. Philip of France
O. Louis of France
P. Vixen

NAME _____ DATE _____

The Lion in Winter by James Goldman

Answer each of the following questions in two or three complete sentences.

1. How does the play show that Eleanor and Henry enjoy the plots that they are constantly hatching against each other?

    _____

    _____

    _____

    _____

2. How is Alais a victim of the plots of the other characters?

    _____

    _____

    _____

3. Why does Geoffrey feel neglected and angry?

    _____

    _____

    _____

    _____

4. What does Eleanor finally admit is the one thing that she really wants?

    _____

    _____

    _____

    _____

5. How does the audience know, at the end of the play, that this family feud is not over?

    _____

    _____

    _____

    _____

CHALLENGE

Write an essay to defend or refute the following statement: Despite their many feuds, Henry II and his Queen Eleanor still love each other deeply.

NAME _____   DATE _____

The House of the Seven Gables by Nathaniel Hawthorne

Select the letter of the word or phrase which correctly completes each statement.

_____ 1. The House of the Seven Gables had been built by (A) Colonel Pyncheon (B) Clifford (C) Matthew Maule (D) Cousin Jaffrey.

_____ 2. In order to seize the land that he desired, Pyncheon had Matthew Maule (A) executed as a wizard (B) run out of town (C) financially ruined (D) thrown into prison.

_____ 3. The people of the town believed that the house was (A) elegant (B) well-built (C) cursed (D) all of the above.

_____ 4. On the day that the house was to have had its first great reception, the Colonel (A) died (B) became governor (C) established his land claim (D) married his new bride.

_____ 5. Hepzibah may be described as (A) homely (B) shy (C) loyal (D) all of the above.

_____ 6. Jaffrey Pyncheon (A) genuinely wants to help Hepzibah (B) dislikes Phoebe (C) looks just like the Colonel (D) is very fond of Clifford.

_____ 7. Hepzibah's closest friend and helper becomes (A) Holgrave (B) Phoebe (C) Cousin Alice (D) Uncle Venner.

_____ 8. Phoebe (A) takes over the shopkeeping chores (B) helps Clifford (C) is a good gardener (D) all of the above.

_____ 9. After his return to the house, Clifford is (A) aggressive and violent (B) childlike (C) a total recluse (D) determined to get revenge.

_____ 10. When Jaffrey wants to see Clifford, Hepzibah (A) faints (B) absolutely refuses (C) begs Jaffrey to leave (D) calls the police.

_____ 11. Holgrave the daguerreotypist (A) has been to Europe (B) has practiced hypnosis (C) writes short stories (D) all of the above.

_____ 12. Alice Pyncheon was destroyed by (A) her father's greed (B) her own poor health (C) Maule's desire for revenge (D) her weak mind.

_____ 13. Uncle Venner may be described as (A) an optimist (B) the town philosopher (C) an eccentric (D) all of the above.

_____ 14. Phoebe has to return home (A) because her mother is ill (B) to finish taking care of some personal matters (C) because she is afraid of Clifford (D) because Jaffrey tells her to leave.

_____ 15. Jaffrey wants Clifford to surrender (A) the combination to the safe (B) the deed to the house (C) the documents regarding the missing land claim (D) the personal letters of Judge Pyncheon.

_____ 16. Jaffrey threatens to send Clifford (A) to an insane asylum (B) back to prison (C) to the hospital (D) out of the country.

_____ 17. Jaffrey Pyncheon dies (A) when Hepzibah shoots him (B) when Clifford strangles him (C) in the same way the Colonel had died (D) of food poisoning.

_____ 18. When they find Jaffrey's body, Clifford and Hepzibah (A) run away (B) notify the constable (C) turn to Holgrave for help (D) hide the body in a closet.

_____ 19. Holgrave views Pyncheon's death as (A) part of the curse (B) a fulfillment of Maule's prophecy (C) a just punishment for Jaffrey's wickedness (D) all of the above.

_____ 20. At end of the novel, the House of the Seven Gables (A) falls into ruin (B) is owned by Phoebe and Holgrave (C) is cared for by Uncle Venner (D) burns down.

150 Great Books

NAME _____ DATE _____

The House of the Seven Gables by Nathaniel Hawthorne

Answer each of the following questions in two or three complete sentences.

1. How is Hepzibah exactly like the house itself?

   _____

   _____

   _____

   _____

2. Tell briefly why the house is supposed to have been cursed.

   _____

   _____

   _____

   _____

3. How does Phoebe's arrival change the lives of Hepzibah and Clifford?

   _____

   _____

   _____

   _____

4. Why did Jaffrey have Clifford sent to prison?

   _____

   _____

   _____

   _____

5. Why are Uncle Venner and Holgrave important characters in the story?

   _____

   _____

   _____

   _____

CHALLENGE

One of Nathaniel Hawthorne's major literary themes is that sin and guilt in one generation greatly affect all future generations. Explain how this theme is illustrated in *The House of the Seven Gables*.

NAME _____ DATE _____

The Scarlet Letter by Nathaniel Hawthorne

Select the letter of the word or phrase which correctly completes each statement.

_____ 1. The setting of the novel is (A) London (B) Virginia (C) Massachusetts (D) New York.

_____ 2. For her crime of adultery, Hester is sentenced to (A) exile (B) wear the letter A (C) death (D) being branded on the forehead.

_____ 3. Chillingworth is the name that is used by Hester's (A) father (B) physician (C) pastor (D) husband.

_____ 4. Arthur Dimmesdale is (A) intellectually brilliant (B) weak and sickly (C) respected by the community (D) all of the above.

_____ 5. Hester earns her living as a (A) seamstress (B) cleaning lady (C) librarian (D) soap- and candlemaker.

_____ 6. Whom does the following quote describe? "She was lady-like too, after the manner of the feminine gentility of those days; characterized by a certain state and dignity." (A) Hester (B) Mistress Hibbins (C) Pearl (D) the governor's wife.

_____ 7. Who or what is being described? "It was the scarlet letter endowed with life." (A) Pearl (B) Hester (C) Dimmesdale's tombstone (D) the letter that Hester wore on her breast.

_____ 8. Who did the following? "Holding his hand over his heart as was his custom, whenever his peculiarly nervous temperment was thrown into agitation." (A) Chillingworth (B) Bellingham (C) Winthrop (D) Dimmesdale.

_____ 9. Who is described in the following way? "At first his expression had been calm, meditative, scholarlike. Now there was something ugly and evil in his face which they had not previously noticed." (A) the sea captain (B) Chillingworth (C) Dimmesdale (D) the Apostle Eliot.

_____ 10. Who did the following? "He has violated in cold blood the sanctity of a human heart." (A) Bellingham (B) Dimmesdale (C) Chillingworth (D) Winthrop.

NAME _____ DATE _____

The Scarlet Letter by Nathaniel Hawthorne

Answer each of the following questions in two or three complete sentences.

1. How is the community wrong in the way that it treats Hester and Pearl?

    _____

    _____

    _____

    _____

2. How does Hester's relationship with the town change as the years pass?

    _____

    _____

    _____

    _____

3. What does Chillingworth's search for revenge do to him?

    _____

    _____

    _____

    _____

4. What happens to Dimmesdale because of his guilt?

    _____

    _____

    _____

    _____

5. Why is the third scaffold scene the most important scene in the novel?

    _____

    _____

    _____

    _____

CHALLENGE

Why is *The Scarlet Letter* often called the first significant psychological novel in American literature?

NAME _____ DATE _____

The Country of the Pointed Firs by Sarah Orne Jewett

Correctly complete each sentence with information from the novel.

1. The town where the story is set is called _____.

2. The narrator goes to the village in order to _____.

3. Almira Todd specializes in _____.

4. Captain Littlepage tells the visitor _____.

5. The narrator enjoys her visit with Mrs. Blackett and William because _____

   _____.

6. During their visit to Green Island, Mrs. Todd tells her friend the story of _____

   _____.

7. The visitor rents the abandoned schoolhouse so she _____.

8. Mrs. Todd enjoys a visit with her friend, _____.

9. Mrs. Todd's main competitor in the village was _____.

10. Mrs. Todd's cousin Joanna had chosen to live alone on Shell-Heap Island because

    _____.

11. During her visit to Shell-Heap Island, the narrator felt _____.

12. Mrs. Todd and her friend make a long trip to _____.

13. The aspects of the family reunion that the visitor enjoys most are _____.

14. Elijah Tilley talks with the visitor about _____.

15. William's girlfriend Esther is a _____.

16. Mrs. Todd and the narrator visit an old lady who believes she is a twin to _____

    _____.

17. The narrator attends the wedding of _____.

18. Esther carries a _____ to her wedding.

19. The story ends as the narrator _____.

20. Mrs. Todd's parting gifts to the summer visitor include _____.

150 Great Books

NAME _____ DATE _____

The Country of the Pointed Firs by Sarah Orne Jewett

Answer each of the following questions in two or three complete sentences.

1. Describe the unique features of Dunnet Landing and the surrounding territory.

   _____

   _____

   _____

   _____

2. What are some of the great strengths of Almira Todd's personality?

   _____

   _____

   _____

   _____

3. Every small village has a few local characters. Who are some of the very odd characters in Dunnet Landing?

   _____

   _____

   _____

   _____

4. What makes Mrs. Blackett such a very special person?

   _____

   _____

   _____

   _____

5. How does the city-bred narrator change as a result of the time that she spends at the Landing?

   _____

   _____

   _____

   _____

CHALLENGE

Discuss some of the important values of life that the city girl learns from Dunnet Landing and its people.

NAME _____ DATE _____

Doctor Zhivago by Boris Pasternak

Select the letter of the word or phrase that correctly completes each statement.

_____ 1. The novel opens with the death of (A) Yuri's father (B) Yuri's mother (C) the Tzar (D) Lara's father.

_____ 2. One witness to the suicide of Yuri's father was (A) Misha Gordon (B) Uncle Nikolai (C) Yuri (D) Mr. Gromeko.

_____ 3. A first sign of the approaching revolution was a massive strike by the (A) railroad workers (B) university students (C) dock workers (D) members of the army.

_____ 4. At the Sventitsky's Christmas party, Lara (A) meets Yuri (B) first meets Komarovsky (C) tries to shoot Komarovsky (D) becomes engaged to Pasha.

_____ 5. After their marriage, Lara and Pasha (A) work on the farm (B) teach school (C) work for the Communist party (D) do hospital work.

_____ 6. An important weather symbol which recurs in the novel is (A) rain (B) sunset (C) snow (D) fog.

_____ 7. After the revolution, Yuri takes his family out of Moscow (A) by train (B) so they can get enough to eat (C) to the estate of Tonia's grandfather (D) all of the above.

_____ 8. The military conflict which ravaged the Russian people was primarily between (A) the Tzar and the peasants (B) rival communist factions (C) Russia and Germany (D) Russia and Japan.

_____ 9. On the estate and Varykino, the family lived mainly by (A) Yuri's selling poetry (B) farming (C) the help of a friend who had government connections (D) cutting lumber.

_____ 10. In Yuriatin, Yuri again sees Lara (A) in the hospital (B) on the street (C) in the library (D) at the railroad station.

_____ 11. On his way back to Tonia and his son, Yuri (A) changes his mind and returns to Lara (B) is captured (C) is shot (D) meets Lara's husband.

_____ 12. One of the cruelest revolutionary commanders is (A) Yuri's brother (B) Lara's husband (C) the son of Zhivago's estate manager (D) Tonia's cousin.

_____ 13. Yuri escapes from the rebel camp (A) on skis (B) in the back of a truck (C) by stealing a horse (D) disguised as a woman.

_____ 14. Lara's letter tells Yuri that (A) her husband is still alive (B) Yuri has a daughter (C) his family has gone back to Moscow (D) all of the above.

_____ 15. Yuri and Lara spend their happiest time (A) in her apartment (B) in Varykino (C) in Moscow (D) in the forest near Yuriatin.

_____ 16. Yuri's family was deported to (A) Berlin (B) London (C) Paris (D) Siberia.

_____ 17. Lara and her daughter were helped to escape by (A) Yuri (B) Komarovsky (C) Strelnikov (D) Misha Gordon.

_____ 18. Before his death, Lara's husband (A) confesses his crimes (B) apologizes to Yuri (C) is reunited with his wife (D) is assured of his wife's love.

_____ 19. The last writing that Yuri Zhivago did was (A) poems (B) novels (C) political pamphlets (D) plays.

_____ 20. Lara (A) later met Yuri's wife (B) was never seen in Moscow again (C) did not know of Yuri's death (D) probably died in a concentration camp.

NAME _____ DATE _____

Doctor Zhivago by Boris Pasternak

Answer each of the following questions in two or three complete sentences.

1. In what ways did Lara and Yuri both have very troubled childhood experiences?

_____

_____

_____

_____

2. What experiences of Zhivago's showed his very poetic reaction to nature?

_____

_____

_____

_____

3. What hardships did the Zhivago family experience on their train trip to the country?

_____

_____

_____

_____

4. When he was captured, why had Yuri decided to leave Lara and return to Tonia?

_____

_____

_____

_____

5. Why are Yuri and Lara so happy during their final days together?

_____

_____

_____

_____

CHALLENGE

Write an essay explaining how *Doctor Zhivago* portrays both the personal revolution of an individual and the general revolution of the Russian nation.

NAME _____ DATE _____

The Winthrop Woman by Anya Seton

In the numbered blanks at the left, write the letter of the matching person or place.

_____ 1. Son-in-law who accused Elizabeth of adultery with Hallet

_____ 2. Elizabeth's father who was an apothecary

_____ 3. Elizabeth's first husband

_____ 4. Weak man who went mad because of his guilty feelings about his past

_____ 5. Had been the boyhood companion of an English nobleman

_____ 6. Dutchwoman who was Elizabeth's neighbor and close friend

_____ 7. Autocratic head of the Winthrop family

_____ 8. Indian who spared Elizabeth's life because she had once saved him

_____ 9. Governor who arranged for Elizabeth's marriage to Hallet

_____ 10. Elizabeth's beloved aunt and substitute mother

_____ 11. Gypsy who told Elizabeth that she would spend her life searching after freedom

_____ 12. Boatman who transported the family from Massachusetts Bay to Greenwich

_____ 13. Elizabeth's jilted fiancé

_____ 14. English country estate of the Winthrop family

_____ 15. Military captain who died defending Elizabeth and Hallet

_____ 16. Woman who was excommunicated for her belief in a theology of grace and inner light

_____ 17. Connecticut peninsula very special to Elizabeth

_____ 18. Elizabeth's worldly companion on the voyage to Massachusetts

_____ 19. Most beloved of the Winthrop sons

_____ 20. Elizabeth's Indian servant and friend

A. Harry
B. Jack
C. Groton
D. John Winthrop
E. Mirabelle Gardiner
F. Telaka
G. Robert Feake
H. Toby Feake
I. Margaret
J. Monakewaygo
K. Thomas Lyon
L. Keofferam
M. William Hallet
N. Peyto
O. Anne Hutchinson
P. Anneke Patrick
Q. Daniel Patrick
R. Stuyvesant
S. Thomas Fones
T. Edward Howes

150 Great Books

NAME _____ DATE _____

The Winthrop Woman by Anya Seton

Answer each of the following questions in two or three complete sentences.

1. Why did Elizabeth find Harry and his friends so fascinating?

_____

_____

_____

_____

2. What character traits did Elizabeth have, even in her childhood, which were very unsuitable for a proper Puritan matron?

_____

_____

_____

_____

3. What political difficulties did John Winthrop have in the Massachusetts Bay Colony?

_____

_____

_____

_____

4. Why were Elizabeth and Robert Feake forced to leave Massachusetts Bay?

_____

_____

_____

_____

5. What difficulties did Elizabeth and Hallet have in legally becoming husband and wife?

_____

_____

_____

_____

CHALLENGE

Discuss why Elizabeth Winthrop was a survivor. How did she battle against the authoritarian systems and the physical difficulties of her society?

NAME _____   DATE _____

Exodus by Leon Uris

In the numbered blanks at the left, write the letter of the matching person, place, or thing.

_____   1. Term for a native-born Jewish Palestinian

_____   2. First document which promised the Jews a homeland in Palestine

_____   3. Ally of Hitler, led the Arab hate-campaign against the Jews

_____   4. American nurse who wanted to stay neutral in the conflict

_____   5. Ship loaded with children that forced the British to give in

_____   6. Walked from Russia to Palestine

_____   7. Retired British general who settled in Palestine and aided the Jewish cause

_____   8. Survived the ghetto of Warsaw and the Nazi concentration camps

_____   9. Jewish terrorist society

_____   10. Female warrior who trained Jewish children in the art of self-defense

_____   11. Leader of the diplomatic negotiations which helped to create the state of Israel

_____   12. Head of the Jewish terrorist organization

_____   13. Communal farms established to reclaim land in Palestine

_____   14. Children's settlement in Galilee where Karen and Kitty lived

_____   15. German Jewish girl who was hidden by a Danish Christian family

_____   16. Worked in an airlift operation to bring Jews to Palestine

_____   17. Organization for illegal Jewish immigration

_____   18. Engineered the mass breakout from the Acre jail

_____   19. Gave his life building a road to lift the seige of Jerusalem

_____   20. Journalist whose story from Cyprus brought the plight of the refugee children to the attention of the world

A. Haj Amin
B. Jordana
C. Foster J. MacWilliams
D. Maccabees
E. Kibbutz
F. Sabra
G. Sutherland
H. Mossad Aliyah Bet
I. Akiva
J. Exodus
K. Ari Ben Canaan
L. Gan Dafna
M. Balfour Declaration
N. Mark Parker
O. Yakov and Jossi Rabinsky
P. Karen Hansen Clemett
Q. Dov Landau
R. Barak Ben Canaan
S. David Ben Ami
T. Kitty Fremont

150 Great Books

NAME _____ DATE _____

Exodus by Leon Uris

Answer each of the following questions in two or three complete sentences.

1. Why did Kitty want so much to take Karen to America?

   _____

   _____

   _____

   _____

2. What were some of the impossible odds facing the Jewish settlers in Palestine?

   _____

   _____

   _____

   _____

3. How does the situation of Taha and the village of Abu Yesha illustrate the human tragedy of the conflict between the Arabs and the Jews?

   _____

   _____

   _____

   _____

4. How did Ari run the *Exodus* operation right under the noses of the British?

   _____

   _____

   _____

   _____

5. How did Dov learn survival? How did Karen help him learn to love?

   _____

   _____

   _____

   _____

CHALLENGE

Write an essay explaining whether Leon Uris is biased or objective in the historical material which he presents. Is Uris too pro-Jewish, and too anti-British and anti-Arab? Does his bias weaken or strengthen the total effectiveness of the novel?

NAME _____ DATE _____

The Friendly Persuasion by Jessamyn West

Place a (+) before each statement that is true and a (0) before each statement that is false.

_____ 1. Jess Birdwell is a Quaker minister.

_____ 2. Mattie showed the same talent for playing the organ that Eliza did.

_____ 3. Enoch was the youngest of the Birdwell's sons.

_____ 4. The Birdwells had one daughter who died in childhood.

_____ 5. Eliza tended to be more superstitious and poetic than Jess did.

_____ 6. When Samantha became Eliza's pet, Jess was caught in a conflict between his love for his wife and his hatred for geese.

_____ 7. Labe understood better than Josh did that Old Alf needed someone to talk to.

_____ 8. To Mattie, Eliza's wedding ring made a sound which represented happiness and marriage.

_____ 9. Josh was wounded by a rifle bullet at the Battle of Finney's Ford.

_____ 10. The Birdwell farm was raided by Morgan's troops.

_____ 11. The buried Bible page represented a link with the Birdwell family past.

_____ 12. Lady was a better-looking horse than Red Rover was.

_____ 13. Eliza got just as emotionally involved in the race with Rev. Godley's horse as Jess did.

_____ 14. Eliza would not let Lafe Millspaugh eat at her table because Lafe refused to wash.

_____ 15. Jess was a great believer in modern, progressive innovations.

_____ 16. Jess realized the state of his own good health when he saw the problems and illnesses of others.

_____ 17. Eliza had done all of the painting on her special vase early one morning when she was first married.

_____ 18. Jess and Eliza were pleased with all of their children's choices of husbands and wives.

_____ 19. "The Illumination" refers in part to Jess's installing of inside electricity.

_____ 20. Before Jess met Homer, Eliza had already died.

150 Great Books

NAME _____ DATE _____

The Friendly Persuasion by Jessamyn West

Answer each of the following questions in two or three complete sentences.

1. What traits of Jess's were not quite in keeping with his Quaker beliefs?

    _____

    _____

    _____

    _____

2. In what ways is Eliza both a practical woman and a woman of deep feeling?

    _____

    _____

    _____

    _____

3. What lesson does Jess learn when he acquires Lady, the mare?

    _____

    _____

    _____

    _____

4. What conflict did Josh Birdwell face when he thought that Morgan's raiders were approaching his home?

    _____

    _____

    _____

    _____

5. How does Jess's occupation as a nurseryman increase his sensitivity to life?

    _____

    _____

    _____

    _____

CHALLENGE

Write an essay describing three objects which have great meaning in Jess and Eliza's married life. Explain the significance of each object.

NAME _____ DATE _____

The Caine Mutiny Court-Martial by Herman Wouk

Correctly complete each sentence with information from the novel.

1. Maryk's position on the *Caine* was _____.

2. The *Caine*'s job in the Navy was _____.

3. Greenwald took the job defending Maryk because _____

   _____.

4. The lawyer for the prosecution was _____.

5. Maryk had taken command of the *Caine* during _____.

6. Keefer's occupation in civilian life was as a _____.

7. Maryk had kept a log of _____.

8. When they went to present the information to the admiral, Keefer _____

   _____.

9. Keith accused Queeg of _____.

10. Queeg had forced Keith to pay for _____.

11. The men said that in landing the Marine forces, Queeg had _____

    _____.

12. Greenwald forces Dr. Lundeen to label Queeg's personality as _____.

13. Besides Maryk himself, the only witness that the defense called was _____.

14. The psychiatrists labeled Queeg as very _____.

15. Maryk obtained most of his knowledge of psychology from _____.

16. Greenwald gets Maryk acquitted by _____.

17. Queeg said that he had been harsh with his men in order to _____.

18. The judge refuses to _____.

19. The party in the last scene is to celebrate _____.

20. Greenwald says that the one most guilty of destructive behavior is _____.

150 Great Books

NAME _____ DATE _____

The Caine Mutiny Court-Martial by Herman Wouk

Answer each of the following questions in two or three complete sentences.

1. Why did Queeg's crew dislike him so intensely?

   _____

   _____

   _____

   _____

2. According to Dr. Bird, how did Captain Queeg's navy command compensate for his psychological problems?

   _____

   _____

   _____

   _____

3. What did the captain do to make Maryk take control of the *Caine*?

   _____

   _____

   _____

   _____

4. How did Keefer use Maryk to get even with Queeg?

   _____

   _____

   _____

5. Why did Greenwald feel that officers like Queeg were important to the Navy?

   _____

   _____

   _____

   _____

CHALLENGE

Write an essay describing how Queeg's appearance on the witness stand wins for Maryk the verdict of not guilty.

150 Great Books

ANSWER KEYS

Elizabeth the Queen by Maxwell Anderson

OBJECTIVE:

1. Penelope
2. Raleigh, Cecil
3. his silver armor
4. Cadiz
5. wage war against Spain
6. Bacon
7. Ireland
8. ambition, pride
9. Essex and her throne
10. her ring
11. they are intercepted
12. disband his army
13. Essex controls the city
14. king
15. has him arrested
16. Essex to send the ring
17. Shakespeare (*Henry IV*)
18. pardon Essex
19. Elizabeth
20. Penelope

SHORT ANSWER:

1. Plots by the Raleigh faction to discredit Essex.
2. His ego. He will not defer to Raleigh.
3. Temper tantrums, fear for her throne.
4. Cheers of the populace—that Essex may be set up as king.
5. His pride—he will not take anything from anyone.

CHALLENGE:

Issue of love for Essex vs. her desire for power. She keeps her throne, but loses the man she loves.

Becket by Jean Anouilh

OBJECTIVE:

1. J
2. A
3. T
4. O
5. B
6. I
7. E
8. M
9. D
10. K
11. G
12. Q
13. S
14. C
15. R
16. F
17. N
18. H
19. P
20. L

SHORT ANSWER:

1. Cares for the suffering of the people.
2. Admires the monk's spirit—sees himself as he might have been.
3. Gives away his wealth and devotes his life to God.
4. Finds a cause to die for.
5. Confused, still caring deeply for Becket, but determined to keep his crown.

CHALLENGE:

Change is greatest in Becket from sensual man to holy man as he defends the honor of God. Henry remains basically stubborn and still dependent and uncertain.

A Tale of Two Cities by Charles Dickens

OBJECTIVE:

1. J
2. R
3. A
4. O
5. D
6. H
7. M
8. S
9. B
10. I
11. N
12. K
13. Q
14. C
15. L
16. F
17. P
18. G
19. E
20. G

ANSWER KEYS (continued)

A Tale of Two Cities by Charles Dickens (continued)

SHORT ANSWER:

1. To tell her that her father has been found.
2. Stryver gets credit for all of Carton's work.
3. Darnay wants change—uncle enjoys all of the evils of class privilege.
4. He is a very gentle, caring person.
5. Threatens to reveal Basard's identity—gets Darnay out by drugging him.

CHALLENGE:

Carton gives his life. Darnay risks his life for Gabelle. Miss Pross sacrifices her hearing to save Lucy.

April Morning by Howard Fast

OBJECTIVE:

1. twenty-four hours
2. argue
3. Levi
4. his grandmother
5. signing the muster book
6. Jonas Parker
7. blacksmith
8. the reverend
9. Moses Cooper
10. the Metonomy Road
11. Solomon Chandler
12. behind rock walls
13. Joseph Simmons
14. fowling pieces, rifles
15. a British private
16. fell asleep
17. Boston
18. Ruth Simmons
19. candles
20. the siege of Boston

SHORT ANSWER:

1. He constantly found fault.
2. Puts his arm around Adam's shoulder and holds him.
3. Talk to the British. The British shot first.
4. So the British would be totally driven out.
5. Change from a boy into a man who could face responsibility.

CHALLENGE:

Involvement in other battles—Bunker Hill, etc. Marriage to Ruth, seeing a new nation founded after the Revolution.

Cimarron by Edna Ferber

OBJECTIVE:

1. D
2. D
3. B
4. D
5. B
6. B
7. B
8. A
9. C
10. C
11. B
12. D
13. A
14. D
15. A
16. C
17. C
18. B
19. C
20. D

SHORT ANSWER:

1. Girl to whom he gave a drink stole it.
2. Flashy dress, ability to shoot, court defense, preaching.
3. Brought up the children, ran the paper, built the family a place in society.
4. Donna married for money, Cim married an Indian.
5. Instant wealth totally turned social values upside down.

CHALLENGE:

Yancy—flashy daring in the middle of every adventure. Sabra—the steady work that built the country.

ANSWER KEYS (continued)

The Great Gatsby by F. Scott Fitzgerald

OBJECTIVE:

1. Nick
2. moves in next door
3. yawning constantly
4. a little fool
5. loud, lavish, crowded, impersonal
6. Valley of Ashes, Dr. T.J. Eckleberg
7. light on Daisy's dock
8. homely, plain, middle class
9. Tom and Myrtle fight
10. Jordan
11. Daisy and Gatsby's courtship
12. her parents refused
13. where it came from
14. Daisy and Gatsby, his house
15. Gatsby's shirts
16. Dan
17. Gatsby's car
18. Tom is with Jordan
19. Daisy, Gatsby
20. he thought Gatsby killed his wife

SHORT ANSWER:

1. They do what they want—don't care who they hurt.
2. Sees the fakeness of the lifestyle.
3. Real name Jay Gatz, no war record, money came from bootlegging.
4. Crude careless bully vs. the caring and refined gentleman.
5. No one came—empty pool vs. the night of the brightly lighted party and the house full of people.

CHALLENGE:

No real depth of human relationships, excessive craze of the jazz-age parties, desolation of the Valley, fight scene in the city apartment, Jordan's indifference.

Johnny Tremaine by Esther Forbes

OBJECTIVE:

1. C
2. B
3. B
4. B
5. D
6. C
7. A
8. A
9. C
10. D
11. B
12. A
13. C
14. A
15. C
16. A
17. B
18. C
19. A
20. A

SHORT ANSWER:

1. Pouring silver into a crucible that cracked.
2. Sullen, idle, restless.
3. Messenger, eavesdropper, spy.
4. Mother was Lyte's niece.
5. To stand up proudly and not be put down by any oppressor.

CHALLENGE:

British as human—Sgt. Gale and Lt. Stranger had jobs they didn't want to do. Happy Rab was killed, Lapham girls separated.

ANSWER KEYS (continued)

The Lion in Winter by William Goldman

OBJECTIVE:

1. D	6. E	11. K	16. O
2. H	7. J	12. B	17. J
3. I	8. M	13. L	18. H
4. N	9. F	14. E	19. G
5. A	10. I	15. C	20. P

SHORT ANSWER:

1. Constant political maneuvers and verbal barbs.
2. Marriage to her as a key to land and power.
3. No one mentions him as king.
4. Her freedom and Henry's love.
5. He will let Eleanor out again for Easter Court.

CHALLENGE:

Deep feelings underneath the barbs, her seen with the jewels, the pleasure both of them find in playing the game.

The House of the Seven Gables by Nathaniel Hawthorne

OBJECTIVE:

1. A	6. C	11. D	16. A
2. A	7. B	12. C	17. C
3. C	8. D	13. D	18. A
4. A	9. C	14. B	19. D
5. D	10. C	15. C	20. B

SHORT ANSWER:

1. Old, musty, shriveled.
2. Maule cursed Pyncheon after the Colonel stole Maule's land.
3. Brings light, beauty, and youth into the house.
4. Clifford took the blame for some of Jaffrey's crooked business dealings.
5. Holgrave a descendant of Maule—he and Phoebe unite the two families. Uncle Venner represents comic-relief view of common people.

CHALLENGE:

Judge's death, retribution for the sins of his ancestors. Clifford and Hepzibah victims of the family curse. Spell broken when Phoebe and Holgrave leave.

The Scarlet Letter by Nathaniel Hawthorne

OBJECTIVE:

1. C	6. A
2. B	7. A
3. D	8. D
4. D	9. B
5. A	10. C

ANSWER KEYS (continued)

The Scarlet Letter by Nathaniel Hawthorne (continued)

SHORT ANSWER:
1. Passed judgment on her heart, not on her actions.
2. They come to accept her, but she withdraws from them.
3. Turns him into a devil.
4. Total physical and mental breakdown.
5. Dimmesdale finally becomes free of his guilt.

CHALLENGE:
Dimmesdale and Chillingworth are physically destroyed by hidden guilt. Hester's beauty fades. For each character, the outside becomes a reflection of the person's inner condition.

The Country of the Pointed Firs by Sarah Orne Jewett

OBJECTIVE:
1. Dunnet Landing
2. write
3. herbs and medicines
4. about his travels
5. simple and peaceful life
6. her love for Nathan
7. can be alone
8. Mrs. Fosdick
9. Dr. Bassett
10. her lover was lost at sea
11. very close to Joanna's spirit
12. the Bowden family reunion
13. conversation and visits with people along the way
14. his dead wife
15. a shepherdess
16. Queen Victoria
17. William and Esther
18. lamb
19. leaves the village
20. some herbs, a coral pin that Nathan had brought home

SHORT ANSWER:
1. Small, peaceful island community, small harbor, bay full of boats.
2. Knowledge of herbs, great understanding of human nature.
3. William, Elijah Tilley, Captain Littlepage.
4. Simple spirit and totally peaceful environment.
5. Spiritual beauty, real values of life.

CHALLENGE:
Various characters represent faithfulness in love, strong family ties, links with the values of the past.

Doctor Zhivago by Boris Pasternak

OBJECTIVE:
1. B
2. A
3. A
4. C
5. B
6. C
7. D
8. B
9. C
10. C
11. B
12. B
13. A
14. D
15. B
16. C
17. B
18. D
19. C
20. D

SHORT ANSWER:
1. Yuri lost his mother, his father disappeared. Lara was victimized by her mother's lover.
2. Beauty of the countryside in all seasons. Groves of woods, fields, snowstorms.
3. Hunger, thirst, filth, crowded conditions.
4. Sense of loyalty and duty.
5. Find private peace in an outer world that is coming apart.

ANSWER KEYS (continued)

Doctor Zhivago by Boris Pasternak (continued)

CHALLENGE:

Yuri and Lara lose and find each other against the background of the social upheaval in Russia. They are finally parted forever by those same social currents.

The Winthrop Woman by Anya Seton

OBJECTIVE:

1. K	6. P	11. N	16. O
2. S	7. D	12. H	17. J
3. A	8. L	13. T	18. E
4. G	9. R	14. C	19. B
5. M	10. I	15. Q	20. F

SHORT ANSWER:

1. Exciting worldly life versus dull Puritanism.
2. Strong, independent personality, love of color, excitement, and adventure.
3. His authority was opposed, the Dudley faction, lost elections, the oppositions of Roger Williams and Anne Hutchinson.
4. Involvement in the Hutchinson affair, accusation of witchcraft.
5. Problems with Feake, opposition of son-in-law, caught in currents of New Amsterdam's politics.

CHALLENGE:

Survived Harry's death, built family and lands despite Feake's weakness, unfulfilled love for Jack, support for Anne Hutchinson, is finally able to marry Hallet.

Exodus by Leon Uris

OBJECTIVE:

1. F	6. O	11. R	16. C
2. M	7. G	12. I	17. H
3. A	8. Q	13. E	18. K
4. T	9. D	14. L	19. S
5. J	10. B	15. P	20. N

SHORT ANSWER:

1. To save Karen from the past, to provide a substitute for the daughter that Kitty had lost.
2. Swamps and rocky land, no social structure, Arab problems, British domination.
3. Friends who had lived together became enemies who fought each other.
4. Stole trucks and uniforms, looked like a genuine British army division.
5. Learned survival in the ghettos and concentration camps. Karen taught Dove to love again.

CHALLENGE:

Uris a pro-Jewish position. Frequently anti-British. Individual characters' actions are strengthened by their beliefs. All are caught in the cross-currents of political and military events.

ANSWER KEYS (continued)

The Friendly Persuasion by Jessamyn West

OBJECTIVE:

1. 0	6. +	11. +	16. +
2. 0	7. +	12. 0	17. 0
3. 0	8. +	13. +	18. 0
4. +	9. 0	14. 0	19. 0
5. 0	10. 0	15. +	20. 0

SHORT ANSWER:

1. Love of music, poetry, fast horses.
2. Excellent homemaker, deeply religious and loving.
3. Appearance is not everything.
4. His Quaker religious beliefs versus the desire to defend his home.
5. Noticed changes of seasons, land, natural beauty.

CHALLENGE:

The vase Eliza had painted, the page from the old family Bible, the wedding ring as a symbol of marriage and maturity.

The Caine Mutiny Court-Martial by Herman Wouk

OBJECTIVE:

1. executive officer
2. a mine sweeper
3. he was ordered to do so
4. Challee
5. a typhoon
6. a novelist
7. Queeg's strange behavior
8. chickened out
9. cruelty to his men
10. a case of liquor
11. taken the ship away too soon
12. paranoid
13. Queeg
14. disturbed
15. Keefer's psychology books
16. breaking down Queeg
17. enforce discipline
18. censure Greenwald
19. publication of Keefer's book
20. Keefer

SHORT ANSWER:

1. Unnecessarily hard on his men for foolish details, punishments too strict for the offenses.
2. By being the absolute authority on his ship.
3. Refused to turn the ship around in a storm.
4. Keefer gave information which made Maryk believe that Queeg was unbalanced.
5. Maintained discipline and helped keep the country's military defenses strong.

CHALLENGE:

Greenwald battered Queeg on the witness stand until the court was convinced that the Captain was mentally unbalanced.

UNIT 4

Other Worlds and Future Times—
Tales of FANTASY and SCIENCE FICTION

SYNOPSES

The Fantastic Voyage
by Isaac Asimov

This novel presents the exciting possibilities and great dangers of scientific advances in medicine. When Benes, a Communist defector carrying critical military secrets, is critically injured in an assassination attempt, a delicate operation is needed to dissolve a blood clot. Scientists decide to use deminiaturization (a process which reduces people and objects to molecular size) to perform the surgery inside the body using a laser beam. The submarine *Proteus* and her military and medical crew are injected into the patient's bloodstream. Asimov's descriptions of the interior of the body are vividly written. Suspense builds as the *Proteus* is attacked by the body's defense system. Human conflicts occur among crew members Michaels, Grant, and Duval. Acts of sabotage make emergency repairs to the ship necessary. When the journey through the arteries is blocked, the medical team outside the body must stop the heart so the ship can pass through. But how long can the patient survive? The entire journey takes place in one hour. Suspense builds for the reader as the critical seconds tick by. Can the blood clot be dissolved before time runs out? Isaac Asimov has written a fantastic and very unusual work of fiction.

Fahrenheit 451
by Ray Bradbury

Montag, a fireman, lives in a future world in which people have become thoughtless robots who are glued to huge television screens. The fireman's task is to seek out caches of hidden books and burn them. Beatty, the fire chief, explains to Montag that people will be happier if they are not upset or forced to think. Montag meets Clarisse, an intelligent and disturbing girl who is the absolute antithesis of his zombie-like wife Mildred. Montag becomes curious enough to begin reading the seditious writings that he has been ordered to destroy. At one fire, he sees an old woman die rather than leave the books that she loves. Classified as a criminal, Montag must escape the relentless mechanical hound. Professor Faber believes that the disturbing ideas are those which help man to remain human. Faber helps Montag to become part of an underground which seeks to preserve past ideas for future thinkers. Using as his title the igniting point of paper, Ray Bradbury states powerfully the importance of saving universal truths for each generation.

Harvey
by Mary Chase

Elwood P. Dowd is a gentle eccentric who talks with an invisible rabbit named Harvey. As the reader becomes involved in this play, Harvey becomes very real. Elwood's sister Veta and her daughter Myrtle Mae feel that Elwood must be put in a sanitarium to save the family from social disgrace. At Chumley's Rest, the private hospital that Veta chooses, a series of comic mixups occurs, and Veta herself is committed by mistake. Harvey affects everyone who comes in contact with him: Dr. Chumley, Dr. Sanderson, and Miss Kelly. Finally Elwood's family agrees to coexist with Harvey. The drama is a lighthearted fantasy which seems to say that reality becomes what we believe it is. In order to remain happy, a man must hold on to his dreams. Students who read this play would also enjoy seeing the film version which starred James Stewart.

2001: A Space Odyssey
by Arthur C. Clarke

How did intelligence begin on earth? This novel opens as Moon-Watcher and his prehistoric friends are influenced by a strange slab that glows with light. Many centuries later space ships explore realms where man has never gone before. Dr. Heywood Floyd and his colleagues must fathom the mystery of the huge TMA-1 monolith that has been discovered on the surface of the moon. The scientists try to determine whether the great slab had been planted as a signaling device by beings with intelligence far superior to man's. When astronauts Bowman and Poole voyage to trace the source of the monolith's mysterious signals, HAL, the space ship's computer, suddenly malfunctions and turns killer. Bowman alone is able to survive after he disconnects HAL's circuits and pilots the ship by hand. On the far side of the stars, Bowman is drawn into the interior of the mysterious monolith. The novel's ending leaves the greatest questions unanswered. What superior beings exist in our universe? Are there other worlds beyond the stars? Clarke's work is challenging reading and would be of particular interest to students who have seen Stanley Kubrick's film adaptation.

Blithe Spirit
by Noel Coward

This sophisticated drama providing a comic view of psychic phenomena is set in a small English village. Charles and Ruth Condimime, to help research a book that Charles is writing, decide to hold a seance. They invite a medium, local eccentric Madame Arcati, to preside over the attempt to contact the spirit world. The fun really begins when Madame Arcati mistakenly calls back the ghost of Charles's first wife Elvira. Charles finds himself in the same house with two wives, one living and one dead. Both women are determined to possess him. Comic dialogue occurs because Elvira is visible and audible only to Charles. Determined to get rid of Elvira, Charles and Ruth again summon Madame Arcati. Meanwhile, Elvira has been plotting to have Charles all to herself. The play's climax comes when Elvira's plan backfires, Madame Arcati's techniques fail, and Charles has twice the problems he had before. Blithe Spirit is a humorous look at the consequences of meddling with forces beyond our control.

Alas, Babylon
by Pat Frank

How will human beings respond when they are caught in the ultimate nightmare—the aftermath of an atomic war? After the world's communications and U.S. government are annihilated, the citizens of Fort Repose, Florida must return to the land to survive. Randy Bragg, pampered member of an aristocratic family, must assert his manhood. Mark, Randy's brother in the Air Force, has sent his wife and children to Fort Repose for their safety. The Henrys, a Negro family who own the property next to Randy's, have the only safe water supply, an artesian well. The electrical system is dead, banks are useless, and the town is totally cut off from the outside world. The total spectrum of human nature—the weak, the strong, the evil and the good—rises to the surface as the various characters respond to the crisis. Dan Gunn, the noble doctor, sacrifices himself for others. Helen Bragg, now a widow, must cope with the death of her husband. Weak banker Edgar Quizzenberry totally collapses when his world is gone. As they try to help others, Randy and Lib McGovern find their love for each other. Alas, Babylon is a strong novel describing human responses to crisis.

Stranger in a Strange Land
by Robert Heinlein

This novel is a strong piece of social satire which would be appropriate for superior students. Mike, the son of earthlings who died on Mars, has been sent to Earth by "The Old Ones," the superiors of Martian intelligence, to determine whether Earth should survive. Mike's good, gentle nature cannot "Grok" (understand) the evil and greed which he finds in mankind. Jubal Harshaw tries to protect Mike from the forces that wish to exploit him. Mike's superior powers, however, help him to defend himself. Everyone who tries to capture him simply vanishes. Heinlein satirizes all political, social, and religious institutions as weak or totally corrupt. Mike becomes a celebrity and, eventually, the leader of his own religious cult. When the new "evangelist" tries to preach his gospel of love, the crowd turns on Mike and tears him to pieces. The base traits of human nature, for the author of this novel, clearly lie beneath a very thin veneer of civilized behavior.

Lost Horizon
by James Hilton

In the aftermath of a revolution in India during the 1940s, four people escape by plane. The craft crashes in the mountains and the pilot is killed. The four passengers are taken to the marvelous kingdom of Shangri-La, where life is lived in total moderation and no one ever grows old. Miss Brinklow, the missionary, Barnard, the man with the secret past, Mallinson, the impulsive engineer, and Conway, the diplomat, all respond in different ways to life in paradise. Conway learns the secrets of Shangri-La during many conversations with the High Lama. Three people adjust to life in the valley. Only Mallinson desires to leave with Lo-Tsen, a beautiful native girl whom he loves. The escape effort provides the climax of the novel's plot. The story ends as Conway, who has left Shangri-La to help Mallinson, seeks to return. James Hilton has provided well-drawn characters and excellent landscape description.

Brave New World
by Aldous Huxley

In the London of the future, people are scientifically produced by cloning, technology is god, and everyone is kept totally happy. Being a misfit in a world where each person is conditioned to fill a specific slot is the ultimate disaster. Bernard Marx is a strange little man who is brilliant, but does not fit in. Yet Lenina finds Bernard strangely fascinating. Together they take a trip to a savage reservation where life follows natural processes. Love, sensitivity, ugliness, and old age replace the sterile life Bernard has known. Bernard finds John the Savage, who was born on the reservation after his mother had been abandoned by a high government official. John speaks the language of Shakespeare and cherishes high ideals of the civilized world about which his mother has told him. Bernard takes John to London, where the young man becomes an instant celebrity. John cannot cope with the coldness of technology or the lack of humanity. He will not live in a state of drug-induced happiness; he claims suffering as a part of being human. At the novel's end, John and Bernard both withdraw from a world with which they can no longer cope. This anti-utopian work shows clearly the ways in which scientific perfection can destroy the beauty and the pain of being human.

The Lion, the Witch, and the Wardrobe
by C.S. Lewis

This allegory, written as a children's fantasy, presents the theological conflict between good and evil. In an English country house, four children find a magic wardrobe which is the entrance to the kingdom of Narnia. The evil forces of the White Witch have taken over the kingdom. Susan, Lucy, Peter, and Edmund battle to defeat the White Witch and free the castle of Cain Paravel. The champion of right is the great lion, Aslan. When Aslan comes, spring returns to Narnia and the land is set free. The ultimate triumph over evil demands the death of Aslan, who is sacrificed to save the weak Edmund from the witch's power. Good has more powerful magic than evil, however, and the forces of Aslan rise in triumph. C.S. Lewis has written a delightful children's tale with a powerful spiritual message. *The Lion, the Witch, and the Wardrobe* is the first volume of Lewis's *Chronicles of Narnia* series.

A Canticle for Leibowitz
by Walter M. Miller

In a post-nuclear world, mankind has returned to the Dark Ages. The monks of St. Leibowitz Abbey struggle to preserve fragments of civilization. While in the desert on a retreat, Brother Francis Gerard has a strange vision. He discovers fragments of documents written by Leibowitz. These strange documents mark the beginning of a new rise for man. Electricity is reinvented and new technology develops. Humanity, however, begins to use this new knowledge for evil purposes. Wars break out, and previous mistakes are repeated. As centuries pass, the various abbots of St. Leibowitz try to stem the rising tide of evil. Finally new atomic weapons threaten to destroy the earth entirely. At the command of Abbot Zerchi, Brother Joshua takes command of a space expedition which will carry a colony of settlers and the order's precious documents to a new planet in a last desperate attempt to save the human race. Walter Miller's powerful plot illustrates that, unless man's destructive tendencies change, the catastrophes of history will be doomed to repetition.

The Hobbit
by J.R.R. Tolkien

This first volume of the *Lord of the Rings* saga tells of Bilbo Baggins, an ordinary peaceloving hobbit who is drawn away from his home and into great adventures by a group of dwarves and by the wizard Gandalf. Bilbo steals from Gollum a magic ring which will make the wearer invisible. The members of the party escape from vicious eagles and from the dungeons of the Elf King. Bilbo and the dwarves battle the dragon Smaug for the treasure of the mountain and possession of the fabulous Arkenstone. The exciting plot concludes with the Battle of Five Armies, a confrontation between the forces of good and the forces of evil. *The Hobbit*'s characters represent the little people who are drawn into life's battles against the negative forces which would oppose them.

NAME _____ DATE _____

The Fantastic Voyage by Isaac Asimov

Select the letter of the word or phrase which correctly completes each statement.

_____ 1. Security arrangements for Benes' defection were handled by (A) Grant (B) Owens (C) Duval (D) Carter.

_____ 2. In the car with Benes when the attack came was (A) Reid (B) Owens (C) Duval (D) Peterson.

_____ 3. Benes was injured by an attack from (A) a laser gun (B) a computerized car (C) a car with a suicide driver (D) a firebomb.

_____ 4. Benes' knowledge was important (A) because only he knew how miniaturization worked (B) his knowledge could help maintain balance with the world's military powers (C) he could provide the names of other enemy agents (D) his knowledge could be used for medical purposes.

_____ 5. The operation on Benes' blood clot was to be done (A) with a scalpel (B) with a laser beam (C) by a Russian surgeon (D) by injecting a special fluid into the brain.

_____ 6. The greatest danger factor in the voyage of the Proteus was (A) the white blood cells (B) the heartbeat (C) the time limitation (D) the contraction of the lungs.

_____ 7. The designer of the Proteus was (A) Michaels (B) Owens (C) Reid (D) Grant.

_____ 8. The total time lapse before deminiaturization would begin was about (A) one day (B) one hour (C) three hours (D) unknown.

_____ 9. The Proteus was injected into the body by (A) use of a saline solution (B) an injection at the base of the neck (C) a hypodermic needle (D) all of the above.

_____ 10. The Brownian motion was caused by (A) molecular movement (B) the heartbeat (C) the action of the red and white blood cells (D) the presence of a foreign substance in the brain.

_____ 11. On board the Proteus, the final authority to make decisions was held by (A) Reid (B) Grant (C) Carter (D) Duval.

_____ 12. When the submarine could not continue its trip through the artery, the only alternative route lay through (A) the ear (B) the heart (C) the lungs (D) the large intestine.

_____ 13. The crew was most fascinated by the body's (A) size (B) complicated structure (C) defense system (D) visual beauty.

_____ 14. The destruction of the Proteus was caused by (A) red corpuscles (B) white corpuscles (C) defensive antibodies (D) fibers of the lung tissue.

_____ 15. Grant was almost killed in the (A) lung (B) heart (C) brain (D) inner ear.

_____ 16. Grant dismantled the radio (A) to provide spare parts for the laser (B) to repair the ship's control panel (C) to avoid contact with the outside (D) to prevent unnecessary sound waves.

_____ 17. The greatest danger to Benes' life occurred when (A) the ship was injected (B) Duval used the laser gun (C) his heart was deliberately stopped (D) the crew began to deminiaturize.

_____ 18. The only romantic relationship in the novel was between Cora and (A) Duval (B) Michaels (C) Grant (D) Owens.

_____ 19. Michaels wanted to destroy the ship (A) so the Russians could have more power (B) because he believed Benes' knowledge was dangerous for the world (C) because he was jealous of Duval (D) because he was insane.

_____ 20. The team emerged from Benes' body through (A) the ear (B) the eye (C) the bloodstream (D) the kidneys.

NAME _____ DATE _____

The Fantastic Voyage by Isaac Asimov

Answer each of the following questions in two or three complete sentences.

1. What were the medical and military possibilities of the deminiaturization process?

   _____
   _____
   _____
   _____

2. Why was saving Benes' life so important to the world?

   _____
   _____
   _____
   _____

3. How is Cora almost killed? How does Grant rescue her?

   _____
   _____
   _____
   _____

4. What role do those in the outside operating room play in the voyage of the *Proteus*?

   _____
   _____
   _____
   _____

5. How does Grant develop as a character and mature as a person during the voyage?

   _____
   _____
   _____
   _____

CHALLENGE

Isaac Asimov is both a scientist and a storyteller. What are some of the specific details that he uses to combine scientific knowledge, narrative skills, and visual pictures as he makes *The Fantastic Voyage* a very exciting novel?

NAME _____ DATE _____

Fahrenheit 451 by Ray Bradbury

Place a (+) before each statement that is true and a (0) before each statement that is false.

_____ 1. The society that is pictured in this novel places great value on personal relationships.

_____ 2. Montag's job as a fireman was to burn books.

_____ 3. Clarisse reminds Montag a great deal of his wife.

_____ 4. Mildred Montag deliberately tried to commit suicide.

_____ 5. Mildred enjoys discussing Montag's work with him.

_____ 6. Montag constantly smells of kerosene.

_____ 7. The mechanical hound is used by the fire department to "smell out" potential criminals.

_____ 8. Mildred has a very clear memory of when she and Montag met.

_____ 9. Montag enjoys the programs in the "parlor" as much as Mildred does.

_____ 10. The old woman dies with her books because Beatty gives her no opportunity to escape.

_____ 11. Beatty believes that burning books makes life simpler for the general population.

_____ 12. The title of the novel refers to the street address of the firehouse.

_____ 13. Montag steals only one book to read.

_____ 14. Mildred enjoys reading the books as much as Montag does.

_____ 15. Professor Faber tries to help Montag answer Beatty's arguments.

_____ 16. The fire alarm for Montag's house was turned in by the next-door neighbors.

_____ 17. Mildred's friends are pleased and amused when Montag reads poetry to them.

_____ 18. Faber tells Montag that the best escape route is along the river and away from the city.

_____ 19. Montag throws the Hound off his scent by planting a book in Beatty's house.

_____ 20. Montag's assignment with the group of hobos is to memorize passages from Shakespeare.

NAME _____ DATE _____

Fahrenheit 451 by Ray Bradbury

Answer each of the following questions in two or three complete sentences.

1. How is Clarisse McClellan contrasted with Montag's wife, Mildred?

   _____

   _____

   _____

   _____

2. Why does Beatty believe that society is better off without books?

   _____

   _____

   _____

   _____

3. According to Faber, why are books so greatly hated and feared?

   _____

   _____

   _____

   _____

4. Describe how Montag manages to escape from the Hound.

   _____

   _____

   _____

   _____

5. How does Granger's group hope to preserve knowledge for another generation?

   _____

   _____

   _____

   _____

CHALLENGE

The woman whose books the firemen have come to burn quotes the words of Latimer, a fifteenth-century religious martyr. "Play the man, Master Ridley; we shall this day light such a candle, by God's grace in England, as I trust shall never be put out" (p. 38).

Discuss what effect this woman's death had on Montag. How *will* her death, through Montag, help to light a candle for the world?

150 Great Books

NAME _____ DATE _____

Harvey by Mary Chase

Place a (+) before each statement that is true and a (0) before each statement that is false.

_____ 1. Veta is concerned about Myrtle Mae's lack of social opportunities.

_____ 2. Veta's mother had divided her property equally between Veta and Elwood.

_____ 3. Elwood P. Dowd is a very gracious, unselfish man.

_____ 4. Myrtle Mae is the only person besides Elwood who is able to see Harvey.

_____ 5. The stage directions for this play are written so the audience sees Harvey, while the actors on stage pretend not to.

_____ 6. Dr. Chumley commits Veta to the hospital by mistake.

_____ 7. Wilson is the strongarm man for the sanitarium.

_____ 8. One subplot of the play is Miss Kelly's romantic interest in Wilson.

_____ 9. Judge Gaffney is the family lawyer.

_____ 10. Elwood leaves his hat and coat lying on the table at Chumley's Rest.

_____ 11. Veta plans to sue Dr. Chumley's hospital.

_____ 12. A pooka is a spirit which has taken animal form.

_____ 13. Harvey remains with Elwood throughout the entire action of the play.

_____ 14. Elwood has a photograph of himself and Harvey.

_____ 15. Dr. Sanderson meets Elwood and Harvey at Charlie's Bar.

_____ 16. Elwood had first seen Harvey leaning against a lamppost.

_____ 17. Harvey had been the name of a childhood friend of Elwood's.

_____ 18. Chumley has plans to capture Harvey for himself.

_____ 19. The cab driver tells Veta that the patients are always more happy and optimistic after they have had their shots at Dr. Chumley's.

_____ 20. At the end of the play, Veta agrees to coexist with Harvey.

NAME _____ **DATE** _____

Harvey by Mary Chase

Answer each of the following questions in two or three complete sentences.

1. What problems does Elwood's strange behavior create for Veta and Myrtle Mae?

    _____

    _____

    _____

    _____

2. Why does the doctor think that Veta should be committed?

    _____

    _____

    _____

    _____

3. How does Dr. Chumley get acquainted with Harvey?

    _____

    _____

    _____

    _____

4. What special powers does Harvey possess?

    _____

    _____

    _____

    _____

5. Why does Veta change her mind about getting rid of Harvey forever?

    _____

    _____

    _____

    _____

CHALLENGE

Write an essay describing the ways that the characterization of Elwood P. Dowd shows that a man's happiness is closely linked to his ability to hang on to his dreams.

NAME _____ DATE _____

2001: A Space Odyssey by Arthur C. Clarke

Select the letter of the word or phrase which correctly completes each statement.

_____ 1. Moon-Watcher's main problem was (A) hunger (B) epidemic (C) drought (D) wild beasts.

_____ 2. The purpose of the great stone slab was to (A) study caveman's responses (B) teach caveman how to develop tools and technology (C) save caveman from extinction (D) program caveman's mind.

_____ 3. Moon-Watcher had begun the mastery of his environment when he (A) planted crops (B) drove out the other tribe (C) gained the power of speech (D) killed the leopard in his cave.

_____ 4. The author implies that man's weapon technology (A) will eventually destroy him (B) made man more civilized (C) made man able to control others (D) made man master of the universe.

_____ 5. Dr. Heywood Floyd goes to Moon Base Clavius (A) to launch a new spaceship (B) to deal with an epidemic (C) to see TMA-1 (D) to conduct experiments to produce more food for mankind.

_____ 6. Floyd's trip to the moon took (A) one day (B) one week (C) two months (D) a year.

_____ 7. Scientists felt that TMA-1 was important because (A) it represented intelligent life beyond earth (B) it showed that the moon had once been inhabited (C) it could be used to transmit radio signals to earth (D) it could be easily dissected to provide important scientific information.

_____ 8. TMA-1 gives its first response when it is (A) cut by lasers (B) exposed to sunlight (C) wired with electrodes (D) analyzed by HAL.

_____ 9. Three crew members of Discovery I (A) were civilians (B) were Russians (C) were to sleep through the first phase of the voyage (D) were to join the flight on a second rescue ship.

_____ 10. The first evidence of trouble in Discovery comes when (A) the earth transmitter seems to malfunction (B) the hatch doors open (C) HAL gives faulty information (D) the hibernation system breaks down.

_____ 11. HAL kills Poole by (A) knocking him off into space (B) cutting off his air supply (C) ripping open Poole's space suit (D) jamming the ship's reentry doors.

_____ 12. HAL attempts to destroy the human crew (A) when Bowman threatens to disconnect him (B) by killing the sleeping members (C) by opening the airlock doors (D) all of the above.

_____ 13. Bowman alone is saved because he is able (A) to get emergency oxygen (B) to get into a space suit (C) to disconnect HAL (D) all of the above.

_____ 14. Discovery's real mission is to (A) map Saturn's terrain (B) trace the source of the TMA-1 signal (C) establish a colony on Jupiter (D) continue on an unmanned course to the stars.

_____ 15. As Bowman continued his mission alone, his main problem was (A) homesickness (B) loneliness (C) silence (D) sleeplessness.

_____ 16. The rings around Saturn appear as (A) sunlight (B) fire (C) stars (D) ice.

_____ 17. On Japetus, Bowman finds (A) another TMA (B) civilized beings (C) Poole's body (D) a gravity force like that of Earth.

_____ 18. The Star Gate beings were those who (A) designed the star system (B) controlled the development of intelligence in the universe (C) had become extinct (D) were the original inhabitants of the earth.

_____ 19. On the inside of TMA, Bowman (A) senses the presence of intelligent life (B) sees a junkyard of abandoned space vehicles (C) seems to be traveling through both time and space (D) all of the above.

_____ 20. The intelligent aliens of Star Gate want to control Bowman's (A) body (B) space ship (C) mind (D) emotions.

150 Great Books

NAME _____ DATE _____

2001: A Space Odyssey by Arthur C. Clarke

Answer each of the following questions in two or three complete sentences.

1. How are Moon Watcher and his tribe changed by their contact with TMA-1?

   _____

   _____

   _____

   _____

2. Why are Floyd and his colleagues so anxious to keep the discovery of TMA-1 a secret?

   _____

   _____

   _____

   _____

3. How do the actions of HAL show the dangers that technology can create?

   _____

   _____

   _____

   _____

4. How does Bowman prove that man is still the master of the computer?

   _____

   _____

   _____

   _____

5. What happens to Bowman at the end of the novel?

   _____

   _____

   _____

   _____

CHALLENGE

Man has long prided himself that with his increased technology he can become master of everything. Write an essay explaining how *2001: A Space Odyssey* shows that man may instead be mastered by intelligence and power which are beyond his own.

NAME _____ DATE _____

Blithe Spirit by Noel Coward

Place a (+) before each statement that is true and a (O) before each statement that is false.

_____ 1. Both Ruth and Charles are serious believers in the powers of the occult.

_____ 2. Charles has invited Madame Arcati to get information for a book that he is writing.

_____ 3. Charles and Elvira were married for fifteen years.

_____ 4. Elvira was a great help to Charles with his writing career.

_____ 5. The Bradmans regard the whole idea of the seance as a joke.

_____ 6. When Elvira arrives, only Charles is able to see and hear her.

_____ 7. Daphne was one of Charles's previous lady friends.

_____ 8. Madame Arcati assures Ruth that she can dematerialize Elvira very easily.

_____ 9. Edith is injured in a fall which was intended for Charles.

_____ 10. The tune "Always" is one of Ruth's favorite melodies.

_____ 11. Elvira plans to kill Ruth in an automobile accident.

_____ 12. In Madame Arcati's second trance, Daphne brings back the wrong wife.

_____ 13. Madame Arcati regards herself as an amateur in dealings with the spirit world.

_____ 14. When they are both ghosts, Ruth and Elvira side together against Charles.

_____ 15. Mrs. Bradman is the medium through whom the wives were called back.

_____ 16. Madame Arcati learns the truth by hypnotizing Edith.

_____ 17. Madame Arcati is absolutely certain that the house is free of spirits forever.

_____ 18. Charles decides to leave the house altogether.

_____ 19. At the end of the play, the spirits of both wives have returned to a peaceful rest.

_____ 20. Light, sound, and special-effects cues are very important to the staging of this play.

150 Great Books

NAME _____ DATE _____

Blithe Spirit by Noel Coward

Answer each of the following questions in two or three complete sentences.

1. How was Charles's marriage to Elvira different from his marriage to Ruth?

   _____

   _____

   _____

   _____

2. How does Elvira's invisibility cause a great deal of confusion?

   _____

   _____

   _____

   _____

3. What mistake does Madame Arcati make in her attempt to return Elvira to the spirit world?

   _____

   _____

   _____

   _____

4. What role does Edith play in all of the confusion?

   _____

   _____

   _____

   _____

5. At the end of the play, how does the audience know that the ghosts of Ruth and Elvira are still present?

   _____

   _____

   _____

   _____

CHALLENGE

Write an essay describing how Noel Coward uses traditional ideas about the supernatural to create comedy, and to make subject matter funny which is usually considered dark and mysterious.

NAME _____ DATE _____

Alas, Babylon by Pat Frank

Place a (+) before each statement that is true and a (0) before each statement that is false.

_____ 1. Most of the novel's action takes place in central Florida.

_____ 2. Randy Bragg always took life more seriously than his brother Mark did.

_____ 3. Mark sends his wife and children to Fort Repose because he believes that they will be safer there.

_____ 4. The war in this novel is begun by a deliberate confrontation between the United States and Russia.

_____ 5. The black citizens of Fort Repose generally have better survival skills than the whites have.

_____ 6. After the bombs are dropped, communications are quickly restored between New York and Washington.

_____ 7. The loss of electricity causes the most serious disruption of life in Fort Repose.

_____ 8. Peyton's eyes are permanently damaged when she looks at the bomb.

_____ 9. Edgar Quizzenberry is a strong man who is able to survive the catastrophe.

_____ 10. "Alas, Babylon" was a code signal that Mark and Randy had first used when they were children.

_____ 11. The citizens of Fort Repose begin to measure time from the day that the bomb had been dropped.

_____ 12. Lib McGovern's mother liked Randy and approved of his marrying her daughter.

_____ 13. Admiral Hazzard was a shortwave expert.

_____ 14. Dan Gunn ran the community's only hardware store.

_____ 15. Fort Repose had an excellent Civil Defense system for emergencies.

_____ 16. Gasoline became one of the most valuable substances.

_____ 17. Helen and Randy were eventually married.

_____ 18. Randy found a source of salt from reading a record in an old diary.

_____ 19. Christmas Eve services were held in an effort to bring the community together.

_____ 20. At the end of the novel, the people of Fort Repose have chosen to leave their community and live elsewhere.

150 Great Books

NAME _____ DATE _____

Alas, Babylon by Pat Frank

Answer each of the following questions in two or three complete sentences.

1. In what ways does Randy assume leadership in this time of crisis?

   _____

   _____

   _____

   _____

2. Describe the accidental events which cause the war to start.

   _____

   _____

   _____

3. In what ways does the value of every commodity suddenly change after the Day?

   _____

   _____

   _____

   _____

4. How are the old community lines of class and color erased as the people of the community struggle to survive?

   _____

   _____

   _____

   _____

5. What are some of the previously old and useless objects which suddenly become very valuable?

   _____

   _____

   _____

   _____

CHALLENGE

People in times of crisis reveal very clearly the strengths and weaknesses of their character. Using various characters from *Alas, Babylon* as examples, write an essay which illustrates the truth of the above statement.

NAME _____ DATE _____

Lost Horizon by James Hilton

Select the letter of the word or phrase which correctly completes each statement.

_____ 1. The young man receives the manuscript of Conway's story from (A) Conway himself (B) Rutherford (C) the British consul (D) Mallinson.

_____ 2. Conway's memory was restored by (A) hypnosis (B) medication (C) music (D) love.

_____ 3. The four passengers left Baskul because of (A) plague (B) famine (C) flood (D) political revolution.

_____ 4. Conway's profession was as a (A) diplomat (B) soldier (C) mining engineer (D) freelance writer.

_____ 5. The passenger most upset about their circumstances was (A) Miss Brinklow (B) Conway (C) Mallinson (D) the pilot.

_____ 6. The passengers learned that they had changed destination from (A) talking to the pilot (B) the length of the flight (C) the direction of the flight (D) the radio transmission that the pilot received.

_____ 7. Shangri-La was located in (A) India (B) China (C) Tibet (D) Eastern Russia.

_____ 8. The life of Shangri-La was governed by (A) democracy (B) asceticism (C) moderation (D) rigid totalitarian control.

_____ 9. The host for the group when they arrived was (A) Chang (B) the High Lama (C) Lo-Tsen (D) Karakal.

_____ 10. Conway learned the history of Shangri-La from (A) Chang (B) old library manuscripts (C) the High Lama (D) Lo-Tsen.

_____ 11. The lamas of Shangri-La had learned the secret of (A) reducing passions (B) retarding the aging process (C) slowing down time (D) all of the above.

_____ 12. Barnard was really (A) a secret agent (B) an army officer (C) a fugitive from justice (D) an agent of the Catholic church.

_____ 13. The High Lama tells Conway that the group will leave the valley (A) not at all (B) when the porters arrive (C) by plane (D) with Chang as a guide.

_____ 14. The least content of the group is (A) Barnard (B) Miss Brinklow (C) Mallinson (D) Conway.

_____ 15. One very unusual part of Conway's experience in Shangri-La was (A) the courtesy he received (B) the freedom he had to move about (C) his free access to the library (D) the number of times that he visited the High Lama.

_____ 16. The man who helped Perrault build Shangri-La was (A) Chang (B) Henschell (C) Briac (D) Andrews.

_____ 17. The High Lama's favorite composer was (A) Chopin (B) Beethoven (C) Mozart (D) Brahms.

_____ 18. The purpose of Shangri-La was (A) a place to find peace (B) a preserve for the world's treasures (C) a refuge from man's destructive tendencies (D) all of the above.

_____ 19. The successor to the High Lama was to be (A) Conway (B) Chang (C) Briac (D) Miss Brinklow.

_____ 20. Conway leaves Shangri-La because of (A) Lo-Tsen (B) Barnard (C) Mallinson (D) Chang.

150 Great Books

NAME _____ DATE _____

Lost Horizon by James Hilton

Answer each of the following questions in two or three complete sentences.

1. How does each of the passengers react when they find out that they have been hijacked?

   _____

   _____

   _____

   _____

2. Why does Conway become the natural leader of the group?

   _____

   _____

   _____

3. What aspects of life in Shangri-La does Conway enjoy most?

   _____

   _____

   _____

   _____

4. Why do Barnard and Miss Brinklow decide to stay?

   _____

   _____

   _____

5. Where do you think Conway has gone at the end of the novel?

   _____

   _____

   _____

   _____

CHALLENGE

Write an essay discussing the aspects of Conway's character which would qualify him for the leadership of Shangri-La.

NAME _____ DATE _____

Stranger in a Strange Land by Robert Heinlein

In the numbered blanks at the left, write the letter of the matching person, place, or thing.

_____ 1. Religious sect whose chief practice was the pursuit of pleasure

_____ 2. Government agent that Mike made disappear in Ben's apartment

_____ 3. A stripper who became a priestess

_____ 4. Spaceship that carried Mike's parents to Mars

_____ 5. Programmed Mike to provide information about Earth

_____ 6. Martian term for death

_____ 7. Maintenance man and mechanical expert

_____ 8. Helped Mike to escape from the hospital

_____ 9. A very special snake

_____ 10. Tattooed lady who was a member of Mike's inner circle

_____ 11. Commander of the Martian expedition

_____ 12. Secretary of the World Federation

_____ 13. Only member of the expedition who spoke Martian

_____ 14. Bishop who was "disincorporated" by Mike

_____ 15. Mike's protector and spiritual father

_____ 16. Died at the hands of an angry mob

_____ 17. A "Fair Witness"

_____ 18. Special place of living and sharing

_____ 19. Newsman whose life was saved by Harshaw

_____ 20. Term for knowledge or understanding

A. Mike
B. Van Tramp
C. Digby
D. Nest
E. Duke
F. Dawn Ardent
G. Honey Bun
H. Mahmoud
I. "Old Ones"
J. Fosterites
K. Gil Berquist
L. Anne
M. Patty
N. Ben Caxton
O. Joseph Douglas
P. Grok
Q. Discorporation
R. Jubal Harshaw
S. Jill
T. *Envoy*

NAME _____ DATE _____

Stranger in a Strange Land by Robert Heinlein

Answer each of the following questions in two or three complete sentences.

1.   Explain the significance of "water brotherhood."

   _____

   _____

   _____

   _____

2.   Why has Mike been sent to Earth? Why is he removed?

   _____

   _____

   _____

   _____

3.   What steps does Jubal take to protect Mike from the evil in human nature?

   _____

   _____

   _____

   _____

4.   How are Mike's Martian values different from Earth values?

   _____

   _____

   _____

   _____

5.   Explain the term "groking." For which of the novel's characters does "groking" seem to be most complete?

   _____

   _____

   _____

   _____

CHALLENGE

Michael Valentine Smith is a stranger to the values and customs of Earth's society. He tells Jubal, "Father, I saw the horrible shape this planet is in, and I grokked, though not in fulness, that I could change it." What human attitudes does Mike try to change? Why do his efforts fail?

NAME _____ DATE _____

Brave New World by Aldous Huxley

Correctly complete each sentence with information from the novel.

1. The "god" of the world society pictured in this novel was _____

   because _____.

2. Each person's place in society was determined by _____.

3. Bokanovsky's process was _____.

4. Lenina finds Bernard interesting because he _____ ,

   and she agrees to go with him to _____

   _____.

5. Bernard Marx was considered a misfit because _____.

6. John the Savage had heard about the wonders of London from _____.

7. The drug used to keep society stabilized was _____.

8. On the reservation, Lenina was horrified by _____.

9. When they returned to London, Linda was _____.

10. John's father was _____.

11. John had learned English by reading _____.

12. Bernard's friend, also a misfit, was _____.

13. To London society, John is _____.

14. The behavior which horrified John most in London society was _____.

15. Bernard became a total social outcast when _____.

16. "Death conditioning" was achieved by _____.

17. John starts trouble at the Hospital for the Dying when _____.

18. The Savage tells the World Controller that he claims the right to _____

    _____.

19. John withdraws to the lighthouse because _____.

20. John becomes world famous when _____

    _____.

NAME _____ DATE _____

Brave New World by Aldous Huxley

Answer each of the following questions in two or three complete sentences.

1. What human emotions are either socially disgraceful or entirely missing in the "brave new world?"

   _____

   _____

   _____

   _____

2. How does this society encourage the consumption of manufactured goods?

   _____

   _____

   _____

   _____

3. In what ways do John's expectations of the "brave new world" fall far short of the reality which he experiences?

   _____

   _____

   _____

   _____

4. Why will Bernard probably be happier in Iceland than in England?

   _____

   _____

   _____

   _____

5. Why does John commit suicide?

   _____

   _____

   _____

   _____

CHALLENGE

Brave New World is called an anti-utopian or negative utopian novel. In what ways is the "ideal society" presented by Aldous Huxley really not so ideal after all?

NAME _____ DATE _____

The Lion, the Witch, and the Wardrobe by C.S. Lewis

Place a (+) before each statement that is true and a (0) before each statement that is false.

_____ 1. The four children in the story live with their parents in a large old country house.

_____ 2. Peter is the first of the children to enter Narnia.

_____ 3. Mr. Tumnus was supposed to tell the White Witch about Lucy's presence in Narnia.

_____ 4. Under the witch's spell, snow falls constantly in Narnia.

_____ 5. Edward, when he comes to Narnia, also meets Mr. Tumnus.

_____ 6. The White Witch takes advantage of Edward's greedy nature, and of his dislike for his brother.

_____ 7. All four of the children enter Narnia when they want to escape from Mrs. McCready and her group of tourists.

_____ 8. The children learn from the Beavers that Aslan is returning to Narnia.

_____ 9. The White Witch's chief power lies in her wand.

_____ 10. Mrs. Beaver is pictured as a motherly, practical housewife.

_____ 11. The children learn of a prophecy which states that Aslan will sit on the throne at Cain Paravel.

_____ 12. When Edmund arrives at the White Witch's house, he is treated kindly, and is given all of the Turkish Delight that he can eat.

_____ 13. One sign of Aslan's returning is a drastic change in Narnia's climate.

_____ 14. According to Aslan's directions, Peter will lead the troops into battle against the White Witch.

_____ 15. Aslan sacrifices his life in exchange for Peter's life.

_____ 16. Lucy and Susan witness the sacrifice of Aslan at the Stone Table.

_____ 17. Lucy and Susan are able to untie the ropes which bind Aslan's body.

_____ 18. Aslan is restored to life by a magic that is greater than the magic of the White Witch.

_____ 19. Aslan has to batter down the gate of the castle in order to set the stone prisoners free.

_____ 20. When the children return to the other side of the wardrobe, they find that several years have passed since they left.

NAME _____ DATE _____

The Lion, the Witch, and the Wardrobe by C.S. Lewis

Answer each of the following questions in two or three complete sentences.

1. What magic qualities does the wardrobe possess?

    _____

    _____

    _____

    _____

2. Contrast Lucy's first visit to Narnia with Edmund's first visit.

    _____

    _____

    _____

    _____

3. How do the Beavers assist the children?

    _____

    _____

    _____

    _____

4. How does Aslan use a more powerful magic to defeat the power of the White Witch?

    _____

    _____

    _____

    _____

5. How does Time in Narnia differ from Time in the world of men?

    _____

    _____

    _____

    _____

CHALLENGE

Define *allegory* as a form of literature. Write an essay to discuss the ways in which *The Lion, The Witch, and the Wardrobe* may be studied as an allegory of the triumph of good over evil.

NAME _____ DATE _____

A *Canticle for Leibowitz* by Walter M. Miller

In the numbered blanks at the left, write the letter of the matching person, place, or thing.

_____ 1. Presented to the Pope the decree for canonization of Leibowitz

_____ 2. King of the plains kingdom who began the new war

_____ 3. New settlement begun by refugees from earth

_____ 4. Discovered the Leibowitz blueprint fragment

_____ 5. Scientist who journeyed to personally inspect the Leibowitz relics

_____ 6. Tomato seller who had been deformed by radioactivity

_____ 7. Invented a treadle machine to produce electric light

_____ 8. Wanted to use euthanasia on the worst of the radiation victims

_____ 9. Wandering Jew who kept seeking the world's deliverer

_____ 10. Attempt to destroy all remains of culture and civilization

_____ 11. Refused to allow drawings to be made of the Abbey's fortifications

_____ 12. Nickname given to the deformed victims of radiation fallout

_____ 13. Scientist who lived in the days before the first nuclear war

_____ 14. Leader of a starship expedition to preserve civilization

_____ 15. Stole the copy instead of a valuable original relic

_____ 16. At first refused to believe in the validity of a novice's great discovery

_____ 17. Collection of ancient documents which had been carefully preserved by the monks

_____ 18. Saint Leibowitz's wife

_____ 19. Abbot who believed that all men should be able to die with dignity

_____ 20. Papal legate who tried to warn the world of the beginning of a new war

A. Brother Francis Gerard
B. Emily
C. Isaac Edward Leibowitz
D. Pope's Children
E. Abbot Arkos
F. Simplification
G. Monsignor Aguerra
H. Robber
I. Marcus Apollo
J. Thon Taddeo
K. Hannegan
L. Benjamin
M. Brother Kronhoer
N. Memorabilia
O. Dom Paulo
P. Brother Joshua
Q. Abbot Zerchi
R. Mrs. Grales
S. Doctor Cors
T. Centaurus Colony

NAME _____ DATE _____

A *Canticle for Leibowitz* by Walter M. Miller

Answer each of the following questions in two or three complete sentences.

1. How did Brother Francis meet the pilgrim? What discovery resulted from this meeting?

   _____

   _____

   _____

   _____

2. What actions of the tribal chiefs begin the second war?

   _____

   _____

   _____

3. Why does Dom Paulo fear the scientific work that the men of his generation are beginning to do?

   _____

   _____

   _____

   _____

4. Why does Brother Joshua doubt his ability to lead the new colony? Why does he finally agree to assume the leadership?

   _____

   _____

   _____

5. How does Abbot Zerchi fight to preserve the dignity of the human being?

   _____

   _____

   _____

   _____

CHALLENGE

Write an essay to decribe some of the methods by which the monks of St. Leibowitz Abbey struggled to preserve civilization. Against what destructive forces were they always forced to battle?

NAME _____ DATE _____

The Hobbit by J.R.R. Tolkien

In the numbered blanks at the left, write the letter of the matching person, place, or thing.

_____ 1. Great confrontation between good and evil

_____ 2. Hobbit relatives who were always interested in adventures

_____ 3. Town of men which was burned by the dragon

_____ 4. Vicious wolves who were allies of the Goblin King

_____ 5. The most valuable object in the dragon's hoard of stolen treasure

_____ 6. Original owner of the magic ring

_____ 7. Forest where Bilbo and the dwarves were captured by the elves

_____ 8. Gave the travelers a map with clues to the mountain's hidden entrance

_____ 9. Saved Bilbo and the dwarves from death by fire

_____ 10. Dragon who guarded the stolen treasure

_____ 11. Bilbo's home address

_____ 12. Saved the dwarves by smuggling them out in empty kegs

_____ 13. Ancient raven who served as a messenger and observer

_____ 14. Wizard who selected Bilbo for the journey

_____ 15. Led the reinforcements of dwarf troops to help the troops in the mountain

_____ 16. Dwarf who was restored to his rightful position of leadership

_____ 17. Bear-shaped man who was served by a host of magical animals

_____ 18. Greatest enemies of both dwarves and men

_____ 19. Archer who killed the dragon with a single arrow

_____ 20. Imprisoned the dwarves in his dungeons

A. Bag-End, Underhill
B. Esgaroth
C. Mirkwood
D. Battle of the Five Armies
E. Roac
F. Dain
G. Arkenstone
H. Beorn
I. Lord of the Eagles
J. Bard
K. Bilbo
L. Elf-King
M. Wargs
N. Goblins
O. Elrond
P. Smaug
Q. Thorin
R. Gollum
S. Gandalf
T. Took

150 Great Books

NAME _____ DATE _____

The Hobbit by J.R.R. Tolkien

Answer each of the following questions in two or three complete sentences.

1. How did Baggins become involved in going adventuring?

   _____

   _____

   _____

   _____

2. Where did Bilbo get his magic ring? What were the ring's special powers?

   _____

   _____

   _____

   _____

3. On what occasions did Gandalf rescue Bilbo and his dwarf companions?

   _____

   _____

   _____

   _____

4. Why did Thorin refuse to give Bard and his men a share of the dragon's treasure?

   _____

   _____

   _____

   _____

5. In what ways was Bilbo different when he returned from his great adventures?

   _____

   _____

   _____

   _____

CHALLENGE

Discuss the ways in which *The Hobbit* represents an allegory of the struggle between good and evil. In what ways does Bilbo represent the experience of the ordinary man?

ANSWER KEYS

The Fantastic Voyage by Isaac Asimov

OBJECTIVE:

1. A	6. C	11. B	16. A
2. B	7. B	12. B	17. C
3. C	8. B	13. D	18. C
4. B	9. D	14. B	19. B
5. B	10. A	15. A	20. B

SHORT ANSWER:

1. Medical—doctors could observe and operate inside the body. Military—arms and troops moved unseen—biological warfare.
2. Possesses important military and intelligence information.
3. Attacked by the body's defense system—he swims out and cuts her loose.
4. Tracked the ship inside the body, stopped the heart to let the ship through, brought the ship out.
5. Becomes emotionally involved in the success of the mission, falls in love with Cora.

CHALLENGE:

Brilliant word pictures of the body's interior, imaginative use of sound effects, suspenseful plot—would they get to the clot in time? Would they get out?

Fahrenheit 451 by Ray Bradbury

OBJECTIVE:

1. 0	6. +	11. +	16. 0
2. +	7. +	12. 0	17. 0
3. 0	8. 0	13. 0	18. +
4. 0	9. 0	14. 0	19. 0
5. 0	10. 0	15. +	20. 0

SHORT ANSWER:

1. Mildred hooked to television, no emotion, totally passive. Clarisse—talkative, active, interested and emotionally alive.
2. So life will be simpler, and people will be happy if they do not have to think.
3. Because every idea will offend someone, because books present ideas which make life more complicated.
4. Plants books in a house and calls in a fire alarm.
5. Memorize passages—each man becomes a living book.

CHALLENGE:

Her death lighted the fire of discontent in Montag, made him want to read, led to his rebellion against the system, and his break for freedom.

Harvey by Mary Chase

OBJECTIVE:

1. +	6. 0	11. +	16. +
2. 0	7. +	12. +	17. 0
3. +	8. 0	13. 0	18. +
4. 0	9. +	14. 0	19. 0
5. 0	10. 0	15. 0	20. +

ANSWER KEYS (continued)

Harvey by Mary Chase (continued)

SHORT ANSWER:

1. Constantly embarrasses all of their friends, makes it impossible for Myrtle Mae to have a normal social life.
2. When she tells him about Elwood and Harvey.
3. Converses with Elwood and Harvey at Charlie's Place.
4. Make people happy and keep dreams alive.
5. Wants to keep the spirit of happiness that Elwood has found.

CHALLENGE:

Elwood is the only content, adjusted character in the play. The other characters become happier as they adjust to Elwood's dreams.

2001: A Space Odyssey by Arthur C. Clarke

OBJECTIVE:

1. A	6. A	11. C, A	16. D
2. D	7. A	12. D	17. A
3. D	8. B	13. D	18. B
4. A	9. C	14. B	19. C
5. C	10. C	15. C	20. C

SHORT ANSWER:

1. Begin to think, make tools, become hunters and killers.
2. Feared the public would panic if they thought that the earth was being watched.
3. Computer goes mad and turns killer.
4. Disconnects the computer and destroys its power.
5. Enters monolith—becomes child world controller.

CHALLENGE:

Man is a small being in a total universe. Intelligences much greater than ours. Knowledge way beyond what man can explain.

Blithe Spirit by Noel Coward

OBJECTIVE:

1. 0	6. +	11. 0	16. +
2. +	7. 0	12. +	17. 0
3. 0	8. 0	13. 0	18. +
4. 0	9. +	14. +	19. 0
5. +	10. 0	15. 0	20. +

SHORT ANSWER:

1. Ruth—steady, sensible, unemotional. Elvira—unpredictable, flighty, passionate.
2. Ruth thinks that Charles is insulting her when he is really talking to Elvira.
3. Brings back the ghost of the wrong wife.
4. The medium through which the supernatural forces work.
5. Throwing things at each other, breaking up the house.

CHALLENGE:

Ghosts are not fearful, but figures of mischief. Murder becomes comic when Elvira's efforts to kill Charles backfire. As ghosts, both Ruth and Elvira remain totally "human."

ANSWER KEYS (continued)

Alas, Babylon by Pat Frank

OBJECTIVE:

1. +	6. 0	11. +	16. +
2. 0	7. +	12. 0	17. 0
3. +	8. 0	13. +	18. +
4. 0	9. 0	14. 0	19. 0
5. +	10. +	15. 0	20. 0

SHORT ANSWER:

1. Takes care of his brother's family, organizes the community supplies and services, defends the town from the highwaymen.
2. Pilot drops a bomb on a Soviet Middle East base by mistake.
3. Checks and bonds worthless, frozen food will not keep, nothing electrical works.
4. Blacks and the whites who live closest to the land help the others to survive.
5. The hand phonograph, old diary for the directions to the salt supply, oil lamps, hand razor.

CHALLENGE:

Edgar—weak and collapses, Porky Logan's greed kills him. Florence, Randy, and Lib able to cope and survive the crisis.

Stranger in a Strange Land by Robert Heinlein

OBJECTIVE:

1. J	6. Q	11. B	16. A
2. K	7. E	12. O	17. L
3. F	8. S	13. H	18. D
4. T	9. G	14. C	19. N
5. I	10. M	15. R	20. P

SHORT ANSWER:

1. Total giving of one person to another, symbolized by the exchange of water.
2. To get information from the "Old Ones." All of the needed information had been gained.
3. Keep him away from the fake religion of the Fosterites, protect him from the politicians who would exploit him and from the curious press.
4. Emphasis on giving, not taking. Always truthful. Human body good for food after death. No sense of sexual embarrassment.
5. Understanding reality to the fullest. Jubal gains this most completely.

CHALLENGE:

The author believes that Mike cannot change earth because human nature is basically greedy and destructive. Mike tries to replace greed and evil with love, and he is destroyed by those that he tries to help.

Lost Horizon by James Hilton

OBJECTIVE:

1. B	6. C	11. D	16. B
2. C	7. C	12. C	17. C
3. D	8. C	13. A	18. D
4. A	9. A	14. C	19. A
5. C	10. C	15. D	20. C

174

ANSWER KEYS (continued)

Lost Horizon by James Hilton (continued)

SHORT ANSWER:
1. Mallinson very upset, Barnard and Miss Brinklow stoic, Conway relaxes and enjoys the experience.
2. In the diplomatic service, had organized the escape from India.
3. Relaxed, no pressure or sense of schedule, time to appreciate the spiritual and the beautiful.
4. Barnard to work a mine, Miss Brinklow to found a mission.
5. Trying to find his way back to Shangri-La.

CHALLENGE:
Conway had exhibited natural leadership abilities. Has great curiosity. Does not feel trapped by being cut off from the outside world. The spiritual is more important than the physical.

Brave New World by Aldous Huxley

OBJECTIVE:
1. Ford, invented the assembly line process
2. decanting and conditioning
3. cloning, assembly-line birth process
4. is different from the others, the Reservation
5. he is smaller, homely, antisocial
6. his mother, Linda
7. somma
8. the dirt, the aged people, the ugliness
9. put under somma in a hospital
10. Director of the Hatchery
11. Shakespeare
12. Hemholtz Watson
13. a novel curiosity
14. no sexual restraint, absence of love
15. the Savage refused to appear
16. taking the children to view the dying as exhibits in a zoo
17. he screams to protect his mother, upsets the "conditioning"
18. be unhappy
19. he can no longer tolerate the society
20. films of his suffering are shown as entertainment

SHORT ANSWER:
1. Family love, motherhood, faithfulness to one person.
2. Programming the children that "ending is better than mending." Always pushing things that are new.
3. John expects Shakespeare noble human who suffers. He finds a world of impersonal, drug-induced happiness.
4. All the other misfits are there.
5. His ultimate act of defiance—to prove himself human.

CHALLENGE:
Suffering part of being human. Conditioned happiness destroys the human's right to be an individual. Right to be a thinking person gone. No meaningful art or literature possible.

The Lion, the Witch, and the Wardrobe C.S. Lewis

OBJECTIVE:
1. 0
2. 0
3. +
4. 0
5. 0
6. +
7. +
8. +
9. +
10. +
11. 0
12. 0
13. +
14. +
15. 0
16. +
17. 0
18. +
19. 0
20. 0

ANSWER KEYS (continued)

The Lion, the Witch, and the Wardrobe by C.S Lewis (continued)

SHORT ANSWER:

1. Is the entrance to Narnia.
2. Lucy meets Mr. Tumnus the good, Edmund is lured by the White Witch's evil powers.
3. Protect them from the agents of the White Witch, feed them, guide them to Aslan.
4. Sacrifices himself to defeat evil, and then is restored to life.
5. Years in Narnia may be only a few minutes in the world of men.

CHALLENGE:

Allegory—characters symbols of abstract ideas or values. Aslan, Christ figure—deliverer from the White Witch's evil. Trees and animals restored to their most noble condition by the power of good.

A Canticle for Leibowitz by Walter M. Miller

OBJECTIVE:

1. G	6. R	11. O	16. E
2. K	7. M	12. D	17. N
3. T	8. S	13. C	18. B
4. A	9. L	14. P	19. Q
5. J	10. F	15. H	20. I

SHORT ANSWER:

1. Out on a retreat in the desert—Leibowitz fragments found in a cave.
2. Beginning of arms buildup, claims on each other's territory.
3. Scientific knowledge will be used to destroy the world all over again.
4. Not sure of his own spiritual qualities. The abbot sends him as the earth is getting ready to destroy itself again.
5. To close down the centers for mercy killing, and to allow people to die with dignity.

CHALLENGE:

Monks preserved fragments of civilization, scientific knowledge. Attempt to build society again. Monks' faith is destroyed by man's desire for power. Faith itself becomes victim of man's base nature.

The Hobbit by J.R.R. Tolkien

OBJECTIVE:

1. D	6. R	11. A	16. Q
2. T	7. C	12. K	17. H
3. B	8. O	13. E	18. N
4. M	9. I	14. S	19. J
5. G	10. P	15. F	20. L

SHORT ANSWER:

1. Dwarves and Gandolf move into his house and talk him into going with them.
2. From Gollum, to be invisible.
3. Help in the battle, from the attack of the wolves and the trees which are on fire.
4. He was the rightful dwarf leader—that the dragon had stolen the treasure from his people.
5. Difficulty settling down, memories of his adventures, dwarves may pop in to visit.

CHALLENGE:

Dwarves and Bilbo confront the dragon in the battle for the treasure. Bilbo is the average man, who uses his intelligence to cope with circumstance. Attains maturity through his experiences.

UNIT 5

In Search of Conscience—
The LITERATURE of SOCIAL ISSUES

SYNOPSES

To Sir With Love
by E.R. Braithwaite

This special story of student-teacher relationships takes place at Greenslade School in London's East End shortly after World War II. Rick Braithwaite cannot get a job as an engineer because he is black. He obtains a job teaching Greenslade's "incorrigibles." This experience changes his life and theirs. "Sir" teaches his students manners, gives them an appreciation for cultures and peoples outside their own, and helps the young adults gain self-respect. Encouraged by his principal, Mr. Florian, "Sir's" teaching tools range from ballet to boxing. The most powerful lessons, however, come from the students' own lives. A young girl grows into a woman by understanding the needs of her mother. The class stands against the racial prejudice of the community to attend the funeral of a black classmate's father. "Sir," in turn, must deal with his own feelings as he falls in love with Gillian, who is white, and must consider if their love is strong enough to withstand the forces that will attack their marriage. This book illustrates the truth that a good teacher both helps students to learn and in turn learns from his or her students.

The Good Earth
by Pearl S. Buck

This epic novel of China in the early nineteenth century traces the rise of Wang Lung's family from peasant to patrician status. Wang and his wife O-lan survive famine, flood, and war to retain the land, which represents to them the source of life. But as Wang's family builds a financial empire, their simple ways are corrupted by the civilization of the city. Wang fails as a parent, and his sons move further from mother earth. The simple values which made the family great are adulterated by greed and the lust for power. Wang himself rejects his faithful wife and becomes infatuated with a beautiful young courtesan. At the end of the novel, Wang's sons stand ready to destroy everything their father has built. Old Wang himself simply wants to return to the land. The author pictures powerfully the survival struggle of the people of China, the values of the simple life, and the corrupting dangers of luxury.

The Chocolate War
by Robert Cormier

Can one individual's rebellion defeat a corrupt system and "dare to disturb the universe?" Jerry Renault, the new boy at Trinity School, accepts his assignment from the Vigils, the school's gang of controllers. He is not to participate in the school's annual chocolate sale. Brother Leon, the school's assistant headmaster, is using the Vigils and their leader Archie Costello in Leon's own drive for power. The authority figures that Cormier pictures are less than ideal role models. Leon is vicious and Brother Eugene is weak. Only Brother Jacques acts to save Jerry from being totally destroyed. The students represent a cross section of human attitudes. The helpless Goober runs away instead of standing up to help Jerry. Totally corrupt Emile Janza, who defiles everything that he touches, is disgusting even to Archie. Jerry Renault dares to defy the system as one man's act of courage. Although Jerry loses his battle, the loner gains nobility as he stands up for what he believes in, even against crushing odds.

I Am the Cheese
by Robert Cormier

As shy, sensitive Adam Farmer bicycles to Vermont to visit his father, the mystery of Adam's past is unraveled. The novel's main story is told through a series of flashbacks. Adam's family had to assume a new identity when his father, a newspaper man, had become a government witness against a crime syndicate. Adam finds out the truth about himself as he is able to link his own memories with a birth certificate in a locked drawer and an overheard phone call. Adam's closest friend, Amy Hertz, brightens the serious side of Adam's nature. But is Amy real? Why is Dr. Brint asking so many questions? Was the mysterious Mr. Gray friend or enemy? Adam himself is now threatened by the evil forces that destroyed his family. Cormier has woven a clever plot by using three different levels of narrative: the bike trip, the interviews with Dr. Brint, and Adam's own memories. This book, like many of Cormier's other novels, has a hero who must struggle against the system. As in the nursery rhyme that his father had sung to him, Adam Farmer becomes the "cheese who stands alone."

The Autobiography of Miss Jane Pittman
by Ernest J. Gaines

This story of one black woman's courageous fight for life and dignity begins during the Civil War and ends during the civil rights demonstrations of the 1960s. Miss Jane, at age 110, tells her own story. Jane and Ned, the child of a black woman killed by Yankee soldiers, escape from the plantation in the aftermath of the Union Army's march through the South. Although she is no longer a slave, Miss Jane lives in the Negro quarters and works as a cook in Mr. Samson's kitchen. Joe Pittman, the man she loves, is killed by a horse. Racial violence claims the life of her adopted son Ned as the young man is trying to build a better life for his people. This novel shows how any reform movement in the first half of the twentieth century was feared by the blacks. The slave mentality still made them fear that their white employers would take away their meager wages, food, and housing. Robert Samson, the young master on the estate, becomes a victim of the South's racial standards. He falls in love with Mary Agnes, a girl with the "taint" of black blood. Despair eventually drives Robert to suicide. Young Jimmy brings new hope to the people of the plantation. He also is killed before the demonstrations that he has planned can take place. After Jimmy's death, Miss Jane, then over one hundred years old, participates in the protest action to give blacks the right to drink at public fountains. Miss Jane's singular life illustrates a century of struggle by black Americans from the chains of slavery to the rights of full citizenship.

Black Like Me
by John Howard Griffin

Journalist John Griffin changes his skin color from white to black by using medication and sun lamp treatments. He then ventures into the deep South during the 1960s to find out how a black man really feels. Griffin begins in New Orleans, a city in which he finds some tolerance. He journeys across the South to Atlanta. The worst experiences of hatred come in Mississippi. Things that a white man would take for granted—getting a drink of water and finding a rest room—are prohibited to a black man. Dealing with the "hate stares" of vicious whites and the loneliness of his isolation from his own family become major problems for Griffin. However, the traveler also finds kindness in a rural family who will share with a stranger their poor home and meager supply of food. Newspaper editor P.D. East agrees to print Griffin's accounts of his experiences. When the articles are published, the explosion of prejudice in Griffin's home town is so great that his family is forced to move. The autobiography shows a very ugly side of American society. In the land of the free, the way a man is treated differs only because he has changed the color of his skin.

A Raisin in the Sun
by Lorraine Hansbury

On the south side of Chicago in the 1940s, the Younger family lives in a crowded, shabby apartment. This powerful play deals with the conflicts which erupt as the family awaits the arrival of Walter Senior's insurance check. Walter Junior struggles for his dreams in a world which constantly frustrates his efforts to achieve manhood. Ruth loves her husband but cannot always understand him. Walter's sister Beneatha wants to express her individuality. She is fascinated by Asagai, a young Nigerian. Lena, the mother, desperately attempting to hold the family together, uses some of the insurance money to make a down payment on a house in an all-white neighborhood. After Walter's lack of judgment causes the loss of the rest of the money in a liquor store venture and the white neighbors threaten the family, Lena is nearly defeated. Walter is then able to assert his manhood for Travis, his young son, who represents the family's hope for the future. A powerful study of modern black Americans, this play is a wonderful story of family love and survival.

The Little Foxes
by Lillian Hellman

Do the meek inherit the earth, or do the vicious devour it? Lillian Hellman's powerful social drama shows some of these devourers at work. Regina Giddens and her brothers, Oscar and Ben Hubbard, are conspiring to make a fortune by building a cotton mill in partnership with a Chicago tycoon. Regina's ailing husband Horace blocks their plans because Horace does not want the town destroyed. Horace and Regina's daughter, Alexandra, side with her father against the Hubbards' plots. Birdie, Oscar's wife, is a pathetic alcoholic who escapes to the bottle and the memories of her girlhood on the plantation. The Hubbards' financial schemes threaten to backfire when Horace discovers that the brothers have "borrowed" some of his stock to use as collateral for their loan. Viciousness becomes personified as Regina allows Horace to die so she can get what she wants. The conspirators begin to threaten each other in attempts to get the lion's share of the money. Alexandra, at the drama's conclusion, asks Regina, "Mama, are you afraid???" This play presents the brutal world of business which seems to be controlled by characters totally lacking in conscience and ethics.

Inherit the Wind
by Jerome Laurence and Robert E. Lee

This play is a fictionalized version of the famous Scopes Monkey Trial, which pitted Clarence Darrow against William Jennings Bryan. As the drama opens, Bertram Cates is on trial in Hillsboro for teaching Darwinism in his science class. The real issue on trial is a man's right to think for himself. Two great legal giants have come to argue the case: Matthew Harrison Brady, champion of Biblical creationism, and Henry Drummond, who appears to the religious forces in the town as the Devil incarnate. Hornbeck, a cynical reporter for a Baltimore newspaper, serves as narrator for the play's action. Caught between the two powerful currents is Rachel Brown, the daughter of the town's fundamentalist minister, who is in love with Bert. The trial in the stuffy courtroom builds to a fever pitch. After all scientific evidence is rejected as irrelevant, Drummond puts Brady on the stand as a witness for the defense. Through Drummond's clever line of questioning, Brady is forced to admit that the Bible is not the only authority for truth. Brady in turn accuses Drummond of attempting to destroy people's faith. Although the court finds Bert guilty, Drummond has won his point and Brady has lost his audience. The right of choice has been much more on trial than Bert Cates has. *Inherit the Wind* is not an antireligious play. The author makes a powerful statement for the right of man to have an open mind.

To Kill a Mockingbird
by Harper Lee

This childhood memory novel is set in Maycomb, Alabama in the 1930s. Scout and Jem, the motherless children of lawyer Atticus Finch, are being brought up by Calpurnia, the motherly Negro housekeeper who will tolerate no foolishness. Scout remembers their childhood playmate Dill, who came from Mississippi each summer. She recalls the neighbors: Miss Maudie, Miss Stephanie Crawford, and cantankerous Mrs. Dubose. The magnet which drew the children's imagination was the mysterious Radley house next door. The reader sees through Scout's eyes the reactions of Maycomb's citizens when their father agrees to defend Tom Robinson, a Negro accused of raping a white girl. Scout and Jem try to defend the family honor with their fists. Their father battles a prejudiced judicial system that will convict the man because his skin is the wrong color. Harper Lee shows the evil in destroying the innocent, that it is "a sin to kill a mockingbird." In the novel's exciting conclusion, Scout's life is saved by a very unexpected friend. The author presents beautifully the relationship between Atticus and his children, the small comic episodes of the neighborhood, and the larger human issues of class and race relationships.

Main Street
by Sinclair Lewis

Nobel prize winner Lewis pictures powerfully the mental and social mediocrity of small town America in the 1920s. Idealistic librarian Carol marries Dr. Will Kennicott and moves to Gopher Prairie. The young bride has starry-eyed visions of turning the town into a cultural oasis. But Carol struggles in vain to bring reform and culture to people who do not want to change. Her marriage to Will becomes more dull with each passing year. In contrast to the Kennicott's boring marriage is the true love of Bea and Miles Björnstam, who have been cast out by Gopher Prairie's "elite." The author's ironic style shows the readers clearly who the "best people" really are. Other victims of the vicious tongues of Gopher Prairie are Fern, the young teacher, and Erik, the sensitive artist. Carol sees in Erik the man she might have had. Although Carol escapes from the town and spends two years in Washington D.C., she eventually returns. Seeing no change in her own time, Carol hopes that things may be different for the next generation. This novel portrays "the village virus," the shallowness and apathy that Lewis saw on every main street in America.

The Crucible
by Arthur Miller

In 1693, Salem, Massachusetts was nearly destroyed by the infamous witchcraft trials. Miller's play presents this town as an example of the passions of greed, hatred, and envy which might destroy any society. The girls, led by Abigail Williams, begin to pretend that they are possessed and to accuse the town's social outcasts. As the hysteria mounts, Abigail seeks to seduce John Proctor, who has already made love to her, and to get even with John's wife Elizabeth for dismissing Abigail from her service. The town parson, Rev. Parris, is locked in a power struggle within his church. Old hatred emerges between the families of Thomas Putnam and Francis Nurse. Rev. Hale is called in as an expert on witchcraft. After he has condemned many to death, Hale realizes that the real evil in Salem lies in the hearts of its citizens. One very pathetic character is Mary Warren, who becomes Abigail's tool. Abigail reduces Mary to a hysteria which leads to John Proctor's arrest and condemnation. At the end of the drama, Proctor finds cleansing for the guilt in his own soul. Written during the McCarthy era, when hysteria was on the march in America, the play shows that a society can be corrupted when sanity is defeated and emotions are out of control.

Animal Farm
by George Orwell

Using the beast fable form, Orwell presents the communist revolution as a dream gone sour. When the animals, led by pigs Napoleon and Snowball, drive out Farmer Jones and his men, the animals have high hopes for a better life. The Animal Commandments are established as just rules for all. After Napoleon drives out Snowball and assumes authoritarian contol, conditions deteriorate. The laws are revised, with the aid of Squealer the propaganda agent, to mean what Napoleon says they mean. All dissent is brutally crushed. Even the loyal horse Boxer is sold to the glue factory when he can no longer produce. In the end, the pig rulers become exactly like the men they have driven out. Orwell personifies the animals to represent the varying attitudes toward communism and capitalism. Students would need to do some background reading on the history of the communist revolution in order to fully appreciate this book. Orwell believed at first that communism would help the working class. He wrote Animal Farm to show that the dream had failed.

Cry, the Beloved Country
by Alan Paton

This epic novel of South Africa, written in 1949, is crucial to a student's understanding of the problems of apartheid, the doctrine of race separation which is destroying South Africa's people. Paton weeps for a land that is being broken because the old tribal roots are disappearing. The young are being lured by the promise of wealth in the cities and in the mines. Stephen Kumalo's family is the author's example of this social breakup. Stephen goes to Johannesburg in search of his son Absalom and his sister Gertrude. Bewildered by the great city, Stephen is aided by a fellow priest, Msimangu. Stephen finds that his sister has become a prostitute. Absalom has been involved in the murder of Arthur Jarvis, son of a wealthy landowner who lives near Stephen's village. Arthur's death was particularly tragic because the young man was working for social reform to benefit both black and white South Africans. Absalom is condemned to be hanged, while the real criminals who planned the murder go free. Stephen's efforts to save his sister fail; Gertrude returns to her former life. Yet Stephen sees a ray of hope when James Jarvis sends a farm expert to help the people of the valley. Real hope for change, however, lies with the next generation, with Gertrude's child and with Arthur Jarvis' young son, "the child with brightness in him." Paton's novel presages the problems facing his country in the 1980s. The author's warning still applies: "The world cannot afford another Johannesburg."

Twelve Angry Men
by Reginald Rose

This television drama opens as a jury of ordinary men begin deliberations to decide the fate of a boy accused of knifing his father. The case seems easy. At first, one man votes "not guilty" because he feels that the case at least deserves to be discussed. The reader never knows the names of these jurors; each is just an average man with a number. As the debate continues, tempers rise. The attitudes of the jury members toward the boy reveal what kind of person each juryman is under the skin. Under closer scrutiny, the testimony of each witness and the validity of each piece of evidence is called into question. Reasonable doubt as to the boy's guilt is clearly established. This play shows the great responsibility that a person on a jury has when he or she is asked to decide the fate of another person. The drama of Rose's plot emerges as these jurymen themselves are made vulnerable by the pressures of the judicial process.

A Majority of One
by Leonard Spigelgass

Mrs. Jacoby, a Jewish lady from Brooklyn, has strong prejudices against the Japanese who killed her son David. When Mrs. Jacoby goes to live in Japan with her daughter and son-in-law, she meets Mr. Asano, a prominent Japanese businessman. His son was also killed in the war. Two lonely people become friends when Mrs. Jacoby approaches Mr. Asano to help in her son-in-law's trade negotiations. However, when Mr. Asano asks her to keep company with him, proposing a serious relationship according to Japanese customs, Mrs. Jacoby refuses. She still thinks too much of her husband Sam to love anyone else. However, when Mr. Asano comes to New York, the two can be friends on a more casual basis. Through Mrs. Jacoby's experience, the author of the play presents the lesson that enemies can become friends. Each person can deal with the prejudices within the self, and can become a very important "majority of one."

The Hiding Place
by Corrie Ten Boom

This true story of one Dutch woman's survival in a German concentration camp shows that faith and love can conquer hate. The peaceful life of the Ten Booms, a family of watchmakers, is shattered when the Germans invade Holland. The family home becomes a hiding place for Jews who are fleeing the holocaust. Until they are captured, Corrie and her family work with the underground to save many lives. Corrie's elderly father dies at the hands of the Germans. Corrie and her sister Betsie suffer greatly, first in a Dutch prison and finally in the German camp at Ravensbruck. The two women survive through their faith in God, a faith which they share with the other prisoners. They experience many examples of human kindness in the midst of the horror. Betsie finally dies from illness and starvation. Corrie, released due to a clerical error, makes her way back home to Holland. After the war, Corrie establishes a new mission to help those whose lives had been shattered by the concentration camp experience. Corrie Ten Boom's biography shows that, even in the worst situations, people of faith can find the strength to survive and to help others.

Native Son
by Richard Wright

Bigger Thomas, a young black man living in Chicago in the 1930s, exists on the edge of explosive frustration. Bigger goes to work for Mr. Dalton, a wealthy philanthropist who wants to give young black boys a chance. Yet, ironically, Dalton also owns the rat-infested tenement in which Bigger and his family are forced to live. Finally the anger inside Bigger explodes. To prove his manhood, he commits two murders. He strangles Mary Dalton and shoves her body into the furnace. The crime is discovered only when one of Mary's earrings is found. As the police close in on him, Bigger also murders his mistress Bessie. The trial becomes a spectacle as the whites of Chicago erupt in rage against all blacks. Buckley, the prosecuting attorney, seeks to make an example of Bigger, and to use the racial hatred of the community to further his own political ambitions. He presents Bigger as nothing more than a vicious animal. In the novel's very didactic conclusion Richard Wright, using the summation of Max, the defense lawyer, claims that society is responsible for Bigger's crimes. The black population has been dehumanized, frustrated, and forced to strike back in anger. Although rather "preachy" in some places, *Native Son* is a powerful social novel by one of America's finest black authors.

NAME _____ DATE _____

To Sir With Love by E.R. Braithwaite

In the numbered blanks at the left, write the letter of the matching person or place.

_____ 1. Narrator of the story

_____ 2. Supposed to be a difficult place to teach

_____ 3. Student whose father died

_____ 4. Opposite of "Sir" in appearance and attitude

_____ 5. Girl that "Sir" intended to marry

_____ 6. Domestic science teacher who understood kids

_____ 7. Developed from a girl into an attractive young woman

_____ 8. Attacked a teacher in gym class

_____ 9. Fat boy that others made fun of

_____ 10. Principal with progressive ideas

_____ 11. Taught the class before "Sir" took over

_____ 12. Defeated by "Sir" in a boxing match

_____ 13. The art teacher

_____ 14. Taught physical education

_____ 15. Stabbed a boy with an antique knife

A. Mrs. Dale-Evans
B. Mr. Florian
C. Greenslade
D. Pamela Dare
E. Denham
F. Weston
G. Buckley
H. Fernman
I. Mr. Bell
J. Rick
K. Potter
L. Gillian
M. Clinty
N. Hackman
O. Seales

NAME _____ DATE _____

To Sir With Love by E.R. Braithwaite

Answer each of the following questions in two or three complete sentences.

1. After Braithwaite left the service, what problems did he have in getting a job?

2. What special circumstances in the lives of the students influenced the ways that they behaved in school?

3. What did "Sir" hope to accomplish by the rules that he established for his class?

4. How did the class change in their interests and attitudes during the year that "Sir" taught them?

5. Why is Pamela Dare a good example of the growth that took place in "Sir's" students?

CHALLENGE

A good teacher both helps his students to learn and learns from his students. Discuss the ways that *To Sir With Love* illustrates the truth of this statement.

NAME _____ DATE _____

The Good Earth by Pearl S. Buck

Select the letter of the word or phrase which correctly completes each statement.

_____ 1. The novel opens on (A) Wang Lung's birthday (B) the day of the great flood (C) Wang Lung's wedding day (D) the day his first son is born.

_____ 2. O-lan has all of the following characteristics except: (A) loyalty (B) physical strength (C) cooking skill (D) talkativeness.

_____ 3. The family is reduced to poverty because of (A) war (B) flood (C) drought (D) the invasion of robber bands.

_____ 4. Wang Lung is forced to sell everything except (A) his oldest daughter (B) his tools (C) his father's bed (D) his land.

_____ 5. The family travels to the South by (A) train (B) foot (C) boat (D) oxcart.

_____ 6. In the city, Wang Lung (A) is a beggar (B) works as a rickshaw carrier (C) enlists in the army (D) negotiates for the purchase of more land.

_____ 7. The gold which begins the family's new life comes from (A) selling land (B) his uncle's kindness (C) a desperate, dying rich man (D) an inheritance from his father.

_____ 8. As his lands and wealth grow, Wang's most dependable assistant is (A) his father (B) Ching (C) his eldest son (D) his uncle's son.

_____ 9. Signs of Wang's increasing prosperity include (A) his son's going to school (B) his buying land from the House of Hwang (C) his hiring laborers to work his land (D) all of the above.

_____ 10. Wang becomes infatuated with Lotus (A) when O-lan dies (B) because he has too much leisure time (C) because she reminds him of O-lan (D) because she is interested in his farming projects.

_____ 11. The reader dislikes Wang most when (A) he refuses to sell his land (B) he brings Lotus to his house (C) he takes O-lan's pearls (D) he beats up his son.

_____ 12. Wang decides that his third son (A) will be a merchant (B) will go to school (C) must remain on the land (D) will become a soldier.

_____ 13. Wang is forced to feed and house his uncle's family because (A) he fears attacks by robbers (B) he has a sense of family obligation (C) O-lan asks him to (D) it is his father's dying request.

_____ 14. The move to the great house in the city represents (A) the change in the family's social position (B) the rejection of simple values (C) the dominance of the sons over the father (D) all of the above.

_____ 15. The family's financial empire is supervised by (A) Wang's uncle (B) the second son (C) the eldest son (D) Wang himself.

_____ 16. In his last years, Wang most wanted (A) grandsons (B) peace (C) a new wife (D) more wealth.

_____ 17. The great house is almost destroyed by (A) quartered soldiers (B) a fire (C) a flood (D) an earthquake.

_____ 18. In his last years, Wang is comforted by (A) Cukoo (B) Lotus (C) Pear Blossom (D) the wife of his son.

_____ 19. Wang spends the last years of his life (A) in the great house (B) in the South (C) in his old house on the land (D) at the teahouse.

_____ 20. At the end of the novel, Wang's sons (A) openly defy their father (B) will obey their father's wishes (C) plan to destroy what Wang has built (D) show great respect for the old ways of life.

NAME _____ DATE _____

The Good Earth by Pearl S. Buck

Answer each of the following questions in two or three complete sentences.

1. How does O-lan give Wang Lung strength during the early years of their marriage?

   _____
   _____
   _____
   _____

2. Why will Wang Lung sacrifice everything to keep his land?

   _____
   _____
   _____
   _____

3. How does Wang's love for O-lan differ from his infatuation with Lotus?

   _____
   _____
   _____
   _____

4. How is Wang a failure as a parent?

   _____
   _____
   _____
   _____

5. By the end of the novel, how has the Lung family become exactly like the House of Hwang?

   _____
   _____
   _____
   _____

CHALLENGE

Write an essay to show how *The Good Earth* illustrates the destructive power of wealth on individuals and human relationships. What important personal values are lost as the emphasis of life is placed on material gain?

NAME _____ DATE _____

The Chocolate War by Robert Cormier

In the numbered blanks at the left, write the letter of the matching person or place. You will use some letters more than once.

_____ 1. Brilliant student who was humiliated and accused of cheating

_____ 2. Sadistic teacher who uses his classroom to exercise his own vicious nature

_____ 3. Natural runner and athlete

_____ 4. Boy used by the Vigils to finally destroy Jerry

_____ 5. Treasurer for the chocolate campaign

_____ 6. Gave assignments for the Vigils

_____ 7. Had to help Goober complete his assignment

_____ 8. Was beaten up by Carter for defying the Vigils

_____ 9. Was forced to tell Brother Leon about Jerry's assignment

_____ 10. Had a nervous breakdown when his classroom was taken apart

_____ 11. Setting for the novel

_____ 12. Became a symbol of one man's rebellion against the system

_____ 13. President of the Vigils

_____ 14. Hardworking pharmacist

_____ 15. History teacher who had been "tipped off" by Archie

_____ 16. Might have to carry out the assignments that he gave to others

_____ 17. His mother had died of cancer

_____ 18. Stopped the fight by turning out the lights

_____ 19. Saw the chocolate campaign as a means to establish control and power

_____ 20. Quit the football team as an act of protest

A. Mr. Renault
B. Trinity
C. Frankie Rollo
D. Brother Jacques
E. Caroni
F. Brian Cochran
G. Carter
H. Janza
I. Bailey
J. Jerry Renault
K. Brother Eugene
L. Obie
M. Brother Leon
N. Archie Costello
O. Goober

NAME _____ DATE _____

The Chocolate War by Robert Cormier

Answer each of the following questions in two or three complete sentences.

1. Why does Jerry continue to refuse the chocolates, even after his assignment from the Vigils is over?

   _____

   _____

   _____

   _____

2. How does Brother Leon plan to use the Vigils for his own purposes?

   _____

   _____

   _____

   _____

3. What is the significance of the "black box" in the Vigils organization?

   _____

   _____

   _____

   _____

4. How is Jerry harrassed by the other students?

   _____

   _____

   _____

   _____

5. What happens at the "raffle"? How is the fight finally stopped?

   _____

   _____

   _____

   _____

CHALLENGE

Jerry Renault is one individual who "dares to disturb the universe." Write an essay explaining how author Robert Cormier gives Jerry a dignity of human spirit, even though Jerry fails in his attempt to fight against the system.

NAME _____ DATE _____

I Am the Cheese by Robert Cormier

Place a (+) before each statement that is true and a (0) before each statement that is false.

_____ 1. As the story opens, Adam is riding a bus to Vermont.

_____ 2. Adam is going to see his father.

_____ 3. Adam instinctively trusts Dr. Brint because of Brint's kindly eyes.

_____ 4. Adam's earliest memories have to do with the sounds and smells of his parents.

_____ 5. During Adam's childhood, the family moved frequently.

_____ 6. Adam remembers "The Farmer in the Dell," because his father sang that song to him frequently.

_____ 7. When the dog attacks him, Adam falls from his bike and lands in the ditch.

_____ 8. Adam's father had protected him from a dog when Adam was a child.

_____ 9. Adam enjoys being with Amy because she makes him feel good about himself.

_____ 10. Every one of Amy's "Numbers" that Adam helps with is successful.

_____ 11. The visiting editor from Rawlings told Amy that he used to work with Adam's father.

_____ 12. Adam shows real courage in the restaurant when he defends the package from Junior Varney and his friends.

_____ 13. Adam learns that his family had to run and hide because Adam's father had a criminal record.

_____ 14. After he finds out the truth about his identity, Adam is very angry because his parents have lied to him.

_____ 15. The greatest fear that the family faces is the fear of the unknown.

_____ 16. Adam's parents were killed in a plane crash.

_____ 17. Amy Hertz never really existed.

_____ 18. Mr. Grey was a true friend who protected the Delmonte family.

_____ 19. On his bike trip, Adam is able to stay at the same motel where he had stayed with his parents.

_____ 20. At the end of the story, Adam and his father are reunited.

NAME _____ DATE _____

I Am the Cheese by Robert Cormier

Answer each of the following questions in two or three complete sentences.

1. How does Adam Farmer (Paul Delmonte) show himself to be a brave person in spite of his many fears?

   _____

   _____

   _____

   _____

2. Why is Adam's relationship with Amy Hertz so special?

   _____

   _____

   _____

   _____

3. Why did Adam's family have to assume a new identity?

   _____

   _____

   _____

   _____

4. What are some of the clues that Adam gets as he begins to learn the truth?

   _____

   _____

   _____

   _____

5. What does Adam's mother mean by the ''Never-Knows''? Why are these the greatest fears of all?

   _____

   _____

   _____

   _____

   _____

CHALLENGE

Paul Delmonte (Adam Farmer) is fighting for survival. How is this fight linked to the title of the novel? Do you believe that the boy will succeed in this struggle? Why or why not?

NAME _____ DATE _____

The Autobiography of Miss Jane Pittman by Ernest J. Gaines

Place a (+) before each statement that is true and a (0) before each statement that is false.

_____   1.   When she died, Miss Jane was 110 years old.

_____   2.   As a slave, Miss Jane had been the cook on her master's plantation.

_____   3.   Most of the story takes place in Mississippi.

_____   4.   After the Emancipation Proclamation, the freed slaves received a great deal of help from the government.

_____   5.   Ned was Miss Jane's son.

_____   6.   Miss Jane was given her name by a Yankee soldier.

_____   7.   Joe Pittman was killed by a horse he was attempting to break.

_____   8.   Ned was attempting to build a school to aid Negro children.

_____   9.   Ned died in a violent flood.

_____ 10.   Living conditions for the freed blacks were not much better than they had been in the days of slavery.

_____ 11.   The sheriff could find no witnesses to testify to Ned's death.

_____ 12.   Religion played an important part in Jane Pittman's life.

_____ 13.   Mary Agnes LeFabre had a very small amount of Negro blood.

_____ 14.   Robert Samson would not tolerate his son having any relationship at all with a Negro woman.

_____ 15.   Mary Agnes encouraged Tee Bob's romantic advances.

_____ 16.   Tee Bob shot himself.

_____ 17.   Jimmy was punished less strictly because Jane and his aunt Lena felt that he had special gifts and abilities.

_____ 18.   Even though Jane was too old to continue cooking for the Samson family, she continued to live in the cook's residence.

_____ 19.   Robert Sampson rented most of his farm acreage to Negro sharecroppers.

_____ 20.   Miss Jane particpated in a civil rights protest which centered around a public drinking fountain.

NAME _____ DATE _____

The Autobiography of Miss Jane Pittman by Ernest J. Gaines

Answer each of the following questions in two or three complete sentences.

1. How did Jane and Ned survive their journey after leaving the plantation?

   _____
   _____
   _____
   _____

2. How did the whites take advantage of the ignorance of the freed blacks?

   _____
   _____
   _____
   _____

3. How did Ned Douglass try to help his people?

   _____
   _____
   _____
   _____

4. How was young Robert Samson a victim of the double standard in Southern society?

   _____
   _____
   _____
   _____

5. What did Miss Jane mean when she said that they knew that Jimmy was "the One"?

   _____
   _____
   _____
   _____

CHALLENGE

In one speech, Ned Douglass told his audience that a black American is different from a nigger, because a black American "cares and will always struggle." Write an essay to illustrate how Miss Jane Pittman is an example of such an American.

NAME _____ DATE _____

Black Like Me by John Howard Griffin

Correctly complete each sentence with information from the novel.

1. Griffin by profession is a _____.

2. In his experiment, Griffin changed only _____.

3. The medical procedure to change the color of Griffin's skin was done in _____
   _____.

4. His skin color changed gradually by using _____
   and _____.

5. The shoeshine man in New Orleans who helped Griffin was named _____.

6. Griffin realized how totally his appearance had changed when _____
   _____.

7. His greatest physical discomforts as a black man came from not being easily able to
   find _____ and _____.

8. Griffin feels that the black man's greatest need is for _____.

9. The man lynched in Mississippi was named _____.

10. The "hate stare" was _____.

11. The "best" Negroes were thought to be _____.

12. Griffin was greatly assisted by a courageous newspaper editor named _____
    _____.

13. The men who gave Griffin rides were mostly interested in _____.

14. Griffin's most wonderful experience as a black came when _____
    _____.

15. The city where Griffin functioned both as a black and as a white was _____.

16. The magazine which first published Griffin's articles was the _____.

17. The most difficult emotional aspect of Griffin's experiment was the _____.

18. The total time that Griffin remained a Negro was about _____.

19. When they found out what Griffin had done, the people of his home town _____
    _____.

20. In order to escape the publicity, Griffin's family had to _____.

150 Great Books

NAME _____ DATE _____

Black Like Me by John Howard Griffin

Answer each of the following questions in two or three complete sentences.

1. Describe the process by which Griffin became a Negro.

_____

_____

_____

_____

2. Why did Griffin make this experiment?

_____

_____

_____

_____

3. How was he treated differently as a black man in New Orleans than he was treated in Mississippi?

_____

_____

_____

_____

4. Describe the public reaction when Griffin's story was published.

_____

_____

_____

_____

5. What does Griffin believe are the greatest dangers in the modern civil rights movement?

_____

_____

_____

_____

CHALLENGE

Write an essay explaining how John Howard Griffin's experiences proved that good or evil in human nature has nothing whatever to do with the color of a man or woman's skin.

NAME _____ DATE _____

A Raisin in the Sun by Lorraine Hansbury

Select the letter of the word or phrase which correctly completes each statement.

_____ 1. The set of the play is supposed to convey a sense of (A) shabbiness (B) over-crowdedness (C) exhaustion (D) all of the above.

_____ 2. The relationship between Ruth and Walter in the first scene may be best described as (A) indifference (B) hostility (C) loving frustration (D) sympathy.

_____ 3. All the characters in Act I are mainly interested in (A) Walter's job (B) Mama's insurance check (C) Travis' report card (D) Ruth's pregnancy.

_____ 4. Walter wants Ruth to (A) loan him some money (B) persuade Lena to give him money (C) be nicer to Beneatha (D) let Travis get an after-school job.

_____ 5. Lena (A) holds the family together (B) spoils Travis (C) doesn't understand the new ideas of the young (D) all of the above.

_____ 6. Beneatha doesn't really like George because he is (A) rich (B) poor (C) snobbish and shallow (D) uneducated.

_____ 7. The news of Ruth's pregnancy (A) makes Walter angry (B) is greeted joyously by everyone (C) makes Lena realize how desperate the situation is (D) is kept a secret.

_____ 8. Beneatha likes Asagai (A) because he understands her real needs (B) because he is African (C) because he brings her nice gifts (D) because he is studying medicine.

_____ 9. Walter feels that no one (A) listens to him (B) loves him (C) trusts him (D) thinks that he can be a success.

_____ 10. George Murchison insults Walter by (A) calling him "boy" (B) telling him he is a drunk (C) using language Walter doesn't understand (D) telling Walter he is stupid.

_____ 11. Mama first talks about the purchase of the house to (A) Ruth (B) Walter (C) Beneatha (D) Travis.

_____ 12. Ruth is concerned when she finds out that the house is (A) small (B) in a white neighborhood (C) too far from her work (D) owned by Lena.

_____ 13. Mama places her trust in Walter by (A) giving him the money to bank (B) putting him in charge of the movers (C) agreeing to meet Willie Harris (D) helping him find a new job.

_____ 14. Walter's dreams include (A) a fine car (B) a good school for Travis (C) a mansion (D) all of the above.

_____ 15. Karl Lindner (A) comes to welcome them to Claybourne Park (B) wants to buy the house back (C) threatens them cause Willie couldn't get the license.

_____ 17. The one who insists that they must move is (A) Mama (B) Ruth (C) Walter (D) Beneatha.

_____ 18. Originally, Walter intended to (A) accept Lindner's money (B) look for another job (C) move into the house anyway (D) go to Africa.

_____ 19. The person whose presence helps Walter stand up to Lindner is (A) Travis (B) Mama (C) Ruth (D) Asagai.

_____ 20. An important symbol for the family's survival is (A) Mama's hat (B) the plant (C) Ruth's ironing board (D) the insurance check.

NAME _____ DATE _____

A Raisin in the Sun by Lorraine Hansbury

Answer each of the following questions in two or three complete sentences.

1. What are some of the problems created by the Younger's crowded living situation?

   _____
   _____
   _____
   _____

2. Why does Beneatha like Asagai better than she likes George?

   _____
   _____
   _____
   _____

3. How does Lena show great courage and strength of character?

   _____
   _____
   _____
   _____

4. Despite their arguments, how does the play show that Walter and Ruth love each other?

   _____
   _____
   _____

5. How does Walter "come into his manhood" at the end of the play?

   _____
   _____
   _____
   _____

CHALLENGE

The title of the play comes from Langston Hughes' poem, "A Dream Deferred." Read this short poem. Write an essay explaining how each of the attitudes expressed in the poem apply to characters in this play.

NAME _____ DATE _____

The Little Foxes by Lillian Hellman

Place a (+) before each statement that is true and a (0) before each statement that is false.

_____ 1. The dinner for Mr. Marshall takes place in Oscar and Birdie's home.

_____ 2. Birdie's family lost Lionnet because Birdie's brothers were too weak to hold on to it.

_____ 3. Alexandra is pleased with the idea of marrying Leo.

_____ 4. The Hubbards are planning a partnership with Marshall to build a cotton mill.

_____ 5. Regina wants to live in New York after the conclusion of the business deal.

_____ 6. Horace Giddens has cancer.

_____ 7. Birdie tries to warn Alexandra and to protect her from the Hubbards' scheming.

_____ 8. Regina forces Ben and Oscar to promise Horace fifty per cent of the mill profits.

_____ 9. When Horace returns home, he agrees at once to cooperate in the mill deal with Marshall.

_____ 10. Oscar Hubbard is pictured as a violent, vicious man.

_____ 11. Horace knows that Leo stole the bonds from the strongbox.

_____ 12. Birdie escapes from ugliness and unhappiness by drinking.

_____ 13. Horace does not want Alexandra to know about the evil and cruelty that exists within the family.

_____ 14. Horace intends to change his will to leave everything to Alexandra.

_____ 15. Horace collapses at the foot of the stairs.

_____ 16. Alexandra knows that her mother is at least partially responsible for her father's death.

_____ 17. Oscar sticks up for Leo when Leo is accused of theft.

_____ 18. Regina threatens to ruin her brothers if they do not give in to her demands for controlling interest in the mill.

_____ 19. Oscar suspects the truth about Regina's guilt in Horace's death.

_____ 20. In this play, the world seems to be controlled by those who are totally lacking in ethics and conscience.

NAME _____ DATE _____

The Little Foxes by Lillian Hellman

Answer each of the following questions in two or three complete sentences.

1. Contrast the personalities of Regina Giddens and Birdie Hubbard.

    _____

    _____

    _____

    _____

2. Why does Horace refuse to cooperate with the Hubbards in their business plans?

    _____

    _____

    _____

    _____

3. How does Regina show that she is just as ruthless as her brothers are?

    _____

    _____

    _____

    _____

4. In what ways is Alexandra more her father's daughter than her mother's daughter?

    _____

    _____

    _____

    _____

5. What evidences are there at the end of the play that Regina may have good reason to be afraid?

    _____

    _____

    _____

    _____

CHALLENGE

The author divides the characters in *The Little Foxes* into three groups: those who eat the earth, those who fight, and those who stand around and watch. Write an essay, placing each of the play's characters into one of these three classifications. Which group seems to be victorious at the end?

NAME _____ DATE _____

Inherit the Wind by Jerome Lawrence and Robert E. Lee
Correctly complete each sentence with information from the play.

1. The atmosphere in Hillsboro before the trial may best be described as _____

   _____.

2. Bertram Cates has been accused of _____.

3. The chief attorney for the prosecution is _____.

4. The attorney for the defense is _____.

5. Hornbeck works for _____.

6. Rachel wants Bert to _____.

7. Brady's main character trait is his _____.

8. When Melinda first sees Drummond, she thinks that he is _____.

9. The court refuses to admit any of Drummond's evidence about _____.

10. Drummond says that what is really on trial is _____.

11. Rachel is very afraid of _____.

12. Drummond calls as his witness for the defense _____.

13. The jury finds Bert Cates _____.

14. The judge sentences Bert _____.

15. At the close of the trial, Brady intends to _____.

16. Brady accuses Drummond of _____.

17. When Brady starts to make his speech, the spectators _____.

18. Cate's bail will be paid by _____.

19. The judge comes back with the news that Brady _____.

20. Rachel Brown has decided to _____.

NAME _____ DATE _____

Inherit the Wind by Jerome Lawrence and Robert E. Lee

Answer each of the following questions in two or three complete sentences.

1. Why is the entire nation interested in the trial of Bert Cates?

   _____

   _____

   _____

   _____

2. Why is the atmosphere in Hillsboro prejudiced against Bert's getting a fair trial?

   _____

   _____

   _____

   _____

3. How is Rachel Brown trapped in the middle of the conflict?

   _____

   _____

   _____

   _____

4. How does Drummond trap Brady with Brady's own logic?

   _____

   _____

   _____

   _____

5. How does Drummond show respect for Brady as an opponent?

   _____

   _____

   _____

   _____

CHALLENGE

Write an essay discussing how man's right to think is on trial in the case of Bertram Cates.

NAME _____ DATE _____

To Kill a Mockingbird by Harper Lee

Select the letter of the word or phrase which correctly completes each statement.

_____ 1. The story is told by (A) Jem (B) Scout (C) Atticus (D) Calpurnia.

_____ 2. Scout got into trouble her first day at school because of (A) Miss Caroline (B) Jem (C) Burris Ewell (D) Walter Cunningham.

_____ 3. Maycomb despised the Ewells because (A) they were crude (B) they were dirty (C) they lived in the town dump (D) all of the above.

_____ 4. The only "mother" that Scout could remember was (A) Aunt Alexandra (B) Calpurnia (C) Miss Maudie (D) Miss Caroline.

_____ 5. The children's imaginations were inspired by (A) Boo Radley (B) the arrival of Dill (C) the books they read (D) all of the above.

_____ 6. In escaping from the Radley house, Jem (A) was shot (B) lost his pants (C) actually saw Boo (D) stole some vegetables.

_____ 7. Boo Radley was (A) dangerous to the children (B) sociable (C) an adult with a child's mind (D) an only child.

_____ 8. Scout's favorite relative was (A) Uncle Jack (B) Cousin Francis (C) Aunt Alexandra (D) Uncle Jimmy.

_____ 9. Mrs. Dubose (A) had a nasty tongue (B) was a very sick old lady (C) helped Scout and Jem to learn patience (D) all of the above.

_____ 10. Tom Robinson was accused of (A) rape (B) murder (C) arson (D) larceny.

_____ 11. In defending Tom, Atticus had to face (A) the hatred of the Ewells (B) a lynch mob (C) the misunderstanding of the community (D) all of the above.

_____ 12. Atticus took Tom's case (A) because Tom was a friend of Calpurnia's (B) because Judge Taylor appointed him (C) because he thought that he could get Tom acquitted (D) because Atticus needed the publicity.

_____ 13. The children watched Tom's trial (A) through the window (B) from the front row (C) from the back of the courtroom (D) from the colored balcony.

_____ 14. Mayella Ewell (A) was trying to get even with Tom (B) wa a victim of her father's cruelty and abuse (C) could speak clearly and logically (D) had actually been raped.

_____ 15. Tom could not have been Mayella's attacker (A) because he was a cripple (B) because he didn't enter the house (C) because he didn't know her (D) because he wasn't strong enough.

_____ 16. Tom was found guilty (A) because he was guilty (B) because he was black (C) because Atticus did a poor job defending him (D) because Bob Ewell's word was well-respected in the community.

_____ 17. Tom (A) was hanged (B) later went free (C) was shot trying to escape (D) was pardoned by Judge Taylor.

_____ 18. The injustice of the Robinson case was presented to the community by (A) Miss Maudie's letter to the paper (B) Mr. Underwood's editorial (C) Miss Gates' speech in class (D) Reverend Sykes' sermon.

_____ 19. On Halloween night, Scout's life was saved by (A) Jem (B) Atticus (C) Boo Radley (D) Sheriff Tate.

_____ 20. Bob Ewell died (A) when Jem stabbed him (B) when Boo stabbed him (C) when he fell on his own knife (D) when he was stabbed by the wires on Scout's costume.

NAME _____ DATE _____

To Kill a Mockingbird by Harper Lee

Answer each of the following questions in two or three complete sentences.

1. Why was Jem's and Scout's relationship with their father so special?

   _____

   _____

   _____

   _____

2. Why was school such a disaster for Scout?

   _____

   _____

   _____

   _____

3. What does Scout learn when she goes to church with Calpurnia?

   _____

   _____

   _____

   _____

4. Even though Atticus wishes to shield them, how do the children become involved in the events surrounding the Tom Robinson case?

   _____

   _____

   _____

   _____

5. Why does Mr. Underwood compare Tom's death to the killing of a mockingbird?

   _____

   _____

   _____

   _____

CHALLENGE

In what ways would the childhood experiences recounted in *To Kill a Mockingbird* help Jean Louise Finch to grow into a compassionate, less prejudiced adult?

NAME _____ DATE _____

Main Street by Sinclair Lewis

Select the letter of the word or phrase which correctly completes each statement.

_____ 1. Carol met and married Will Kennicott when she was (A) a teenager (B) a college student (C) a young librarian (D) an office worker in Washington.

_____ 2. Carol's idealism became focused on (A) slum clearance (B) small-town reform (C) education (D) temperance.

_____ 3. After she had been in Gopher Prairie for a few months, Carol's main feeling was (A) entrapment (B) indifference (C) anger (D) enjoyment.

_____ 4. The person whose initial reaction to Gopher Prairie was most opposite to Carol's was (A) Erik's (B) Bea Sorenson (C) Sam Clark (D) Fern Mullins.

_____ 5. Carol realizes that the town accepts her only because (A) her husband is one of them (B) she is a college student (C) she is young and intelligent (D) they agree with her ideas about small-town reform.

_____ 6. Kennicott's interests included all of the following except (A) automobiles (B) agriculture (C) land speculation (D) hunting.

_____ 7. Carol's closest female friend in Gopher Prairie was (A) Maud Dyer (B) Mrs. Bogart (C) Vida Sherwin (D) Juanita Haycock.

_____ 8. Carol's first party was seen by the town as (A) overdone (B) pretentious (C) Carol's attempt to show off (D) all of the above.

_____ 9. The most ironic name that Lewis uses for a town organization is (A) Thanatopsis (B) Jolly Seventeen (C) Bon-Ton (D) Gopher Prairie Drama Society.

_____ 10. Carol tries to improve all of the following except (A) the Baptist Church (B) the town hall (C) the school (D) the library.

_____ 11. The dullness of small-town life is also understood by (A) Kennicott (B) Guy Pollock (C) Sam Clark (D) Mrs. Champ Clark.

_____ 12. Victims of Gopher Prairie's prejudices include all of the following except: (A) Maud Dyer (B) Miles Bjornstam (C) Bea Soronson (D) Fern Mullins.

_____ 13. Erik's father blames his son's problems on (A) the Jolly Seventeen (B) Carol (C) Erik's employer (D) Dr. Kennicott.

_____ 14. The most vicious hypocrite in the town is (A) Vida Sherwin (B) Aunt Bessie (C) Mrs. Bogart (D) Mrs. Champ Clark.

_____ 15. Carol is drawn to Eric because she feels that they are both (A) sensitive (B) artistic (C) outcasts (D) intelligent.

_____ 16. The most positive element in Carol's life is (A) her husband (B) her son (C) the Jolly Seventeen (D) Thanatopsis.

_____ 17. Carol and Kennicot have their most serious quarrel over (A) Erik (B) Fern Mullins (C) building a new home (D) Harry Blausser's improvement campaign.

_____ 18. Carol finds her desire for a larger world in (A) New York (B) Washington (C) Minneapolis (D) Los Angeles.

_____ 19. When Kennicott comes to visit Carol, he (A) courts and woos her (B) demands that she return home (C) makes fun of her work (D) asks her for a divorce.

_____ 20. At the end of the novel, Carol sees the continuation of her hopes in (A) her children (B) the new school building (C) the new library (D) the revival of her love for Kennicott.

NAME _____ DATE _____

Main Street by Sinclair Lewis

Answer each of the following questions in two or three complete sentences.

1. What dreams does Carol have for Gopher Prairie? How are these dreams reduced to frustrations during the first years of her marriage?

_____

_____

_____

_____

2. How is the marriage of Bea and Miles more real than the marriage of Carol and Kennicott?

_____

_____

_____

_____

3. Why is Carol's attraction to Erik destined to produce heartbreak?

_____

_____

_____

_____

4. What is the "Village Virus"? Why is it so deadly to Carol Kennicott?

_____

_____

_____

_____

5. How does Fern Mullins become a victim of everything that is evil in Gopher Prairie?

_____

_____

_____

_____

CHALLENGE

Write an essay discussing the character development of Carol Kennicott. How does she change from a starry-eyed idealist to a mature woman who can cope with reality? What are some of the experiences which produce these changes?

NAME _____ DATE _____

The Crucible by Arthur Miller

Correctly complete each sentence with information from the play.

1. Parris had frequent conflicts with his congregation about _____.

2. _____ had learned the techniques of witchcraft on the island of _____.

3. Abigail and the girls had been caught by Parris when they were _____.

4. Elizabeth Proctor had fired Abigail because _____.

5. The character who best presents the voice of common sense in the rising hysterics is _____.

6. Thomas Putnam's enemies in his land disputes were _____ and _____.

7. Parris has sent for Reverend Hale because _____.

8. Ruth Putnam accuses Rebecca Nurse of _____.

9. The relationship between John and Elizabeth Proctor at the beginning of Act II may best be described as _____.

10. Mary Warren is afraid of Abigail because _____.

11. When Hale asks Proctor to repeat the commandments, the one that John misses is _____.

12. Elizabeth knows that Abigail has accused her of witchcraft so that _____ _____.

13. Giles Corey and Francis Nurse try to save their wives by _____.

14. _____ is the chief justice of the court.

15. When Mary Warren tries to tell the truth, Abigail _____.

16. Hale quits the court because _____.

17. Hale tries to get Rebecca and John to confess so that _____.

18. Elizabeth's life is saved because _____.

19. Giles Corey dies by _____ because he will not _____.

20. John will not sign the confession because _____.

150 Great Books

NAME _____ DATE _____

The Crucible by Arthur Miller

Explain in two or three sentences the meaning of each of the following quotes or character descriptions.

1. "He have his goodness now. God forbid that I should take it from him."

   _____
   _____
   _____
   _____

2. "A strikingly beautiful girl with an endless capacity for dissembling."

   _____
   _____
   _____
   _____

3. "Elizabeth, your justice would freeze beer."

   _____
   _____
   _____
   _____

4. "We are only what we always were, but naked now . . . and God's icy wind will blow."

   _____
   _____
   _____
   _____

5. "In his presence, a fool felt his foolishness instantly."

   _____
   _____
   _____
   _____

CHALLENGE

The Salem witchcraft trials resulted in the destruction of a society. Describe the roots of hate, jealousy, and greed which were the real forces behind the hysterics. Discuss the characters which best illustrate these attitudes.

NAME _____ DATE _____

Animal Farm by George Orwell

Place a (+) before each statement that is true and a (0) before each statement that is false.

_____ 1. Snowball had the dream which envisioned the ideal animal society.

_____ 2. Jones was a cruel farmer who abused and neglected his animals.

_____ 3. The basic principle of the revolution at the beginning was that some animals were superior to other animals.

_____ 4. Major led the battle to drive Jones and his men from the farm.

_____ 5. Snowball was a better speaker and organizer than Napoleon was.

_____ 6. Education was an important part of the animals' revolutionary program.

_____ 7. Napoleon favored the building of the windmill, while Snowball opposed it.

_____ 8. Snowball returned to Animal Farm several times after Napoleon's dogs drove him off.

_____ 9. Benjamin was the perfect example of the hard worker who believed everything that he was told.

_____ 10. The animals successfully defended the farm at the Battle of the Cowshed.

_____ 11. Clover was lured away from Animal Farm by her love of sugar and bright ribbons.

_____ 12. Squealer was responsible for changing the Animal Commandments to justify everything that the pigs did.

_____ 13. Napoleon himself took the responsibility for the accidental destruction of the first windmill.

_____ 14. Napoleon used Mr. Pilkington as a agent to trade for the necessities that Animal Farm could not produce.

_____ 15. As time passed, the lifestyle of the average animal improved substantially.

_____ 16. All errors and problems were blamed on Snowball.

_____ 17. Napoleon and his pigs continued to encourage the other animals by frequently singing "Beasts of England."

_____ 18. All the animals were allowed to drink some of the whiskey that was produced on the farm.

_____ 19. No animals ever challenged Napoleon's authority.

_____ 20. Boxer was the animal who was most betrayed by the revolution he had believed in.

NAME _____ **DATE** _____

Animal Farm by George Orwell

Answer each of the following questions in two or three complete sentences.

1. Describe the animals' utopian vision of an ideal society.

    _____

    _____

    _____

    _____

2. How did Napoleon gain absolute control of Animal Farm?

    _____

    _____

    _____

    _____

3. In what specific ways was Squealer valuable as a propaganda expert?

    _____

    _____

    _____

    _____

4. How did life on Animal Farm gradually change for the average animal?

    _____

    _____

    _____

    _____

5. How did the pigs finally become just like the men they had driven out?

    _____

    _____

    _____

    _____

CHALLENGE

Write an essay discussing Orwell's use of personification. How do the characteristics of the various animals represent traits evident in human nature?

NAME _____ DATE _____

Cry, the Beloved Country by Alan Paton

In the numbered blanks at the left, write the letter of the matching person or place.

_____ 1. Stephen's guide and closest friend in Johannesburg

_____ 2. Skilled speaker who had been corrupted by his love for power

_____ 3. God

_____ 4. Kumalo's home village

_____ 5. Struck Jarvis's houseboy on the head with a crowbar

_____ 6. Organizer of the bus boycott to protest a rate increase

_____ 7. Said that he fired his gun because he was afraid

_____ 8. Reverend, pastor

_____ 9. Brought up Gertrude's child as her own son

_____ 10. English priest who married the girl to Absalom

_____ 11. Planned to build a new church for the people of the village

_____ 12. Jarvis's brother-in-law whose opinions represent the views of the South African white community

_____ 13. Returned to a life of crime and prostitution

_____ 14. Stephen's tribe

_____ 15. Came to the valley to teach scientific farming methods

_____ 16. Title of respect used by the blacks for a white man

_____ 17. Gave Stephen and Gertrude a place to live in Johannesburg

_____ 18. Powerful writer who believed that South Africa must recognize the humanity of her black population

_____ 19. Absalom's landlady

_____ 20. Lawyer for the defense

A. Umfundisi
B. Umnumzana
C. John Kumalo
D. Johannes Pafuri
E. Gertrude
F. Mr. Carmichael
G. Father Vincent
H. John Harrison
I. Arthur Jarvis
J. Ndotsheni
K. James Jarvis
L. Msimangu
M. Mrs. Mkize
N. Absalom
O. Mrs. Lithebe
P. Zulu
Q. Tixo
R. Napoleon Letsitsi
S. Mrs. Kumalo
T. Dubula

NAME _____ DATE _____

Cry, the Beloved Country by Alan Paton

Answer each of the following questions in two or three complete sentences.

1. Describe Kumalo's initial reactions when he arrives in Johannesburg.

    _____

    _____

    _____

    _____

2. Contrast Stephen Kumalo and his brother John.

    _____

    _____

    _____

    _____

3. How does Stephen's family represent the breakdown of the South African tribal system?

    _____

    _____

    _____

    _____

4. How do Msimangu and Mrs. Lithebe represent goodness and humanity against a background of injustice and evil?

    _____

    _____

    _____

5. How are both Absalom Kumalo and Arthur Jarvis victims of the social evils of South Africa?

    _____

    _____

    _____

    _____

CHALLENGE

Write an essay describing the hopes which Alan Paton has for his country. Where does Paton believe that the fulfillment of these hopes lies?

NAME _____ DATE _____

Twelve Angry Men by Reginald Rose

In the numbered blanks at the left, write the letter of the matching person or place. Some letters may be used more than once.

_____ 1. Was himself the product of a slum environment

_____ 2. Charged the jury that their vote had to be unanimous

_____ 3. Eyesight was called into question

_____ 4. Insists from the beginning that the jury members take some time to give the case a fair hearing

_____ 5. Wanted to get done quickly so he could get to a baseball game

_____ 6. Inexperienced and lax, appointed by the court

_____ 7. Setting for most of the play

_____ 8. Verified from his experience that the old man could not have heard the body fall because of the noise from the train

_____ 9. The most violent member of the group, capable of being a killer himself

_____ 10. Man of weak opinions, changed his vote twice because he was easily swayed by the others

_____ 11. Oldest member of the jury, identified with the old man's need for respect and attention

_____ 12. Most cultured of the jury members

_____ 13. Had been declared by a psychiatrist as being capable of killing

_____ 14. Could not have moved fast enough to see the boy run away

_____ 15. Bigot, who saw the boy as one of "them"

_____ 16. Timed the reenactment of the old man's walk to the hall

_____ 17. An immigrant who took his responsibilities to democracy very seriously

_____ 18. Tried to keep the tempers of the others under control

_____ 19. Brought in the pieces of evidence for examination

_____ 20. Violent man who had served a term in prison

A. #8
B. The old man
C. The boy's lawyer
D. The boy's father
E. #3
F. #7
G. #10
H. #4
I. The foreman
J. #5
K. #11
L. #6
M. #9
N. Woman witness
O. Guard
P. #12
Q. #2
R. The judge
S. The defendant
T. The jury room

NAME _____ DATE _____

Twelve Angry Men by Reginald Rose

Answer each of the following questions in two or three complete sentences.

1. Why does #8 vote "not guilty" on the first ballot?

    _____

    _____

    _____

    _____

2. How does the attitude of #8 toward the boy and the crime contrast with the attitude of #10?

    _____

    _____

    _____

    _____

3. Why does #5 understand, better than any of the others, the feelings of the defendant?

    _____

    _____

    _____

    _____

4. Why does the author of the play give the jury members numbers instead of names?

    _____

    _____

    _____

    _____

5. Why is #7 really the weakest of the jury members when the final vote comes?

    _____

    _____

    _____

    _____

CHALLENGE

The true nature of a person's character emerges when that person is subjected to stress and pressure. Select three of the jurors and describe how true character comes out in the pressure of the jury room.

NAME _____ DATE _____

A Majority of One by Leonard Spigelgass

Correctly complete each sentence with information from the play.

1. Jerry Black works for _____.

2. Jerry and Alice have just received a transfer to _____.

3. Essie Rubin is concerned about the quality of her neighborhood because _____
   _____.

4. Mrs. Jacoby has strong feelings against the Japanese because _____
   _____.

5. Jerry and Alice want Mrs. Jacoby to _____
   _____.

6. When Mrs. Jacoby first meets Mr. Asano, she _____.

7. Mr. Asano tells Mrs. Jacoby that his son and daughter _____
   _____.

8. Jerry is concerned about Mrs. Jacoby's friendship with Mr. Asano because _____
   _____.

9. Eddie, the Japanese houseboy, says that he is losing face because _____
   _____.

10. As a girl, Mrs. Jacoby had come to America from _____.

11. Jerry is upset because the trade negotiations have _____.

12. Mrs. Jacoby decides to help Jerry by _____.

13. Mrs. Jacoby tells Mr. Asano that his company needs to _____.

14. Alice and Jerry have called the military police to _____.

15. Among the gifts that Mr. Asano gives Mrs. Jacoby are _____
    and _____.

16. Mr. Asano asks Mrs. Jacoby to _____.

17. Mrs. Jacoby refuses because _____.

18. Mrs. Jacoby decides that she wishes to _____.

19. In the concluding scene of the play, Mr. Asano _____.

20. Mrs. Jacoby and Mr. Asano decide to _____.

NAME _____ DATE _____

A *Majority of One* by Leonard Spigelgass

Answer each of the following questions in two or three complete sentences.

1. How does Mrs. Jacoby illustrate her motherly instincts on the sea voyage?

   _____
   _____
   _____
   _____

2. Why do Jerry and Alice insist that Mrs. Jacoby accompany them?

   _____
   _____
   _____
   _____

3. What danger of the diplomatic service is Mrs. Jacoby warned about?

   _____
   _____
   _____
   _____

4. What does Mrs. Jacoby's dinner with Mr. Asano accomplish?

   _____
   _____
   _____
   _____

5. Why can Mrs. Jacoby and Mr. Asano be friends in New York easier than they could be in Japan?

   _____
   _____
   _____
   _____

CHALLENGE

Write an essay showing how the plot of this play illustrates Jerry Black's statement: "If you want to stop prejudice, you've got to stop it in yourself" (p. 124).

150 Great Books

NAME _____ DATE _____

The Hiding Place by Corrie Ten Boom

In the numbered blanks at the left, write the letter of the matching person or place.

_____ 1. Organization of Dutchmen who collaborated with the Germans

_____ 2. German officer who arranged a reunion for the family in an Amsterdam prison

_____ 3. Where Corrie grew up

_____ 4. Helped supply the underground with hundreds of needed ration cards

_____ 5. Was imprisoned for playing the Dutch national anthem

_____ 6. German death camp where Betsie died

_____ 7. Holland's first licensed woman watchmaker

_____ 8. Prisoner-foreman in the radio factory

_____ 9. Strange-shaped old house where refugees could be hidden

_____ 10. Prison hospital worker who got the women medicine and vitamins

_____ 11. Dutch policeman who helped the underground

_____ 12. Means "Grandfather," children's nickname for Corrie's father

_____ 13. Code name used by the underground to protect each person's identity

_____ 14. Relative who wrote tracts and was a champion of various social causes

_____ 15. Sister with a special kind of love, even for their German captors

_____ 16. Man that Corrie loved

_____ 17. Managed to smuggle in a blue sweater to keep Betsie warm

_____ 18. Nickname for the man who became the head of the underground operation

_____ 19. Corrie's brother, an ordained minister

_____ 20. Old watchmaker who was persecuted by the young German, Otto

A. Beje
B. Haarlem
C. Tante Jans
D. Opa
E. Christoffels
F. Peter
G. Wilhelm
H. Betsie
I. Nollie
J. Corrie
K. Karel
L. NSB
M. Fred Koornstra
N. Rolf
O. "Pickwick"
P. Mr. Smit
Q. Ravensbruck
R. Mien
S. Mr. Mooman
T. Lieutenant Rahms

NAME _____ DATE _____

The Hiding Place by Corrie Ten Boom

Answer each of the following questions in two or three complete sentences.

1. How was Corrie's father a great influence in the community?

   _____

   _____

   _____

   _____

2. How was Corrie's disposition different from Betsie's?

   _____

   _____

   _____

   _____

3. What methods did the Ten Booms use to hide and protect their Jewish friends?

   _____

   _____

   _____

   _____

4. What examples of human kindness did Corrie find, even in the horror of the prisons and the concentration camp?

   _____

   _____

   _____

   _____

5. What kind of new work did Corrie begin after her release from prison?

   _____

   _____

   _____

   _____

CHALLENGE

Corrie Ten Boom believes that the strength to survive will be given as that strength is needed. Write an essay giving some examples from her experiences which prove this statement to be true.

NAME _____ DATE _____

Native Son by Richard Wright

In the numbered blanks at the left, write the letter of the matching person.

_____ 1. Entered Mary's room and smelled the liquor

_____ 2. Found escape and consolation in her religion

_____ 3. Police officer who was injured by Bigger in his attempt to evade capture

_____ 4. Delivered Mary's trunk to the railroad station

_____ 5. Used the publicity of Bigger's trial to advantage in a campaign for reelection

_____ 6. Owned the tenement building in which Bigger and his family lived

_____ 7. Black minister who tried to help Bigger

_____ 8. Bigger's younger sister

_____ 9. Friend who shared Bigger's movie fantasies

_____ 10. Wore valuable earrings that were inherited from her grandmother

_____ 11. Murdered by Bigger because she endangered his escape

_____ 12. White delicatessen owner whom the boys intended to rob

_____ 13. Treated Bigger as an equal by shaking hands with him

_____ 14. One of the men who discovered Mary's body in the furnace

_____ 15. Pled with the court to spare Bigger's life because Bigger was himself a victim

_____ 16. Witnessed Bigger's disposal of Mary's body

_____ 17. Private investigator employed by Mary's father

_____ 18. Was attacked by Bigger because he sensed Bigger's fear

_____ 19. Dalton housekeeper who was kind to Bigger

_____ 20. Helped Bigger kill a large black rat

A. White Cat
B. Mrs. Thomas
C. Buddy
D. Mr. Blum
E. Vera
F. Peggy
G. Mr. Dalton
H. Gus
I. Mrs. Dalton
J. Jan
K. Mary
L. Britten
M. Bigger
N. Toorman
O. Hammond
P. Max
Q. Buckley
R. Bessie
S. Jack
T. Jerry

NAME _____ DATE _____

Native Son by Richard Wright

Answer each of the following questions in two or three complete sentences.

1. What were some causes of Bigger's feelings of frustration?

   _____

   _____

   _____

   _____

2. In what ways was Mary Dalton's death an accident?

   _____

   _____

   _____

   _____

3. Why was Jan's and Mary's behavior toward him very confusing to Bigger?

   _____

   _____

   _____

   _____

4. How did the police finally capture Bigger?

   _____

   _____

   _____

   _____

5. Why did Buckley insist that Bigger must die for his crimes?

   _____

   _____

   _____

   _____

CHALLENGE

Write an essay summarizing Max's arguments, which represent Richard Wright's philosophy, that society itself is responsible for the crimes of Bigger Thomas.

ANSWER KEYS

To Sir With Love by E.R. Braithwaite

OBJECTIVE:

1. J	6. A	11. N
2. C	7. D	12. E
3. O	8. K	13. M
4. F	9. G	14. I
5. L	10. B	15. H

SHORT ANSWER:

1. Couldn't find a job as an engineer—was rejected because he was black. Prejudice was always hidden.
2. Broken homes, had to work at a very young age, grew up fighting for survival.
3. To bring order to the class, to teach them respect for others.
4. Interest in customs and cultures of other countries, museums, music, ballet.
5. Grows from a girl into a woman, new understanding of her mother's situation, willing to defy prejudice to take flowers to the black family.

CHALLENGE:

Students learn to be ladies and gentlemen. Learn the realities of a world outside their own. "Sir" learns to understand their view of life, to receive their love and affection.

The Good Earth by Pearl S. Buck

OBJECTIVE:

1. C	6. B	11. C	16. B
2. D	7. C	12. C	17. A
3. B	8. B	13. A	18. C
4. D	9. D	14. D	19. C
5. A	10. B	15. C	20. C

SHORT ANSWER:

1. Plows the earth with him, looks after his aged father, helps the family survive the flood, keeps the family together in the city so they can return to the land.
2. Land is the link with the past and the hope for the future.
3. Love of shared experience versus physical infatuation.
4. Dictates what his sons must do, gives them no choice, fails to educate them in the traditional values.
5. Corrupted by wealth and luxury, removal from the land to the city, total loss of the old ways.

CHALLENGE:

Novel chronicles the destruction of the Oriental family ideals. Wang deserts O-lan for Lotus. Sons become alienated from the father. The uncle and his son join the robbers. After Wang's death the sons will take over and the land will be gone.

222

ANSWER KEYS (continued)

The Chocolate War by Robert Cormier

OBJECTIVE:

1. I	6. N	11. B	16. N
2. M	7. L	12. J	17. J
3. O	8. C	13. G	18. D
4. H	9. E	14. A	19. M
5. F	10. K	15. D	20. O

SHORT ANSWER:

1. Becomes his act of individual defiance against the system.
2. Leon's main desire for control. Plans to use the Vigils as a tool to exercise this control.
3. If the leader draws the black spot, he must complete the assignment.
4. Obscene phone calls, destruction of the poster in his locker, art project gets "lost."
5. Boys gang up to fight Jerry. He is brutally beaten. Brother Jacques turns out the lights.

CHALLENGE:

Theme of the book is individual rights against a corrupt system. Even though he is beaten by overwhelming odds, Jerry gains nobility by his refusal to give in. Jerry's strength in opposition to the weaker boys who allow themselves to be controlled.

I Am the Cheese by Robert Cormier

OBJECTIVE:

1. 0	6. +	11. 0	16. 0
2. +	7. 0	12. 0	17. +
3. 0	8. +	13. 0	18. 0
4. +	9. +	14. 0	19. 0
5. 0	10. 0	15. +	20. 0

SHORT ANSWER:

1. He saves his package, he fights to get his bike back.
2. He relaxes with her and talks about himself. He has fun in her "capers."
3. His father testified against organized crime.
4. Two birth certificates, the editor who does not know his family, the aunt that he didn't know he had.
5. Her fears for their future. Never knowing when Mr. Gray would tell them to move again.

CHALLENGE:

Phrase from "Farmer in the Dell," "the cheese stands alone." Must fight Brint, the drugs, the system which wants to destroy him. Perhaps he can't survive, but he will fight to the end, just like he continued to struggle on his bike trip.

The Autobiography of Miss Jane Pittman by Ernest J. Gaines

OBJECTIVE:

1. +	6. +	11. 0	16. 0
2. 0	7. +	12. +	17. 0
3. 0	8. +	13. +	18. 0
4. 0	9. 0	14. 0	19. 0
5. 0	10. +	15. 0	20. +

ANSWER KEYS (continued)

The Autobiography of Miss Jane Pittman by Ernest J. Gaines (continued)

SHORT ANSWER:

1. Ate stolen potatoes and corn, kept hidden from gangs of killers, followed the river.
2. Made them sign papers that they couldn't read, kept them on plantations doing menial jobs and living in terrible conditions.
3. To educate the blacks, to better their lives.
4. A white man couldn't marry a black, but could keep her as his mistress. Robert really loved Mary Agnes. Suicide was the only way out.
5. The deliverer who could provide the leadership for real social change.

CHALLENGE:

Maintained her pride, even when she was a slave. Fought to keep Ned and herself alive. Rose to the position of trusted servant to the Samson family. In her old age, she was willing to participate in the civil rights struggle.

Black Like Me by John Howard Griffin

OBJECTIVE:

1. a journalist
2. his skin color
3. New Orleans
4. medication and sunlamp treatments
5. Sterling Williams
6. looking in the mirror
7. restrooms, drinking fountains
8. economic advancement
9. Parker
10. the look whites gave blacks
11. those with the lightest skin
12. P.D. East
13. Negro's sex life
14. shared the cabin with the black family
15. Montgomery, Alabama
16. *Sepia*
17. loneliness
18. six months
19. burned him in effigy
20. move somewhere else

SHORT ANSWER:

1. Medication from a dermatologist, sunlamp treatments, dye to darken the area around his face and eyes.
2. To find out how being black really felt.
3. New Orleans—ignored or politely put in his place. Mississippi—treated like an animal or a curiosity.
4. Family had to leave town. Articles received well by some, but attracted the fury of the southern whites.
5. That the Negroes will become as angry and as racist as the whites are.

CHALLENGE:

Good whites—P.D. East, the girl in the bookstore, the monks. Good blacks—the family who took him in, Sterling Williams, the shoeshine man. Bad whites—the bus driver, the lady ticket seller, the sexually curious. Bad blacks—Christophe, the man on the bus. The only way that Griffin was any different was in his skin color. Not his morals, manners, or education.

A Raisin in the Sun by Lorraine Hansbury

OBJECTIVE:

1. D	6. C	11. D	16. A
2. C	7. C	12. B	17. B
3. B	8. A	13. A	18. A
4. B	9. A	14. D	19. A
5. D	10. C	15. B	20. B

ANSWER KEYS (continued)

A Raisin in the Sun by Lorraine Hansbury (continued)

SHORT ANSWER:

1. No privacy, everything shabby, no room for Travis to sleep, emotional pressures of overcrowding.
2. Asagai—genuine and caring. George is a fake and a snob.
3. Buys a house in the white neighborhood. Tries to keep the family together.
4. Each wants the best for the other. Ruth feels the helplessness of Walter's frustration— Walter wants to fulfill his great dreams for his family.
5. He defies Lindner and says that the family will move into their house.

CHALLENGE:

The failure of old Walter's hopes—the dream which dries up. Festering—Beneathea's anger. Stinking—fakeness of George. Crusting over—Lena's feelings of failure. Heavy load—reaction to Ruth's pregnancy. Explode—Walter's blowup at George.

The Little Foxes by Lillian Hellman

OBJECTIVE:

1. 0	6. 0	11. +	16. +
2. +	7. +	12. +	17. 0
3. 0	8. 0	13. 0	18. +
4. +	9. 0	14. 0	19. 0
5. 0	10. +	15. 0	20. +

SHORT ANSWER:

1. Regina—dominating and vicious. Birdie—dependent and victimized.
2. He will not participate in their destructive greed.
3. She allows Horace to die so she can have her way.
4. She is caring, has a sense of morality.
5. Oscar suspects the truth about Horace's death.

CHALLENGE:

The Hubbards and Regina are the eaters. Horace and Alexandra are the fighters. Birdie stands helplessly and watches.

Inherit the Wind by Jerome Lawrence and Robert E. Lee

OBJECTIVE:

1. a carnival	7. egotism	13. guilty	17. leave
2. teaching evolution	8. the devil	14. $100 fine	18. Hornbeck's newspaper
3. Brady	9. scientific theory	15. make a speech	19. is dead
4. Drummond	10. the right to think	16. destroying people's faith	20. leave her father and go with Bert
5. *Baltimore Sun*	11. her father		
6. give up and quit	12. Brady		

SHORT ANSWER:

1. Drama of the confrontation between Brady and Drummond.
2. Bible-preaching forces controlled the town. No room for any dissenting opinion.
3. Caught between her loyalty to her father and her love for Bert.
4. Tricks Brady into admitting that perhaps the Bible might not be the only authority.
5. Eulogizes Brady's lost greatness—scene of weighing the copy of the Bible with the copy of Darwin.

ANSWER KEYS (continued)

Inherit the Wind by Jerome Lawrence and Robert E. Lee (continued)

CHALLENGE:

Play presents the right to think about alternatives. The open mind of Bert opposed to the closed attitude of the community. Desmond's triumph—the right to think. Brady's tragedy—the brilliant speaker but the closed mind.

To Kill a Mockingbird by Harper Lee

OBJECTIVE:

1. B	6. B	11. D	16. B
2. D	7. C	12. B	17. C
3. D	8. A	13. D	18. B
4. B	9. D	14. B	19. C
5. D	10. A	15. A	20. B

SHORT ANSWER:

1. Talks to them on adult level, answers their questions, reads to them and makes time for them.
2. Tries to explain about the Cunninghams, gets into trouble because she can read and write. Generally bored with the whole thing.
3. That Calpurnia is different with the blacks, that race prejudice exists on both sides.
4. Kids get called names and get into fights at school, watch the trial from the colored balcony.
5. Senseless destruction of that which is innocent.

CHALLENGE:

Tom Robinson case, learning to see the reality of prejudice. Courage from Mrs. Dubose. At the missionary society—how to keep her head in time of crisis. Not to believe hearsay, to understand the other person's situation—Boo Radley.

Main Street by Sinclair Lewis

OBJECTIVE:

1. C	6. B	11. B	16. B
2. B	7. C	12. A	17. D
3. A	8. D	13. B	18. B
4. B	9. B	14. C	19. A
5. A	10. A	15. C	20. A

SHORT ANSWER:

1. To make Gopher Prairie a model small town. They are satisfied with the status quo.
2. They share a life and love and care for each other.
3. Erik has the gentleness and sensitivity that Will lacks.
4. The entrapment of the small town. The mind and the spirit will die.
5. She is driven out. Her life is destroyed by the evil minds and vicious tongues.

CHALLENGE:

Begins with high ideals, but is disillusioned by experience. Tries to make a difference and fails. Rejects Erik's love—escapes to Washington. Returns to life with Will. Sees hope for a difference in her children.

ANSWER KEYS (continued)

The Crucible by Arthur Miller

OBJECTIVE:

1. his salary, the deed to his house
2. Tituba, Barbados
3. dancing naked in the woods
4. Elizabeth knew of Abigail's affair with John
5. Rebecca Nurse
6. Francis Nurse, Giles Corey
7. he was a witch-craft expert
8. killing her children
9. cold, suspicious
10. Abigail threatens her
11. adultery
12. Abigail can have John
13. bringing a petition to the court
14. Danforth
15. turns and accuses her
16. the whole thing has gone out of control
17. their lives can be saved
18. she is pregnant
19. being crushed, confess
20. he wants to keep his name

SHORT ANSWER:

1. Proctor found nobility and a freedom from guilt through death.
2. Abigail could totally change her personality to fit any situation.
3. Elizabeth never really forgave John.
4. The real motives for people's behavior would come out.
5. Proctor made others uncomfortable because he could see through their actions.

CHALLENGE:

Putnam's hatred for Nurse over church fight. Putnam greed for land. Abigail's jealousy and desire for John, desire for revenge against Elizabeth. Parris' paranoia.

Animal Farm by George Orwell

OBJECTIVE:

1. 0
2. +
3. 0
4. 0
5. +
6. +
7. 0
8. 0
9. 0
10. +
11. 0
12. +
13. 0
14. 0
15. 0
16. +
17. 0
18. 0
19. 0
20. +

SHORT ANSWER:

1. Society where all animals would be equal and all would receive the reward for their work.
2. Destroyed the plans for the windmill, drove out Snowball, used the dogs to keep control.
3. Changed all of the commandments and rules to fit what Napoleon wanted.
4. Became much worse—harder work, fewer benefits for the masses, privilege to pigs alone.
5. Lived in the house, drank liquor, used whips to keep the others in line.

CHALLENGE:

Lust for power—Napoleon. Unquestioning loyalty—Boxer. Opportunist—Squealer. Vanity—Molly. Entire book is an allegory to illustrate how the communist revolution failed. Average life was worse—new ruling class replaced the old.

ANSWER KEYS (continued)

Cry, the Beloved Country by Alan Paton

OBJECTIVE:

1. L	6. T	11. I	16. B
2. C	7. N	12. H	17. O
3. Q	8. A	13. E	18. I
4. J	9. S	14. P	19. M
5. D	10. G	15. R	20. F

SHORT ANSWER:

1. Confusion at the size and noise, grief for what the city has done to his family.
2. Stephen faithful to God and traditional values. John a political opportunist with no morals left.
3. Lured to the city and into crime for money. Controlled by fear. Old ways gone with nothing to replace them.
4. Msimangu—helped Stephen find his son. Lawyer took Absalom's case free. Mrs. Lithebe tried to help Gertrude and the girl.
5. Absalom victim of the white man's greed destroying the society. Arthur killed by one of the blacks that he wished to help.

CHALLENGE:

Restoration of the land and the tribe. Meaning for the individual life in spiritual values. Hope in understanding, in the new generation like Arthur Jarvis' son.

Twelve Angry Men by Reginald Rose

OBJECTIVE:

1. J	6. C	11. M	16. Q
2. R	7. T	12. H	17. K
3. N	8. L	13. S	18. I
4. A	9. E	14. B	19. O
5. F	10. P	15. M	20. D

SHORT ANSWER:

1. He feels that they should at least discuss the case.
2. #8 remains openminded. #10 is sure that the boy is guilty.
3. He came from the same kind of background.
4. They represent a typical cross-section of human attitudes.
5. He changes his vote just to get the whole thing over with—no convictions.

CHALLENGE:

#3 hatred for his own son comes out, and his violence as he attacks #8. #10 total bigot—hatred for "those kind of people." #9 little man who has always been ignored—identified with the man who testifies to get attention. #11 sensitive because he was a refugee.

ANSWER KEYS (continued)

A Majority of One by Leonard Spigelgass

OBJECTIVE:

1. U.S. State Department
2. Japan
3. blacks and Puerto Ricans are moving in
4. her son was killed in the war
5. go to Japan
6. snubs him
7. were killed by the American forces
8. Asano will use that friendship in the negotiations
9. Mrs. Jacoby does all the work
10. Russia
11. totally broken off
12. going to see Mr. Asano
13. diversify
14. find Mrs. Jacoby
15. kimono, a set of china
16. keep company with him
17. thinks too much of Sam
18. go home to New York
19. has dinner with Mrs. Jacoby
20. be friends and enjoy each other's company

SHORT ANSWER:

1. Concern for Mr. Asano's health, for everyone's welfare.
2. So they can look after her.
3. Being offered friendship by people who want favors in return.
4. Gets him to compromise and reopen the talks.
5. Their friendship will not be bound by Japanese custom or linked to Jerry's job.

CHALLENGE:

Mrs. Jacoby and Mr. Asano are both able to see each other as individuals, not as members of nations in the war. Jerry learns of his own prejudices created by his job.

The Hiding Place by Corrie Ten Boom

OBJECTIVE:

1. L
2. T
3. B
4. M
5. F
6. Q
7. J
8. S
9. A
10. R
11. N
12. D
13. P
14. C
15. H
16. K
17. I
18. O
19. G
20. E

SHORT ANSWER:

1. He shared his faith with his neighbors, loved children.
2. Betsie—more at peace with herself, the homemaker, able to find beauty anywhere. Corrie—more of a rebel, found love for their enemies more difficult.
3. Building of the fake room, obtaining fake ration cards, installing the warning system to be sounded if the Germans came.
4. Hospital worker who gave them vitamins, the lieutenant who let them see their family, the care of the prisoners for each other.
5. Helping persons who had been displaced by the war.

CHALLENGE:

Being able to enjoy the company of the ants, Bible classes in the concentration camp, emotional survival after Betsie's death, strong faith in God and the power of love, learning to forgive those who had persecuted them.

ANSWER KEYS (continued)

Native Son by Richard Wright

OBJECTIVE:

1. I	6. G	11. R	16. A
2. B	7. O	12. D	17. L
3. T	8. E	13. J	18. H
4. M	9. S	14. N	19. F
5. Q	10. K	15. P	20. C

SHORT ANSWER:

1. Being shut out from all opportunities and the quality of life that was available to the whites.
2. Bigger meant to keep her from crying out, but he smothered her instead.
3. He was used to being kept "in his place." They treated him like an equal.
4. By a manhunt through the entire city. Finally trapped him on a rooftop.
5. Because Bigger was a horrible animal. Because he was being helped by socialist and communist factions. He represented a danger to the white man's status quo.

CHALLENGE:

The American system dominated by the whites had kept Bigger down. Limits on his life. Slum living conditions. Blacks kept as more an animal or a boy than a man. Loss of hope and opportunity produced the frustration which led to violence.

UNIT 6

The Triumph of the Spirit—
OVERCOMING HANDICAPS

SYNOPSES

Strong at the Broken Places
by Max Cleland

Cleland's autobiography shows that a man can resume a normal life after he has had a catastrophic injury. A specialist in radio and electronics work for the Army, Max lost both legs and one arm when he stepped on a live grenade while serving in Vietnam. Determined to function again, he spent months in the hospital recovering from his injuries and receiving physical therapy. He learned to walk with artificial limbs, to use a hook as a hand, and to drive a specially equipped automobile. Cleland's greatest obstacles were psychological. He had to believe in himself, even when his family and friends were embarrassed by his handicap and treated him like a freak. Max decided to enter Georgia politics to prove that a handicapped person could fully participate in all of life's activities. After losing his bid for the U.S. House of Representatives, Cleland was appointed by President Carter to head the Federal Veterans Administration. This book is the account of a man who freed himself from self-pity and "broke reality into manageable proportions" so he could live a productive life one day at a time.

I Heard the Owl Call My Name
by Margaret Craven

Mark, a young priest who is dying of cancer, is sent by his bishop to serve the Church in the small Indian village of Kingcome Inlet in northwestern Canada. By living with these simple people close to the cycles of nature, Mark learns to prepare for death. At first he is regarded suspiciously as an outsider. But gradually, as Mark shares with his people the life and death crises of their existence, he becomes one of them. He learns to value the elderly and to understand the old tribal ways. Mark pities the tragedy of Gordon who is totally alienated from the ways of his people by living in the city. By sharing life and relating to nature, Mark is ready "when the owl calls his name."

Ice Castles
by Leonore Fleischer

Alexis Winston wants to become a champion figure skater. Yet Lexie must learn the cost that is required to become a winner. Marcus, her father, does not want his daughter to enter the competitions because he fears he will lose Lexie as he has lost her mother. Nick, the boy she really loves, cannot keep up with the world of competition. Beulah, Lexie's hometown coach, wants Lexie to have the success that she herself was denied. After Lexie's first competition, Deborah Mackland, a professional coach, offers to promote the young skater's career. Glory has a high price; as Lexie becomes an important skater, personal relationships fall by the wayside. After Lexie is blinded in a freak accident, Deborah abandons her because the coach cannot allow herself to become emotionally involved. After a period of deep emotional withdrawal, Lexie is persuaded by Beulah, Nick, and her father to attempt skating again. Lexie finds her own triumph as she finds that skating is no longer a means of escape, and that she can cope with the world on human terms.

233

The Miracle Worker
by William Gibson

Can any child who is blind and deaf be taught to communicate with the outside world? Helen Keller, striken by a childhood illness, is like a little wild animal with a strong desire to learn. Having exhausted all other options, Helen's parents hire a half-blind young teacher from Boston, Miss Annie Sullivan. As she teaches Helen, Annie battles Helen's stubborn will, the pity of the family, and the ghosts of her own past. Annie is determined that Helen will learn. The teacher says that "giving up is my idea of original sin." An epic battle ensues. Helen and Annie leave the dining room in wreckage, but Helen does fold her napkin. Annie wants more. Neatness is not enough; Helen must *know*. The breakthrough comes as Helen feels water running through her fingers and is able to associate the thing with the word. The play presents some powerful educational issues. How much can a handicapped child be expected to learn? "What can be done to disinter the human spirit?" Students who read *The Miracle Worker* may also want to read Helen's biographical tribute to Miss Sullivan, *Teacher*.

I Never Promised You a Rose Garden
by Joanne Greenberg

Seventeen-year-old Deborah Blau lives constantly with family pressure, and is never able to quite measure up to the expectations of her parents and grandparents. Deborah's mind retreats into the hidden world of Yr, which has its own population and vocabulary. As their daughter becomes almost totally removed from reality, Deborah's parents are forced to place her in a mental hospital. The forces in the hidden world which desire to punish Deborah are making her dangerously self-destructive. Dr. Fried, or "Furii," Deborah's psychiatrist, struggles to help Deborah gain "full weight" (to come back from her retreat to live fully in the world of reality). Life in the hospital is an up–and–down cycle for Deborah. Even during her sickest periods, she shows signs of great intelligence and sensitivity. As Deborah's condition improves, she and her friend Carla are able to leave the hospital for short periods. She learns Latin and Greek from Miss Coral, one of her fellow patients. The novel has its comic moments as Carla and Deborah learn how to outwit the hospital staff. With Dr. Fried's help, Deborah is able to finish high school. She can believe that reality, with all of its problems, is better than escape into the darkness of insanity. The novel is a powerful look at the problems of mental illness, the kinds of therapy that can be used, and the ways in which the patient must finally heal himself or herself.

Ordinary People
by Judith Guest

Conrad Jarrett's suicide attempt shattered the fragile structure of his family. Conrad returns from the hospital and tries to put his life back together. The novel deals with the effects of the boy's problems on his father Calvin, his mother Beth, and on Conrad himself. Dr. Berger, Conrad's psychiatrist, helps Conrad cope with his problems at school, his guilt feelings over the death of his brother Buck, and his failure to communicate with his mother. Calvin tries to make up for past failures by supplying his son with things. His mother Beth cannot respond because of her own deep emotional needs. The most helpful person in Conrad's life is Jeannine, a girl he meets at school. The boy's fragile balance is almost destroyed when Karen, a friend that he had met in the hospital, commits suicide. Calvin finally seeks some help for himself and his son. Beth simply continues to run away. This book shows that, in an average family, people can hurt others unintentionally. Each individual must then find his or her own road back.

Death Be Not Proud
by John Gunther

This loving biography tells the story of newsman Gunther's fifteen-year-old son Johnny, who was stricken with a brain tumor. The father tells what a special, sensitive person Johnny was and how his optimism helped his parents cope with his death. Even while undergoing painful physical treatments, Johnny retained his patience and his sense of humor. Through tutors and home study, he was able to return for graduation with his class from Deerfield Academy. Gunther says that his son was able to discuss life honestly and openly, and to appreciate the good things in every day. Part of the book contains excerpts from Johnny's diaries. His wide variety of interests included philosophy, chemistry, and chess. This book also expresses the feelings of a father and mother who must stand by helplessly as a malignant disease takes its course. Courage is needed by both the parents and the son. Although containing medical details which might be difficult for some students, *Death Be Not Proud* is a great statement of victory and life.

Susan's Story
by Susan Hampshire

A famous English stage and television actress, Susan Hampshire suffers from dyslexia. This birth defect makes learning difficult by causing severe reading difficulties, motor function, and directional problems. The section of the brain which controls these functions sends incorrect directions to the muscles and the eyes. During her childhood, Susan became ashamed of her inability to read easily. She was able to hide her handicap through her talents as a comic, musician and actress. As she sought serious theatrical roles, reading scripts and learning lines became increasingly more difficult. When she admitted her problem, Miss Hampshire was able to find help and to realize that dyslexia does not indicate any lack of intelligence. She developed a special code which greatly aided her in reading and memorization. The actress's greatest triumph came when she starred as Fleur in the BBC's Masterpiece Theater series adaptation of *The Forsyte Saga*. Susan's personal struggles have also included the breakup of her marriage and the death of her mother. This autobiography is a very honest book. By admitting to the public that she suffers from dyslexia, Miss Hampshire hopes to prove to others that this handicap can be overcome.

The Old Man and the Sea
by Ernest Hemingway

In this short novel, one old man's battle with a great fish becomes a symbol for Hemingway of the struggle of every man against the forces of the universe. Old Santiago, who has fished for forty days and caught nothing, finally hooks the great marlin. Even as he struggles with the fish, the old man has great respect for the sea creature. After the fish is caught, the old man must tow the creature home beside his small boat. In battling the sharks as they attack the fish, Santiago loses his harpoon and his knife. When he arrives in port, the old man has only the skeleton of the fish, which is swept out like garbage with the tide. But the old man's spirit is not broken. He hangs on to the very end, and continues to dream of grand adventures.

Flowers for Algernon
by Daniel Keyes

Charlie Gordon is a moron who does menial work in a bakery and attends a special night class for retarded adults. Because of his great desire to learn, Charlie is selected for experimental surgery which, if successful, will turn him into a genius. Like the white mouse Algernon, who has had a similar operation, Charlie becomes a guinea pig for Dr. Nehmur and Dr. Strauss. After his surgery, his escalating intelligence creates serious social and psychological problems for Charlie. He desires love, but cannot understand his own physical drives. He learns that the people who he thought were his friends are really making fun of him. A rapidly increasing memory brings flashbacks of his abusive mother and his tortured childhood. The peak of Charlie's intelligence marks the peak of his loneliness. He discovers a flaw in the scientific procedure: he will lose everything he has gained. As his abilities rapidly wane, Charlie prepares for his own death as he carefully buries Algernon. Told by Charlie himself in each stage of his progress and regression, the novel powerfully presents the need of every person, regardless of intelligence, for love and acceptance.

Eric
by Doris Lund

Mrs. Lund writes graphically of her son Eric's battle with leukemia. A star soccer player, Eric was as determined to beat his illness as he was to win on the playing fields of Yale. Eric's mother writes honestly of her own feelings. Eric violently rejected his mother's efforts to pamper or protect him. Eric's friends, as well as his brothers and sisters, were made stronger by Eric's determination to make every day count. Even in the hospital, Eric's optimism and sense of humor helped many on his ward at Ewig Eight. During his three-year fight against a fatal disease, Eric Lund gave hope to many. This book also tells how the Lunds, since Eric's death, have helped other patients by donating blood platelets. *Eric* is a mother's special tribute to a very special son.

Requiem for a Heavyweight
by Rod Serling

Mountain McClintock is a has-been boxer with no other skills with which to make a new life. Written for television, this play shows Mountain's efforts to maintain his self-respect as time and his physical condition have robbed him of the only career he knows. To pay off some gambling debts, Maish, Mountain's manager, wants to force the boxer to become a clownish wrestler. Maish seeks to manipulate Mountain by making him feel gratitude for past favors. Army, the trainer, feels compassion for the man who has never "taken a fall." Grace, a girl that Mountain meets at the employment office, wants to make the ex-boxer feel like a person instead of a piece of meat. The drama's conclusion provides hope as Mountain breaks free of Maish, returns to his native Tennessee, and finds the possibility of a new life working with children.

One Day in the Life of Ivan Denisovich
by Alexander Solzhenitsyn

How does a man remain human in the hell of a Siberian concentration camp? Shukhov, imprisoned for eight years for undetermined political crimes, has learned that his survival depends on cooperation with the system. The whole camp runs on an elaborate system of payoffs and bribery. One must satisfy the guards, the cooks, and the gang boss. As the author presents his characters, the prisoners become definite individuals, and yet they are representative of every man. Positive human values emerge as the prisoners help each other obtain food and work as a team to lay bricks in the arctic temperatures. At day's end, Shukhov is satisfied. He considers himself lucky not to have been placed in solitary and to have been able to get enough to eat. The Soviet Union's latest Nobel prize winner has created a microcosmic picture of the strength of man's spirit to triumph over oppression.

Cannery Row
by John Steinbeck

The cannery district of Monterey, California is the home of society's dropouts, outcasts, and misfits. Ironically, some of these very misfits personify the most noble traits of human goodness. Mack and the boys, members of a hobo commune, decide to give a party for Doc, the community's resident physician and philosopher. After the first party wrecks Doc's laboratory, the boys make another attempt. They must first, however, go on a frog hunt to finance the enterprise. The bumbling efforts of each character in this book are based on good intentions. Dora, the madame of the local brothel, contributes twice as much as anyone else to charity. Dora's girls become nurses when an epidemic hits the community. Steinbeck's series of vignettes of life on Cannery Row mixes comedy with pathos. The short book is a fine piece of local color illustrating the common denominators of human behavior. Steinbeck says that "everywhere in the world are Mack and the boys."

The Pearl
by John Steinbeck

Kino, a simple pearl fisherman, finds the dream of a lifetime, the great pearl of the world. However, his dreams of a new life are destroyed by the forces of evil and greed which attack his great discovery. After Kino refuses a very low price for his pearl from a system of crooked pearl buyers, the fisherman defies the system and decides to journey to the city to sell the pearl himself. The attempt at independence costs Kino his home, his boat, and his son. The luster in the pearl is changed to a sickly gray. Kino and his wife, their lives now destroyed, now throw the gem back into the ocean. This short novel is a powerful parable of the dangers of greed and the evil in human nature.

On Golden Pond
by Ernest Thompson

This powerful twentieth-century drama is an affirmation of life and love in old age. Norman and Ethel Thayer have been spending summers on Golden Pond in Maine for many years. The play takes place during the summer in which Norman celebrates his eightieth birthday. Ethel tries to cheer Norman up, but the old man is determined to enjoy his misery. The love between these two people is wonderfully presented by the comic give and take between them, and in the way that Ethel comforts Norman like a frightened child when he becomes lost on a familiar road. When their daughter Chelsea comes to visit, Ethel tries to establish a truce in the long war between father and daughter. Billy, the young son of the man that Chelsea intends to marry, spends the summer, and brings life and youth back into Norman's existence. In a powerful concluding scene, Ethel and Norman both realize the strength of their love in the face of their own mortality. This play strongly states that love is not the exclusive province of the young.

The Other Side of the Mountain
by E.G. Valens

Jill Kinmont is a strictly trained athlete at the height of her skiing career with hopes for the 1976 Olympics. That dream ends when Jill falls on a jump and breaks her neck. Jill's victories in the aftermath of her accident show her to be a winner in human terms. After winning an initial battle with self-pity, Jill works to strengthen the muscles that she has left. Her friend Audra Jo, who has had polio, helps Jill cope with the psychological impact of her paralysis. The two men in Jill's life react very differently. Bud Warner, with whom Jill had shared love and the enthusiasm of skiing, left her because he could not handle Jill's changed situation. Dick Beuk, a pilot and a daredevil skier, gave Jill the love and support needed to help her come back. Jill has to go on alone after Dick is killed in a plane crash. Jill's greatest obstacle in her desire to become a teacher is to convince school authorities that she could manage in a classroom. After being given a chance to teach, Jill reaches out to children with learning problems. Jill Kinmont's experiences have changed her from an athletic personality into a full person.

The Bridge of San Luis Rey
by Thornton Wilder

This short novel won the author his second Pulitzer prize. In seventeenth-century Peru, the collapse of a bridge killed five people. Brother Juniper, a devout but insignificant monk, determines to discover the divine purpose behind the accident. Why these five? As omniscient narrator, the author tells us what Brother Juniper could never know, the inner secrets of each heart. The Marquesa de Montemayor, thought by Lima society to be an eccentric alcoholic, was really a literary genius. Her maid Pepita looked after the Marquesa and prevented others from taking advantage of her. The Abbess Madre Maria, who had sent Pepita to the Marquesa, wished Pepita to carry on the work at the convent. When Pepita dies, the Abbess must carefully search her own motives. Manuel and Esteban were inseparable brothers until Manuel becomes involved with the actress La Perichole. Esteban's plans to find solace by going to sea are ended when the bridge collapses. La Perichole, a handsome actress who charmed even the viceroy, was coached by Uncle Pio. The old man fulfilled his own desires by perfecting his protégée's acting. When small-pox destroyed the actress's beauty, Uncle Pio persuaded Camila to give him her young son to educate. But these plans were all ended by the fall of the bridge. Brother Juniper's "Why?" is never answered. But the stories of these characters provide a look into the human heart, which is controlled by one passion or another.

The Skin of Our Teeth
by Thornton Wilder

This unusual drama presents the progress of mankind in spite of the various catastrophes of history. Mr. and Mrs. Antrobus, their daughter Gladys and son Henry, who serve as representatives of the human race, survive ice, flood, and war. The entire history is narrated by Sabina, an ironic maid who comments freely on human frailty. The play shows a mixture of the good and evil in history. Mr. Antrobus is the inventor who is working on the wheel and the alphabet. Mrs. Antrobus' strong domestic instincts help the family to survive each successive crisis. In Act III, Gladys' child represents the hope that life will continue. Son Henry, however, bears the mark of Cain, the destructive tendencies of mankind. The struggle will continue. In her concluding speech, Sabina says that "The end of this play isn't written yet." Thornton Wilder, however, is an optimist who believes that we will make it through, if only "by the skin of our teeth."

NAME _____ DATE _____

Strong at the Broken Places by Max Cleland

Place a (+) before each statement that is true and a (0) before each statement that is false.

_____ 1. Cleland is a native of Massachusetts.

_____ 2. While he was in high school, Max excelled at everything that he attempted.

_____ 3. When he entered the army, Max was sent to Vietnam immediately after he finished his training.

_____ 4. Cleland's specialty in the service was radio and electronics work.

_____ 5. Max was a major when he was injured.

_____ 6. Max was injured by shot from enemy aircraft guns.

_____ 7. Cleland lost both of his legs and one of his arms.

_____ 8. Cleland received his first surgical treatment at a military hospital in Manila.

_____ 9. Max chose to have his physical therapy at the veterans hospital nearest his home.

_____ 10. One of Max's biggest problems was in dealing with the ups and downs of his emotions.

_____ 11. The "snake pit" referred to a hospital ward for those who had been injured in combat.

_____ 12. Life inside the hospital was easier for Max than life outside.

_____ 13. Jon Peters was another wounded man who helped and encouraged Max.

_____ 14. Max was able to stand by himself the first time that he was outfitted with artificial limbs.

_____ 15. Max's first set of artifical legs were made of plastic and steel.

_____ 16. Max was a successful candidate for the U.S. House of Representatives.

_____ 17. Max found real peace when he let God help him with his problems.

_____ 18. Max Cleland was appointed head of the Veterans Administration by President Lyndon Johnson.

_____ 19. Max has worked to make the public more aware of the problems that returning veterans face.

_____ 20. Max now wears his artificial limbs whenever he appears in public.

NAME _____ DATE _____

Strong at the Broken Places by Max Cleland

Answer each of the following questions in two or three complete sentences.

1. How was Max Cleland injured?

    _____
    _____
    _____
    _____

2. Why did the reactions of his friends and family make Max uncomfortable?

    _____
    _____
    _____
    _____

3. What were the three greatest physical handicaps that Max overcame in his battle for rehabilitation?

    _____
    _____
    _____
    _____

4. Why did Max decide to enter politics?

    _____
    _____
    _____
    _____

5. What did Max mean when he said that he had to learn to "break reality down into manageable proportions?"

    _____
    _____
    _____
    _____

CHALLENGE

Write an essay describing some of the ways that Max Cleland became "strong at the broken places."

NAME _____ DATE _____

I Heard the Owl Call My Name by Margaret Craven

Select the letter of the word or phrase which correctly completes each statement.

_____ 1. The novel takes place in (A) New England (B) northwestern Canada (C) Siberia (D) Alaska.

_____ 2. The main character is a (A) fisherman (B) bishop (C) Indian chief (D) priest.

_____ 3. Mark's hardest task as he comes to the village is (A) to rebuild the church (B) to make new converts (C) to win the Indians' trust and acceptance (D) to make the Indians more civilized.

_____ 4. Mark's pilot and closest friend is (A) Jim (B) Caleb (C) Gordon (D) Keetah.

_____ 5. Mark's first friends in the village were (A) the old men (B) Martha and Mrs. Hudson (C) two small children (D) Gordon and Keetah.

_____ 6. Mark learns to value the elderly people of the village because (A) they come to church most regularly (B) they bring him gifts of food (C) they have the knowledge of the old tribal customs (D) they teach him the native language.

_____ 7. The bishop sends Mark to Kingcome Inlet (A) to help Mark prepare for his own death (B) because the Indians need help (C) because the previous priest has resigned (D) because all of the other parishes are full.

_____ 8. Life in the village of Kingcome is centered around (A) the cycles of nature (B) government hunting and fishing regulations (C) the church calendar (D) the school year.

_____ 9. The one member of the community who refuses to belong is (A) Sam (B) the constable (C) the teacher (D) Mrs. Hudson.

_____ 10. Contact with the outside world comes from (A) the visits of the bishop (B) the arrival of the hospital ship (C) the visits of the RCMP (D) all of the above.

_____ 11. Mark knows that the villagers have accepted him when (A) they bring him loaves of fresh bread (B) they offer to help build a new vicarage (C) they take him fishing (D) they take him to the old burial grounds.

_____ 12. The greatest damage to the people of the tribe comes from (A) floods (B) landslides (C) poor fishing catches (D) the white man's civilization.

_____ 13. The person in the story who least understood the culture of the villagers was (A) the teacher (B) the lady anthropologist (C) Caleb (D) the bishop.

_____ 14. The person who departed most from the Indian ways was (A) Gordon (B) Jim (C) Keetah (D) Mrs. Hudson.

_____ 15. Mark dies (A) of cancer (B) from drowning (C) in a landslide (D) from an accidental gunshot wound.

NAME _____ DATE _____

I Heard the Owl Call My Name by Margaret Craven

Answer each of the following questions in two or three complete sentences.

1. What difficult physical conditions does Mark find when he comes to the village?

   _____

   _____

   _____

   _____

2. What advice does Caleb give Mark about working with the Indians before Mark goes to his new parish?

   _____

   _____

   _____

   _____

3. Why do the villagers totally accept Mark after the death of Gordon's mother?

   _____

   _____

   _____

   _____

4. After he goes to school, why can Gordon never really come back home?

   _____

   _____

   _____

   _____

5. Explain how the title of the novel relates to the story.

   _____

   _____

   _____

   _____

CHALLENGE

Discuss some of the significant ways in which Mark comes to terms with life and with death as he serves as the priest in Kingcome Inlet.

150 Great Books

NAME _____ DATE _____

Ice Castles by Leonore Fleischer

Select the letter of the word or phrase which correctly completes each statement.

_____ 1. When the novel opens, Alexis Winston is (A) twelve (B) sixteen (C) eight (D) twenty.

_____ 2. Lexie enjoys skating most (A) at Beulah's rink (B) on the pond at the farm (C) at Broadmoor (D) in the Regional competitions.

_____ 3. Nick had dropped out of college (A) because he was a poor student (B) because he had been drafted by a professional hockey team (C) because he really didn't know what he wanted to do with his life (D) because he wanted to be with Lexie.

_____ 4. At first, Marcus did not want Lexie to enter the skating competitions because (A) he was afraid that he would lose her (B) he was afraid that she would be injured (C) he was jealous of her relationship with Nick (D) he thought that skating was too expensive.

_____ 5. Beulah wanted Lexie to succeed as a skater because (A) Beulah herself had failed (B) Beulah wanted fame as a coach (C) Beulah wanted to make money from Lexie's skating (D) Beulah wanted to spite Marcus.

_____ 6. The most difficult part of the Regionals for Lexie was (A) the compulsory figures (B) the introduction to the judges (C) the long program (D) the short program.

_____ 7. When she began coaching Lexie, Deborah Mackland felt that Lexie's biggest handicap was (A) her age (B) her lack of talent (C) the jealousy of the other skaters (D) her lack of money.

_____ 8. Deborah wanted to coach Lexie because (A) it was a challenge (B) it would enhance her own reputation (C) she felt that Lexie had real talent (D) all of the above.

_____ 9. As she became more famous as a skater, Lexie lost (A) her poise (B) her most important personal relationships (C) her ability to be at ease with people (D) her gratitude to Deborah.

_____ 10. Brian Dockett fell in love with Lexie because (A) she reminded him of Deborah (B) she was so fresh and natural (C) she was good for his public image (D) she was a natural champion.

_____ 11. When she saw Ceciel Monchet fall, Lexie (A) turned to Brian for help (B) became a terrified child (C) decided to give up skating (D) refused to finish the Christmas telecast.

_____ 12. Lexie's encounter with Nick after her win at the Sectionals (A) left her frightened and confused (B) took the joy out of her victory (C) made her realize that she still loved Nick (D) all of the above.

_____ 13. Lexie's accident occurred (A) when she skated on a rink that was too small (B) when she tried to escape her hurt by skating (C) when she crashed into a chair (D) all of the above.

_____ 14. Deborah leaves after Lexie's accident because (A) Marcus told her to (B) she had no feeling for Lexie (C) she knew that Lexie would never skate again (D) she was afraid of becoming emotionally involved.

_____ 15. When she returns home after the accident, Lexie (A) needs physical therapy (B) goes into total withdrawal (C) goes back to school (D) talks frequently with Brian.

_____ 16. The person who starts Lexie on the road to recovery is (A) Beulah (B) Marcus (C) Nick (D) Brian.

_____ 17. Lexie regains her self-confidence (A) with help from Marcus (B) by skating with Nick (C) by daily workouts at Beulah's rink (D) all of the above.

_____ 18. Lexie does not want the crowd at the Regionals to know that she is blind because (A) she does not want pity (B) she is afraid they will reject her entry (C) Beulah tells her not to tell them (D) all of the above.

_____ 19. The first person at the Regionals to discover that Lexie is blind is (A) Brian (B) Deborah (C) the chief judge (D) Annette Brashlout.

_____ 20. The biggest change in Lexie at the end of the novel is that (A) her skating technique has improved (B) she knows that Nick loves her (C) she no longer needs to use skating as an escape (D) she knows that she has her father's love and support.

NAME _____ DATE _____

Ice Castles by Leonore Fleischer

Answer each of the following questions in two or three complete sentences.

1. What is the significance of the skating dress that Lexie wears in her first Regional competition?

   _____

   _____

   _____

   _____

2. Why is Marcus Winston so reluctant to let his daughter become part of the world of competitive skating?

   _____

   _____

   _____

   _____

3. Why is Deborah Mackland's relationship with Lexie closer than Deborah's relationships with other skaters that she has coached?

   _____

   _____

   _____

   _____

4. Why does Nick stay away from Lexie for so long after Lexie is injured?

   _____

   _____

   _____

   _____

5. What part does Marcus play in helping Lexie learn to cope with the world again?

   _____

   _____

   _____

   _____

CHALLENGE

Write an essay explaining how *Ice Castles* illustrates the sacrifices, in terms of personal needs and human relationships, that must be made for any athlete to become a champion.

NAME _____ DATE _____

The Miracle Worker by William Gibson

Correctly complete each sentence with information from the novel.

1. Helen Keller was made blind and deaf by _____.

2. _____ is willing to do anything to help Helen.

3. Annie Sullivan had been a student at _____.

4. Annie's own difficulties in life included _____.

5. Flashbacks in the play are used to relate _____.

6. One of the play's subplots includes the conflict between _____

   and _____.

7. The children at the school gave Annie _____ and Helen a _____.

8. Helen causes the family problems because _____.

9. The first thing Annie must teach Helen is _____.

10. Annie tries to communicate with Helen by _____.

11. In the breakfast scene, Annie and Helen _____.

12. Annie wants to separate Helen from the family because _____.

13. _____ agrees to learn the hand alphabet to help Annie.

14. The captain agrees to give Annie _____ weeks alone with Helen in _____.

15. Annie says that her idea of original sin is _____.

16. After Helen returns, the Kellers are pleased because _____.

17. At her first meal at home again, Helen _____.

18. The first word that Helen understands is _____.

19. A very important prop in the final scene is _____.

20. At the end of the play, Kate sends Helen _____.

NAME _____ DATE _____

The Miracle Worker by William Gibson

Answer each of the following questions in two or three complete sentences.

1. What signs of intelligence does Annie see in Helen?

   _____

   _____

   _____

   _____

2. What are Annie's greatest strengths in dealing with Helen?

   _____

   _____

   _____

3. Why does Annie say that the Kellers' pity is one of Helen's greatest problems?

   _____

   _____

   _____

   _____

4. Explain Annie's statement: "Obedience is the gateway through which knowledge enters the mind of a child."

   _____

   _____

   _____

   _____

CHALLENGE

Discuss why Annie Sullivan was an effective teacher, especially for a handicapped child like Helen.

NAME _____ DATE _____

I Never Promised You a Rose Garden by Joanne Greenberg

In the numbered blanks at the left, write the letter of the matching person or place.

_____ 1. Taught Deborah the essentials of Latin and Greek

_____ 2. Essence of self, which Deborah believed was poisonous to all around her

_____ 3. Suffered because Deborah received all of the family's attention

_____ 4. Rented Deborah a room when Deborah was an outpatient

_____ 5. Deborah's most constant imaginary companion

_____ 6. Place of total blackout and insensibility

_____ 7. Patient who almost never spoke

_____ 8. Deborah's mother

_____ 9. The hidden world

_____ 10. Means "fire-touch." Deborah's name for her doctor

_____ 11. Ward attendant who had real care and concern for the patients

_____ 12. Was forced to live on the charity of his father-in-law

_____ 13. Patient who went home and committed suicide

_____ 14. Used Deborah as a tool to carry out his anger against a cruel world

_____ 15. Identified with the "kids" in their desire to escape

_____ 16. Deborah's close friend in the hospital

_____ 17. Gave Deborah a piece of wood which represented a small piece of herself

_____ 18. Voice that warned Deborah of the dangers in the real world

_____ 19. English doctor who could not identify with Deborah's problems

_____ 20. Patient who had made it to the outside, and became a symbol of hope to the others

A. Nganon
B. Carmen
C. Esther
D. Mrs. King
E. Yr
F. Censor
G. Suzy
H. Pit
I. Dr. Fried
J. Jacob
K. Pop Blau
L. Anterrabae
M. Furii
N. Carla
O. Doris Rivera
P. Miss Coral
Q. Dr. Royson
R. Sylvia
S. Doctor Halle
T. Quentin

NAME _____ DATE _____

I Never Promised You a Rose Garden by Joanne Greenberg

Answer each of the following questions in two or three complete sentences.

1. What specific experiences in Deborah's childhood had forced her to seek refuge in an imaginary world?

_____
_____
_____
_____

2. How do Deborah's parents react to her illness and hospitalization?

_____
_____
_____
_____

3. Why is Dr. Fried able to reach Deborah when others fail?

_____
_____
_____
_____

4. Even in her sickest times, how does Deborah show signs of both intelligence and caring?

_____
_____
_____
_____

5. What choice does Deborah have to make at the end of the novel? What does she mean by the phrase, "full weight"?

_____
_____
_____
_____

CHALLENGE

Write an essay describing the strengths that Deborah Blau has gained from her experience which will help her in the fight for identity and survival in the real world.

NAME _____ DATE _____

Ordinary People by Judith Guest

Place a (+) before each statement that is true and a (0) before each statement that is false.

_____ 1. The novel opens while Conrad is still in the hospital.

_____ 2. Buck, Conrad's brother, had been killed in an automobile accident.

_____ 3. The family attempts to cover the problems that they all have by pretending that everything is normal.

_____ 4. The story is told primarily through the viewpoint of Conrad and Beth.

_____ 5. Conrad's favorite extracurricular activity is the school choir.

_____ 6. Conrad attempted suicide because he felt guilty for his brother's death.

_____ 7. Cal is trapped between his love for his wife and his love for his son.

_____ 8. Arnold Bacon had been Conrad's psychiatrist while he was in the hospital.

_____ 9. To all their friends, Cal and Beth seem to have the perfect marriage.

_____ 10. Dr. Berger recognizes that Conrad needs to get in touch with his own feelings.

_____ 11. Karen is a girl that Conrad meets at choir practice.

_____ 12. Conrad's dreams frequently involve feelings of being trapped.

_____ 13. Conrad tells his mother when he quits the swim team.

_____ 14. Beth's major concern is for Conrad's welfare.

_____ 15. Conrad finally succeeds in his efforts to communicate with his mother.

_____ 16. Conrad's relationship with Jeannine is one of the most positive aspects of his life.

_____ 17. Calvin and Beth go to Dr. Berger together to seek family counseling.

_____ 18. The family Christmas celebration heals many old emotional wounds.

_____ 19. Conrad's beating up Lazenby is really an explosion of all the feelings that have been penned up inside him.

_____ 20. At the end of the novel, Calvin and Beth are attempting to build a new life.

NAME _____ DATE _____

Ordinary People by Judith Guest

Answer each of the following questions in two or three complete sentences.

1. Why did Conrad Jarrett try to commit suicide?

   _____

   _____

   _____

   _____

2. How does Dr. Berger help Conrad build a new life?

   _____

   _____

   _____

   _____

3. How does Calvin try to relieve his guilt feelings about Conrad's problems?

   _____

   _____

   _____

   _____

4. What does Beth mean when she says that she is being manipulated?

   _____

   _____

   _____

   _____

5. Why is Beth's situation at the end of the novel more hopeless than either Conrad or Calvin's situation?

   _____

   _____

   _____

   _____

CHALLENGE

Cal had said to his son, Buck, "People get hurt without anyone meaning it." Explain how the Jarrett family's story illustrates the truth of this statement.

Death Be Not Proud by John Gunther

Correctly complete each sentence with information from the novel.

1. Gunther states in his preface that his purpose for writing this book is _____

   _____.

2. Two of Johnny's first artistic interests were _____

   and _____.

3. In school, Johnny had great difficulty with _____.

4. Johnny's favorite subjects were _____

   and _____.

5. The private school that Johnny attended was _____.

6. By profession, John Gunther, Sr., is _____.

7. The first symptoms of Johnny's tumor were _____.

8. The chief doctor on Johnny's case was _____.

9. The surgeons could not remove the tumor because _____.

10. Johnny wrote a letter and received a reply from the famous scientist, _____.

11. "The flap" was left by the surgeons in Johnny's scalp so _____.

12. The prefix "glio-" before a tumor means that _____.

13. One of the new treatments given Johnny was injections of _____.

14. Dr. Max Gerson attempted to treat Johnny with _____.

15. During his illness, Johnny kept up with his schoolwork by _____.

16. Johnny's favorite game was _____.

17. For several months Johnny made great improvement. The reason for this was ____

    _____.

18. One of Johnny's greatest achievements was his return to _____

    for _____.

19. Two physical effects of Johnny's illness were _____

    and _____.

20. The flowers at Johnny's funeral gave great evidence that _____.

NAME _____ DATE _____

Death Be Not Proud by John Gunther

Answer each of the following questions in two or three complete sentences.

1. In what ways was John Gunther, Jr., a very unusual person?

   _____

   _____

   _____

   _____

2. How do you know that Johnny and his father were very close?

   _____

   _____

   _____

   _____

3. What was Johnny's special relationship with his mother?

   _____

   _____

   _____

   _____

4. In what unusual ways did Johnny manage to pass his preparatory school courses?

   _____

   _____

   _____

5. What insights into Johnny's personality are provided by the letters and diary entries which are included in the book?

   _____

   _____

   _____

   _____

CHALLENGE

How did the way that Johnny Gunther faced his illness and approaching death help those around him? How did Johnny show that he cared more for the feelings of others than he cared for his own pain?

NAME _____ DATE _____

Susan's Story by Susan Hampshire

Place a (+) before each statement that is true and a (0) before each statement that is false.

_____ 1. Dyslexia is a condition that one has from birth.

_____ 2. The dyslexic person has problems with reading and spelling, but no major problems with physical coordination.

_____ 3. Susan Hampshire's first teacher was her mother.

_____ 4. Both of Susan's sisters were also dyslexic.

_____ 5. Susan learned at an early age to use her acting ability to disguise her reading and spelling problems.

_____ 6. Susan and her brother lived with their father most of the time.

_____ 7. The family traveled a great deal when Susan was young.

_____ 8. Being dyslexic made Susan feel more helpless when she was a child than it did when she was an adult.

_____ 9. Usually only one side of the brain is affected by dyslexia.

_____ 10. Susan's first real acting role was in a television series.

_____ 11. Susan had a normal social life when she was a teenager.

_____ 12. Susan enjoyed working as an assistant stage manager and doing ordinary off-stage tasks.

_____ 13. Susan was very upset when she was told by a doctor that she suffered from "word blindness."

_____ 14. Susan gradually developed her own code for reading and understanding play scripts.

_____ 15. Susan's trip to Hollywood to start a movie career was a great success.

_____ 16. One of Susan's greatest accomplishments was getting her driver's license.

_____ 17. Susan's marriage to Pierre Granier-Deferre is still happy and stable.

_____ 18. Most of Miss Hampshire's greatest film successes have been adaptations of British novels for television.

_____ 19. An important turning point in Miss Hampshire's life was her visit with Dr. Albert Schweitzer.

_____ 20. Miss Hampshire now has two children.

150 Great Books

NAME _____ DATE _____

Susan's Story by Susan Hampshire

Answer each of the following questions in two or three complete sentences.

1. What unusual experiences in Miss Hampshire's childhood greatly helped her later career?

   _____

   _____

   _____

   _____

2. Why does Susan Hampshire have to work so much harder than most actresses?

   _____

   _____

   _____

   _____

3. Why was Susan's mother an important influence in her daughter's life?

   _____

   _____

   _____

   _____

4. What are some of the major difficulties that all dyslexics have in common?

   _____

   _____

   _____

   _____

5. What efforts is Miss Hampshire now making to help those with problems similar to her own?

   _____

   _____

   _____

   _____

CHALLENGE

In what ways is Susan Hampshire a fine example of the principle that determination and effort can help people to cope, even with very serious handicaps?

NAME _____ DATE _____

The Old Man and the Sea by Ernest Hemingway

Correctly complete each sentence with information from the novel.

1. The part of the world where this story takes place is _____.

2. The old man has fished for _____ days without catching anything.

3. The boy stopped going fishing with the old man because _____ _____.

4. Sardines and tuna were used by these fishermen for _____.

5. The old man's name was _____ ; the boy's name was _____.

6. The old man is very interested in the sport of _____ ; his great hero is _____.

7. The boy takes care of the old man by _____ and _____.

8. The old man dreams about _____.

9. The old man personifies the sea as _____ because _____.

10. The old man can tell where the fish are by _____.

11. The old man's fishing tackle consists of a series of _____ and _____.

12. The old man battles the great fish for _____ days.

13. During the battle with the fish, the old man wishes most that _____ _____.

14. The old man is concerned over the injury to _____.

15. The total length of the huge fish is _____ feet.

16. The old man finally kills the fish with _____.

17. Because the boat is so small, the old man must get the fish home by _____.

18. The old man kills the first shark with _____ and the second shark with _____.

19. The old man can no longer defend the fish against the sharks after _____ _____.

20. At the end of the story, the skeleton of the great fish is _____ _____.

NAME _____ DATE _____

The Old Man and the Sea by Ernest Hemingway

Answer each of the following questions in two or three complete sentences.

1. Briefly describe the relationship between the boy and the old man.

   _____

   _____

   _____

   _____

2. How does the old man show his love for and understanding of the sea?

   _____

   _____

   _____

   _____

3. Why does the old man call the great fish, "his brother"?

   _____

   _____

   _____

   _____

4. Why does the old man continue to battle the sharks, even though he realizes that the battle is hopeless?

   _____

   _____

   _____

   _____

5. What is the significance of the old man's dreams about the lions?

   _____

   _____

   _____

   _____

CHALLENGE

Write an essay describing the way that Hemingway affirms, in *The Old Man and the Sea*, his belief in the significance of every human being, regardless of whether the person wins or loses the battle that he or she fights.

NAME _____ DATE _____

Flowers for Algernon by Daniel Keyes

Select the letter of the word or phrase which correctly completes each statement.

_____ 1. Charlie Gordon had been selected for the experiment because of his (A) good looks (B) artistic ability (C) desire to learn (D) family references.

_____ 2. The story is told through (A) Dr. Strauss' reports (B) Charlie's journal (C) Miss Kinnian's school records (D) newspaper accounts of the convention.

_____ 3. The men at the bakery (A) make fun of Charlie (B) play tricks on Charlie (C) are cheating their boss (D) all of the above.

_____ 4. Rose Gordon had most wanted her son to be (A) famous (B) musical (C) artistic (D) normal.

_____ 5. Charlie's closest friend at the Institute was (A) Bert (B) Dr. Strauss (C) Fay (D) Alice.

_____ 6. Charlie learns the reality of his childhood (A) from Norma (B) through a series of memory flashbacks (C) from his father (D) from Mr. Donner.

_____ 7. As his intelligence increases, Charlie becomes (A) easier to get along with (B) nervous (C) more confused and upset (D) happier and more at peace with himself.

_____ 8. As his intelligence increases, Charlie's greatest problems are in (A) reading (B) social adjustment (C) spelling (D) remembering.

_____ 9. At the convention in Chicago, Charlie (A) feels like a prize exhibit (B) greatly identifies with Algernon (C) realizes that his intelligence will not last (D) all of the above.

_____ 10. Charlie sees himself most clearly (A) in characters he reads about (B) in the retarded boy in the restaurant (C) in the mirror images (D) in films of his earlier behavior.

_____ 11. Dr. Guarino (A) had been kind to Charlie (B) had used straps to hold Charlie down (C) was a quack who did not help (D) all of the above.

_____ 12. Charlie's regression meant that (A) he would be slightly less intelligent (B) his intelligence would remain at the same level (C) he would be worse off than he was before the experiment (D) he would not be able to learn any more languages.

_____ 13. When he visited his father, Charlie (A) identified himself (B) got a haircut (C) told Matt about Rose (D) gave Matt a copy of his book.

_____ 14. The report explaining the final result of the experiment comes from (A) Bert (B) Charlie (C) a panel of psychiatrists (D) Beekman University.

_____ 15. Charlie's mother (A) lives with his sister Norma (B) treats Charlie like a child (C) is seriously mentally unbalanced (D) all of the above.

_____ 16. Charlie is anxious to find his parents (A) because he knows that time is running out for him (B) so that he can introduce them to Alice (C) so that he can help them financially (D) so that he can get permission for another experiment.

_____ 17. As he begins to regress, Charlie lives with (A) Matt (B) Bert (C) Mr. Donner (D) Alice.

_____ 18. Charlie visits the Warren Home (A) so that he can know what is ahead for him (B) so that he can write an article about the work they do (C) so that he can get a job on the staff (D) so that he can find someone who will understand his problems.

_____ 19. Charlie buries Algernon (A) in the backyard (B) in a shoebox (C) so that Algernon will not be thrown into the incinerator (D) all of the above.

_____ 20. At the end of the novel, Charlie (A) is happy (B) feels that he has a lot of friends (C) thinks about Algernon (D) all of the above.

NAME _____ DATE _____

Flowers for Algernon by Daniel Keyes

Answer each of the following questions in two or three complete sentences.

1. How did Charlie get his job at the bakery?

   _____

   _____

   _____

   _____

2. How does Charlie's personality change as his intelligence increases?

   _____

   _____

   _____

   _____

3. Why was Charlie's relationship with Alice so difficult for both of them?

   _____

   _____

   _____

   _____

4. How did Matt Gordon try to protect his son from Rose's rage? Why did Matt fail?

   _____

   _____

   _____

   _____

5. When he learned that the regression would come, why did Charlie decide to return to work at the Institute?

   _____

   _____

   _____

   _____

CHALLENGE

Explain how the following quote from the novel presents a tremendous truth about human nature, and applies in particular to the problems that Charlie Gordon encounters: "The mind absorbed in and involved in itself as a self-centered end, to the exclusion of human relationships, can lead only to violence and pain" (p. 174).

150 Great Books

NAME _____ DATE _____

Eric by Doris Lund

Correctly complete each sentence with information from the novel.

1. Eric's major sports interest was _____.

2. The greatest positive factor that kept Eric alive in his battle against leukemia was
   _____.

3. Mrs. Lund's greatest problem during Eric's illness was _____.

4. Eric's brother's and sisters' names were _____ ,
   _____ and _____.

5. Eric's treatment was done at _____ Hospital.

6. A drug used for Eric's treatment was _____ , which was
   then very expensive and very experimental.

7. The three stages in the treatment of leukemia were called _____ ,
   _____ , and _____.

8. One of Eric's greatest thrills was his trip to _____
   with _____.

9. Remission means _____.

10. Mrs. Lund worked as a _____.

11. The doctor who was Eric's closest friend was _____.

12. Eric and Mary Lou met when _____.

13. At the end of his junior year in college, Eric was elected _____.

14. The patients in Ewig Eight nicknamed themselves _____.

15. Plasmapheresis was the process of _____.

16. During his hospitalization periods, Eric created the imaginary character of _____
    _____.

17. Eric had a total of _____ remissions, over a period of _____.

18. Eric told the nurses' symposium that what leukemia patients needed most was __
    _____.

19. The elderly lady on his ward who became Eric's friend was _____.

20. After Eric's death, his body was _____.

150 Great Books

NAME _____ DATE _____

Eric by Doris Lund

Answer each of the following questions in two or three complete sentences.

1. What mental attitudes of Eric's helped to prolong his life?

    _____

    _____

    _____

    _____

2. Why did Eric and his mother frequently have conflicts?

    _____

    _____

    _____

    _____

3. How did Eric help the other patients on Ewig Eight?

    _____

    _____

    _____

    _____

4. What other staff members and patients on Ewig Eight helped Eric?

    _____

    _____

    _____

    _____

5. How has the Lund family continued to support the work at Memorial Hospital since Eric's death?

    _____

    _____

    _____

    _____

CHALLENGE

Describe how Eric's philosophy of "Tomorrow is a long way off" helped Eric and those who loved him as they fought the battle against leukemia.

NAME _____ DATE _____

Requiem for a Heavyweight by Rod Serling

Select the letter of the word or phrase that correctly completes each statement.

_____ 1. As the play opens, Mountain (A) is number five in the heavyweight rankings (B) has just won a fight (C) has been badly beaten (D) is considering retirement.

_____ 2. Maish needs money (A) to pay Army's salary (B) to pay Mountain's medical expenses (C) to pay off a debt to the mob (D) to train a new fighter.

_____ 3. Orders for Mountain to stop fighting come from (A) Maish (B) Mr. Fox (C) Mr. Henson (D) the doctor.

_____ 4. Maish's main concern is for (A) Mountain's reputation (B) Mountain's feelings (C) Army's feelings (D) his own survival.

_____ 5. In the scene with Foxy, Maish shows that he (A) will change his loyalties very quickly (B) cannot easily be tricked (C) has a thorough knowledge of boxing (D) all of the above.

_____ 6. The small bar is nicknamed "the graveyard" because (A) on the wall are plaques to the memory of dead fighters (B) has-beens come here to relive the past (C) it is the oldest building on the street (D) it is next to a cemetery.

_____ 7. Mountain was given his nickname because of his (A) height (B) home state (C) weight (D) ability to withstand physical punishment.

_____ 8. Mountain's chief personality trait is his (A) aggressiveness (B) selfishness (C) pride and loyalty (D) desire to be a winner.

_____ 9. Mountain's relationship with Maish may be best described as (A) trusting (B) dependent (C) childlike (D) all of the above.

_____ 10. Mountain feels that he must get a job (A) to help Maish (B) to regain his self-respect (C) to pay back a loan (D) to have something to do with his time.

_____ 11. Grace wants most to help Mountain (A) get a job (B) gain some self-esteem (C) work with children (D) be independent of Maish.

_____ 12. Mountain had never dated because (A) he didn't have time (B) Maish wouldn't let him (C) he didn't want anyone to hurt him (D) he was in training.

_____ 13. Army didn't want Maish to turn Mountain into a wrestler because (A) there was no money in wrestling (B) wrestling would destroy Mountain's pride (C) Army was afraid that Mountain would get hurt (D) the doctor had forbidden Mountain to wrestle.

_____ 14. Wrestling would destroy Mountain's pride because (A) it was dangerous (B) the bouts were fixed (C) the costumes would make him look silly (D) he wasn't smart enough to learn the holds.

_____ 15. To force Mountain's cooperation in the wrestling scheme, Maish appeals to Mountain's (A) feelings of guilt (B) sense of obligation (C) feelings of personal loyalty (D) all of the above.

_____ 16. Mountain walks out on Maish when he learns that (A) Parelli is a crook (B) the match is fixed (C) Maish had bet against him (D) Grace has found him a job.

_____ 17. Army (A) was once himself a fighter (B) sends Mountain home (C) asks Grace to help Mountain (D) all of the above.

_____ 18. Grace helps Mountain most by (A) giving him a ticket to Tennessee (B) finding him work (C) giving him hope (D) getting him out of the bar.

_____ 19. Maish gains some measure of self-respect at the end of the play by (A) apologizing to Mountain (B) finding Army another job (C) refusing to become a crooked manager (D) paying off his gambling debts.

_____ 20. At the end of the play, Mountain (A) becomes a wrestler (B) finds the possibility of a new life (C) marries Grace (D) shoots himself.

NAME _____ DATE _____

Requiem for a Heavyweight by Rod Serling

Answer each of the following questions in two or three complete sentences.

1. Why does the doctor insist that Mountain stop fighting?

    _____

    _____

    _____

    _____

2. How is Maish's attitude toward Mountain contrasted with Army's attitude?

    _____

    _____

    _____

    _____

3. Why is Maish so desperate to turn Mountain into a wrestler?

    _____

    _____

    _____

    _____

4. How does Maish take advantage of Mountain's loyal nature?

    _____

    _____

    _____

    _____

5. How does Mountain's relationship with Grace provide hope for Mountain's future?

    _____

    _____

    _____

    _____

CHALLENGE

In order to survive psychologically, every person must have a measure of self-respect. Write an essay describing how Mountain's boxing career has robbed him of his self-respect. Then describe how, in the conclusion of the play, Mountain finds hope for regaining his self-esteem.

NAME _____ DATE _____

One Day in the Life of Ivan Denisovich
by Alexander Solzhenitsyn

Correctly complete each sentence with information from the novel.

1. Shukhov has been in the concentration camp for _____ years.

2. As a punishment for staying in bed too long, Shukhov has to _____.

3. Shukhov's prison number is _____ ; his group number is _____.

4. The prisoners' meals consist entirely of _____ and _____.

5. Before he leaves camp, Shukhov hides his bread by _____.

6. The most important person in the prisoner's life is his _____.

7. The man in prison for his faith is _____.

8. _____ has rich friends and frequently receives packages from home.

9. _____ had once been a military officer and had visited with admirals in the British navy.

10. _____ is the disciplinary officer who has the power to sentence men to the cells.

11. Before the men leave camp for work, they have to _____.

12. The job for the day is _____.

13. Shukhov has a _____ hidden at the worksite.

14. _____ is a prisoner who is always trying to scrounge something from the others.

15. Shukhov takes great personal pride in _____.

16. The men work after it gets dark because _____.

17. The whole crew is detained at the worksite because _____.

18. Shukhov is able to smuggle into the camp _____.

19. When they return to the camp Shukhov gets extra food by _____.

20. Shukhov feels that this has been a good day because _____.

NAME _____ DATE _____

One Day in the Life of Ivan Denisovich
by Alexander Solzhenitsyn

Answer each of the following questions in two or three complete sentences.

1. What are some of the ways that the prisoners try to beat the system?

   _____
   _____
   _____
   _____

2. Why is Tyurin a good gang boss?

   _____
   _____
   _____

3. How does the whole camp work on a "pay-off" system?

   _____
   _____
   _____
   _____

4. What do these men in prison value most?

   _____
   _____
   _____
   _____

5. How is Alyoshka's attitude about imprisonment different from Shukhov's attitude?

   _____
   _____
   _____
   _____

CHALLENGE

Write an essay describing the ways that Ivan Denisovich (Shukhov) manages to retain the goodness of his humanity while existing in a totally dehumanizing situation.

NAME _____ DATE _____

Cannery Row by John Steinbeck

In the numbered blanks at the left, write the letter of the matching person or place.

_____ 1. Pet adopted by Mack and the boys

_____ 2. The area's main industry

_____ 3. Financially sharp grocery store owner

_____ 4. Incorrectly named by a confused mother

_____ 5. Lived in a boiler that had been rejected by the cannery

_____ 6. Unofficial leader of the local hobo group

_____ 7. Nursed the sick during the influenza epidemic

_____ 8. Constantly experimented with various forms of artistic expression

_____ 9. Dora's "bouncer"

_____ 10. Retarded man who was protected by Doc

_____ 11. Owner of the frog pond

_____ 12. Home of Mack and the boys

_____ 13. Owner of the Bear Flag Restaurant

_____ 14. Gave tea parties for cats

_____ 15. Mechanical genius who fixed Lee's truck, and then landed in jail

_____ 16. Filled in as the part-time bartender at La Ida

_____ 17. Enjoyed traveling the coast collecting marine specimens

_____ 18. One of Dora's girls who broke her arm

_____ 19. Doc's home

_____ 20. Setting for the story

A. Lee Chong
B. Eddie
C. Mack
D. Dora Flood
E. Palace Flophouse and Grill
F. Western Biological Laboratory
G. Hazel
H. Henri
I. Mr. and Mrs. Sam Malloy
J. Frankie
K. Gay
L. Darling
M. Dora's Girls
N. Doc
O. Mary Talbot
P. Alfred
Q. Monterey
R. The Captain
S. Phyllis Mae
T. Hediondo Cannery

NAME _____ DATE _____

Cannery Row by John Steinbeck

Answer each of the following questions in two or three complete sentences.

1. By what process did Mack and the boys furnish their home?

   _____
   _____
   _____
   _____

2. Why did they decide to give Doc a party?

   _____
   _____
   _____
   _____

3. Why was the first party such a disaster? Why was the second one a success?

   _____
   _____
   _____
   _____

4. Why is the frog-hunting scene a fine example of Steinbeck's use of comedy?

   _____
   _____
   _____
   _____

5. How does this novel show the good in those people that society usually terms evil or social rejects?

   _____
   _____
   _____
   _____

CHALLENGE

Steinbeck says, "Everywhere in the world there are Mack and the boys." Write an essay which explains how the various characters in *Cannery Row* illustrate traits which are common to human nature.

NAME _____ DATE _____

The Pearl by John Steinbeck

Place a (+) before each statement that is true and a (0) before each statement that is false.

_____ 1. As the story opens, Kino is contented with his life.

_____ 2. Kino's little girl is bitten by a scorpion.

_____ 3. The doctor deliberately makes the baby sick.

_____ 4. The doctor willingly treats anyone who comes to him.

_____ 5. The pearl that Kino finds is large and beautiful.

_____ 6. No one in the town knows that Kino has found the perfect pearl.

_____ 7. The pearl buyers agree on a system which is designed to cheat people.

_____ 8. The pearl buyers offer Kino a fair price for his pearl.

_____ 9. Kino's greatest dream is for his son to have an education.

_____ 10. The whole village knows about Kino's good fortune.

_____ 11. Kino's brother urges him to take his pearl to the city.

_____ 12. Kino accidentally puts a hole in the bottom of his boat.

_____ 13. Juana wants to throw the pearl back into the sea.

_____ 14. Kino kills a man to protect his pearl.

_____ 15. Kino finally decides to accept the price that the buyers have offered.

_____ 16. Kino's son is shot when the child cries out in the night.

_____ 17. Kino kills the man who killed his child.

_____ 18. Kino is able to beat the system.

_____ 19. Kino's wife is loyal to her husband to the end.

_____ 20. Kino and his family take the pearl and go to live in a different town.

NAME _____ DATE _____

The Pearl by John Steinbeck

Answer each of the following questions in two or three complete sentences.

1. What hopes and dreams does Kino have when he finds the pearl?

    _____
    _____
    _____
    _____

2. How are his dreams destroyed?

    _____
    _____
    _____
    _____

3. Why does the pearl, which had been beautiful, suddenly begin to look evil and ugly?

    _____
    _____
    _____
    _____

4. What do Kino and Juana finally do with the pearl?

    _____
    _____
    _____
    _____

5. State in your own words the themes that Steinbeck is presenting in this novel.

    _____
    _____
    _____
    _____

CHALLENGE
Write an essay describing some of the ways that instant wealth might destroy a person's life.

NAME _____ DATE _____

On Golden Pond by Ernest Thompson

Place a (+) before each statement that is true and a (0) before each statement that is false.

_____ 1. Ethel and Norman Thayer are both in their 80s.

_____ 2. The Thayers have been spending their summers on Golden Pond for many years.

_____ 3. The action of the play spans about three months.

_____ 4. The summer girls' camp on the lake is still operational.

_____ 5. Charlie had been in love with Chelsea since both of them were kids.

_____ 6. Norman is obsessed with the idea of dying.

_____ 7. Elmer was one of Ethel's childhood sweethearts.

_____ 8. Chelsea had joined the high-school basketball team so that Norman would be proud of her.

_____ 9. When he goes alone for a walk in the woods, Norman becomes lost and frightened.

_____ 10. Norman converses comfortably with Chelsea's boyfriend Bill.

_____ 11. Chelsea has come to Norman's birthday party because her mother wrote and asked her to come.

_____ 12. Ethel enjoys going fishing as much as Billy and Norman do.

_____ 13. Billy and Norman both enjoy the time that they spend together.

_____ 14. Bill comes back with Chelsea when she returns to pick up Billy.

_____ 15. Chelsea and Bill were married while they were in Europe.

_____ 16. *On Golden Pond* has several different set locations.

_____ 17. Norman suffers a fatal heart attack just as they are about to close up the cottage.

_____ 18. Norman and Ethel agree to spend the winter with Chelsea and Bill in California.

_____ 19. Ethel feels the reality of death when she believes that Norman may really be in danger.

_____ 20. The play ends with a promise of hoped-for return.

NAME _____ DATE _____

On Golden Pond by Ernest Thompson

Answer each of the following questions in two or three complete sentences.

1. How does Norman Thayer play the part of a grouchy old man to the hilt?

_____

_____

_____

_____

2. How does Ethel show that she completely understands all of Norman's moods?

_____

_____

_____

_____

3. What caused the problems between Norman and Chelsea?

_____

_____

_____

_____

4. How does spending time with Billy help Norman?

_____

_____

_____

_____

5. What does the cottage on Golden Pond represent to Norman and Ethel?

_____

_____

_____

_____

CHALLENGE

Write an essay explaining how the relationship of Norman and Ethel Thayer shows the qualities of love which grow and last over a long period of time.

NAME _____ DATE _____

The Other Side of the Mountain by E.G. Valens

In the numbered blanks at the left, write the letter of the matching person or place.

_____ 1. Cared for Jill during her long convalescence

_____ 2. Wrote the story of Jill's recovery for *Life* magazine

_____ 3. The mountain where Jill first trained and practiced

_____ 4. Jill's friend, a promising young skier who was stricken with polio

_____ 5. An elderly caller who brought Jill chocolates, stamps, and postcards

_____ 6. Where Jill learned to use the muscles that were still functional

_____ 7. Jill's hometown in Colorado

_____ 8. Olympic woman skier who gave Jill help and inspiration

_____ 9. Loved Jill, but left her because he could not handle her handicap

_____ 10. Became Olympic champ after Jill was injured

_____ 11. Helped Jill to use her intellect to study, and to write

_____ 12. Jill's ski coach and second father

_____ 13. City where Jill attended the Olympics

_____ 14. Played Jill in the film about her accident

_____ 15. Special tool developed to help Jill eat

_____ 16. Jill's brother, also a ski champion

_____ 17. Jill's therapist, later Audra Jo's husband

_____ 18. The Kinmont's ranch

_____ 19. Pilot and daredevil skier who gave Jill love and support

_____ 20. Sold his ranch to help pay Jill's medical expenses

A. Audra Jo Nicholson
B. Linda Meyers
C. Dave McCoy
D. Rocking K
E. Mammoth
F. Bob
G. Marilyn Hassett
H. Andrea Mead Lawrence
I. Dick Buek
J. June Kinmont
K. Bill Kinmont
L. Bud Werner
M. California Rehabilitation Center
N. Spork
O. Lee Baumgarth
P. Bishop
Q. Cortina
R. Mr. Hardy
S. Lee Zadroga
T. Jan Mason and Burke Uzzle

NAME _____ DATE _____

The Other Side of the Mountain by E.G. Valens

Answer each of the following questions in two or three complete sentences.

1. What were some of the ways that Jill developed her body to become a championship skier?

_____

_____

_____

_____

2. Describe the circumstances of Jill's accident.

_____

_____

_____

_____

3. Contrast Dick's reaction to Jill's injury with Bud's reaction.

_____

_____

_____

_____

4. How did Audra Jo help Jill cope with her feelings?

_____

_____

_____

_____

5. What were some of the greatest obstacles that Jill had to overcome in her desire to be a teacher?

_____

_____

_____

_____

CHALLENGE

Before her accident, Jill Kinmont's only thoughts were being a skiing champion. Discuss the ways that Jill showed herself, after the accident, to be a real winner in human terms, even though she was physically paralyzed.

150 Great Books

NAME _____ DATE _____

The Bridge of San Luis Rey by Thornton Wilder

Correctly complete each sentence with information from the novel.

1. The novel is set in _____ in the _____ century.

2. Brother Juniper wanted to investigate the lives of the victims to prove that _____
   _____.

3. The Marquesa de Montemayor had a great gift for _____.

4. The Marquesa's greatest desire was _____.

5. Madre Maria was training Pepita to _____.

6. The Perichole was forced by the Viceroy to _____.

7. Pepita would not send the letter that she had written to the Abbess because _____
   _____.

8. Just before her death, the Marquesa was determined to _____
   _____.

9. A division comes in the relationship between Manuel and Esteban when _____
   _____.

10. Camila hires Manuel to _____.

11. Manuel's death is caused by _____.

12. Captain Alvarado spent all his time at sea to escape from _____
    _____.

13. Captain Alvarado was not killed when the bridge fell because _____
    _____.

14. Uncle Pio's three great desires in life were for _____
    _____ and _____.

15. Uncle Pio trained Camila to be a great actress by _____.

16. After Camila retired from the theater, she _____.

17. Camila's son _____ suffered from _____.

18. Camila's beauty was destroyed by _____.

19. Uncle Pio persuades Camila to let him _____.

20. After his great book was finished, Brother Juniper _____.

150 Great Books

NAME _____ DATE _____

The Bridge of San Luis Rey by Thornton Wilder

Answer each of the following questions in two or three complete sentences.

1. What are some of the ironic contrasts between the Marquesa's life and her letters?

_____

_____

_____

_____

2. How did Pepita help the Marquesa?

_____

_____

_____

3. How did Esteban begin to find his own identity after Manuel's death?

_____

_____

_____

_____

4. How did Uncle Pio's life with Camila fulfill all of his deepest desires?

_____

_____

_____

_____

5. What effects did Pepita's death have on Madre Maria?

_____

_____

_____

_____

CHALLENGE

"Epiphany" is defined as a new moment of insight or awareness which changes a person's life. Select three characters from *The Bridge of San Luis Rey* who had such learning experiences. What did each person learn? How was each person changed?

NAME _____ DATE _____

The Skin of Our Teeth by Thornton Wilder

Correctly complete each sentence with information from the play.

1. The character who acts as narrator of the play is _____.

2. Mr. Antrobus has already invented _____

   and is working on _____.

3. In Act I, the human race is about to be wiped out by _____.

4. Mrs. Antobus's main concerns are for _____.

5. As a reward for his service, Mrs. Antrobus gives the telegraph boy a _____.

6. Henry Antrobus represents the human tendency for _____.

7. The people that Antrobus wants to save from the cold represent _____.

8. At the end of Act I, Sabina asks the audience to _____.

9. The setting for Act II shifts to _____.

10. In his election speech, Mr. Antrobus states that the human race will _____

    _____.

11. The character who speaks the author's philosophy in Act II is _____.

12. Antrobus and Sabina are making plans to _____.

13. Antrobus's radio speech is interrupted by _____.

14. At the end of Act II, the human race needs to be saved from _____.

15. At the beginning of Act III, humanity has just survived _____.

16. Mr. Fitzpatrick comes to inform the audience that _____.

17. Sabina brings Mrs. Antrobus the news that _____.

18. Hope for the future is represented in Act III by _____.

19. Confrontation between good and evil in Act III comes in the dialogue between

    _____ and _____.

20. Sabina's speech at the end of the play is linked with _____.

NAME _____   DATE _____

The Skin of Our Teeth by Thornton Wilder

Answer each of the following questions in two or three complete sentences.

1. What catastrophe does the human race survive in each act of this play?

    _____

    _____

    _____

    _____

2. What is the significance of the mark on Henry's face? How is this significance carried through the entire play?

    _____

    _____

    _____

    _____

3. What positive and negative traits of motherhood are displayed by Mrs. Antrobus?

    _____

    _____

    _____

    _____

4. What is the significance of the books mentioned in Acts I and III?

    _____

    _____

    _____

    _____

5. Explain Sabina's final statement: "The end of this play isn't written yet."

    _____

    _____

    _____

    _____

CHALLENGE
Write an essay discussing the traits of the human race illustrating the author's belief that we will survive by the "skin of our teeth." Which characters in the play reveal these traits? What character traits that will endanger that survival does this play also illustrate?

150 Great Books

ANSWER KEYS

Strong at the Broken Places by Max Cleland
OBJECTIVE:

1. 0	6. 0	11. +	16. 0
2. +	7. +	12. +	17. +
3. 0	8. 0	13. 0	18. 0
4. +	9. 0	14. +	19. +
5. 0	10. +	15. 0	20. 0

SHORT ANSWER:
1. Picked up a live grenade in Vietnam.
2. They were embarrassed by his disability and made him feel like a freak.
3. To walk with artificial limbs, to use his hook as a hand, to drive a special car.
4. To show the world that a handicapped person could participate in life, to help other handicapped people.
5. To deal with life's experiences and problems one day at a time.

CHALLENGE:

Stronger in spirit as he overcame physical handicaps. Learning to walk, psychological adjustment to his injuries, freeing himself from self-pity.

I Heard the Owl Call My Name by Margaret Craven
OBJECTIVE:

1. B	6. C	11. B
2. D	7. A	12. D
3. C	8. A	13. B
4. A	9. C	14. A
5. C	10. D	15. A

SHORT ANSWER:
1. Primitive lifestyle, church and vicarage in ruins.
2. Not to try to push white ideas, to allow the Indians to teach him.
3. Because he has really come to share in their suffering.
4. Gordon has adopted too many of the white man's ways.
5. Owl is the death symbol. Mark is preparing for his death.

CHALLENGE:

Relates to the cycles of nature. Values his people for their simple approach to living. Death becomes a natural part of life. He has shared death with his people, and can now accept his own.

Ice Castles by Leonore Fleischer
OBJECTIVE:

1. B	6. A	11. A	16. A
2. B	7. A	12. D	17. D
3. C	8. D	13. D	18. A
4. A	9. B	14. D	19. A
5. A	10. B	15. B	20. C

ANSWER KEYS (continued)

Ice Castles by Leonore Fleischer (continued)

SHORT ANSWER:

1. The same dress that Beulah had worn in competition years before.
2. He is afraid he will lose her as he lost her mother.
3. She came to really care for Lexie, wanted the underdog to win.
4. He thinks Lexie loves Brian, he feels helpless to cope with her blindness.
5. He sets her free to attempt skating again, gets Beulah to help her.

CHALLENGE:

Lexie loses Nick, sacrifices a normal social life for hours of disciplined practice. Normal life gives way to the demands for athletic perfection.

The Miracle Worker by William Gibson

OBJECTIVE:

1. a childhood illness
2. Kate
3. Perkins Institute
4. blindness, the death of Jimmy
5. Annie's childhood
6. James and his father
7. dark glasses, the doll
8. creates chaos in the house, is totally spoiled
9. discipline
10. hand alphabet
11. fight, totally wreck the dining room
12. she can't teach because of their interference
13. Kate
14. two weeks, the garden house
15. giving up
16. she is clean and well-behaved
17. starts all over again
18. *water*
19. the pump
20. to Annie

SHORT ANSWER:

1. Temper tantrums, stealing the key, mimics everything that is spelled into her hands.
2. Her youth, her physical strength and determination, her knowledge of what it is to be blind.
3. They pamper her, don't expect her to learn, don't discipline her.
4. No child can learn anything who is constantly given his own way.

CHALLENGE:

Annie is emotionally strong, cares enough for Helen to make her be as much as she can become, refuses to give up. Expects Helen to learn.

I Never Promised You a Rose Garden by Joanne Greenberg

OBJECTIVE:

1. P
2. A
3. G
4. D
5. L
6. H
7. R
8. C
9. E
10. M
11. T
12. J
13. B
14. K
15. S
16. N
17. I
18. F
19. Q
20. O

SHORT ANSWER:

1. Failure to live up to parents' and grandfather's expectations. Sought escape from family stress situation into an imaginary world.
2. They think it is their fault.
3. Helps by sharing herself. Does not allow Deborah to enjoy her illness or feel sorry for herself.
4. Closeness with Carla, learning with Miss Coral, relationships with the various attendants.
5. Will she give up her imaginary kingdom of Yr? To live totally in the world of reality.

ANSWER KEYS (continued)

I Never Promised You a Rose Garden by Joanne Greenberg (continued)

CHALLENGE:

Ability to act independently proves to her that she is a good person. Success in finishing high school. Belief that reality, even with all of its problems, is better than escape.

Ordinary People by Judith Guest

OBJECTIVE:

1. 0	6. +	11. 0	16. +
2. 0	7. +	12. +	17. 0
3. +	8. 0	13. 0	18. 0
4. 0	9. +	14. 0	19. +
5. +	10. +	15. 0	20. 0

SHORT ANSWER:

1. Guilt feelings over Buck's death, failure to live up to his parents' expectations.
2. By being available, by listening, by helping him learn to keep control of his world.
3. By giving him things, especially the car.
4. Feels trapped by the demands of both her husband and son.
5. She won't get any help but runs away instead.

CHALLENGE:

Conrad feels a failure as a son. Christmas scene attempt at normality is a catastrophe. Cal wants to reach his son, gives him things instead. Conrad attempts to reach his mother, but she cannot respond.

Death Be Not Proud by John Gunther

OBJECTIVE:

1. present the account of Johnny's illness
2. music and painting
3. neatness and getting things done on time
4. chemistry and physics
5. Deerfield
6. a newspaper correspondent
7. stiff neck, violent headaches
8. Dr. Traeger
9. spread too far into the brain
10. Einstein
11. the pressure could be relieved
12. a fatal tumor
13. mustard gas
14. diet and vitamins
15. studying at home
16. chess
17. unknown
18. Deerfield, graduation
19. blindness and loss of motor coordination
20. he had a great number of friends

SHORT ANSWER:

1. His spirit, determination, acceptance of his illness, emotional maturity.
2. Shared interest in his father's work.
3. Cared and read to him, discussed his approaching death openly and honestly.
4. Tutors, correspondence courses.
5. Total awareness of what was happening, appreciation of every good thing in life.

CHALLENGE:

He gave strength to his parents and to other patients. Endured pain, but kept his sense of humor. This humor helped his parents.

ANSWER KEYS (continued)

Susan's Story by Susan Hampshire

1. +	6. 0	11. 0	16. +
2. 0	7. +	12. +	17. 0
3. +	8. 0	13. +	18. +
4. 0	9. +	14. +	19. +
5. +	10. 0	15. 0	20. 0

SHORT ANSWER:
1. Traveling, being taken to the dance studio, early association with theatrical people.
2. Reading difficulties—must spend much more time studying scripts. Blocking problems because of poor directional sense.
3. Much music and art, relaxed home life, positive attitude toward the good to be found in each day.
4. Reading difficulties, letter reversals, motor and directional problems.
5. Admitting publicly that she is dyslexic. Helping others to admit their disabilities, working to raise funds for special educational opportunities.

CHALLENGE:
Struggles to rise to the top of the acting profession, coping emotionally with a difficult personal life including the death of her mother and the failure of her marriage. She now uses her reputation as a way to help others.

The Old Man and the Sea by Ernest Hemingway

OBJECTIVE:
1. Cuba
2. forty
3. his parents wouldn't allow him to
4. bait
5. Santiago Manolin
6. baseball, Joe DiMaggio
7. feeding him, covering him with a blanket
8. the beauties of Africa
9. woman, so changeable
10. birds
11. a series of hooks and sticks
12. three
13. the boy was not with him
14. his hands
15. five feet longer than his boat
16. harpoon
17. towing it beside the boat
18. harpoon, his knife
19. he loses the knife
20. swept out with the tide

SHORT ANSWER:
1. Boy loves the old man's dreams. Boy reminds the old man of his youth.
2. Sea as a woman. He respects and understands all of her moods.
3. Respect for the fish's size and strength.
4. To protect his fish as long as he can.
5. He will continue to dream of great adventures.

CHALLENGE:
Old man becomes a symbol of the courage of each person. Even though he loses, he hangs in until the end.

Flowers for Algernon by Daniel Keyes

OBJECTIVE:
1. C	6. B	11. D	16. A
2. B	7. C	12. C	17. D
3. D	8. B	13. B	18. A
4. D	9. D	14. B	19. D
5. A	10. B	15. D	20. D

ANSWER KEYS (continued)

Flowers for Algernon by Daniel Keyes (continued)

SHORT ANSWER:

1. Donner promised Charlie's uncle to care for Charlie.
2. More confused, angry, realizes that others are laughing at him.
3. Becoming aware of his manhood. Mental maturity far above emotional maturity.
4. Protect him from injury, try to find doctors to help him. Charlie's life is in danger, he takes Charlie away.
5. To chronicle the results of the experiment before his intelligence was gone.

CHALLENGE:

Rose Gordon's self-centeredness—totally destructive. Charlie's need for love—Fay and Alice. Charlie's need to find his family before time runs out. When Charlie is most intelligent, he is most isolated and alone.

Eric by Doris Lund

OBJECTIVE:

1. soccer
2. Eric's determination to beat the disease
3. her desire to protect him
4. Meredith, Mark, Jennifer
5. Memorial
6. asparaginase
7. protocol, maintenance, consolidation
8. California, Eddie
9. disease temporarily under control
10. free-lance writer
11. Dr. Monroe Dowling
12. she was his private nurse
13. captain of the soccer team
14. Murphy's mob
15. separating platelets from plasma
16. Ralph, the elephant
17. six, three years
18. hope
19. Mrs. Hardy
20. given to Cornell Medical Center

SHORT ANSWER:

1. Willingness to live one day at a time, and to face life realistically.
2. She was over-protective, he needed his freedom.
3. By his positive attitudes in helping them fight.
4. Mary Lou, Murphy, Mrs. Hardy.
5. Continued blood donations to help others.

CHALLENGE:

Got everything they could out of each experience: Christmas, soccer games, vacations, birthdays.

Requiem for a Heavyweight by Rod Serling

OBJECTIVE:

1. C
2. C
3. D
4. D
5. D
6. B
7. B
8. C
9. D
10. A
11. B
12. C
13. B
14. B
15. D
16. C
17. D
18. C
19. C
20. B

284

ANSWER KEYS (continued)

Requiem for a Heavyweight by Rod Serling (continued)

SHORT ANSWER:

1. Fears permanent damage to his head and eyes.
2. Army cares, Maish sees him as a commodity to sell.
3. He needs money to pay off the mob.
4. Makes Mountain feel guilty to become a wrestler.
5. Offers him hope, makes him feel like a person.

CHALLENGE:

Begins to lose fights, becomes a piece of meat. He cannot sacrifice his pride. Grace makes him feel human. Hope for the future with kids like the boy on the train.

One Day in the Life of Ivan Denisovich by Alexander Solzhenitsyn

OBJECTIVE:

1. eight
2. mop the floor
3. S-856, 104
4. bread and mush
5. sewing it into his mattress
6. gang boss
7. Alyoshka
8. Caesar
9. The Captain
10. Volkovay
11. be frisked
12. building a wall
13. trowel
14. Fetyukov
15. his brick work
16. they mix too much mortar
17. one man is missing because he has fallen asleep
18. a piece of metal
19. standing in the package line for Caesar
20. has had double rations, is not in the cells

SHORT ANSWER:

1. Hiding tools and pieces of metal, plotting for extra food.
2. Gets the most rations and the best work assignments for his men.
3. Bribes for guards, cooks, those in offices, those in charge of the mail.
4. Extra food, free time, solitude, sleep.
5. Deep faith in God versus just simple day-by-day survival.

CHALLENGE:

Help for others to get food, sharing of packages, cooperation of the work teams to get the job done, sympathy when others suffer.

Cannery Row by John Steinbeck

OBJECTIVE:

1. L
2. T
3. A
4. G
5. I
6. C
7. M
8. H
9. P
10. J
11. R
12. E
13. D
14. O
15. K
16. B
17. N
18. S
19. F
20. Q

ANSWER KEYS (continued)

Cannery Row by John Steinbeck (continued)

SHORT ANSWER:

1. Getting pieces of junk from the dump.
2. Because he is such a good guy.
3. They get into a fight and break up the house. Doc gives a party for them.
4. Chase the frogs into the nets with flashlights, sell frogs to Doc to finance his party.
5. Prostitutes and social outcasts help others. Doc's care for Frankie.

CHALLENGE:

Human nature everywhere a mixture of good and evil. Dora's girls become nurses. Mack and the boys don't work and are outcasts, yet are capable of great caring.

The Pearl by John Steinbeck

OBJECTIVE:

1. +	6. 0	11. +	16. +
2. 0	7. +	12. 0	17. +
3. +	8. 0	13. +	18. 0
4. 0	9. +	14. +	19. +
5. +	10. +	15. 0	20. 0

SHORT ANSWER:

1. He will have a rifle, they will be married, his son will go to school.
2. The greed of the pearl buyers, the doctor, and the trackers.
3. Because it has caused Coyotito's death.
4. Throw it back into the sea.
5. Evil in man will destroy hope.

CHALLENGE:

Any sudden gain of wealth that brings out the greed in others and is destructive to happiness and human relationships.

On Golden Pond by Ernest Thompson

OBJECTIVE:

1. 0	6. +	11. +	16. 0
2. +	7. 0	12. 0	17. 0
3. +	8. 0	13. +	18. 0
4. 0	9. +	14. 0	19. +
5. +	10. 0	15. +	20. +

SHORT ANSWER:

1. With the operator, with Charlie, with Bill.
2. Humors him, protects him when he is confused and helpless.
3. She wanted to please him, but never could.
4. He learns how to relate to someone.
5. The total continuity of their years of marriage.

CHALLENGE:

Puts up with the faults of the other person, protects and cares, finds pleasure in shared memories and little things.

ANSWER KEYS (continued)

The Other Side of the Mountain by E.G. Valens

OBJECTIVE:

1. J	6. M	11. S	16. F
2. T	7. P	12. C	17. O
3. E	8. H	13. Q	18. D
4. A	9. L	14. G	19. I
5. R	10. B	15. N	20. K

SHORT ANSWER:

1. Swimming, jogging, foot exercises through tires, horseback riding.
2. Fell on a jump and broke her neck.
3. Bud left her—could not cope, Dick stayed and helped.
4. Audra had polio—dealt with her own handicap, so she could help Jill.
5. None of the schools thought that Jill could manage in a classroom situation.

CHALLENGE:

Jill learned to handle her disability and her emotions. Got rid of self-pity. Reached out to children with learning disabilities. Became a person instead of an athletic personality.

The Bridge of San Luis Rey by Thornton Wilder

OBJECTIVE:

1. Peru, 17th century
2. there was purpose in the accident
3. writing beautiful letters
4. gain her daughter's love
5. take over her work
6. apologize to the Marquesa
7. she feels it is not noble
8. pray for the health of her daughter's child
9. Manuel becomes attracted to Camila
10. write her letters
11. blood poisoning
12. his own unhappy memories
13. he went down with the luggage
14. theater, Spanish literature, beautiful women
15. constantly criticizing her performances
16. retire to the country
17. Don Jaime, epilepsy
18. smallpox
19. take Jaime to be educated
20. is burned at the stake

SHORT ANSWER:

1. Letters show a woman of wit and culture; she was seen by society as a demented drunk.
2. Looking after her, preventing others from taking advantage of her.
3. Agreeing to leave with Captain Alvarado.
4. Love of women, literature, and theater. He lived a substitute life through her.
5. Got over her focus on the importance of her work. Learned about disinterested love.

CHALLENGE:

Camila learns to love, comes to work with Madre Maria. Marquesa's daughter learns the truth about her mother. Madre Maria learns disinterested love. Captain Alvarado learns that life must go on.

ANSWER KEYS (continued)

The Skin of Our Teeth by Thornton Wilder

OBJECTIVE:

1. Sabrina
2. the wheel, the alphabet
3. ice
4. her children
5. a needle
6. killing, evil
7. arts, literature, history
8. burn the chairs to save humanity
9. Atlantic City
10. survive, triumph
11. fortune-teller
12. run away together
13. storm warnings
14. the flood
15. war
16. some actors are ill; there will be replacements
17. Mr. Antrobus is coming home
18. Gladys's baby
19. Henry and his father
20. the beginning

SHORT ANSWER:

1. Ice age, flood, war.
2. Mark of Cain—the first killer—symbol of the violent tendencies in man.
3. Cares and loves her children, is totally possessive of them.
4. The great books of world culture.
5. The human race will continue going through the same process.

CHALLENGE:

Mr. Antrobus—inventiveness, sheltering culture, continuing technical progress. Mrs. Antrobus—domestic instincts which help the family to survive. Henry—the evil in man which endangers that survival.

UNIT 7

The Top of the Ladder—

Stories of PROFESSIONAL SUCCESS and ACHIEVEMENT

SYNOPSES

Life and Death in the Coral Sea
by Jacques-Yves Cousteau

This book recounts one of the many expeditions of Cousteau, the French explorer whose searches have provided knowledge of one of man's last great frontiers—the ocean's floor. His ship, the *Calypso*, on this particular mission, went (during the 1960s) to explore the coral formations in the Red Sea area and near the islands in the Indian Ocean. Cousteau was horrified to see how much the plant and animal life in the sea bed had deteriorated since his previous visit to the area. Living coral had been reduced to a mass of dead gray by oil spills from tankers and sewage dumped from ocean liners. Illustrated by beautiful photographs, the book recounts the adventures of the *Calypso*'s crew as they filmed the undersea marvels. Divers had fish and eels eating out of their hands. Cousteau also describes new equipment and techniques which make man able to explore at greater depths than ever before. The thesis of this book is the statement of Cousteau's fear that man may destroy the balance of life in the ocean if the sea is continually used as a garbage dump. The explorer advocates the establishment of sanctuaries to protect the coral structures and the animals which live in them. Cousteau's interesting account of this very unusual exploration would particularly interest students of marine science or biology.

Babe: The Legend Comes to Life
by Robert Creamer

Babe Ruth, a man whose name is synonymous with baseball greatness, began his playing career at an orphanage in Baltimore. His life totally changed when George Hermann Ruth joined his first professional team when he was twenty. Babe's career paralleled the formation of professional baseball. Rivalry between owners of various clubs made regulations necessary. This need resulted in the formation of the American and National leagues. First with the Boston Red Sox and later with the New York Yankees, Babe Ruth helped to change the style of the game. Off the field, Babe caused great problems for his managers by his after-hours antics. Babe's marriage was wrecked by his love of fast living. After his playing days were over, Babe's reputation as a playboy kept him from getting a job as a manager. In the ballpark his performances were geared to please the fans. He first pitched and then played first base. His real triumphs came at the plate, as the home run king. This biography contains an excellent account of the formative years of baseball, and of Babe Ruth, one of the game's brightest stars.

Citizen Tom Paine
by Howard Fast

This fictionalized biography portrays the down-and-out Englishman whose fiery rhetoric sparked the American Revolution. Paine was abused as a child. His wife died in poverty in the gin mills of London. On the advice of Benjamin Franklin, Paine came to America. His alliance with printer Robert Bell resulted in "The Crisis Papers," which put heart into the American cause during the dark years of 1776-1777. Paine was a social misfit, whose crude manners, sloppy dress, and excessive drinking were an embarrassment to aristocrats Washington and Jefferson. Paine could establish no roots, although he ached to belong. He rejected love because he was too insecure to maintain a lasting relationship. After peace came, Paine no longer belonged in America. He went to England to stir up the lower classes there. After being driven from England as a traitor, Paine went to France. At first Paine was hailed as a hero in the emotional excesses of the new French Republic. After the Revolution in the 1790s became more extreme, Paine was imprisoned. He was freed after Napoleon came to power. Paine returned to America to be condemned as an atheist, and to die broken and unknown. Although leading a tragic personal life, Tom Paine was a firebrand of ideas. He became a citizen of the world when he said, "Where revolution is, there is my country."

I Always Wanted to Be Somebody
by Althea Gibson

As she paved the way for other black athletes in the 1950s and 1960s, tennis champion Althea Gibson made the long journey from the streets of Harlem to the center court at Wimbledon, England. She became toughened as a child, learning to box so she could hold her own in gang battles. Inspired by her idol Sugar Ray Robinson, Althea fought the racial prejudice which denied her access to court facilities and tournaments. Assisted by friends who gave her opportunities to attend school and encouraged by her coach Sidney Llwellyn, Althea fought her way upward. She managed to establish herself on equal terms with all athletes, black and white. She had many adventures and made many friends as she toured the world playing exhibition tennis for the U.S. State Department. Finally she became a Wimbledon champion, honored at a luncheon given by the mayor of New York. Gibson's story shows that her quest for excellence was aided by her determination to succeed. She feels it is more important to be a top player than simply to become a racial symbol.

All Creatures Great and Small
by James Herriot

Working as a veterinarian in Yorkshire, England in the 1930s was, for James Herriot, unsettling at best. Herriot tells with humor of his boss, Sigfried Farnon, who was totally disorganized and always blamed everyone else for his mistakes. Herriot had many harrowing experiences as he traveled to isolated farms and had to work with the most primitive equipment. Another difficulty was the superstition of the farmers, who distrusted any new technique. Herriot presents a wonderful cast of Yorkshire characters: Tristan, Sigfried's playboy brother, Mrs. Pumphrey, whose pampered dog Tricki adopted James as his "uncle," Mr. Cranford, who tried to collect on a fake insurance claim, and Mrs. Hall, the wonderful housekeeper who looked after the young doctors. An important part of this autobiography is a love story. When James meets and marries Helen, their honeymoon turns into a round of emergency house calls. This firsthand picture of the irregularities of a vet's life and the local color of rural England make this book well worth reading.

Teacher: Anne Sullivan Macy
by Helen Keller

As a companion to *The Miracle Worker*, this book is Helen Keller's tribute to Teacher, the woman whose dedication unlocked Helen's mind. Teacher used every ounce of her strength and all of her own failing eyesight to help Helen become an independent person. Teacher opposed special institutions for the handicapped because she felt that such places cut people off from the real world. When Helen attended Radcliffe College, she had difficulty obtaining Braille books. Teacher read to her the texts that were not available. Learning to type provided Helen with an increased measure of independence. As she helped Helen, Anne Sullivan also battled her own mood swings and bouts with depression. The two women shared a love of dogs and poetry. They faced catastrophe together when a fire destroyed many of their precious manuscripts. After Anne's death, Polly Thompson became Helen's companion. During World War II, the two women traveled the world to encourage those who were handicapped or injured. Anne's determination to learn and to be free lived on in Helen, as the pupil continued to carry on the teacher's work. *Teacher* shows by the example of Anne Sullivan how love and dedication can make all the difference.

Joseph
by Joyce Landorf

This novel is a fictionalized retelling of the Biblical success story of Joseph, the Hebrew dreamer who became prime minister of Egypt. The story traces the influence that the women in his life had on the development of Joseph's personality. His mother Rachel taught her son the ways of God and how to exercise special mystical gifts. Sherah, wife of Joseph's elder brother Judah, was Joseph's friend during his teenage years. She wove, at the request of his father Jacob, Joseph's coat of many colors, which stirred the envy of his brothers when the garment set Joseph apart as the special son. As a result of his brothers' jealousy, Joseph was sold into Egyptian slavery. After he rose to become overseer of the house of Potiphar, Joseph had to cling to his moral principles and resist the love of Khumet, Potiphar's wife. After being imprisoned on false pretenses, Joseph is freed when he interprets the king's strange dreams. After becoming governor general of Egypt, Joseph is supported by his loving wife Asenath. The young man is reconciled with his family after he confronts the brothers who betrayed him. A story of one man's preparation for greatness, *Joseph* combines well the narrative of the Bible with an excellent account of the historical Egyptian background.

Auntie Mame
by Jerome Lawrence and Robert E. Lee

This comedy, based on the book by Patrick Dennis, is a marvelous tribute to human optimism. In the 1920s, orphaned Patrick Dennis is thrust into the madcap world of his loving, but very eccentric, Auntie Mame. For both Mame and Patrick, the relationship is love at first sight. Mame feels that the boy should experience life firsthand. She battles the efforts of Mr. Babcock, who has been appointed Patrick's trustee, to imprison the boy's mind. When the financial world collapses in 1929, Mame goes to work. While selling roller skates, Mame meets the love of her life, Beauregard Burnside. During a trip to Beau's plantation, Mame wins the hearts of his southern family when she outrides the fox in the hunt. Beau and Mame spend their married life on a long honeymoon, until Beau is killed in an avalanche. Meanwhile, Patrick, attending exclusive schools and colleges, is turning into a snob. After Mame returns to New York, she meets the upper-crust Upsons, parents of Patrick's fiancée Gloria. Meanwhile, Mame has a new cause to work on. Having encouraged her secretary, Agnes Gooch, to experiment with life, Mame must now help Agnes cope with the consequences. In the play's hilarious concluding scene, Mame gives an intimate family dinner which reveals what phonies the Upsons really are. A wonderful play, *Auntie Mame* illustrates the philosophy that life should be lived to its fullest.

The Contender
by Robert Lipsyte

Two black teenagers, Alfred Higgins and his friend James, both need a way out of Harlem. James begins to escape through drugs; that escape begins to destroy him. Alfred finds a better way. He begins training at Mr. Donatelli's gym to become a boxer. His aunt Pearl doesn't understand Alfred's choice, but she does understand his need for a dream. Alfred learns self-discipline by attending workouts, jogging and restricting his diet. He is encouraged by his boss, Mr. Epstein (who had been a boxer himself), and by his friend Spoon, a former fighter who is now a teacher. Although Alfred is successful in a few fights, Donatelli will not allow him to go on because the risk of injury is too great. Alfred, however, has found his self-respect. Spoon encourages him to go to school so he can have a profession when his boxing career is over. James is reaping the consequences of his choice. Alfred learns that his friend is hooked on heroin and is in trouble with the police. After finding James hiding in a cave, Alfred persuades his friend to go to the authorities for help. *The Contender* is a powerful novel about the consequences of decisions.

My Life
by Golda Meir

This powerful autobiography tells of the Russian immigrant girl who became Prime Minister of Israel. Golda's family emigrated from Russia to Milwaukee, Wisconsin when Golda was a child. As a teenager, Golda became increasingly involved in Zionist and labor activities. After marrying Morris Meyerson, Golda and her husband emigrated to Palestine in the 1920s. Life was hard, but Golda loved the challenge. As she became increasingly involved in labor politics in the 1930s, Golda's marriage fell apart. Although she and Morris remained friends, Golda chose to put the cause of the Jewish state above her personal life. Mrs. Meir describes from her personal experience the struggle against the Arabs and the British which resulted in the formation of the state of Israel in 1948. After working as a fundraiser in the 1950s to make Americans aware of Israel's cause, Mrs. Meir entered the government. She describes the loneliness of this very public life. Golda became Labor Minister, Foreign Minister, and finally Prime Minister. She expresses the anger she felt when other nations did not fulfill their promises to Israel. She feels that the nation can never compromise, especially with the Arab extremists, even if Israel has to fight alone. My Life, a book for students who are good readers, presents the personal history of one woman who has made a great impact on her world.

The Death of a Salesman
by Arthur Miller

This powerful social drama presents the personal history of Willy Loman, a little man whose life is being crushed and who has nothing to live on except the crumbs of past dreams. Because he can no longer cover his New England sales territory, Willy's salary is taken away. He is finally fired by the son of his former boss because Willy can no longer produce. His sons, Happy and Biff, are also failures; one is a playboy and the other is a thief. Willy's wife Linda is desperately trying to hold her husband's world together. She vainly cries out that a human being is being destroyed, but no one is taking notice. The play's plot includes a series of flashbacks which show Willy's past hopes and Biff's disillusionment when the young man finds his father in a Boston hotel room with a prostitute. At the play's end, Willy commits suicide as his only way out. Miller's play is strong drama, the account of a little man devoured by an inhuman system.

The Greatest Story Ever Told
by Fulton Oursler

This account of the life of Jesus of Nazareth is well-adapted from the Gospels. Jesus, the special Son, has solid family training as he is instructed by his father, Joseph, in the traditions of the Jewish religion and in the trade of a carpenter. At the age of thirty, Jesus begins his ministry and chooses the men who will help Him. Although the common people welcome His teachings as words of hope, the political leaders see Jesus as a threat and begin plotting His destruction. This plotting leads to betrayal by one of His own disciples, arrest, condemnation, and death on a Roman cross. After Jesus's death, however, Annas, one of the priests who plotted the teacher's destruction, states that the Jewish leaders may have made a mistake. The ideas that Jesus preached, the lessons of love instead of legalism, become stronger after His death and will go on forever. Oursler's very readable account of the life and words of Jesus help the reader to understand why the life of this one man had such an impact on the world.

The Teahouse of the August Moon
by John Patrick

This comedy is set on the island of Okinawa during the late 1940s, the period of American occupation after World War II. Captain Fisby, who has failed at every assignment the Army has given him, is sent to Tokobi to carry out Plan B, to turn the small village into a model of democracy. Fisby finds that the town educates him, since he finds there a peace and wisdom that do not need American help. The town is set on a firm economic base as the natives manufacture brandy from sweet potatoes. Fisby totally adopts the village ways and accepts the gift of a geisha girl Lotus Blossom. Instead of building a school, Fisby builds a teahouse. The horrified military authorities order Fisby to tear down the teahouse and accuse him of failing to follow military procedure. The officers quickly reverse their decision when they learn that a congressional committee is coming to examine Tokobi as a model of economic stability. This play provides a comic look at the tendency of Americans to impose "civilization" on people who may themselves be more civilized in the long run.

The Paper Lion
by George Plimpton

To get an inside look at professional football, reporter Plimpton "joined" the Detroit Lions. He attended training camp, went through the strenuous physical routines, and sat through classes. The reporter learned that playing football requires mental skill as well as physical prowess. The playbook becomes a most important part of each player's equipment. Plimpton shared the players' love of practical jokes. He sweated with the rookies on "The Night of the Squeaky Shoes," when those who did not make the grade were cut from the squad. Although Plimpton was listed as a quarterback, he had to practice his plays by throwing to the neighborhood kids who haunted the playing field. His helmet never did fit properly. Plimpton was allowed to play briefly in an intersquad game; he fumbled every play he attempted. George could not play in a regular game because the commissioner was afraid he would be seriously injured. This book provides a special look at the team spirit of football, with which the players supported each other on the field and off. Plimpton's experiences had both comic and serious moments. He learned that winning was done by the team unit, not by one star or individual.

My Name is Asher Lev
by Chaim Potok

This novel presents the tortured world of a young Jewish artist whose talent comes into conflict with his family and his faith. Asher's family came to New York from the U.S.S.R. during the 1960s. His parents are Zionists, involved in helping other Jews escape from the U.S.S.R. As a child, Asher shows strong intuitive sense and a great talent for drawing. Mr. Krinsky, a neighborhood store owner and Asher's "father substitute," helps the boy understand what being Jewish really means. Although Asher's father feels that the boy's drawings are sacrilege, the Rebbe, leader of the congregation, understands this special talent and makes arrangements for Asher to study with Jacob Kahn. Kahn teaches Asher important principles of art and life. Asher's first exhibit is a great success. However, he finds that his audiences do not always want to see the feelings he has painted. When Asher's greatest exhibit includes a Crucifixion scene and his parents see themselves in the painting, the family violently repudiates the young artist. Asher, however, must go on with his work. His art becomes an act of religious expression intended to bring God into the sufferings of all men. This novel would be appropriate for students who are good readers, especially those who have special artistic or musical gifts.

The Camera Never Blinks
by Dan Rather with Mickey Hershowitz

Rather began studying journalism at a small southern college with Hugh Cunningham. Cunningham taught his students to be on the spot, to go where the news was. Rather's book gives a firsthand account of his career. He barely escaped Hurricane Carla on the coast of Texas. This daring reporting gave him a national reputation. Rather later had narrow escapes in Vietnam. He was in Dallas when Kennedy was shot in 1963. He became the favorite target of the Nixon White House because of Rather's many confrontations with the President's men during the Watergate era. Rather acknowledges his debt to Hugh Kendrick, who helped him learn the techniques of foreign reporting when Dan was on assignment in London. His friend Morris Frank helped by telling Rather that the real future in communications was in television, not radio. Veteran newsman Walter Cronkite served as a great example of the honest communicator. Rather also pays tribute to his wife Jean, who copes with the demands that Dan's job makes on their family life. For Dan Rather, television shows the world as it is. "The camera never blinks." A newsman must be daring enough to go after the story, wherever it is. Rather provides a good example of such a newsman, who will stick to his guns under pressure and present the news as he honestly sees it. His book is a superb look inside the world of mass communications.

Go Up for Glory
by Bill Russell

This book is the public and personal account of the great star of the Boston Celtics. The star describes growing up in Louisiana and California. He first played college basketball at the University of San Francisco. Next came an Olympic gold medal won at the games in Melbourne, Australia. Playing professionally for coach Red Auerbach, Russell developed the special technique of throwing opponents off guard by making them move out of their accustomed patterns. Besides the excitement of the game, Russell also writes about the loneliness he felt while the team was on the road. In some southern cities, Bill was forced to stay at a separate hotel from his teammates because he was black. He also had to battle the pain of arthritis. This is a very optimistic personal memoir. As an athlete and as a black man, Bill Russell has found his maturity. He believes that America can best serve blacks by providing an open economic system in which each citizen, regardless of color, can reach for his or her best. The book gives the reader both the excitement of the basketball court and the opinions of Bill Russell, the man.

Anchorwoman
by Jessica Savitch

Because she broke ground for women to attain top positions in communications, Jessica Savitch was an important pioneer of the 1960s and 1970s. Her first jobs were modeling and doing commercials. When Jessica desired to become a serious news reporter, she was told that there was "no room for broads in broadcasting." Jessica finally got a job with a CBS affiliate station in Houston. Male reporters and cameramen, however, were reluctant to work with her. She overcame their prejudices by providing coverage which was sensitive and significant. Professional success came very suddenly. Jessica learned the importance of creating an image as a newscaster. She became a news anchorwoman in Philadelphia. Jessica then gained national exposure when she was assigned by CBS to the 1972 election night coverage. Savitch's book acknowledges those who helped her career. Joan Showalter of CBS helped her create a television image. Reporters Charles Osgood and Ed Bradley taught her the principles of newswriting and copy editing. *Anchorwoman* contains both humorous and serious moments. Jessica had to learn to laugh at her own mistakes. She also had to resume her career after having to cope with her husband's suicide. Jessica Savitch's death in 1983 was a great loss to the communications industry. Her legacy was an open door for women to compete equally with men for top posts as newscasters.

Babe Didrikson: The World's Greatest Woman Athlete
by Gene Schoor

Babe Didrikson Zaharias was a champion in many sports, among them track and field, basketball, and golf. She was the first woman to win, in the 1930s, multiple Olympic medals in track and field events. In golf, Babe was a real pioneer. In the 1940s, she helped to establish ladies' professional golf, and to help the sport grow to tournament proportions. Her beloved husband George was her most important fan. Never the remote athlete, Babe talked with the fans and was loved by people wherever she went. Babe's greatest victory came in her fight against cancer. Twice she returned to play tournament golf after she had had surgery. She was the first American woman to win the British Open. Babe's story provides an example of a woman who did what others said could not be done. She fought for life until her death at the age of forty-five. Because her example still stands for courage, the trophy honoring America's finest women athletes is named for Babe Didrikson Zaharias.

Pygmalion
by George Bernard Shaw

This play pokes fun at the pretensions of British society as the plot recounts the success of a phonetics teacher who transforms a flower girl into a duchess. When Henry Higgins finds Eliza Doolittle sitting in the gutter at Covent Garden, he makes a bet with his friend Pickering that he can pass the girl off as nobility in high society in six months. Eliza wins Higgins' bet, but totally surprises the professor by rebelling against his total indifference to her as a person. Higgins is shocked to learn that his flower girl has feelings, and that she has the nerve to criticize *his* bad manners. After Eliza leaves him, Higgins learns how much he really misses her. A great source of comedy in the play is Eliza's cockney father Alfie, who mocks the code of traditional morality. Shaw presents the superficial nature of all social distinctions made by class labeling. The only difference, Eliza states, "between a lady and a flower girl is not how she acts, but how she is treated." *Pygmalion* is typical of Shaw's ironic attitude toward the failings of the human race.

The Prime of Miss Jean Brodie
by Muriel Spark

Jean Brodie, an instructor at the Marcia Blaine School in Edinburgh in the 1930s, is famous for her eccentric teaching methods. Miss Brodie battles the system and her archenemy Miss McKay to control the minds of "her girls." She also uses the girls as intermediaries in her love affairs with Mr. Lloyd, the art teacher, and Mr. Lowther, the singing teacher. Being in her prime, Miss Brodie totally captivates the minds of those around her. Finally, Sandy, one of Miss Brodie's special girls, rebels, and betrays the teacher to the school authorities. As a teacher, Miss Brodie was a failure because she only encouraged her students to copy her thought patterns. Her success, however, came in teaching her girls to be different so that they could escape from the mold into which she herself had poured them.

The Playboy of the Western World
by John M. Synge

As the play opens, Christy Mahon gains instant status when he arrives in a small Irish village and announces to everyone that he has just killed his father. Christy becomes particularly attractive to Pegeen, since the stranger seems to be a total foil to the ineffectual Shawn whom she had intended to marry. Christy continues to live up to his heroic reputation until his father, very much alive, arrives in town. The son had merely hit the old man with a hoe. Christy turns out to be not the great playboy but an average man who had lost his temper. This comedy shows that sometimes strength of character can be created as a reflection of the way that others see us. People can be very disappointed when truth turns out to be much less exciting than fantasy. Synge's play presents fine Irish local color and excellent dialogue for comic effects.

The House of Mirth
by Edith Wharton

Lily Bart has been educated to be a beauty in high society. After her father's financial failure and her mother's death, Lily has no skills. She is left at the mercy of her aunt, Mrs. Penniston. Lily becomes involved with a social set whose standards and customs she cannot afford. Her only hope is a wealthy marriage. Lily's one real relationship is with Lawrence Seldon, who understands Lily because both of them are social outsiders. Lily is fond of Seldon, but she loves high society more. Getting increasingly into debt, Lily is used and betrayed by her rich friends. She is disinherited when her aunt learns of her gambling. Lily's circumstances go from bad to worse, since she cannot hold a job and becomes ill. Now she can only watch her former friends as the society folk parade up Fifth Avenue in their elaborate carriages. Lily gains nobility that these others will never know as she manages to pay all of her debts and refuses to stoop to blackmail. After Lily's suicide, Seldon looks on her shattered beauty and realizes too late that he really loved her. The author's title for this novel is highly ironic. Wharton knew all too well that the New York society in which she herself had lived was cruel, wasteful, and superficial. Although Lily Bart is destroyed by this viciousness, she is above them all at the end because she dies obligated to no one.

NAME _____ DATE _____

Life and Death in a Coral Sea by Jacques-Yves Cousteau

Place a (+) before each statement that is true and a (0) before each statement that is false.

_____ 1. Coral is a complex system of both plant and animal life.

_____ 2. Cousteau and his men first began exploring the Red Sea in 1951.

_____ 3. Although the *Calypso*'s crew is international, much of the money for the expeditions comes through contracts with the United States government.

_____ 4. Sharks are the only real danger to divers working in deep ocean water.

_____ 5. One great key to the *Calypso*'s success has been the teamwork of the men involved.

_____ 6. *Calypso* was built in Great Britain for service in World War II.

_____ 7. One big problem was finding enough storage space for all of the necessary scientific equipment.

_____ 8. The "Sea Fleas" each held two men at a time.

_____ 9. Divers were able to transmit the human voice from depths below 200 feet.

_____ 10. Cousteau found that the coral formations had changed little from his previous visits.

_____ 11. The islands of the Indian Ocean are largely uninhabited.

_____ 12. "Rapture of the deep" occurs when too much oxygen gets into the blood.

_____ 13. Oil tankers pose one of the greatest threats to the survival of undersea life.

_____ 14. In spite of the Mid-East War of 1967, the work of the *Calypso* continued without interruption.

_____ 15. The creatures of the undersea world are more active in the daytime than they are at night.

_____ 16. Cousteau has found proof that the water level of the Indian Ocean is lower now than it was in prehistoric times.

_____ 17. The United States has established a sanctuary to preserve coral life off the coast of California.

_____ 18. Parrot fish helped to build coral reefs by creating large quantities of sand.

_____ 19. Traveling in schools helps to protect sea creatures from natural enemies.

_____ 20. Cousteau and his men helped the Navy raise several sunken ships to the surface.

NAME _____ DATE _____

Life and Death in a Coral Sea by Jacques-Yves Cousteau

Answer each of the following questions in two or three complete sentences.

1. What special features were added to the *Calypso* to make her more suitable for the task of underwater exploration?

   _____

   _____

   _____

   _____

2. Why is the coral of the Red Sea especially vulnerable to the killing forces of man's civilization?

   _____

   _____

   _____

   _____

3. How did Cousteau's men become at home both on the water and in it?

   _____

   _____

   _____

   _____

4. What difficulties did the divers encounter in their efforts to film the world under the sea?

   _____

   _____

   _____

   _____

5. What new kinds of equipment did Cousteau's team pioneer which made it possible for them to explore greater depths of the ocean world?

   _____

   _____

   _____

   _____

CHALLENGE

Write an essay summarizing Cousteau's fears for the safety of the sea. What changes does he say that man must make if the coral world is to survive for another generation?

NAME _____ DATE _____

301

Babe: The Legend Comes to Life by Robert W. Creamer

Select the letter of the word or phrase which correctly completes each statement.

_____ 1. Babe Ruth was a native of (A) Baltimore (B) Boston (C) Chicago (D) New York.

_____ 2. Ruth's father (A) died in World War I (B) abandoned his wife and children (C) ran a saloon (D) was also a baseball player.

_____ 3. The person most responsible for Ruth's adolescent character development was (A) his grandfather (B) Brother Matthias (C) Jack Dunn (D) Father Benson.

_____ 4. Ruth first played professional baseball in (A) Baltimore (B) Boston (C) Washington (D) New York.

_____ 5. Ruth joined his first professional team when he was (A) sixteen (B) twenty (C) nineteen (D) twenty-three.

_____ 6. The greatest threat to Dunn's Baltimore team was (A) poor managing (B) a rival baseball team (C) poor players (D) a poor playing field.

_____ 7. Ruth got the nickname "Babe" (A) at St. Mary's school (B) while he played with the Red Sox (C) during his first year's spring training (D) as a kid on the streets.

_____ 8. The first position Ruth played was (A) catcher (B) pitcher (C) center field (D) first base.

_____ 9. Ruth became most famous for (A) his wide swing (B) his batting stance (C) his frequent strike-outs (D) his fielding ability.

_____ 10. Ruth's first major league manager was (A) Lannin (B) Dunn (C) Shore (D) Carrigan.

_____ 11. Off the field, Ruth became known for (A) his practical jokes (B) his appetite (C) his escapades with women (D) all of the above.

_____ 12. Ruth first helped a team win a pennant in (A) Providence (B) New York (C) Boston (D) Baltimore.

_____ 13. Ruth's batting ability included great (A) speed (B) distance (C) strength (D) all of the above.

_____ 14. Ruth was sold to the New York Yankees by (A) Lannin (B) Frazee (C) Yawkee (D) Ruppert.

_____ 15. The 1918 season was shortened when (A) the weather was bad (B) all of the players expected to be drafted (C) players were ordered to do work that was necessary to the war (D) the players went on strike.

_____ 16. Helen Ruth (A) shared all of her husband's life (B) committed suicide (C) was treated by Babe with tragic indifference (D) divorced Babe.

_____ 17. Barrow's quarrel with Ruth concerned Babe's (A) night life (B) salary (C) batting stance (D) position in the line-up.

_____ 18. Babes salary figure of $80,000 was higher than (A) the manager's (B) the club owner's (C) the President of the United States (D) the president of US Steel.

_____ 19. The biggest disappointment of Ruth's life was (A) the failure of his marriage (B) his failure to get a managing position (C) his physical illness (D) having to take a cut in salary.

_____ 20. The people Ruth was always closest to were (A) children (B) coaches (C) other ball players (D) reporters.

NAME _____ DATE _____

Babe: The Legend Comes to Life by Robert W. Creamer

Answer each of the following questions in two or three complete sentences.

1. How did becoming a baseball player change young George Ruth's life?

   _____

   _____

   _____

   _____

2. Why was Babe Ruth so difficult for various managers to deal with?

   _____

   _____

   _____

   _____

3. How did the game of baseball change in the 1920s?

   _____

   _____

   _____

   _____

4. Why was Ruth's marriage to Helen a failure?

   _____

   _____

   _____

   _____

5. In what ways were Ruth's last years filled with disappointment and tragedy?

   _____

   _____

   _____

   _____

CHALLENGE

Discuss the ways that Babe Ruth changed the game of baseball. Why was he indeed a "legend"?

NAME _____ DATE _____

Citizen Tom Paine by Howard Fast

In the numbered blanks at the left, write the letter of the matching person or place.

_____ 1. Seemed to abandon Paine when he was a prisoner in France

_____ 2. Paine's first employer in America

_____ 3. Paine's hometown in England

_____ 4. Paine's young wife who died of TB

_____ 5. People that Paine lived with just before his death

_____ 6. Paine's "small book"

_____ 7. Paine's English printer who was accused of treason

_____ 8. Loved Paine and nursed him back to health

_____ 9. Leader of the extremist faction in the French Revolution

_____ 10. Series of pamphlets written to inspire the American troops

_____ 11. First urged Paine to go to America

_____ 12. Inspired Paine to write for the revolutionary cause

_____ 13. Written during the French Revolution

_____ 14. Boyhood friend of Paine's who was hanged

_____ 15. American printer of Paine's pamphlets

_____ 16. Commander of the American troops at Lexington

_____ 17. Work published and banned in England

_____ 18. Farmer whose life represented to Paine the best of the American ideal

_____ 19. Poet and painter friend of Paine's in England

_____ 20. Gave Paine the key to the Bastille

A. Franklin
B. Robert Aitken
C. Alec Stivvens
D. Colonel Parker
E. Mary Lambert
F. Jefferson
G. Jacob Rumpel
H. *Common Sense*
I. Robert Bell
J. *Crisis Papers*
K. Washington
L. Irene Roberdeau
M. *Rights of Man*
N. Thetford
O. Lafayette
P. Jordan
Q. William Blake
R. Danton
S. *Age of Reason*
T. Bonnevilles

NAME _____ DATE _____

Citizen Tom Paine by Howard Fast

Answer each of the following questions in two or three complete sentences.

1. What experiences in Paine's early life helped to make him a revolutionary?

_____

_____

_____

_____

2. What special contributions did Paine make to the American Revolution?

_____

_____

_____

_____

3. Why did Paine's revolutionary ideas fail in England?

_____

_____

_____

_____

4. Why was Paine first accepted and then rejected in France?

_____

_____

_____

_____

5. Why was Paine never able to find personal love and security?

_____

_____

_____

_____

CHALLENGE

Support with evidence from this book that Thomas Paine was indeed a "citizen of the world."

NAME _____ DATE _____

I Always Wanted to Be Somebody by Althea Gibson

In the numbered blanks at the left, write the letter of the matching person or place.

_____ 1. Gave a luncheon in Althea's honor

_____ 2. Section of New York where Althea grew up

_____ 3. Governing organization for American amateur tennis

_____ 4. Team tennis tournament where Althea represented the United States

_____ 5. Provided a home and tennis instruction for Althea while she finished high school

_____ 6. Black athlete who was Althea's childhood idol, and later her friend

_____ 7. Presented Althea with her first Wimbledon trophy

_____ 8. Most important American tennis tournament

_____ 9. Woman tennis champion who was Althea's inspiration

_____ 10. Althea's tennis coach

_____ 11. Theater in Harlem where Althea attended movies and stage shows

_____ 12. Relative with whom Althea lived as a child

_____ 13. Althea's close English friend

_____ 14. Where Althea went to college

_____ 15. The world series championship of tennis

_____ 16. Where Althea had a job as a physical education instructor

_____ 17. Althea's traveling companion on the world tour for the U.S. State Department

_____ 18. Man who first introduced Althea to court tennis

_____ 19. Althea's second family with whom she lived in New Jersey

_____ 20. Traveled with Althea on a tour to Australia

A. Apollo
B. Wightman Cup
C. Mayor Robert F. Wagner
D. Queen Elizabeth
E. Shirley Fry
F. Angela Buxton
G. Karol Fageros
H. Sydney Llewellyn
I. Lincoln University
J. Darbens
K. USLTA
L. Dr. Hubert Eaton
M. Florida A. & M.
N. Alice Marble
O. Buddy Walker
P. Forest Hills
Q. Wimbledon
R. Aunt Daisey
S. Sugar Ray Robinson
T. Harlem

NAME _____ DATE _____

I Always Wanted to Be Somebody by Althea Gibson

Answer each of the following questions in two or three complete sentences.

1. How did Althea learn to survive on the streets of New York?

   _____

   _____

   _____

   _____

2. What were some of the important influences in changing Althea from a young rebel into a serious athlete?

   _____

   _____

   _____

   _____

3. Describe Althea's feelings about living and attending school in the South.

   _____

   _____

   _____

   _____

4. Why was her Asian tour for the State Department an important turning point in Althea Gibson's career?

   _____

   _____

   _____

   _____

5. What does Althea Gibson herself consider to be her major strengths and weaknesses as an athlete?

   _____

   _____

   _____

   _____

CHALLENGE

Describe Althea Gibson's attitudes toward being the first black woman to win the world championship of tennis. Which does she feel is more important, breaking a color barrier or achieving excellence in her sport?

NAME _____ DATE _____

All Creatures Great and Small by James Herriot

In the numbered blanks at the left, write the letter of the matching person or place.

_____ 1. Ran the village pub

_____ 2. Tried to collect on a fake insurance claim

_____ 3. The village "playboy"

_____ 4. The housekeeper for the doctors

_____ 5. Eccentric rich lady who spoiled her pets

_____ 6. Stingy Scottish vet for whom James had to work occasionally

_____ 7. James' boss

_____ 8. Sickly woman who loved her dogs and cats like people

_____ 9. House where James lived

_____ 10. Superefficient secretary

_____ 11. Sigfried's best friend in college

_____ 12. James's wife

_____ 13. Adopted James as his "uncle"

_____ 14. Disposed of all the dead animals

_____ 15. Area of England where the book takes place

A. Sigfried Farnon
B. Tristan
C. Helen
D. Mrs. Hall
E. Mrs. Pumphrey
F. Miss Hardbottle
G. Tricki
H. Yorkshire Dales
I. Miss Stubbs
J. Stewie Brannon
K. Skedale
L. Mr. Worley
M. Angus Grier
N. Jeff Mallock
O. Mr. Cranford

NAME _____ DATE _____

All Creatures Great and Small by James Herriot

Answer each of the following questions in two or three complete sentences.

1. What were James' first impressions when he arrived to interview for his job as assistant veterinarian?

    _____

    _____

    _____

    _____

2. List three real hardships which were connected with James' work.

    _____

    _____

    _____

    _____

3. Contrast the personalities of James and Tristan.

    _____

    _____

    _____

    _____

4. Why was working with Sigfried sometimes so difficult for James?

    _____

    _____

    _____

    _____

5. Describe briefly the countryside where this book is set.

    _____

    _____

    _____

    _____

CHALLENGE

How are the personality qualities which make James Herriot a good vet shown in this autobiography?

NAME _____ DATE _____

Teacher: Anne Sullivan Macy by Helen Keller

Correctly complete each sentence with information from the novel.

1. Helen compares the struggle to overcome her handicap to the climbing of _____.

2. Helen uses the term _____ to describe herself before Annie's arrival.

3. Among the first things that Teacher taught Helen were to _____ and to _____.

4. During Helen's adolescence, Teacher used her limited eyesight to read the literature and research about _____.

5. Teacher encouraged Helen to read and memorize _____.

6. Helen was accused of _____ in one of the stories that she published.

7. Teacher opposed special institutions for blind children because _____.

8. Helen's greatest handicap at Radcliffe was _____.

9. Helen lost the first biography of Teacher that she had written when _____.

10. The animals that Teacher loved most were _____ and _____.

11. Helen was greatly influenced by the religious ideas of _____.

12. The skill that made Helen most independent was _____.

13. To make money, Teacher and Helen appeared for several years in _____.

14. As Teacher's sight failed, Helen's helper and companion became _____.

15. Teacher spent a very happy holiday alone in _____.

16. Teacher's major disposition problem was _____.

17. Aside from the Braille alphabet, Helen believed that the greatest invention for the blind was _____.

18. After 1921, Helen worked for the cause of _____.

19. Teacher accepted an honorary degree from _____.

20. After Teacher's death, the first long trip that Helen took was to _____.

NAME _____ DATE _____

Teacher: Anne Sullivan Macy by Helen Keller

Answer each of the following questions in two or three complete sentences.

1. How did Teacher's own experiences aid her in teaching Helen?

    _____

    _____

    _____

    _____

2. Why did Teacher insist on treating Helen as a normal person?

    _____

    _____

    _____

    _____

3. What accusations were brought against Teacher that angered Helen?

    _____

    _____

    _____

    _____

4. What was the strongest difference of opinion between Teacher and Helen?

    _____

    _____

    _____

    _____

5. How has Helen Keller's work grown to encompass the world?

    _____

    _____

    _____

    _____

CHALLENGE

Write an essay describing the special qualities of Anne Sullivan Macy that lived on in Helen Keller.

NAME _____ DATE _____

Joseph by Joyce Landorf

In the numbered blanks at the left, write the letter of the matching person or place.

_____	1. Was unjustly accused of rape
_____	2. Wife of Jacob who was most skilled in domestic duties
_____	3. Gave his son-in-law the wrong daughter as the first bride
_____	4. City destroyed by Jacob's sons for revenge against their sister
_____	5. Egyptian name given to Joseph
_____	6. Died when her second son was born
_____	7. King's wife who loved to play matchmaker
_____	8. Rachel's servant who bore Jacob two sons
_____	9. Joseph's loving Egyptian wife
_____	10. Maker of the coat of many colors
_____	11. Place sacred to Jacob where God appeared to him in dreams
_____	12. Had been trained in her youth to be a temple dancer
_____	13. Butler who had been helped by Joseph in the prison
_____	14. Made the small statues of Laban's gods
_____	15. Eldest son of Jacob who lost his birthright through violent behavior
_____	16. Potiphar's steward, later Joseph's interpreter
_____	17. Wise high priestess of the goddess Hathor
_____	18. Maimed so that he could not function as a husband
_____	19. Scribe who was Joseph's childhood tutor
_____	20. Worked fourteen years for the woman that he really loved

A. Zaphnath-paaneah
B. Essa
C. Asenath
D. Metenu
E. Makara
F. Khnumet
G. Amset
H. Joseph
I. Potiphar
J. Sherah
K. Reuben
L. Shechem
M. Sapher
N. Bilhah
O. Jacob
P. Rachel
Q. Leah
R. Bethel
S. Aaron
T. Laban

NAME _____ DATE _____

Joseph by Joyce Landorf

Answer each of the following questions in two or three complete sentences.

1. How did Laban and Jacob trick each other?

    _____

    _____

    _____

    _____

2. In what ways were Joseph and his mother Rachel alike?

    _____

    _____

    _____

    _____

3. Why did Sherah leave the tents of Jacob's sons?

    _____

    _____

    _____

    _____

4. What did Joseph mean when he told Khnumet that she was his "Schechem"?

    _____

    _____

    _____

    _____

5. Why was Asenath the perfect mate for Joseph?

    _____

    _____

    _____

    _____

CHALLENGE

Write an essay describing the ways in which Joseph's experiences as a boy and as a man prepared him for his role as prime minister of Egypt.

NAME _____ DATE _____

Auntie Mame by Jerome Lawrence and Robert E. Lee

In the numbered blanks at the left, write the letter of the matching person or place.

_____ 1. Mame's trusted Irish housekeeper

_____ 2. Editor hired to help Mame write her autobiography

_____ 3. Famous British actress from Pittsburgh

_____ 4. Becomes Patrick's wife

_____ 5. Is adopted by his aunt after his father dies

_____ 6. Official of the Knickerbocker Bank

_____ 7. Traveled to India with Auntie Mame

_____ 8. The great love of Mame's life

_____ 9. Died at the Chicago Athletic Club

_____ 10. A very restricted Connecticut suburb

_____ 11. Faithful Japanese houseboy

_____ 12. Played with Bunny Bixler in a pingpong tournament

_____ 13. Burnside's plantation

_____ 14. Arranged for Mame to ride Lightning Rod

_____ 15. Headmaster of a very progressive school in Greenwich Village

_____ 16. Worked one Christmas selling roller skates

_____ 17. Mame's secretary

_____ 18. Jewish cellist who founded a home for refugee children

_____ 19. Mame's one role in the theater

_____ 20. Scene of Mame's "intimate family dinner"

A. Patrick
B. Ralph Divine
C. Vera Charles
D. Lady Iris
E. Ito
F. Beekman Place
G. Peckerwood
H. Beauregard Burnside
I. Mr. Babcock
J. Nora
K. Sally Cato
L. Epstein
M. Mountebank
N. Pegeen Ryan
O. Gloria Upson
P. Agnes Gooch
Q. Michael Dennis
R. Edwin Dennis
S. Brian O'Bannion
T. Mame

NAME _____ DATE _____

Auntie Mame by Jerome Lawrence and Robert E. Lee

Answer each of the following questions in two or three complete sentences.

1. Describe Patrick's introduction to his Auntie Mame.

_____

_____

_____

_____

2. How did Mame and Babcock conflict over Patrick's education?

_____

_____

_____

_____

3. How does the Christmas scene show the love among Mame, Patrick, Nora, and Ito?

_____

_____

_____

_____

4. Why is Mame upset over Patrick's choice of Gloria as a wife?

_____

_____

_____

_____

5. How does Mame succeed in opening Patrick's eyes when she gives her little family dinner?

_____

_____

_____

_____

CHALLENGE

Write an essay showing how Mame Dennis Burnside is an illustration of her own theory that life should be lived to its fullest.

NAME _____ DATE _____

The Contender by Robert Lipsyte

Place a (+) before each statement that is true and a (0) before each statement that is false.

_____ 1. James is Alfred's brother.

_____ 2. Going to the movies is one way that Alfred and James escape from reality.

_____ 3. James had helped Alfred through a great family crisis.

_____ 4. James and Major beat Alfred up because Alfred refused to help them rob the Epsteins' store.

_____ 5. Alfred and James go to Donatelli's gym together.

_____ 6. Aunt Pearl approves of Alfred's interest in boxing.

_____ 7. Boxing, for Alfred, is one way to fulfill his desire to become someone special.

_____ 8. Alfred's Uncle Wilson feels that vocational education offers the best opportunities for a black boy.

_____ 9. Jelly is a good example of the self-discipline that a fighter needs.

_____ 10. Lou Epstein, Alfred's boss, had once been a fighter.

_____ 11. Mr. Donatelli takes great precautions so that his fighters will not be injured.

_____ 12. Spoon helped Alfred to understand that education was important.

_____ 13. Alfred learns that James has become a heroin addict.

_____ 14. Alfred is arrested when he goes to Coney Island with Sonny and Major in a stolen car.

_____ 15. Alfred loses his first fight.

_____ 16. A sign of Alfred's success is a robe with his name on the back.

_____ 17. Before each fight, Alfred has a rest and a good meal at Mr. Donatelli's apartment.

_____ 18. During his fight with Rivera, Alfred is hurt because he fails to protect himself properly.

_____ 19. Donatelli urges Alfred to go on to a long boxing career.

_____ 20. At the end of the story, Alfred agrees to protect James from being arrested by the police.

NAME _____ DATE _____

The Contender by Robert Lipsyte

Answer each of the following questions in two or three complete sentences.

1. What negative elements of life in Harlem can Alfred escape if he becomes a boxer?

    _____

    _____

    _____

    _____

2. What does Alfred learn from going to see Willie Streeter fight?

    _____

    _____

    _____

    _____

3. What types of self-discipline does Alfred need to exercise if he is to become a boxer?

    _____

    _____

    _____

    _____

4. Why have Alfred and James been so close? How is this closeness broken?

    _____

    _____

    _____

    _____

5. How does Spoon help Alfred plan for his future?

    _____

    _____

    _____

    _____

CHALLENGE

Success or failure in life is determined in part by the choices that an individual makes for himself. Write an essay to discuss how James's life is destroyed by his wrong choices, and the ways in which Alfred begins to build his life by making the right ones.

NAME _____ DATE _____

My Life by Golda Meir

Select the letter of the word or phrase which correctly completes each statement.

_____ 1. Golda Meir was born in (A) Poland (B) Russia (C) Germany (D) Milwaukee.

_____ 2. The phrase "goldene medina" refers to (A) the afterlife (B) the land of Israel (C) America as a place of opportunity (D) the beauty of the Jewish law.

_____ 3. The first Zionist in Golda's family was (A) her grandmother (B) her father (C) her mother (D) her sister Sheyna.

_____ 4. As a teenager in Milwaukee, Golda became very involved in (A) relief work (B) the Republican party (C) the rising labor movement (D) the Jewish Defense League.

_____ 5. Morris Meyerson first introduced Golda to (A) concerts and poetry (B) the writings of Karl Marx (C) the Jewish Talmud (D) Labor Zionism.

_____ 6. The Balfour Declaration established (A) peace with the Arabs (B) the state of Israel (C) British recognition of the need for a Jewish homeland (D) a standardized policy of immigration.

_____ 7. Difficulties of Golda's early life in Palestine included (A) fleas and bedbugs (B) inadequate housing (C) difficulty in finding a job (D) all of the above.

_____ 8. During the time she lived on the kibbutz, Golda was *not* involved in which of the following? (A) cooking and kitchen management (B) raising poultry (C) cattle breeding (D) politics.

_____ 9. The Histadrut was the organization for (A) Jewish labor (B) religious conservatives (C) industrial pioneers (D) pacifists.

_____ 10. Golda's marriage did not work because (A) she did not love Morris (B) Morris left her for another woman (C) she and Morris disagreed politically (D) service to the country became more important than Golda's personal life.

_____ 11. Jews in Palestine could not help the European Jews who were being threatened by Hitler because (A) the British would not permit open immigration (B) there was no more room for new people in Palestine (C) there was no transportation to bring the refugees in (D) Jews in Palestine were preoccupied with their own problems.

_____ 12. The Haganah was (A) Israel's parliament (B) the Jewish defense organization (C) the political opposition (D) Mrs. Meir's political party.

_____ 13. Mrs. Meir's major task in the United States during the 1950s was as a (A) representative at the U.N. (B) negotiator for arms sales (C) speaker and fund-raiser (D) trade and cultural representative.

_____ 14. Mrs. Meir feels that the single strongest leader during the early years of Israel's statehood was (A) Ben-Gurion (B) Dyan (C) Sharrett (D) Begin.

_____ 15. Golda's longest term of political office was as (A) Ambassador to Russia (B) Labor Minister (C) Foreign Minister (D) Prime Minister.

_____ 16. Significant needs of the new immigrants to Israel included (A) housing (B) language study (C) becoming economically self-sufficient (D) all of the above.

_____ 17. According to Mrs. Meir, Israel's most dangerous enemy was (A) Nasser (B) Hussein (C) Assayd (D) King Feisel.

_____ 18. She feels that Israel's most significant foreign contributions have been made in (A) Russia (B) China (C) Africa (D) Latin America.

_____ 19. Israel was caught offguard by the Arabs during the Yom Kippur War because of the lack of (A) troops (B) planes (C) adequate intelligence (D) foreign allies.

_____ 20. Mrs. Meir's greatest grief while she was Prime Minister was caused by (A) the destruction of Jerusalem's holy places (B) the suffering of Israeli families (C) the failure of Israel's allies to come to her defense (D) the destruction of Israeli farm land.

NAME _____ DATE _____

My Life by Golda Meir

Answer each of the following questions in two or three complete sentences.

1. How did Golda's experiences as a child in Russia influence her feelings about the Zionist movement?

   _____

   _____

   _____

   _____

2. What difficulties did Golda and her family have in getting to Palestine?

   _____

   _____

   _____

   _____

3. Why did the British "White Paper" infuriate the Jews of Palestine?

   _____

   _____

   _____

   _____

4. What special part did Golda's two children have in her life?

   _____

   _____

   _____

   _____

5. Why does Mrs. Meir feel that Israel cannot compromise, even to the demands of allies like the United States?

   _____

   _____

   _____

   _____

CHALLENGE

Write an essay explaining some of the most significant achievements of Golda Meir's fifty-year political career. In what ways is she a powerful symbol of the growth of the state of Israel?

NAME _____ DATE _____

The Death of a Salesman by Arthur Miller

Correctly complete each sentence with information from the play.

1. Willy Loman's sales territory covered _____.

2. Willy did not like his neighborhood any more because _____.

3. The greatest moment of Biff Loman's life had been _____.

4. Biff had not gone on to college because _____.

5. Willy says that a salesman's most important assets are _____ and _____.

6. Willy feels that Biff is a failure because _____.

7. Bernard had succeeded and become _____.

8. Biff agrees to see _____ to ask for a job.

9. Willy's brother Ben got rich by _____.

10. The one solid, steady member of the Loman family is _____.

11. Willy has to keep borrowing money from _____.

12. Biff had been fired from each job he had for _____.

13. Howard Wagner has humiliated Willy by _____.

14. When Willy asks for a New York job, Howard _____.

15. The coil attached to the gas heater shows that Willy _____.

16. _____ offers Willy a job, but Willy refuses.

17. In the Boston hotel, Biff had found _____.

18. Biff and Happy abandon their father _____.

19. Willy dies by _____.

20. On the day that Willy died, Linda had _____.

NAME _____ DATE _____

The Death of a Salesman by Arthur Miller

Answer each of the following questions in two or three complete sentences.

1. What are Willy's happiest memories of his sons?

    _____

    _____

    _____

    _____

2. How do Willy's memories contrast with the reality of his present life?

    _____

    _____

    _____

    _____

3. How is Happy a dreamer like his father?

    _____

    _____

    _____

    _____

4. How does Linda Loman try to protect her husband?

    _____

    _____

    _____

    _____

5. How was Biff's life changed by his one visit to his father in Boston?

    _____

    _____

    _____

    _____

CHALLENGE

Write an essay showing how the experiences of Willy Loman show the terrible things that can happen to a little man whom nobody really notices.

NAME _____ DATE _____

The Greatest Story Ever Told by Fulton Oursler

In the numbered blanks at the left, write the letter of the matching person or place.

_____ 1. Most outspoken and aggressive of the Apostles

_____ 2. Warned her husband not to condemn an innocent man

_____ 3. Powerful political boss of the Jewish hierarchy

_____ 4. Tax collector who became the Apostle Matthew

_____ 5. Priest who was struck dumb until his son was born

_____ 6. King who imprisoned and executed John the Baptist

_____ 7. Had a child in her old age

_____ 8. High priest who engineered Jesus' arrest and trial

_____ 9. Sisters who were close friends of Jesus

_____ 10. Innkeeper's wife who assisted at Jesus' birth

_____ 11. City where Jesus established his preaching headquarters

_____ 12. Treasurer of the disciples' group

_____ 13. Jewish leader who came to speak to Jesus at night

_____ 14. Member of the Sanhedrin who spoke in Jesus's defense

_____ 15. Lived in the wilderness and ate locust and wild honey

_____ 16. Merchant friend of Joseph who became Barrabas the revolutionary

_____ 17. Where Jesus was arrested

_____ 18. Father of Mary

_____ 19. Got her revenge when her daughter danced

_____ 20. Taught the child Jesus the stories of the Old Testament heroes

A. Annas
B. Caiphas
C. Joseph of Arimathea
D. Procula
E. Samuel
F. Sarah
G. Levi
H. Judas Iscariot
I. Joseph
J. Zachary
K. Herodias
L. Elizabeth
M. Joachim
N. Capernaum
O. Peter
P. Gethsemane
Q. Herod Antipas
R. John the Baptist
S. Mary and Martha
T. Nicodemus

NAME _____ DATE _____

The Greatest Story Ever Told by Fulton Oursler

Answer each of the following questions in two or three complete sentences.

1. Why was Joseph the carpenter a good father for the boy Jesus?

    _____
    _____
    _____
    _____

2. What preparations did Jesus make for the beginnings of His ministry?

    _____
    _____
    _____
    _____

3. Why were the Jewish officials so determined to destroy Jesus?

    _____
    _____
    _____
    _____

4. Why was Jesus so popular with the common people?

    _____
    _____
    _____
    _____

5. After Jesus' death, why did Annas believe that they may have made a mistake?

    _____
    _____
    _____
    _____

CHALLENGE

Write an essay summarizing the reasons why Jesus of Nazareth made such a great impact on the society in which He lived.

NAME _____ DATE _____

The Teahouse of the August Moon by John Patrick

Correctly complete each sentence with information from the play.

1. The setting for the play is the island of _____.

2. The narrator for the beginning of each act is _____.

3. The Occupation commander is _____.

4. In all of his previous jobs, Captain Fisby has _____.

5. The village Fisby is sent to is _____.

6. Fisby's job in that village is to _____.

7. The manual used by all Occupation officers is entitled _____.

8. The August moon is supposed to bring a man _____.

9. Lady Astor is the name given to _____.

10. The authority symbol for the mayor of the village is _____.

11. Mr. Oshira's special craft is in making _____.

12. Purdy sends Captain McLean to the village to _____.

13. Fisby gets the village on a sound economic basis when he helps the people manufac-
    ture and sell _____ made from _____.

14. The special "present" that Fisby receives is _____.

15. Instead of a school, Fisby builds the villagers a _____.

16. Lotus Blossom teaches the other village women to _____.

17. Captain McLean gets involved in the village project because he is interested in __

    _____.

18. When Colonel Purdy comes to the village, he orders that _____.

19. Purdy changes his mind when _____.

20. The villagers can easily rebuild the teahouse because _____.

NAME _____ DATE _____

The Teahouse of the August Moon by John Patrick

Answer each of the following questions in two or three complete sentences.

1. What is the attitude of the villagers toward the various armies that have conquered them?

   _____

   _____

   _____

   _____

2. Why does Fisby see this village assignment as a chance to redeem himself?

   _____

   _____

   _____

   _____

3. How is Fisby gradually conquered by those that he is supposed to have conquered?

   _____

   _____

   _____

   _____

4. Why is the teahouse so important to the village?

   _____

   _____

   _____

   _____

5. Why does Fisby refuse to marry Lotus Blossom and take her back to America?

   _____

   _____

   _____

   _____

CHALLENGE

Write an essay explaining the ways that the people of Tokobi are more sensible and civilized than those who have come to "civilize" them.

NAME _____ DATE _____

The Paper Lion by George Plimpton

Correctly complete each sentence with information from the novel.

1. Plimpton wanted to play with the Lions so that he _____.

2. The position Plimpton played was _____.

3. Plimpton's unusual piece of equipment at practices was his _____.

4. The head coach of the Lions was _____.

5. One method of hazing the rookie football players was _____.

6. Practical jokes played in the Lion's dormitories included _____.

7. Training camp was conducted at _____.

8. The players' work time in training camp was divided between _____
   and _____.

9. The piece of equipment that Plimpton had the most trouble with was _____
   _____.

10. The night that the squad cuts were made was called _____.

11. The largest tackle on the Lions' team was named _____.

12. Plimpton practiced his plays by _____.

13. The only actual game that Plimpton played in was _____.

14. The Lion player suspended for a year for gambling was _____.

15. Plimpton did not play in the game against the Cleveland Browns because _____
    _____.

16. Aside from his equipment, the pro player's most valuable possession is _____.

17. _____ was the Lions' equipment manager.

18. The coach put Plimpton in charge of _____.

19. _____ was the Lions' general manager.

20. Plimpton officially represented the Lions at _____.

NAME _____ DATE _____

The Paper Lion by George Plimpton

Answer each of the following questions in two or three complete sentences.

1. How did the players accept Plimpton's presence with the team?

_____

_____

_____

_____

2. Besides physical strength, what other abilities does a pro football player need?

_____

_____

_____

_____

3. What were some of the conditioning exercises and practice drills that were used in training camp?

_____

_____

_____

_____

4. How did Wilson's method of team discipline differ from the method used by Brown, the Cleveland coach?

_____

_____

_____

_____

5. Describe Plimpton's performance during his one game appearance.

_____

_____

_____

_____

CHALLENGE

Write an essay describing the team spirit that George Plimpton found among the Lions' team members. How was this spirit created? Why was this spirit so important to the team's success?

NAME _____ DATE _____

My Name Is Asher Lev by Chaim Potok

Select the letter of the word or phrase which correctly completes each statement.

_____ 1. Asher's family originally came from (A) Poland (B) Russia (C) France (D) Vienna.

_____ 2. In his early drawings, Asher's most frequent subject was (A) the Rebbe (B) his mother (C) his father (D) his mythical ancestor.

_____ 3. Asher's mother suffered a breakdown when (A) her brother died (B) her husband left for Europe (C) she saw Asher's paintings in the gallery (D) she studied too hard.

_____ 4. The family member who gave Asher most encouragement was (A) his mother (B) his uncle (C) his aunt (D) his father.

_____ 5. His mother decided (A) to return to college (B) to study Russian history and culture (C) to finish her dead brother's work (D) all of the above.

_____ 6. Asher first learned the reality of Jewish suffering from (A) Krinsky (B) the Rebbe (C) Uncle Yaakov (D) his father.

_____ 7. Asher's entire childhood was dominated by (A) the Rebbe (B) his schoolwork (C) his drawing (D) his love of nature.

_____ 8. A major crisis comes in the family when Asher (A) refuses to go to Vienna (B) meets Jacob Kahn (C) does poorly in school (D) does not want to study French.

_____ 9. Asher's father feels that painting is (A) sacrilegious (B) foolishness (C) evil (D) all of the above.

_____ 10. Asher horrifies his schoolmates when he (A) draws in a sacred book (B) reads the New Testament (C) fails Talmud (D) takes art lessons.

_____ 11. Arrangements for Kahn to be Asher's teacher are made by (A) his mother (B) the Rebbe (C) Anna Schaeffer (D) Uncle Yitzchok.

_____ 12. Asher is most upset by (A) his parents' quarrels (B) his mother's illness (C) his father's absences (D) his nightmares.

_____ 13. Asher learns his painting techniques by (A) copying great masterpieces (B) visiting museums and galleries (C) drawing nudes (D) all of the above.

_____ 14. Mrs. Lev's main struggles lie in (A) her studies (B) her memories of her brother (C) her husband's frequent absences (D) the conflict between her husband and her son.

_____ 15. Asher's work is presented to the public by (A) Jacob Kahn (B) Anna Schaeffer (C) Yudel Krinsky (D) Chagall.

_____ 16. The most important period of Asher's studies with Kahn was (A) Sunday afternoon (B) summer in Provincetown (C) a trip to Chicago (D) a month in Florence.

_____ 17. Asher's first real studio is a gift from (A) the Rebbe (B) Jacob Kahn (C) his uncle (D) Anna Schaeffer.

_____ 18. Asher saw the world as (A) a happy place (B) a place of pain and suffering (C) a model for his art (D) a place with no sense or meaning.

_____ 19. Asher's family reacted to the Crucifixion paintings with (A) pride (B) horror (C) shame and pain (D) indifference.

_____ 20. Asher leaves his family at the direction of (A) the Rebbe (B) his father (C) Krinsky (D) his mother.

NAME _____ DATE _____

My Name Is Asher Lev by Chaim Potok

Answer each of the following questions in two or three complete sentences.

1. Why was Asher as a child closer to his mother than he was to his father?

    _____

    _____

    _____

    _____

2. In what ways did Yudel Krinsky become a father figure to Asher?

    _____

    _____

    _____

    _____

3. What did Kahn mean when he told Asher that the purpose of art is to give "permanence to feeling"?

    _____

    _____

    _____

    _____

4. Why did Asher fear his artistic gifts?

    _____

    _____

    _____

    _____

5. Why are Asher's attempts to explain his paintings to his father doomed to failure?

    _____

    _____

    _____

    _____

CHALLENGE

Write an essay explaining the causes of Asher Lev's central conflict between being a Jew and being an artist. What are some of the ways in which Asher attempts to resolve this conflict?

NAME _____ DATE _____

The Camera Never Blinks by Dan Rather with Mickey Herskowitz

In the numbered blanks at the left, write the letter of the matching person or place.

_____ 1. Assassin of John F. Kennedy

_____ 2. Dan Rather's co-anchor on *60 Minutes*

_____ 3. Fearless cameraman who traveled with Rather to the "top of the world" in Tibet

_____ 4. Hurricane that helped to make Rather's career

_____ 5. Where Rather had his first real experience with racial violence

_____ 6. Female newscaster with whom Rather had several unpleasant encounters

_____ 7. Rather's first employer on radio

_____ 8. "Grand old man" of American newscasters

_____ 9. Assignment that Rather wanted so that he could be where the action was

_____ 10. First black college student in Mississippi

_____ 11. Most famous newscaster of World War II

_____ 12. Nixon aide who hated all reporters

_____ 13. Believed by Rather to be one of the best speakers of our century

_____ 14. Mrs. Rather

_____ 15. Senior reporter who gave good advice when Rather was sent to London

_____ 16. Shot the only existing films of the Kennedy assassination

_____ 17. Press secretary to Richard Nixon

_____ 18. Rather's college journalism professor

_____ 19. Friend who suggested to Rather that the real future for a career was in television rather than in radio

_____ 20. Scene of Kennedy's death

A. Mike Wallace
B. Walter Cronkite
C. Carla
D. Jean
E. Ron Ziegler
F. Lee Harvey Oswald
G. Hugh Cunningham
H. Pastor Lott
I. Alexander Kendrick
J. Morris Frank
K. James Meredith
L. Oxford, Mississippi
M. Parkland Hospital
N. Martin Luther King
O. Zapruder
P. Carl Sorensen
Q. Vietnam
R. H.R. Haldeman
S. Barbara Walters
T. Edward R. Murrow

NAME _____ DATE _____

The Camera Never Blinks by Dan Rather with Mickey Herskowitz

Answer each of the following questions in two or three complete sentences.

1. What important concepts did Dan Rather gain from Hugh Cunningham? How did this knowledge help to shape Rather's career?

   _____
   _____
   _____
   _____

2. How do the events narrated in this book show that Dan Rather is not afraid of danger or conflict?

   _____
   _____
   _____
   _____

3. Name three of the biggest stories in Rather's career, and tell how each one helped his personal advancement.

   _____
   _____
   _____
   _____

4. Why does Rather call Vietnam "the television war"?

   _____
   _____
   _____
   _____

5. Why did Rather hesitate to leave his White House assignment and go to New York?

   _____
   _____
   _____
   _____

CHALLENGE

Discuss what you feel are some of the major strengths and weaknesses of Dan Rather's personality which are presented in *The Camera Never Blinks*.

NAME _____ DATE _____

Go Up for Glory by Bill Russell

Correctly complete each sentence with information from the novel.

1. Russell spent his early boyhood in _____.

2. In order to get a better job, Bill's father moved the family to _____.

3. The first black hero of Bill's boyhood was _____.

4. In his school days, Bill was always in the shadow of _____.

5. Bill played college basketball at _____.

6. In order to keep his scholarship, an athlete must _____.

7. Bill's college team was called "The Homeless Dons" because _____.

8. Russell won an Olympic gold medal at the games held in _____.

9. Russell's greatest off-court problem as a professional player is _____.

10. His greatest fear is _____.

11. Russell's greatest single professional rival is _____.

12. The man most responsible for founding the NBA was _____.

13. Russell's coach with the Celtics is _____.

14. Russell's business investments include _____.

15. Russell believes that the best way to beat an opponent on the court is _____.

16. The city in which Russell as a player experienced the most racial harrassment was

_____.

17. Later in his career, Russell suffered great pain from _____.

18. According to Russell, the most important thing for every black man is to _____

_____.

19. He believes that the black community in the United States must not _____.

20. Russell's unique contribution to the cause of civil rights in Florida was _____

_____.

NAME _____ DATE _____

Go Up for Glory by Bill Russell

Answer each of the following questions in two or three complete sentences.

1. According to Russell, how do teachers have both positive and negative influence on black children?

   _____

   _____

   _____

   _____

2. Why does Russell feel that the college scholarship system encourages students to cheat?

   _____

   _____

   _____

   _____

3. What does Russell mean by the "quota system" in professional basketball?

   _____

   _____

   _____

   _____

4. Why did Russell invest money in Liberia?

   _____

   _____

   _____

   _____

5. What personal experiences of racial discrimination did Russell have while he played for the Celtics?

   _____

   _____

   _____

   _____

CHALLENGE

Write an essay explaining why Russell feels that the issue of civil rights is really an issue of human rights. What does Russell see as possible solutions to the problem of racial hatred?

NAME _____ DATE _____

Anchorwoman by Jessica Savitch

Place a (+) before each statement that is true and a (0) before each statement that is false.

_____ 1. Jessica's interest in broadcasting began when she was in high school.

_____ 2. Jessica's parents were very much in favor of their daughter having a career in the communications industry.

_____ 3. Jessica's life was greatly changed when her father died.

_____ 4. Because she saw many other women broadcasters on television, Jessica decided to work in television rather than in radio.

_____ 5. When Jessica went to college, very few schools had any courses to train students in radio and television communications.

_____ 6. Jessica's first college job was with the campus radio station.

_____ 7. The professors at Ithaca College gave Jessica a great deal of encouragement to pursue her career goals.

_____ 8. Jessica earned most of her living in the early years of her career modeling and doing commercials.

_____ 9. Jessica's first network job was with NBC.

_____ 10. She got her first real television field experience with a station in Houston, Texas.

_____ 11. Many male cameramen did not want to cover a story accompanied by a female reporter.

_____ 12. Makeup and wardrobe for television are equally complicated for both male and female newspeople.

_____ 13. Jessica Savitch was one of the first female news anchorpersons in the nation.

_____ 14. Jessica's professional success came very suddenly.

_____ 15. Jessica's personal life was for the most part happy and stable.

_____ 16. Jessica Savitch believed that when a reporter covered an in-depth story, he/she must become involved in the experiences of that story.

_____ 17. Television's rating system is not important in the TV news department.

_____ 18. Jessica Savitch was very sensitive to audience criticism of her work.

_____ 19. Jessica's first major assignment in Washington, D.C. was at the White House.

_____ 20. According to Jessica Savitch, presidential election-night coverage is the most important assignment in making or breaking the career of a reporter.

NAME _____ DATE _____

Anchorwoman by Jessica Savitch

Answer each of the following questions in two or three complete sentences.

1. What difficulties did Jessica Savitch have in getting into broadcasting at all?

_____

_____

_____

_____

2. How does this book show that Miss Savitch was very sensitive to the human aspects of the stories that she reported?

_____

_____

_____

_____

3. How do her experiences illustrate the problems that television's technology can create for the reporters and anchorpeople?

_____

_____

_____

_____

4. Name three people who helped Jessica Savitch's career. What did each person contribute to her personal or professional growth?

_____

_____

_____

_____

5. What events related in this book show that Jessica Savitch had a keen sense of humor?

_____

_____

_____

_____

CHALLENGE

Jessica Savitch died in 1983, a year after *Anchorwoman* was published. What would you consider to be Miss Savitch's greatest contributions to her industry and her greatest legacy to other women desiring careers in television?

NAME _____ DATE _____

Babe Didrikson: The World's Greatest Woman Athlete
by Gene Schoor

Place a (+) before each statement that is true and a (0) before each statement that is false.

_____ 1. Babe's family came to the United States from Sweden.

_____ 2. All of the Didriksons were interested in sports.

_____ 3. Babe was the youngest child in her family.

_____ 4. Babe's first Olympic competition was in track and field events.

_____ 5. Babe played on a ladies baseball team that was sponsored by a Dallas insurance company.

_____ 6. Babe won three gold medals in the 1932 Olympics.

_____ 7. After the Olympics, Babe earned money doing a theatrical act.

_____ 8. Babe's debut in the movies was a great success.

_____ 9. Babe made her first real money in sports as a basketball player.

_____ 10. Babe found that she could not be a real success as a tennis player because she could not hit the ball hard enough.

_____ 11. Golf great Bobby Jones influenced Babe in her decision to become a golfer.

_____ 12. During the 1930s and 1940s, many ladies were active in amateur golf.

_____ 13. In whatever sport she competed, Babe never had very much personal contact with the fans.

_____ 14. George Zaharias was a boxer.

_____ 15. After George and Babe were married, George always accompanied Babe on her tournament appearances.

_____ 16. Babe's greatest single golf tournament was played in Great Britain.

_____ 17. After Babe had her first surgery, she never played golf again.

_____ 18. Betty Dodd was Babe's closest friend.

_____ 19. Babe died at the age of sixty-five, ten years after she had retired from golf.

_____ 20. The trophy honoring America's outstanding women athletes is named for Babe Didrikson Zaharias.

NAME _____ DATE _____

Babe Didrikson: The World's Greatest Woman Athlete
by Gene Schoor

Answer each of the following questions in two or three complete sentences.

1. How did Babe's family give her moral support as she began to develop her athletic skills?

   _____

   _____

   _____

   _____

2. Why was Babe's appearance at the AAU Track and Field Championship such a great triumph?

   _____

   _____

   _____

   _____

3. Why was Babe able to relate so well to people everywhere?

   _____

   _____

   _____

   _____

4. Why was winning the British Women's Amateur Golf Championship such an important victory for Babe?

   _____

   _____

   _____

   _____

5. How did Babe's marriage to George give her support and help as an athlete?

   _____

   _____

   _____

   _____

CHALLENGE

Write an essay to discuss the character traits of Babe Didrikson Zaharias which made her a champion. How did she show these same character traits in her battle against cancer?

NAME _____ DATE _____

Pygmalion by George Bernard Shaw

Place a (+) before each statement that is true and a (0) before each statement that is false.

_____ 1. Higgins and Eliza first meet at the opera.

_____ 2. Higgins can determine a man's birthplace by the man's accent.

_____ 3. Eliza at first thinks that Higgins is a policeman.

_____ 4. Pickering and Higgins have met on several previous occasions.

_____ 5. Eliza offers to pay Higgins one pound per week if he will give her speech lessons.

_____ 6. Higgins says that a duchess generally speaks better English than a lady in a flower shop does.

_____ 7. Doolittle comes to Wimpole Street because he is concerned for his daughter's safety.

_____ 8. Doolittle feels that having too much money will ruin his spirit of independence.

_____ 9. Eliza finds in Higgins the perfect model in speech and manners.

_____ 10. Mrs. Pearce takes a very motherly concern for Eliza's welfare.

_____ 11. Higgins finds Eliza to be a very slow pupil.

_____ 12. Mrs. Higgins is anxious to have all of her friends meet her famous son.

_____ 13. Freddy is totally charmed by Eliza's conversation.

_____ 14. While talking with Freddy, Eliza unconsciously reverts to the vocabulary of her lower-class upbringing.

_____ 15. Doolittle is very pleased to have become a gentleman of fortune.

_____ 16. The language expert at the Embassy announces to everyone that Eliza is a Russian princess.

_____ 17. Eliza decides to marry Colonel Pickering.

_____ 18. Higgins and Pickering flatter and compliment Eliza because she has done so well in her public appearances.

_____ 19. Mrs. Higgins feels that Henry's behavior toward Eliza is without excuse.

_____ 20. Higgins justifies his behavior by saying that he is the same with everybody else.

NAME _____ DATE _____

Pygmalion by George Bernard Shaw

Answer each of the following questions in two or three complete sentences.

1. Why does Higgins agree to teach Eliza?

    _____

    _____

    _____

    _____

2. Why does Higgins call Doolittle an "original moralist"?

    _____

    _____

    _____

    _____

3. What is the difference between Pickering's manners and Higgins' manners?

    _____

    _____

    _____

    _____

4. Why does Eliza blow up at Higgins after the ball?

    _____

    _____

    _____

    _____

5. Explain Eliza's statement: "The difference between a lady and a flower girl is not how she acts, but in how she is treated."

    _____

    _____

    _____

    _____

CHALLENGE

Look up the mythological story of Pygmalion and Galatea. In what ways does Shaw change the plot and the outcome in writing the story of Higgins and Eliza?

NAME _____ DATE _____

The Prime of Miss Jean Brodie by Muriel Spark

Place a (+) before each statement that is true and a (0) before each statement that is false.

_____ 1. Marcia Blaine was a girls' school in New York City.

_____ 2. The Brodie "set" had six members.

_____ 3. Miss Brodie taught English literature in the senior school.

_____ 4. Mary Macgregor died in a train wreck while she was on her way to Spain.

_____ 5. Mr. Lowther was the great love of Jean Brodie's life.

_____ 6. Miss Brodie lost all contact with the members of her "set" after the girls moved on to another class.

_____ 7. Miss Brodie taught her girls very little of the subject matter that was supposed to be a part of the Marcia Blaine curriculum.

_____ 8. Miss MacKay had Miss Brodie dismissed when she found out about Miss Brodie's relationship with Mr. Lloyd.

_____ 9. Sandy later became a famous author and a nun.

_____ 10. Miss Brodie was a staunch opponent of Hitler.

_____ 11. Miss Brodie frequently went to visit Teddy Lloyd and his wife.

_____ 12. Mr. Lowther eventually married Miss MacKay.

_____ 13. Miss Brodie took her girls on various expeditions to different parts of the city.

_____ 14. Miss Brodie was betrayed by Jenny.

_____ 15. Miss Brodie had few close friends among the members of the teaching faculty.

_____ 16. The plot of the novel is a combination of narrative and flashbacks.

_____ 17. Miss Brodie eventually died in a nursing home.

_____ 18. Miss Brodie drank heavily.

_____ 19. Rose became Mr. Lloyd's mistress as a substitute for Miss Brodie.

_____ 20. Miss Brodie spent most of her vacation time traveling in Europe.

NAME _____ DATE _____

The Prime of Miss Jean Brodie by Muriel Spark

Answer each of the following questions in two or three complete sentences.

1. Why were Jean Brodie's teaching methods highly suspect at Marcia Blaine School?

_____
_____
_____
_____

2. Why was Miss Brodie against "team spirit"?

_____
_____
_____
_____

3. Why was Mary Macgregor such a misfit in Miss Brodie's group?

_____
_____
_____
_____

4. What did Miss Brodie mean by "her prime"?

_____
_____
_____
_____

5. Why did Mr. Lowther marry Miss Lockhart?

_____
_____
_____
_____

CHALLENGE

Write an essay describing Jean Brodie's influence on the members of her "set." How was that influence positive? How was it negative?

NAME _____ DATE _____

The Playboy of the Western World by John M. Synge

Place a (+) before each statement that is true and a (0) before each statement that is false.

_____ 1. Before she sees Christy, Pegeen is planning to marry Shawn.

_____ 2. From the beginning of the play, Shawn is characterized as a coward.

_____ 3. Christy had shot his father in a barroom brawl.

_____ 4. Shawn had first seen Christy lying in a ditch by the road.

_____ 5. No one really believed Christy when he told them that he had killed his father.

_____ 6. The Widow Quin wholly approves of Christy's marrying Pegeen.

_____ 7. The village girls are afraid of Christy and will not come near him.

_____ 8. Christy greatly enjoys his new reputation as a killer.

_____ 9. Pegeen found an account in the newspaper of Christy's attack on his father.

_____ 10. The priest refuses to give permission for Shawn to marry Pegeen.

_____ 11. Christy's speeches to Pegeen are extremely poetic.

_____ 12. Christy's father had planned to marry the Widow Casey.

_____ 13. Shawn tried to bribe Christy into leaving the village.

_____ 14. Old Mahon describes his son as a man who drank too much and was very aggressive with women.

_____ 15. Widow Quin agrees to help Christy escape from his father.

_____ 16. In the race, Christy is badly beaten by some of the other village boys.

_____ 17. Michael James prefers Shawn to Christy as a son-in-law.

_____ 18. Philly Cullen is highly suspicious of all of Christy's story.

_____ 19. The arrival of the police prevents Christy from being hanged by a village mob.

_____ 20. At the end of the play, Christy returns home with his father.

©1986 J. Weston Walch, Publisher

150 Great Books

NAME _____ DATE _____

The Playboy of the Western World by John M. Synge

Answer each of the following questions in two or three complete sentences.

1. Why does Pegeen find Christy so very attractive?

_____

_____

_____

_____

2. How is Shawn contrasted with Christy?

_____

_____

_____

_____

3. What really happened between Christy and his father?

_____

_____

_____

_____

4. Why does the Widow Quin agree to help Christy hide the truth?

_____

_____

_____

_____

5. How does Christy change as the play progresses to almost become the man that the villagers think he is?

_____

_____

_____

_____

CHALLENGE

Write an essay showing how this play illustrates that people easily believe what they want to be true, and are very disappointed when truth proves to be less exciting than fantasy.

NAME ———————————————————————— DATE ——————————

The House of Mirth by Edith Wharton

Select the letter of the word or phrase which correctly completes each statement.

—————— 1. Lily Bart's main problem was always a lack of (A) money (B) beauty (C) family connections (D) manners.

—————— 2. The man who most genuinely cared for Lily was (A) Rosedale (B) Gus Trenor (C) Seldon (B) George Dorset.

—————— 3. Lily's chances for social success were greatly damaged in her childhood by (A) lack of a real education (B) her father's death (C) her mother's false sense of values (D) all of the above.

—————— 4. A major pastime of Lily's social set was (A) riding horseback (B) bridge (C) dancing (D) going to concerts.

—————— 5. Seldon and Lily are attracted to each other because (A) they understand each other (B) both are outsiders (C) they don't have to pretend with each other (D) all of the above.

—————— 6. Lily's greatest enemy is (A) Bertha Dorset (B) Judy Trenor (C) Grace Stepney (D) Mrs. Penniston.

—————— 7. Lily accepts financial help from (A) Gus Trenor (B) Seldon (C) Percy Gryce (D) Rosedale.

—————— 8. Lily's only hope for real independence is (A) her inheritance from her aunt (B) a rich marriage (C) getting a good job (D) winning at bridge.

—————— 9. Lily is forced to face the reality of her situation when (A) her aunt dies (B) Bertha abandons her in Europe (C) Seldon refuses to see her (D) Trenor tries to seduce her.

—————— 10. In the novel's climax, Seldon draws the wrong conclusion when he (A) sees Lily leaving Trenor's townhouse (B) does not get an answer to his letter (C) finds out that Lily has met with Rosedale (D) learns that Lily has Bertha's letters.

—————— 11. The one who tries to help Lily in an hour of great need is (A) Gerty Farish (B) Judy Trenor (C) Grace Stepney (D) Mrs. Wellington Bry.

—————— 12. Lily's aunt is most horrified by (A) Lily's clothing bills (B) Lily's gambling debts (C) Lily's friendship with Rosedale (D) Lily's accepting money from Gus Trenor.

—————— 13. When abandoned in Europe, Lily is rescued by (A) George Dorset (B) Gus Trenor (C) Seldon (D) the Duchess.

—————— 14. Lily refuses to use the letters to destroy Bertha because (A) she feels sorry for George (B) she loves Seldon (C) she hopes to get back into Bertha's good graces (D) she feels that blackmail is immoral.

—————— 15. Lily tries to earn a living (A) as a model (B) making hats (C) as a restaurant hostess (D) as a newspaper correspondent.

—————— 16. Lily's declining circumstances are seen in (A) the place where she lives (B) her poor health (C) her total aloneness (D) all of the above.

—————— 17. Lily increasingly seeks escape through (A) sleep-inducing drugs (B) liquor (C) Seldon's companionship (D) increased spending.

—————— 18. When she visits Seldon for the last time, Lily (A) tells him that she loves him (B) asks to borrow money (C) tells him that she is ill (D) burns Bertha's letters.

—————— 19. New York society, as presented in *The House Of Mirth*, was (A) cruel and unfeeling (B) wasteful (C) superficial and selfish (D) all of the above.

—————— 20. Lily shows herself to be above all the others when she (A) repays Trenor's money (B) burns Bertha's letters (C) will not become Rosedale's mistress (D) all of the above.

NAME _____ DATE _____

The House of Mirth by Edith Wharton

Answer each of the following questions in two or three complete sentences.

1. How is Lily Bart different from the other women in her social set?

    _____

    _____

    _____

    _____

2. How do the events of her childhood help to shape Lily's fate?

    _____

    _____

    _____

    _____

3. In what ways is her beauty both an asset and a liability?

    _____

    _____

    _____

    _____

4. How do Lily's fortunes decline after her quarrel with Bertha Dorset?

    _____

    _____

    _____

    _____

5. What are Lily's last actions before her death? How do these actions set her free?

    _____

    _____

    _____

    _____

CHALLENGE

Discuss the ways in which Lily Bart both creates her own problems and is also the victim of circumstances which are beyond her control.

ANSWER KEYS

Life and Death in a Coral Sea by Jacques-Yves Cousteau

OBJECTIVE:

1. +	6. 0	11. +	16. 0
2. 0	7. +	12. 0	17. 0
3. 0	8. 0	13. +	18. 0
4. 0	9. 0	14. 0	19. +
5. +	10. 0	15. 0	20. 0

SHORT ANSWER:

1. Double thick hull, longer nose, special underwater observation chamber.
2. Plant and animal life have no defense system against the oil waste and use of the ocean as a garbage dump.
3. Each man functioned in his special area, yet worked as a team. Used small subs for sea exploring. Made friends with fish and eels.
4. Fish got in the way, problem of carrying photographic equipment, danger from sharks.
5. Aqualungs for depth exploring, two-man subs, "sea fleas" for individual exploring.

CHALLENGE:

Civilization is destroying plant and animal life by upsetting natural balance. Man must stop using sea as a sewer. Possible great food supply from the sea. Man must care for the sea. Set aside preserves to prevent extinction of sea life forms.

Babe: The Legend Comes To Life by Robert W. Creamer

OBJECTIVE:

1. A	6. B	11. D	16. C
2. C	7. C	12. A	17. A
3. B	8. B	13. D	18. C
4. A	9. A	14. B	19. B
5. B	10. D	15. C	20. A

SHORT ANSWER:

1. Took him out of the boys' home, made him an individual.
2. Refusal to accept team discipline and stick to training rules.
3. Beginning of organized leagues, specialized players in one position, lower scoring games with emphasis on the long ball.
4. He didn't include her in his life, left her for other women.
5. Couldn't get a managing position because of his reputation of being uncooperative.

CHALLENGE:

Became a personality. Sparkle of his personal life. Homerun style and ballpark performance geared to please the fans. He was baseball's first "star."

Citizen Tom Paine by Howard Fast

OBJECTIVE:

1. K	6. H	11. A	16. D
2. B	7. P	12. F	17. M
3. N	8. L	13. S	18. G
4. E	9. R	14. C	19. Q
5. T	10. J	15. I	20. O

ANSWER KEYS (continued)

Citizen Tom Paine by Howard Fast (continued)

SHORT ANSWER:

1. Abuse by the Squire, running away from home, his wife dying in poverty, seeing his friend hanged.
2. Fiery rhetoric which inspired the troops and got the American people to support the cause.
3. Too revolutionary, work with miners and unions made the government fear him.
4. First seen as a hero, then rejected as the revolution turned violent.
5. No roots in one place. Too emotionally insecure to establish any lasting relationships.

CHALLENGE:

Total spread of his ideas wherever man wanted to be free—England, France, America. Belonged to no single nation.

I Always Wanted to Be Somebody by Althea Gibson

OBJECTIVE:

1. C	6. S	11. A	16. I
2. T	7. D	12. R	17. G
3. K	8. P	13. F	18. O
4. B	9. N	14. M	19. J
5. L	10. H	15. Q	20. E

SHORT ANSWER:

1. Learned to fight, box, hold her own on the streets.
2. Dr. Eaton gave her a home and kept her in school, example of Sugar Ray Robinson, living with the Darben family.
3. Opportunities severely limited because she was black. No access to white facilities.
4. Accepted on equal terms with other athletes, not just as a black.
5. Strengths are her great determination to succeed, practice and self-discipline. Weaknesses—an emotional person, self-discipline sometimes difficult, needs the help of her coaches.

CHALLENGE:

Quest for sports' excellence primary. More important to be the best athlete that she can than to be recognized as a racial symbol.

All Creatures Great and Small by James Herriot

OBJECTIVE:

1. L	6. M	11. J
2. O	7. A	12. C
3. B	8. I	13. G
4. D	9. K	14. N
5. E	10. F	15. H

ANSWER KEYS (continued)

All Creatures Great and Small by James Herriot (continued)

SHORT ANSWER:
1. Total confusion, mass of barking dogs, Sigfried not around, confused introduction to various ladies.
2. Very few roads, difficult travel and primitive working conditions, the superstitions of the farmers.
3. James—steady and hard working, Tristan—the irresponsible playboy.
4. Absolutely unpredictable and disorganized, blamed the others for his mistakes.
5. Widely scattered farms, small villages, gently rolling hills, great natural beauty.

CHALLENGE:
Ability to cope with all emergencies, willing to help anytime, anywhere, real caring for the farmers and their problems, ability to make on-the-spot decisions, good medical background, love of adventure, physical stamina.

Teacher: Anne Sullivan Macy by Helen Keller

OBJECTIVE:
1. Acropolis
2. the Phantom
3. laugh and play
4. helping the handicapped
5. poetry
6. plagiarism
7. they needed to be independent
8. few books available in Braille
9. their house burned
10. dogs, horses
11. Swedenborg
12. typing
13. vaudeville
14. Polly Thompson
15. Puerto Rico
16. mood swings and depression
17. talking books
18. American Foundation for the Blind
19. Temple University
20. Japan

SHORT ANSWER:
1. She knew what blindness was like.
2. So that Helen could learn and respond like a normal person.
3. Charged that Teacher controlled and manipulated Helen.
4. Religion—Helen believed in an afterlife; Annie did not.
5. Traveled bringing encouragement to handicapped people and those injured in the war.

CHALLENGE:
Determination to learn and be a free person, love of poetry and nature, love of dogs, caring for the feelings and hurts of others.

Joseph by Joyce Landorf

OBJECTIVE:
1. H
2. Q
3. T
4. L
5. A
6. P
7. E
8. N
9. C
10. J
11. R
12. F
13. B
14. S
15. K
16. D
17. G
18. I
19. M
20. O

ANSWER KEYS (continued)

Joseph by Joyce Landorf (continued)

SHORT ANSWER:

1. Laban tricked Joseph with the wrong wife. Jacob tricked Laban so that Jacob owned the strongest of the flocks.
2. Sensitive, dreamer, desire to know God.
3. Because Joseph's brothers sold him into slavery.
4. Place where a moral choice had to be made.
5. Dreamer, spiritually oriented, sensitive, supportive, gentle.

CHALLENGE:

Learning from his mother, survival of the experience of slavery, management experience in the house of Potiphar, survival in prison, lack of bitterness, no desire for revenge.

Auntie Mame by Jerome Lawrence and Robert E. Lee

OBJECTIVE:

1. J	6. I	11. E	16. T
2. S	7. Q	12. O	17. P
3. C	8. H	13. G	18. L
4. N	9. R	14. K	19. D
5. A	10. M	15. B	20. F

SHORT ANSWER:

1. Arrives at Beekman Place in total chaos of one of Mame's gigantic parties.
2. Mame wanted experience through living. Babcock wanted stuffy prep school education.
3. Even though the wealth is gone, they give what little they have with love.
4. Mindless, brainless, society dame. Mame wants a real woman for Patrick.
5. Shows Patrick what stuffy snobs the Upsons are. That her world is more real.

CHALLENGE:

Mame is caring, wacky and willing to try anything, able to cope when the bottom fell out, real love for Beau, shows no sign of losing her zest for life, even in old age.

The Contender by Robert Lipsyte

OBJECTIVE:

1. 0	6. 0	11. +	16. +
2. +	7. +	12. +	17. 0
3. +	8. +	13. +	18. +
4. 0	9. 0	14. 0	19. 0
5. 0	10. +	15. 0	20. 0

SHORT ANSWER:

1. Crowded slums, drugs, liquor.
2. Simply winning is not enough. One must do one's best to become a real contender.
3. Jogging, enough sleep and proper diet, working out at the gym to develop boxing skills.
4. Shared the experiences of their childhood hurts. James gets involved in drugs, turns to crime to pay for his habit.
5. To go to school, to have a profession after his boxing career is over.

ANSWER KEYS (continued)

The Contender by Robert Lipsyte (continued)

CHALLENGE:

James—a life of dependency, drugs, bad company, no goals, no escape. Alfred—gained independence and respect—hard work and self-discipline, goals and hope for a future.

My Life by Golda Meir

OBJECTIVE:

1. B	6. C	11. A	16. D
2. C	7. D	12. B	17. A
3. D	8. C	13. C	18. C
4. C	9. A	14. A	19. C
5. A	10. D	15. B	20. B

SHORT ANSWER:

1. Constant fear of attacks, hunger, Zionist attitudes of her sister.
2. Mutiny of ship's crew, spoiled food, lost luggage, terrible train travel conditions.
3. Shut out immigration to Palestine at the time when European Jews needed to be rescued.
4. Companionship and support.
5. Compromise will weaken Israel's position and strengthen her enemies. Nation must stand alone against world opinion.

CHALLENGE:

Work to make life better on the kibbutz, helping the laboring class as the country got established, fund-raising, foreign contacts, crisis times as prime minister. Woman of determination and strength to succeed in hardship. Very caring for people.

The Death of a Salesman by Arthur Miller

OBJECTIVE:

1. New England
2. houses were closing in
3. playing football at Ebbetts Field
4. flunked high-school math
5. being known and liked
6. he hadn't made any money
7. a lawyer
8. Bill Oliver
9. mining diamonds
10. Linda
11. Charley
12. stealing
13. taking away his salary
14. fired Willy
15. thought about suicide
16. Charley
17. another woman with his father
18. at the steakhouse
19. smashing up his car
20. made the last house payment

SHORT ANSWER:

1. Biff playing football, polishing the car, swinging on the trees in the neighborhood.
2. Happy memories of past success, a total failure in the present.
3. Goes from one grand dream to another—no grasp of reality.
4. Take care of him, help him to continue believing in himself.
5. Sees the reality of his father when he finds Willy with the prostitute.

CHALLENGE:

Willy loses the respect of his sons. His business reputation is gone and he is fired when he can no longer produce. Commits suicide because he sees no way to restore his self-respect.

ANSWER KEYS (continued)

The Greatest Story Ever Told by Fulton Oursler

OBJECTIVE:

1. O	6. Q	11. N	16. E
2. D	7. L	12. H	17. P
3. A	8. B	13. T	18. M
4. G	9. S	14. C	19. K
5. J	10. F	15. R	20. I

SHORT ANSWER:

1. Recognized the child as a special gift from God. Taught Him the traditions of the Jewish fathers and the trade of a carpenter.
2. Fasting, prayer, choosing men to help in His mission.
3. They viewed Jesus as a threat to their religious structure control and their political alliance with the Romans.
4. Healing, feeding, lessons of love instead of legalism.
5. Jesus became martyr. The power of His ideas became stronger after His crucifixion.

CHALLENGE:

Jesus gave the world a faith that worked in daily life. He had an attractive, loving personality. He lifted and loved those who were rejected by life or trampled under by the system.

The Teahouse of the August Moon by John Patrick

OBJECTIVE:

1. Okinawa
2. Mr. Sakini
3. Colonel Purdy
4. made a mess of everything
5. Tokobi
6. bring them democracy
7. Plan B
8. wisdom
9. the goat
10. a white coat
11. lacquered cups
12. analyze Fisby
13. brandy, sweet potatoes
14. geisha girl, Lotus Blossom
15. teahouse
16. be geisha girls
17. agriculture
18. the still be broken up, teahouse torn down
19. congressmen are coming to examine the village
20. they have simply hidden the panels

SHORT ANSWER:

1. Passive acceptance of whoever the conqueror was.
2. He had failed in every single assignment.
3. Totally relaxed military regulations and accepted the ways of the villagers.
4. Center of socialization, symbol of civilization and success.
5. He wants her to stay as she is, not to become Americanized.

CHALLENGE:

They live with what they have. Their style of life is relaxed and easy. They care for each other. Oriental stoicism makes much more sense than Western push.

The Paper Lion by George Plimpton

OBJECTIVE:

1. could write about how it felt to play football
2. quarterback
3. his notebook
4. George Wilson
5. singing school songs
6. scaring each other with masks
7. Cranbrook
8. practice, class instruction
9. his helmet
10. Night of the Squeaky Shoes
11. Night Train Laine
12. playing pass with the kids
13. inter-squad game in Pontiac
14. Alex Karras
15. the commissioner wouldn't let him
16. his playbook
17. Freddy Macklem
18. the rookie variety show
19. Edwin Anderson
20. the pre-season player draft

ANSWER KEYS (continued)

The Paper Lion by George Plimpton (continued)

SHORT ANSWER:

1. With good humor at his mistakes, accepted him as one of them.
2. Mental coordination for field maneuvers, understanding stock plays and patterns, mental anticipation of what the opposing man may do.
3. Jogging, calisthenics, passing and tackle practices, inter-squad scrimmage.
4. Brown—strict discipline. Wilson—emphasized self-discipline, players on their own.
5. Inter-squad pre-season scrimmage, played quarterback badly, muffed every play.

CHALLENGE:

Lions functioned as a team. Spirit created in training camp. Jokes and stories in dormitories, working as a unit on the field. Team members needed a sense of each other's reactions and responses. Acted like cheerleaders for each other. Winning done by the unit, not by one star or individual.

My Name Is Asher Lev by Chaim Potok

OBJECTIVE:

1. B	6. A	11. B	16. B
2. B	7. A	12. A	17. C
3. A	8. A	13. D	18. B
4. B	9. D	14. D	19. C
5. D	10. A	15. B	20. A

SHORT ANSWER:

1. Mother was with him, but his father was away. Mother shared his sensitive nature.
2. Asher spent time at the store. Learned about the experience of being Jewish.
3. Putting one's feelings into visual form so that those feelings may be shared by others.
4. He would draw without realizing what he was doing. Others did not want to see the feelings that he painted.
5. Father viewed painting the Crucifixion as a betrayal of his Jewishness. Hated Asher's putting the family figures in the paintings.

CHALLENGE:

Study and expression of art replaced study of Talmud or involvement in Zionism. Asher tried to make his art an act of religious expression, to bring God to the suffering of all men.

The Camera Never Blinks by Dan Rather with Mickey Herskowitz

OBJECTIVE:

1. F	6. S	11. T	16. O
2. A	7. H	12. R	17. E
3. P	8. B	13. N	18. G
4. C	9. Q	14. D	19. J
5. L	10. K	15. I	20. M

SHORT ANSWER:

1. To get out of the classroom and go where the news was happening. Rather developed skill in on-the-spot reporting.
2. Hurricane danger in Galveston, battlefield in Vietnam, center of conflict with the Nixon White House.
3. Hurricane Carla made him a nationally known name. Vietnam gave him battlefield experience. Kennedy assassination coverage got him moved to Washington.
4. Americans for the first time saw the realities of war in their living rooms.
5. Afraid it would look like he was running away from the attacks of the Nixon organization.

352

ANSWER KEYS (continued)

The Camera Never Blinks by Dan Rather with Mickey Herskowitz
(continued)

CHALLENGE:

Daring, willingness to go after the story wherever it was. Personal strength to stick to his guns under pressure. Weaknesses—taking of risks, not always working through the chain of command.

Go Up for Glory by Bill Russell

OBJECTIVE:

1. Louisiana
2. California
3. Henri Christophe of Haiti
4. His brother Charlie
5. University of San Francisco
6. win
7. they had no gym
8. Melbourne, Australia
9. loneliness
10. dying in a plane crash
11. Wilt Chamberlain
12. Walter Brown
13. Red Auerbach
14. rubber plantation
15. make him move out of his usual pattern
16. St. Louis
17. arthritis
18. know his manhood
19. compromise
20. conducting the first integrated basketball clinics

SHORT ANSWER:

1. Encourage the student by making him reach, or discourage him by putting him down.
2. They must win. Often do not have the needed academic skills to keep their scholarships or the time to study.
3. So many black players per team.
4. His family roots were there.
5. Having to stay in separate hotels from his white teammates and to eat in separate restaurants.

CHALLENGE:

To give adulthood and meaning to each person in an open economic system which lets each person become what he can be. Give each black his identity. Begin with the children.

Anchorwoman by Jessica Savitch

OBJECTIVE:

1. +	6. +	11. +	16. +
2. 0	7. 0	12. 0	17. 0
3. +	8. +	13. +	18. +
4. 0	9. 0	14. +	19. 0
5. +	10. +	15. 0	20. +

SHORT ANSWER:

1. No openings for women. Men would not work with her. Didn't think that women could handle themselves in news or project a good image.
2. Felt the suffering of people that she had to interview in disaster or accident stories.
3. Problems with getting on-the-spot film. Always had to look neat and well-groomed. Problems of make-up and dress for TV image more critical for a woman.
4. Jack Pakino gave her a break as a disc jockey. Joan Showalter (personnel director for CBS) taught Jessica how to create a TV image. Charles Osgood and Ed Bradley—help with copywriting and news editing.
5. Jessica could laugh at her own difficulties and mistakes. She got stuck in the Beemobile. Jokes on her inexperience—"chickenhouse" in Texas episode.

ANSWER KEYS (continued)

Anchorwoman by Jessica Savitch (continued)

CHALLENGE:

Jessica Savitch was the groundbreaker. She proved that a woman could be a news personality. Her legacy was the opening of the door for women to compete equally with men in the industry.

Babe Didrikson: The World's Greatest Woman Athlete by Gene Schoor

OBJECTIVE:

1. 0	6. +	11. +	16. +
2. +	7. +	12. 0	17. 0
3. +	8. 0	13. 0	18. +
4. +	9. +	14. 0	19. 0
5. 0	10. 0	15. 0	20. +

SHORT ANSWER:

1. Family participated in all kinds of sports, gave Babe moral support for her ambitions.
2. First to win multiple medals in several different track and field events.
3. Not an aloof star personality. Willing to be approachable.
4. First American woman to win the tournament.
5. Moral support and love through her golf career. Stayed close by her through her illness.

CHALLENGE:

Determination and desire to excel. Did what others said could not be done. True both in her career and helped her battle with cancer.

Pygmalion by George Bernard Shaw

OBJECTIVE:

1. 0	6. 0	11. 0	16. 0
2. +	7. 0	12. 0	17. 0
3. +	8. +	13. +	18. 0
4. 0	9. 0	14. 0	19. +
5. 0	10. +	15. 0	20. +

SHORT ANSWER:

1. As a challenge, to win his bet with Pickering.
2. His ideas were so far from those generally accepted by society.
3. Pickering showed Eliza how to be a lady. Higgins taught her language, but was a terrible example in behavior.
4. He ignored her—treated her like an object.
5. People become what those around them expect them to be.

CHALLENGE:

Galatea simply remained a living object who responded to her creator's love. Eliza becomes a total person when she rebels against Higgins' domination.

The Prime of Miss Jean Brodie by Muriel Spark

OBJECTIVE:

1. 0	6. 0	11. 0	16. +
2. +	7. +	12. 0	17. +
3. 0	8. 0	13. +	18. 0
4. 0	9. +	14. 0	19. 0
5. 0	10. 0	15. +	20. +

354

ANSWER KEYS (continued)

The Prime of Miss Jean Brodie by Muriel Spark (continued)

SHORT ANSWER:
1. She didn't teach the accepted curriculum.
2. It broke her influence and gave her girls other allegiances.
3. Physically uncoordinated, not very bright.
4. The peak experiences of the best years of her life.
5. He wanted to settle down with a wife. He was tired of Miss Brodie manipulating him.

CHALLENGE:
Positive influence as she stimulated her girls' imagination. Negative—Miss Brodie was a manipulator. Tried to work out her frustrations though the girls. To pour them into a mold, from which they had to escape.

The Playboy of the Western World by John M. Synge

OBJECTIVE:

1. +	6. 0	11. +	16. 0
2. +	7. 0	12. 0	17. 0
3. 0	8. +	13. +	18. +
4. +	9. 0	14. 0	19. 0
5. 0	10. 0	15. +	20. +

SHORT ANSWER:
1. He was much more exciting than anyone else around.
2. Scared, dependent, dull, weak.
3. Hit him on the head and left him in the field.
4. She also wanted a man.
5. He begins to believe the glamorous image that the people give him.

CHALLENGE:
Each time the story was told, Christy got more glamorous and villagers got more excited. Disappointed when the glamour of the murder turned out to be an ordinary quarrel.

The House of Mirth by Edith Wharton

OBJECTIVE:

1. A	6. A	11. A	16. D
2. C	7. A	12. D	17. A
3. D	8. B	13. C	18. D
4. B	9. D	14. B	19. D
5. D	10. A	15. B	20. D

SHORT ANSWER:
1. No money, totally dependent on others.
2. Bankruptcy and the death of her father.
3. Attractive to men, becomes the victim of other women's jealousy.
4. No one in society wants anything to do with her. Doesn't get her aunt's money. Can't hold a job.
5. Burns Bertha's letters to Seldon. Repays Gus' money. Is obligated to nobody.

CHALLENGE:
Plays the games of the rich when she can't afford them. Refuses to realistically face her financial situation. Lives on future expectations. Becomes a victim of her useless upbringing and of Bertha Dorset's viciousness.

UNIT 8

Who Done It???

Tales of the DARK and MYSTERIOUS

SYNOPSES

The Innocents
by William Archibald

This dramatic adaptation of Henry James' novel *The Turn of the Screw* opens as Miss Giddens arrives to be governess to Miles and Flora. The new governess is concerned over the children's strange and secretive behavior. She soon finds herself involved in the macabre world of the supernatural. The ghosts of Miss Jessel, the previous governess, and Quint, the handyman, have possessed the bodies of Miles and Flora and are using the children to carry on a love affair from beyond the grave. Miss Giddens sees the ghost of Quint, which has come for Miles. Knowing that the evil influence must be broken, Miss Giddens sends Flora away, and is determined to free Miles from Quint's clutches. In the drama's climactic scene, the governess forces Miles to tell the truth and to face Quint's spirit. Although Miles is freed, he falls dead in Miss Giddens' arms. This unusually tense drama of haunting probes the influence that the dead can have on the living.

The Chalk Garden
by Enid Bagnold

As the play opens, Mrs. St. Maugham is interviewing candidates for post of governess to her troubled granddaughter, Laurel. A bright girl of fourteen, the child lies, is generally impertinent, and sets fires. Miss Madrigal, an applicant with no references but with a compelling manner, is hired because she can also help Mrs. St. Maugham with the garden, in which nothing will grow. Because the governess will say nothing about her past, Laurel's curiosity is aroused by Madrigal's secretive nature. When the Judge, an old friend of Mrs. St. Maugham's, comes to lunch, the secret is revealed. Madrigal had been tried for murder and had served time in prison. Madrigal's concern for Laurel comes from the governess' own experience. As a child, Madrigal had been such a compulsive liar that nobody believed her when she told the truth. When Laurel's mother Olivia comes to claim her child, Madrigal urges the grandmother to let Laurel go. Laurel needs a mother, not a life of sterility, a "chalk garden." As the play ends, the mystery of Miss Madrigal remains. Was she guilty or innocent of the crime? This play combines suspense with fine characterization.

Where Are the Children?
by Mary Higgins Clark

Set on present-day Cape Cod, this novel recounts the life of Nancy Harmon Eldridge who had been accused seven years before of murdering her two children. Nancy had been acquitted because Rob Legler, the chief prosecution witness, had disappeared. After settling on Cape Cod and beginning a new life as the wife of Ray Eldridge, Nancy's nightmare begins again. Her two new children, Missy and Michael, are kidnapped by the mysterious Courtney Parrish. Parrish also sends an account of Nancy's past to the newspapers. Nancy is immediately accused again. By a series of flashbacks, the author presents Nancy's troubled life: her strange marriage to Carl Harmon, the death of her mother, and the deaths of her first two children, Peter and Lisa. Meanwhile, Parrish has taken Michael and Missy to "The Lookout," a large house above the sea. As the search for the children continues, minor characters provide important clues. Jonathan Knowles, who is writing a book on unsolved crimes, comes to assist. Dr. Lendon Miles, who had been in love with Nancy's mother, tries by hypnosis to unlock Nancy's troubled mind. Dorothy Prentiss finds Missy's red mitten. Parrish is finally identified as Nancy's first husband, Carl, who was thought to have drowned. The author's weather descriptions are excellent. Snow and sleet add to the suspense in an exciting chase scene up to "The Lookout." There Ray and Nancy rescue their children from Parrish's clutches. This novel is easy reading, but is an excellent suspense yarn that will hold the student's attention.

And Then There Were None
by Agatha Christie

In this well-constructed novel, a group of ten people receive mysterious invitations to spend a holiday on Indian Island off the south coast of England. After the guests are trapped on the island by a violent storm, they begin dying one by one. A series of ten small china statues sits on a table in the hall. After each murder, one more statue disappears. The last to die is Judge Wargrave, whose death is really a suicide. The solution to the mystery is found in a manuscript later located in a fishing boat. The Judge, himself dying of cancer, had resolved to punish the others, each of whom had committed a crime for which the criminal could not be prosecuted by law. Some of these crimes had been deliberate. Others were the result of carelessness. Vera Claythorne had killed for the man she loved. Dr. Armstrong's crime had been medical malpractice. The Judge acts as the instrument of justice to balance the scales. This fascinating yarn holds the reader's attention. The solution remains a mystery until the very end.

The Mousetrap
by Agatha Christie

This suspense thriller is the longest-running drama on the London stage. The setting is Monkswell Manor, which owners Giles and Molly are determined to run as a guesthouse. When a snowstorm hits, the owners are trapped with their guests: Mrs. Boyle, Miss Caswell, Christopher Wren, Major Metcalf, and Mr. Paravicini. When a brutal murder is reported to have been committed in the neighborhood, circumstantial evidence makes many of the characters look guilty. Mrs. Boyle is then strangled in the library. The tune of "Three Blind Mice" is heard being picked out on the piano. Police Sergeant Trotter arrives, and appears to be working on the case. The involvement of several characters is established in a case involving the death of a child on a nearby farm. The farmer's wife is already dead. Mrs. Boyle was the magistrate who had sent the orphans to live at the farm. Molly, the third "mouse" in the trap, was the teacher who did nothing to prevent the situation. The man who poses as a policeman is really the insane killer, who desires to avenge his brother's death. Major Metcalf, really the policeman, saves Molly's life. Many of the characters who appear most guilty in the drama have no connection with the case at all. This complex mystery, in typical Christie style, makes all look guilty until proven innocent.

Jamaica Inn
by Daphne Du Maurier

This novel is set in the mysterious world of eighteenth-century Cornwall. After her mother's death, young Mary Yellan goes to live with her aunt and uncle at Jamaica Inn, a mysterious public house on the moors. Joss Merlyn, her aunt's husband, bullies his wife and drinks to excess. Mary becomes aware of illegal activities at the inn when she finds a locked room and hears wagons moving in the night. The strange nocturnal activities, Mary learns by following her uncle, are those of wreckers. These men remove the coast light markers. Ships are then wrecked on the rocks, and the bandits can collect their cargo. Mary is strangely attracted to her uncle's brother, Jem Merlyn, but she fears that he too is a criminal. After finding the inn ransacked and her uncle and aunt murdered, Mary seeks the help of Squire Bassett, the village magistrate, and the strange young church rector, Francis Davey. After Mary learns that Davey is the real leader of the crime ring, Davey attempts to escape with Mary as hostage. Jem, however, arrives to rescue her. *Jamaica Inn* has many elements of suspense, as the apparent "good guys" become the villains. Mary is a strong character who faces danger without fear. Cornish customs and landscape descriptions also help to make this book interesting reading.

Rebecca
by Daphne Du Maurier

The novel is narrated by the second wife of Maxim deWinter, owner of the great estate at Manderley. After a whirlwind courtship and marriage in Monte Carlo, the insecure bride returns to Manderley to live under the shadow of Max's first wife, Rebecca. The young wife is befriended by Frank Crawley, the estate manager, and by Max's sister, Beatrice. Her fear and insecurity mount, however, as she is intimidated by the menacing housekeeper, Mrs. Danvers. Exploring Rebecca's small cottage near the shore, the bride finds clues which indicate that Rebecca was not the paragon she had seemed to be. Mrs. Danvers' evil intentions are clear when she persuades the girl to copy a ball gown from one of the Manderley portraits. The gown is exactly the one that Rebecca had worn. Rebecca's boat is found in the bay. Proof indicates that the boat had been deliberately sunk. Although Max now stands accused of murder, the young bride learns how evil Rebecca really was and that Max loves only her. The novel ends with Mrs. Danvers' departure and the ashes of Manderley filling the night sky.

Angel Street (Gas Light)
by Patrick Hamilton

In this powerful suspense drama, Bella Manningham believes that she is going mad. Her husband treats her cruelly, constantly accusing his wife of hiding or losing things. However, every evening when Manningham goes out, Bella notices that the lights dim and come up again just before her husband returns. One evening, Mrs. Manningham is visited by police detective Rough. Rough tells her that this house was the scene of the murder of Alice Barlow. Rough has reason to believe that Manningham is the killer, and that he spends his evenings on the upper floor of the house searching for Mrs. Barlow's missing rubies. As Rough searches the room, he assures Bella of her sanity by finding all of the things that she was supposed to have lost. Rough finds the rubies, which Bella had unknowingly removed from an old brooch. With the help of Elizabeth, the housekeeper, Rough sets a trap for Manningham. After Manningham is arrested, Bella threatens to cut her husband's throat. At the play's end, the killer is captured. The reader is left wondering, however, if Bella had indeed gone over the edge into insanity.

Arsenic and Old Lace
by Joseph Kesselring

This hilarious mystery-comedy tells of two sweet old ladies, Abbey and Martha Brewster, who have poisoned eleven visitors with elderberry wine and have buried the corpses in the cellar. Mortimer, the nephew, is horrified to learn of the aunts' activities. The aunts view the killings as acts of charity because the victims they select are lonely and homeless. An addition to the comedy is Teddy Brewster, who thinks that he is Theodore Roosevelt and that he is building the Panama Canal in the basement. Jonathan, another nephew with criminal tendencies, arrives to set up his illegal operations in the aunts' home. The whole hilarious mess reaches a climax as Mortimer tells the police the truth, but the officers refuse to believe him. The concluding action becomes such a farce that the aunts seem to be the sanest people in the cast.

Cloud of Witness
by Dorothy L. Sayers

This complex case for Sayers' amateur detective, Lord Peter Wimsey, has serious family overtones. Lord Peter's brother Gerald has been accused of shooting Denis Cathcart, the fiancé of their sister, Lady Mary. The murder took place during a house party at the family mansion. All of the guests begin to look guilty. As Lord Peter investigates, he finds that Gerald is romantically involved with Mrs. Grimethorpe, a farmer's wife whose husband is insanely jealous. Gerald is too much of a gentleman to use the love letter which would provide him with an alibi. Lady Mary did not love Cathcart at all, but was planning to run away with Goyles, a young socialist. Lord Peter risks his own life in the investigation. He is shot in the shoulder and almost swallowed in a bog of quicksand. Many minor crimes and complex motives are uncovered as Wimsey and his valet Bunter search through the "clouds of witness." Cathcart's death finally turns out to be suicide. This complex mystery novel makes excellent use of settings in English country houses and on vast moors. Although this book is more difficult than any of Agatha Christie's, *Cloud of Witness* would be enjoyed by a good reader who is a mystery fan.

Nine Coaches Waiting
by Mary Stewart

This combination of mystery story and Cinderella fairy tale opens as Linda Martin comes to Chateau Valmy to be governess to young Phillipe. Leon Valmy, Phillipe's uncle, is a powerful man who intrigues Linda. She soon learns, however, that Leon and his wife Heloise will stop at nothing to gain control of the estate. Young Phillipe is in great danger, since only he stands in their way. Linda is also becoming romantically involved with Leon's dashing brother, Raoul. After several attempts are made on Phillipe's life, Linda learns the truth from one of the servants. She attempts to take Phillipe away from the chateau and get him safely to the home of his other uncle Hippolyte, who is due home from the East. Linda's loyalty to Phillipe conflicts with her own feelings because she believes that Raoul is involved in the plot to kill the child. The plot gains momentum as Linda and Phillipe evade their pursuers and journey through the French countryside to safety. In the romantic conclusion, Raoul is cleared of all involvement, and he and Linda are reunited. Mary Stewart's fine descriptions and characterizations make this an excellent novel of love and romance.

NAME _____ DATE _____

The Innocents by William Archibald

Select the letter of the word or phrase which correctly completes each statement.

_____ 1. As the play opens (A) Miles and Flora are playing together (B) the stage is in total darkness (C) Miss Giddens is expected to arrive (D) Mrs. Grose is supervising the housecleaning.

_____ 2. Miss Giddens walks up from the gate (A) to surprise the children (B) to look at the garden (C) because she was dropped off by mistake (D) to observe the house.

_____ 3. The children's uncle (A) visits them frequently (B) does not want to be bothered with them (C) prefers Miles to Flora (D) has no children of his own.

_____ 4. Miss Giddens first sees Quint (A) at the window (B) on the balcony (C) in the garden (D) on the staircase.

_____ 5. Miles comes home from school (A) for a vacation (B) because he is ill (C) because he has been asked to leave (D) to keep Flora company.

_____ 6. Mrs. Grose tells Miss Giddens that Quint and Miss Jessel (A) are dead (B) were lovers (C) were close to the children (D) all of the above.

_____ 7. Mrs. Grose refuses to believe (A) in ghosts (B) that Quint was evil (C) that Miles may be in danger (D) that the uncle is indifferent to the children.

_____ 8. The ghost of Miss Jessel is seen by (A) Miles (B) only Flora (C) Mrs. Grose (D) Flora and Miss Giddens.

_____ 9. Miss Giddens (A) calls a doctor (B) telephones Miles' school (C) writes to the children's uncle (D) consults a local clergyman.

_____ 10. Miss Giddens believes that Miles and Flora (A) were tools of Quint and Miss Jessel (B) are still being used (C) are in the grip of supernatural forces (D) all of the above.

_____ 11. The beginning of Act II is different from the beginning of Act I in (A) the set (B) the weather (C) the characters (D) the costumes.

_____ 12. Miss Giddens plans to leave because she feels (A) angry (B) helpless (C) frightened (D) underpaid.

_____ 13. Important props in Act II include (A) playing cards (B) crayons (C) flowers (D) books.

_____ 14. Miss Giddens sends Flora (A) to a hospital (B) to school (C) to her uncle (D) to the next village.

_____ 15. When the ghost of Miss Jessel appears (A) Flora becomes angry and frightened (B) Mrs. Grose sees her (C) Miles sees her (D) the ghost of Quint also is seen.

_____ 16. Mrs. Grose says that Quint died (A) of typhoid (B) in a duel (C) in an accident (D) when he was murdered.

_____ 17. Miss Giddens wants to (A) teach Miles (B) punish Miles (C) free Miles (D) send Miles back to school.

_____ 18. The letter that Miss Giddens had written was stolen by (A) Miles (B) Quint (C) Flora (D) Mrs. Grose.

_____ 19. After Flora and Mrs. Grose leave (A) the stage becomes brilliantly lighted (B) both ghosts appear (C) Miles assumes Quint's personality (D) Miles continues to tell lies.

_____ 20. Miles is set free (A) by telling the truth (B) by facing Quint's ghost (C) by death (D) by all of the above.

NAME _____ DATE _____

The Innocents by William Archibald

Answer each of the following questions in two or three complete sentences.

1. How do Miss Giddens and Mrs. Grose both show concern for Miles and Flora?

   _____

   _____

   _____

   _____

2. How does the behavior of Miles and Flora differ from the behavior of normal children?

   _____

   _____

   _____

   _____

3. How had Quint and Miss Jessel used Miles and Flora? How do the ghosts continue to use them?

   _____

   _____

   _____

   _____

4. How does Miles's manner change in Act II when he is alone with Miss Giddens?

   _____

   _____

   _____

   _____

5. How is Miles finally set free?

   _____

   _____

   _____

   _____

CHALLENGE

Write an essay describing the special sound and light effects required for a production of this play. How does light alternate with darkness to provide contrast in the various scenes?

NAME _____ DATE _____

The Chalk Garden by Enid Bagnold

Place a (+) before each statement that is true and a (0) before each statement that is false.

_____ 1. The entire action of the play takes place in Mrs. St. Maugham's home.

_____ 2. Madrigal presents excellent references when she applies for the job as Laurel's governess.

_____ 3. Laurel is about eight years old.

_____ 4. Before Madrigal arrived, Maitland had been Laurel's most constant companion.

_____ 5. Laurel's mother, who has remarried, does not want Laurel to live with her.

_____ 6. Pinkbell had been Mrs. St. Maugham's former butler.

_____ 7. Mrs. St. Maugham had a large household staff because she entertained frequently.

_____ 8. Laurel's curiosity is aroused by Madrigal's secretive nature.

_____ 9. Mrs. St. Maugham's garden is one of the most beautiful showplaces in the county.

_____ 10. The Judge recognizes Madrigal immediately.

_____ 11. Laurel detests Madrigal and demands that Mrs. St. Maugham fire her.

_____ 12. Madrigal had been placed in charge of the prison garden.

_____ 13. The Judge describes for Laurel how he appears in court.

_____ 14. Maitland had once been in prison.

_____ 15. Laurel guesses that Madrigal has a secret by the initials on the paintbox.

_____ 16. Connie Dolly Wallis had been convicted for the murder of her mother.

_____ 17. Madrigal says that Laurel reminds her of herself as a child.

_____ 18. Because Miss Wallis had been such a liar, no one believed her when she told the truth.

_____ 19. Madrigal urges Laurel not to go to live with her mother.

_____ 20. At the end of the play, Madrigal confesses to Mrs. St. Maugham that the verdict of guilty was true.

NAME _____ DATE _____

The Chalk Garden by Enid Bagnold

Answer each of the following questions in two or three complete sentences.

1. What kinds of behavior made Laurel such a difficult child?

   _____

   _____

   _____

   _____

2. In what ways is Madrigal different from the other candidates for the post of governess?

   _____

   _____

   _____

   _____

3. What is the conflict between Olivia and her mother?

   _____

   _____

   _____

   _____

4. How does Madrigal's behavior at the luncheon give away her identity?

   _____

   _____

   _____

   _____

5. Why does Mrs. St. Maugham want Madrigal to stay with her after Laurel leaves?

   _____

   _____

   _____

   _____

CHALLENGE

Discuss the double meaning in the title of the play. How is Mrs. St. Maugham's garden a reflection of her life?

NAME _____ DATE _____

Where Are the Children? by Mary Higgins Clark

Correctly complete each sentence with information from the novel.

1. The setting of the novel is in _____.

2. Seven years before, Nancy Harmon Eldridge had been accused of _____.

3. Jonathan Knowles was writing a book about _____.

4. Nancy had been freed because _____.

5. Courtney Parrish kidnapped _____ ,

   and took them to _____.

6. Nancy's past was exposed to the community by _____.

7. Dr. Lendon Miles came from _____

   to help Nancy because _____.

8. Chief Coffin searched for the children by _____ and _____.

9. Parrish established an alibi for himself at the time of the kidnapping by _____.

10. Parrish's plans for the children were interrupted by _____

    and _____.

11. Rob Legler returned from Canada in an attempt to _____.

12. Miles tried to help Nancy recall the past by _____.

13. John Kragopolis became suspicious because _____.

14. Michael escaped from Parrish when _____.

15. A clue to the children's whereabouts came when _____.

16. Nancy's mother had been killed by _____

    because _____.

17. Pedophilia is _____.

18. _____ gave the police the first clue that Parrish was really Carl Harmon.

19. Harmon intended to _____ the children by

    _____.

20. The children were saved by _____.

150 Great Books

NAME _____ DATE _____

Where Are the Children? by Mary Higgins Clark

Answer each of the following questions in two or three complete sentences.

1. How had Nancy Harmon tried to hide her past identity?

    _____

    _____

    _____

    _____

2. What steps did Courtney Parrish take to set up "the perfect crime"?

    _____

    _____

    _____

    _____

3. Why was the use of flashbacks important in the story?

    _____

    _____

    _____

    _____

4. Why does the kidnapping immediately become national news?

    _____

    _____

    _____

    _____

5. Name three minor characters who are important in saving the children's lives and clearing Nancy. What contributions does each one make?

    _____

    _____

    _____

    _____

CHALLENGE

Discuss the ways that Mary Higgins Clark uses setting and weather to create the mood and build the suspense in *Where Are the Children?*

NAME _____ DATE _____

And Then There Were None by Agatha Christie

Place a (+) before each statement that is true and a (0) before each statement that is false.

_____ 1. All of the invited party members made the trip from London to the coast together.

_____ 2. Emily Brent had been hired as Mrs. Owens' secretary.

_____ 3. Dr. Armstrong was at the height of his medical career.

_____ 4. Fred Narracott was a guest who was invited to Indian Island.

_____ 5. All of the invited guests had committed crimes for which the law could not prosecute them.

_____ 6. Mr. and Mrs. Rogers had worked for Mr. Owens before.

_____ 7. Vera Claythorne had committed murder for the man that she loved.

_____ 8. Philip Lombard felt guilty because he had left twenty Africans to die.

_____ 9. Three of the guests were killed by drugs or poisons.

_____ 10. General Macarthur had a great desire to escape from Indian Island.

_____ 11. Vera Claythorne was the last of the guests to die.

_____ 12. Emily Brent shot Philip Lombard.

_____ 13. After the Rogers' death, the survivors took turns doing the cooking.

_____ 14. Judge Wargrave's "murder" in the library was a fake.

_____ 15. Blore died by drowning.

_____ 16. Scotland Yard was able to solve the Indian Island case through information gained from the people in a nearby village.

_____ 17. Isaac Morris was really the tenth murder victim.

_____ 18. Judge Wargrave really committed suicide.

_____ 19. The Judge felt a deep sense of guilt after he had killed all of the others.

_____ 20. The case was finally solved by a manuscript that was found in a fishing boat.

368

NAME _____ DATE _____

And Then There Were None by Agatha Christie

Answer each of the following questions in two or three sentences.

1. Why was U.K. Owen mysterious? What did the name really stand for?

_____

_____

_____

_____

2. Describe the role that the weather plays in building the suspense of the story.

_____

_____

_____

_____

3. Which of the guests had committed crimes which were the result of accident or carelessness, rather than deliberate malice?

_____

_____

_____

_____

4. According to the Judge's manuscript, what was his motive for arranging the murders on Indian Island?

_____

_____

_____

_____

5. Explain the connection between the killings, the nursery rhyme, and the set of china statues.

_____

_____

_____

_____

CHALLENGE

Write an essay explaining why you believe, or do not believe, that Judge Wargrave was right in taking the administration of justice into his own hands. Even though each of the victims may have been guilty, did Wargrave have the moral right to act as executioner?

NAME _____ DATE _____

The Mousetrap by Agatha Christie

Place a (+) before each statement that is true and a (0) before each statement that is false.

_____ 1. Giles and Molly had had previous experience in the hotel business.

_____ 2. The snow contributes to both the atmosphere and the plot of the play.

_____ 3. Mrs. Boyle is the only guest who did not have a reservation.

_____ 4. Mrs. Stanning had been murdered with a carving knife.

_____ 5. Sergeant Trotter arrives at Monkswell Manor in a jeep.

_____ 6. Wren offers to help Molly with the cooking.

_____ 7. The child who died in the Longacre Farm abuse case was a little girl.

_____ 8. Suspense builds as the author provides motive and opportunity for each of the characters.

_____ 9. One important clue is a notebook.

_____ 10. Miss Caswell had been responsible for sending the three children to Longacre Farm.

_____ 11. Sergeant Trotter told the others that the heavy snow had knocked down the telephone wires.

_____ 12. Molly finds a bus ticket which indicates that Giles had been in London on the day of the murder.

_____ 13. Molly knew nothing about Giles' family or background when she married him.

_____ 14. The father of the abused children had died of alcoholism.

_____ 15. Trotter tells each person to return to the spot where he or she had been when Mrs. Boyle was killed.

_____ 16. Molly is the killer's third intended victim.

_____ 17. Christopher Wren is really a policeman in disguise.

_____ 18. Giles was the other brother of the Longacre Farm children.

_____ 19. Kathy recognizes her brother by a gesture of his hand in his hair.

_____ 20. Paravicini really had nothing to do with the case at all.

150 Great Books

NAME _____ DATE _____

The Mousetrap by Agatha Christie

Answer each of the following questions in two or three complete sentences.

1. What difficulties do Molly and Giles have in making Monkswell Manor into a suitable guesthouse?

_____

_____

_____

_____

2. Which of the play's characters had no involvement whatever with the case of the child who had died at Longacre Farm?

_____

_____

_____

_____

3. In what ways did Molly and Mrs. Boyle contribute indirectly to Jimmy's death?

_____

_____

_____

_____

4. How does Miss Caswell act to save Molly's life?

_____

_____

_____

_____

5. How is the nursery rhyme, "Three Blind Mice," related to the action of the play?

_____

_____

_____

_____

CHALLENGE

Write an essay describing the ways that Agatha Christie makes each of her characters look guilty. How does this guilt add to the surprise when the identity of the actual killer is revealed?

NAME _____ DATE _____

Jamaica Inn by Daphne Du Maurier

Select the letter of the word or phrase which correctly completes each statement.

_____ 1. Mary goes to live at Jamaica Inn (A) after her mother dies (B) after her father dies (C) when she is married (D) when Aunt Patience writes to invite her.

_____ 2. The attitude of the country people toward the Inn and its landlord seems to be (A) fear (B) appreciation (C) jealousy (D) indifference.

_____ 3. Joss Merlyn is (A) a bully (B) a smuggler (C) an alcoholic (D) all of the above.

_____ 4. Mary sees her first evidence of the Inn's illegal trade (A) in the bar (B) when the wagons unload (C) in the locked room (D) when the Squire comes to find Joss.

_____ 5. Mary finds her aunt to be (A) angry and aggressive (B) nervous and afraid (C) part of the smuggling operation (D) just as Mary had remembered her.

_____ 6. One of the smugglers is hanged when (A) he wants more money (B) he threatens to turn informer (C) he wants to take over the leadership (D) he objects to committing murder.

_____ 7. Jem Merlyn is (A) a horse thief (B) twenty years younger than Joss (C) strangely attractive to Mary (D) all of the above.

_____ 8. Mary first reveals her suspicions about the smugglers to (A) Francis Davey (B) Jem (C) Squire Bassett (D) Richards.

_____ 9. Jem best shows his cleverness when he (A) outwits his brother (B) sells the Squire his own horse (C) breaks a window at the Inn (D) abandons Mary at the Christmas fair.

_____ 10. The wreckers get illegal cargoes by (A) putting up fake lights (B) moving the signal buoys (C) killing the sailors who make it to shore (D) all of the above.

_____ 11. The wreckers lose their cargo on Christmas Day because (A) Jem stops them (B) Mary informs the police (C) they stay on the beach after dawn (D) the Squire brings the constable.

_____ 12. Harry the pedlar suggests that (A) Joss is a poor leader (B) he wants more money (C) Joss should leave the Inn (D) Joss is not the boss of the operation.

_____ 13. After getting lost on the Moors, Mary is picked up by (A) Davey (B) Jem (C) Joss (D) Richards.

_____ 14. Joss Merlyn seems most to fear (A) Jem (B) Squire Bassett (C) Mary's suspicions (D) someone mysterious and unknown.

_____ 15. After escaping from the Inn, Mary goes first for help to (A) Bassett (B) Davey (C) Jem (D) the police in Bodmin.

_____ 16. Mary's companion on her return to the Inn is (A) Harry (B) Richards (C) Bassett (D) Jem.

_____ 17. Both Mary's uncle and aunt have (A) left the Inn (B) been strangled (C) been stabbed (D) been shot.

_____ 18. Mary first learns of Davey's twisted mind from (A) an overheard conversation (B) his letters (C) his housekeeper (D) his drawings.

_____ 19. Davey is unable to escape with Mary because (A) his horse goes lame (B) Mary signals the police (C) they are trapped in the mist (D) he drowns in the bog.

_____ 20. Mary is offered a job and a home (A) at the Inn (B) with the Squire's family (C) in her native village (D) in Bodmin.

150 Great Books

NAME _____ DATE _____

Jamaica Inn by Daphne Du Maurier

Answer each of the following questions in two or three complete sentences.

1. How does the weather add to the atmosphere in *Jamaica Inn?*

    _____

    _____

    _____

    _____

2. What effects does Joss Merlyn's personality have on his wife?

    _____

    _____

    _____

    _____

3. In what ways does Jem Merlyn both attract and repel Mary?

    _____

    _____

    _____

    _____

4. How does the Squire finally get the evidence that he needs to end the wreckers' operations?

    _____

    _____

    _____

    _____

5. How does Mary Yellan show herself to be a young woman of courage and intelligence?

    _____

    _____

    _____

    _____

CHALLENGE

Discuss the plot twists and elements of surprise that the author uses in *Jamaica Inn*. How does she lead the reader to expect one conclusion, while another is really true? Why is her use of these twists successful?

NAME _____ DATE _____

Rebecca by Daphne Du Maurier

Select the letter of the word or phrase which correctly completes each statement.

_____ 1. The novel begins (A) in Scotland (B) in Monte Carlo (C) with a dream sequence (D) at Manderley.

_____ 2. The narrator is (A) Max deWinter (B) Mrs. Danvers (C) deWinter's second wife (D) an objective third person.

_____ 3. Mrs. Van Hopper was (A) crude and offensive (B) a social snob (C) an American (D) all of the above.

_____ 4. Max and the young girl get well acquainted (A) by having dinner (B) by going driving (C) by dancing (D) by playing tennis.

_____ 5. The narrator's feelings about Rebecca included (A) fear (B) curiosity (C) jealousy (D) all of the above.

_____ 6. The bride and groom return to Manderley (A) at night (B) in the spring (C) with no one knowing they were coming (D) in midsummer.

_____ 7. The new Mrs. deWinter is most intimidated by (A) Mrs. Danvers (B) Jasper (C) Frith (D) Beatrice.

_____ 8. During her first interview with Mrs. Danvers, the bride (A) tries to make friends (B) criticizes the redecorating job (C) takes over the management of the house (D) says that she wants a room overlooking the sea.

_____ 9. Life at Manderley makes the new bride feel (A) shy (B) incompetent (C) haunted by Rebecca's ghost (D) all of the above.

_____ 10. The bride learns about the close relationship between Rebecca and Mrs. Danvers from (A) Max (B) Frith (C) Robert (D) Beatrice.

_____ 11. The bride finds Rebecca's abandoned cottage when she (A) goes there with Max (B) asks Ben for directions (C) follows Jasper (D) gets directions from Mrs. Danvers.

_____ 12. She learns the story of Rebecca's drowning from (A) Frank Crawley (B) Max (C) Mrs. Danvers (D) Jack Flavell.

_____ 13. The suggestion for the bride's ball gown comes from (A) the bishop's wife (B) Mrs. Danvers (C) Lady Crowan (D) Beatrice.

_____ 14. The girl realizes how totally she has been tricked when (A) she sees the fury on Max's face (B) she sees Mrs. Danvers' expression of triumph (C) Beatrice tells her that Rebecca had worn the same dress (D) all of the above.

_____ 15. Mrs. Danvers tries to force the young wife (A) to go back to France (B) to get a divorce (C) to commit suicide (D) to move out of Manderley.

_____ 16. Questions about Rebecca's death arise when (A) her boat is found (B) Flavell brings in new evidence (C) Mrs. Danvers decides to testify (D) Ben tells what he has seen.

_____ 17. Max tells his wife that he (A) hated Rebecca (B) shot Rebecca (C) sank Rebecca's boat (D) all of the above.

_____ 18. The claim that Rebecca's boat sank by accident was refuted by (A) Colonel Julyan (B) Captain Searles (C) Mr. Tabb (D) Frank Crawley.

_____ 19. Dr. Baker's evidence proved that (A) Rebecca was insane (B) Rebecca had been critically ill (C) Frank had killed Rebecca (D) Rebecca had committed suicide.

_____ 20. At the end of the novel (A) Mrs. Danvers had disappeared (B) Manderley was on fire (C) the deWinters had decided to leave for Europe (D) all of the above.

NAME _____ DATE _____

Rebecca by Daphne Du Maurier

Answer each of the following questions in two or three complete sentences.

1. How was the second Mrs. deWinter contrasted with Rebecca?

_____

_____

_____

_____

2. How does Mrs. Danvers deliberately make the new bride feel frightened and inadequate?

_____

_____

_____

_____

3. What clues does old Ben provide in the mystery of Rebecca's death?

_____

_____

_____

_____

4. How was Max's marriage to Rebecca a total pretense?

_____

_____

_____

_____

5. Why does Max say that Rebecca laughed when he shot her?

_____

_____

_____

_____

CHALLENGE

How does the author develop the character of the second Mrs. deWinter? Through what experiences does she change from a frightened girl into a mature woman?

NAME _____ DATE _____

Angel Street (Gas Light) by Patrick Hamilton

Correctly complete each sentence with information from the play.

1. As the play opens, Manningham has agreed to take his wife to _____.

2. Bella is very jealous of _____.

3. Manningham has accused his wife of _____.

4. He treats Mrs. Manningham like _____.

5. The servant most loyal to Mrs. Manningham is _____.

6. Rough has learned what goes on in the Manningham household from _____.

7. Rough had first been involved in the Barlow case when _____.

8. Manningham's real name is _____.

9. Mrs. Manningham can tell when her husband is coming home because _____.

10. Alice Barlow's killer did not find _____.

11. In Manningham's locked desk, Rough finds _____.

12. Manningham really spends his evenings searching for _____.

13. Rough finds the rubies in _____.

14. Manningham is attracted to _____.

15. Manningham becomes angry when he finds _____.

16. Manningham tricks his wife into coming downstairs by telling her _____.

17. Manningham threatens to have his wife _____.

18. Rough arrests Manningham for _____.

19. In the last scene, Mrs. Manningham threatens her husband with _____.

20. As the play closes, the audience is not sure _____.

NAME _____ DATE _____

Angel Street (Gas Light) by Patrick Hamilton

Answer each of the following questions in two or three complete sentences.

1. Why does Bella Manningham think that she is losing her mind?

   _____

   _____

   _____

   _____

2. How had Rough connected Manningham to the Barlow case?

   _____

   _____

   _____

   _____

3. What evidence does Rough find that Manningham is trying to drive his wife mad?

   _____

   _____

   _____

   _____

4. How do they accidentally find the rubies?

   _____

   _____

   _____

   _____

5. How is Bella's sanity really in doubt in the last scene?

   _____

   _____

   _____

   _____

CHALLENGE

Write an essay describing the special technical effects which would be necessary to a production of *Angel Street*.

NAME _____ DATE _____

Arsenic and Old Lace by Joseph Kesselring

Place a (+) before each statement that is true and a (0) before each statement that is false.

_____ 1. As the play opens, Reverend Witherspoon is visiting with the aunts.

_____ 2. Teddy thinks that he is Theodore Roosevelt.

_____ 3. Mortimer Brewster is an actor.

_____ 4. The aunts have become famous in the neighborhood for their acts of charity.

_____ 5. The first of the aunts' victims had really died of pneumonia.

_____ 6. The aunts killed their victims with poisoned tea.

_____ 7. The poisons came from an old laboratory in the house.

_____ 8. The aunts are on very good terms with the local police officers.

_____ 9. Aunt Martha had killed Mr. Hoskins by herself.

_____ 10. Mortimer saves Mr. Gibbs' life.

_____ 11. The aunts call in Elaine's father to conduct the funeral services for each of their victims.

_____ 12. Jonathan and Mortimer got along very well when they were boys.

_____ 13. Jonathan and Dr. Einstein plan to set up their criminal operations in the aunts' home.

_____ 14. Mr. Spenalzo is the aunts' thirteenth victim.

_____ 15. Abby and Martha agree that Mr. Spenalzo should be buried in the cellar with the others.

_____ 16. Officer Klein forces Mortimer to listen to the plot of a play that the officer has written.

_____ 17. Jonathan and Einstein are both captured and returned to prison.

_____ 18. When Lieutenant Rooney hears about the thirteen bodies, he orders an immediate search of the cellar.

_____ 19. Elaine is very upset when she learns that Mortimer is not really a member of the Brewster family.

_____ 20. Mr. Witherspoon becomes another "victim" of the aunts' charity.

150 Great Books

NAME _____ DATE _____

Arsenic and Old Lace by Joseph Kesselring

Answer each of the following questions in two or three complete sentences.

1. How does Mortimer react when he learns that his sweet old aunts are murdering people?

    _____

    _____

    _____

    _____

2. Why do the police refuse to believe the truth when it is told to them?

    _____

    _____

    _____

    _____

3. How does Teddy's insanity contribute to the plot of the play?

    _____

    _____

    _____

    _____

4. Why do the aunts view their killings as acts of "charity"?

    _____

    _____

    _____

    _____

5. How do the aunts prevent Mr. Witherspoon from taking Teddy to Happy Dale?

    _____

    _____

    _____

    _____

CHALLENGE

Write an essay describing some of the plot tricks that the author uses in *Arsenic and Old Lace* to make murder and insanity seem comic to the audience.

NAME _____ DATE _____

Clouds of Witness by Dorothy L. Sayers

In the numbered blanks at the left, write the letter of the matching person or place.

_____ 1. Peter Wimsey's mother

_____ 2. Went to Paris to find important evidence

_____ 3. Overheard the Duke arguing with Cathcart

_____ 4. Could have provided the Duke with an alibi

_____ 5. Lied at the inquest to protect the man that she planned to elope with

_____ 6. Wrote to the Duke to warn him about Cathcart

_____ 7. Tried for murder in the House of Lords

_____ 8. Insanely violent, jealous man

_____ 9. Where Peter identified Goyles

_____ 10. Engaged to Lady Mary

_____ 11. Wimsey's valet and assistant

_____ 12. Had the right to try its own members in all felony cases

_____ 13. Gerald's defense attorney

_____ 14. Cathcart's French mistress who abandoned him and went to America

_____ 15. Wealthy, urbane, amateur detective

_____ 16. Rather stupid houseguest of the Duke

_____ 17. Swampy bog which nearly claimed two lives

_____ 18. Shot Wimsey in the shoulder

_____ 19. Found strange stains on her mistress' skirt

_____ 20. Scene of the murder

A. Duke of Denver
B. Riddlesdale
C. Bunter
D. Inspector Parker
E. Ellen
F. Denis Cathcart
G. Peter Wimsey
H. Mrs. Grimethorpe
I. Tommy Freeborn
J. Peter's Pot
K. Sir Impey Biggs
L. Goyles
M. Simone Vonderaa
N. Lady Mary
O. Dowager Duchess
P. Mr. Grimethorpe
Q. House of Lords
R. Soviet Club
S. Freddy Arbuthnot
T. Mr. Pettigrew-Robinson

NAME _____ DATE _____

Clouds of Witness by Dorothy L. Sayers

Explain in two or three sentences the importance of each of the following clues to the final solution of the mystery.

1. The jeweled cat

   _____

   _____

   _____

   _____

2. The stains on the skirt

   _____

   _____

   _____

   _____

3. The missing letter

   _____

   _____

   _____

   _____

4. The stolen license plates

   _____

   _____

   _____

   _____

5. The imprint of a suitcase

   _____

   _____

   _____

   _____

CHALLENGE

Write an essay to discuss the ways in which *Clouds of Witness* proves that what may seem to be the obvious solution to a situation is not necessarily the true solution.

150 Great Books

NAME _____ DATE _____

Nine Coaches Waiting by Mary Stewart

In the numbered blanks at the left, write the letter of the matching person or place.

_____ 1. Cooperated with her husband in the plans to poison Phillipe

_____ 2. Local village druggist

_____ 3. Fought constantly with his father about money

_____ 4. Town near the Valmy estate

_____ 5. Jealous maid who spread rumors about Linda and Raoul

_____ 6. Is compared to a fallen demon king

_____ 7. Leon's estate, managed by Raoul

_____ 8. English housekeeper

_____ 9. Got Linda her job with the Valmys

_____ 10. First told Linda of the murder plot

_____ 11. Phillipe's father who was killed in a plane crash

_____ 12. House where Phillipe and Linda ended their flight from Valmy

_____ 13. Still was waiting for the sound of his parents' returning automobile

_____ 14. Leon Valmy's first wife, Raoul's mother

_____ 15. English forester who comes to Linda's aid

_____ 16. Pretended not to speak or understand French in order to get her job

_____ 17. Orphanage where Linda grew up

_____ 18. Scene of the grand Easter ball

_____ 19. Youngest of the Valmy brothers, an archeologist

_____ 20. Tried to shoot Phillipe in the woods

A. Thonon
B. Etienne
C. Heloise
D. Phillipe
E. Leon
F. Linda
G. Bernard
H. Berthe
I. Albertine
J. Mrs. Siddons
K. William Blake
L. Hippolyte
M. Raoul
N. Villa Mireille
O. Bellevigne
P. Chateau Valmy
Q. Lady Benchley
R. Constance Butcher
S. Deborah
T. Monsieur Garcin

NAME _____ DATE _____

Nine Coaches Waiting by Mary Stewart

Answer each of the following questions in two or three complete sentences.

1. Why is Linda Martin so anxious to return to France?

    _____

    _____

    _____

    _____

2. What are Linda's first feelings about Leon Valmy? How do these feelings later prove correct?

    _____

    _____

    _____

    _____

3. What warning does Florimond give Linda at the Easter ball?

    _____

    _____

    _____

    _____

4. What details of the murder plot does Linda learn from Berthe?

    _____

    _____

    _____

    _____

5. How does Heloise Valmy attempt to justify the attempts to murder Phillipe?

    _____

    _____

    _____

    _____

CHALLENGE

Write an essay describing Linda Martin's internal conflict between her responsibility for Phillipe and her love for Raoul. In what ways does she show her strength and maturity as she handles this situation?

ANSWER KEYS

The Innocents by William Archibald

OBJECTIVE:

1. C	6. D	11. B	16. C
2. B	7. C	12. B	17. C
3. B	8. D	13. A	18. A
4. C	9. C	14. C	19. C
5. C	10. D	15. A	20. D

SHORT ANSWER:

1. Miss Giddens' concern over their uncle's indifference. Mrs. Grose has motherly concern for their welfare.
2. Very adult conversation, intense secretiveness.
3. To carry on their love affair. The ghosts had invaded the bodies of the children.
4. Becomes openly sinister. The personality of Quint comes through.
5. He is free of the ghost, but he is dead.

CHALLENGE:

Light and shadow for the appearance of the ghosts. Music also used for the supernatural. Dim lighting important in night scenes and scenes on the staircase.

The Chalk Garden by Enid Bagnold

OBJECTIVE:

1. +	6. +	11. 0	16. 0
2. 0	7. 0	12. +	17. +
3. 0	8. +	13. +	18. +
4. +	9. 0	14. +	19. 0
5. 0	10. 0	15. +	20. 0

SHORT ANSWER:

1. Setting fires, general impertinence and excessive curiosity. Tendency to lie and exaggerate.
2. Less of a governess stereotype. Much more in control. A woman of mystery with strength.
3. Over who will be in control. Olivia rebelled against her mother to live her own life.
4. Comments and responses about what happens in court from the prisoner's point of view.
5. To help care for her garden and to relieve her loneliness.

CHALLENGE:

Laurel's life is like the garden. Cannot grow in shallow soil without love. Mrs. St. Maugham's life is also barren. She needs to relate and to be needed.

Where Are the Children? by Mary Higgins Clark

OBJECTIVE:

1. Cape Cod
2. murdering her children
3. unsolved murder trials
4. Rob Legler ran away, not enough evidence
5. Missy and Michael, the Lookout
6. newspaper article
7. New York, he had been in love with Nancy's mother
8. dragging the lake, setting up roadblocks
9. going to the store at the same time every day
10. Dorothy and John Kragopolis
11. blackmail Nancy
12. hypnosis
13. rubber duck in the full tub
14. lights went out
15. Dorothy found the mitten
16. Carl, she suspected the truth
17. sexual involvement with children
18. Neal Kinnon
19. kill, drowning
20. Ray Eldridge

ANSWER KEYS (continued)

Where Are the Children? by Mary Higgins Clark (continued)

SHORT ANSWER:

1. Moved to Cape Cod, took a new name, cut and dyed her hair.
2. Residence in the house, established alibi in the community, sent the article to make Nancy look guilty, watched the house through the telescope.
3. Accounts the death of the first children, episode with Legler, the death of Nancy's mother.
4. Article in the paper reveals Nancy's identity and links her with the other children's deaths.
5. John Kragopolis becomes suspicious of Parrish, Giddens sees Legler in the woods, Neal recognizes Carl Harmon as Courtney Parrish.

CHALLENGE:

Rain, sleet give eerie atmosphere. Sleet storm and icy roads make the final chase to the Lookout more dangerous.

And Then There Were None by Agatha Christie

OBJECTIVE:

1. O	6. O	11. +	16. O
2. O	7. +	12. O	17. +
3. +	8. O	13. O	18. +
4. O	9. +	14. +	19. O
5. +	10. O	15. O	20. +

SHORT ANSWER:

1. No one had ever met him. Identity unknown.
2. Trapped by the storm, electricity cut off, no way off the island.
3. Lombard abandoned his men in India. Armstrong—medical malpractice. Emily Brent—cruel dismissal of servant led to suicide.
4. To get revenge for the crimes for which the law cannot punish the criminals.
5. As each one died, a statue from the set disappeared.

CHALLENGE:

Wide variety of answers possible. Does any man have the right to play God with the lives of others? The Judge took that right. His own desire to commit murder made him guilty also. But he felt absolutely no guilt at all.

The Mousetrap by Agatha Christie

OBJECTIVE:

1. O	6. +	11. O	16. +
2. +	7. O	12. O	17. O
3. O	8. +	13. +	18. O
4. O	9. +	14. O	19. +
5. O	10. O	15. O	20. +

ANSWER KEYS (continued)

The Mousetrap by Agatha Christie (continued)

SHORT ANSWER:

1. No help to do cooking or housework, difficulty with the heating system, isolation by the storm.
2. Paravicini—really only a petty thief, Metcalf a policeman, Giles and Christopher—no connection.
3. Molly—school teacher who ignored the plea for help. Mrs. Boyle—the magistrate who sent the children to the farm.
4. She tells Georgie that she is his sister—quiets him down.
5. He had already killed the farmer's wife and Mrs. Boyle. Molly was the third mouse in the trap.

CHALLENGE:

Giles and Molly both have been on mysterious errands. Molly knows little about her husband. Paravicini—the stock villain. Wren—nervous type, very mysterious. Only Trotter who seems so normal is really insane.

Jamaica Inn by Daphne Du Maurier

OBJECTIVE:

1. A	6. D	11. C	16. B
2. A	7. D	12. D	17. C
3. D	8. A	13. A	18. D
4. B	9. B	14. D	19. C
5. B	10. D	15. B	20. B

SHORT ANSWER:

1. Storm when Mary arrives. She gets lost in the fog. The wreckers work in storms and darkness.
2. She is terrified constantly and very secretive.
3. Finds him attractive, but is afraid of him because she thinks that he is like his brother.
4. Brings the constable to raid the inn, tracks and captures Davey.
5. She listens and observes. Goes for help in spite of the danger. Determined to outwit her uncle and his friends. Recognizes the truth when she finds the drawings.

CHALLENGE:

One who seems most guilty is Jem. Davey who seems the safest is really the most evil. Uses exciting chase scenes. Builds suspense by letting the reader know events only as Mary knows them.

Rebecca by Daphne Du Maurier

OBJECTIVE:

1. C	6. D	11. C	16. A
2. C	7. A	12. A	17. D
3. D	8. A	13. B	18. C
4. B	9. D	14. D	19. B
5. D	10. D	15. C	20. D

ANSWER KEYS (continued)

Rebecca by Daphne Du Maurier (continued)

SHORT ANSWER:
1. Rebecca the perfect hostess, ideal society woman. Second wife sensitive, shy, inexperienced.
2. Cold hostile manner, forced tour of Rebecca's room. Trick with the ball gown to make Max angry.
3. He saw Rebecca at the cottage. Saw Max put her body into the boat.
4. Outwardly perfect—inwardly thoroughly morally rotten.
5. Because she was dying, she wanted him to kill her. Her last act of getting even.

CHALLENGE:
From a scared child to a mature woman. She stands by her husband in time of crisis, and becomes sure of Max's love when she knows the truth about Rebecca.

Angel Street (Gas Light) by Patrick Hamilton

OBJECTIVE:
1. the theater
2. Nancy
3. losing things
4. a disobedient child
5. Elizabeth
6. Nancy's boyfriend
7. he was a rookie policeman
8. Sidney Power
9. the lights come up
10. the rubies
11. her brooch, a letter from her relatives
12. the rubies
13. in the vase
14. Nancy
15. his desk has been forced open
16. the dog has been hurt
17. put into an insane asylum
18. murder
19. a razor
20. whether Mrs. Manningham is sane or not

SHORT ANSWER:
1. Things keep disappearing, her husband keeps accusing her.
2. He had seen Sidney Power. He saw Manningham when the couple moved back into the neighborhood.
3. All the things she had supposedly lost he had really hidden.
4. In the vase, they had fallen out of the pin.
5. Threatens him with a razor and enjoys it. Would she really have killed him?

CHALLENGE:
Many light cues important. Raising and lowering of gas to coincide with Manningham's entrances and exits.

Arsenic and Old Lace by Joseph Kesselring

OBJECTIVE:
1. 0
2. +
3. 0
4. +
5. 0
6. 0
7. +
8. +
9. 0
10. +
11. 0
12. 0
13. +
14. 0
15. 0
16. 0
17. +
18. 0
19. 0
20. +

ANSWER KEYS (continued)

Arsenic and Old Lace by Joseph Kesselring (continued)

SHORT ANSWER:
1. Totally horrified when he finds the body. The need to protect them because he thinks they are crazy.
2. The aunts are sweet old ladies who are well-known in the neighborhood for good deeds.
3. Thinks he is Roosevelt. Digging the graves in the cellar becomes digging the Panama Canal.
4. The victims are homeless and they have no one.
5. They give Witherspoon some of the poisoned wine.

CHALLENGE:

Teddy and his bugle interrupt at several key points in the action—as Jonathan and Einstein are going to drink the wine. The police are totally incompetent. Action becomes a farce as characters constantly run in and out. The crazy aunts seem the sanest people in the cast.

Clouds of Witness by Dorothy L. Sayers

OBJECTIVE:

1. O	6. I	11. C	16. S
2. D	7. A	12. Q	17. J
3. T	8. P	13. K	18. L
4. H	9. R	14. M	19. E
5. N	10. F	15. G	20. B

SHORT ANSWER:
1. Found in the garden by Wimsey and Parker. Belonged to Cathcart. Thrown by Cathcart before he died.
2. Found on Lady Mary's skirt by her maid, Ellen. Proved that she had been on the muddy walk.
3. Love letter from Mrs. Grimethorpe—would have provided the Duke with an alibi, but he was too much of a gentleman to use it.
4. Stolen from Rev. Nathaniel Foulis—on the motorcycle that Goyles used to escape from the scene of the crime.
5. Lady Mary carried it when she came down to elope with Goyles. Set it down in the mud.

CHALLENGE:

Everyone looked guilty. The Duke had quarreled with Cathcart. Lady Mary was in the garden. Wimsey and Bunter expose what is not visible. Many minor crimes and other motives. The murder was really a suicide.

Nine Coaches Waiting by Mary Stewart

OBJECTIVE:

1. C	6. E	11. B	16. F
2. T	7. O	12. N	17. R
3. M	8. J	13. D	18. P
4. A	9. Q	14. S	19. L
5. I	10. H	15. K	20. G

ANSWER KEYS (continued)

Nine Coaches Waiting by Mary Stewart (continued)

SHORT ANSWER:

1. She had spent her childhood there. Fond memories of her father.
2. A fallen archangel. She sees him as a man who will stop at nothing to get what he wants.
3. Beware of Raoul and his advances.
4. Bernard and Leon are involved in a plot to kill Phillipe.
5. Leon had put so much into the estate that he had a right to it. Phillipe was in the way.

CHALLENGE:

She believes Raoul to be involved. She puts her responsibility above her feelings. Protects Phillipe by taking him first to Blake's cabin and then to his uncle Hippolyte's house.

UNIT 9

Relived Memories—
CHILDHOOD REMEMBERED

SYNOPSES

A Death in the Family
by James Agee

Set in a small American town in the 1920s, this powerful novel deals with responses to death from an adult's and from a child's point of view. The novel's plot is told by an omniscient narrator. The commentary on the plot comes through the mind of a child. Rufus Follett's father Jay is killed in a car accident. Adult attitudes toward Jay's death vary greatly. His wife Mary, helped by her aunt Hannah, clings to her religious faith. Mary's brother Andrew questions the reason behind such a senseless tragedy. Walter Starr, the handyman, best understands the feeling of the children, Rufus and Catherine. Walter lets the children view the funeral procession so they may say goodbye to their father. Flashbacks relate Rufus' memories of his parents—the swish of his mother's skirts and the smell of his father's pipe. Internal narrative gives the child's thoughts as he senses the tension of the adults after his father is killed. Rufus instinctively cares for his little sister, and absorbs the feelings of the situation without really understanding the reason. Agee, in this novel, gives a sensitive account of a child's efforts to deal with reality.

Little Women
by Louisa May Alcott

This nineteenth-century classic tells the story of the March girls, who are growing up in Concord, Massachusetts in the years during and after the Civil War. Meg, Jo, Amy, and Beth try to help their mother and to follow the models of virtue in *Pilgrim's Progress*. Their next door neighbor, Laurie Laurence, becomes like their brother. The girls are fond of music and drama, but not so fond of housework. Wealthy Aunt March tries to run the family, but her efforts are firmly resisted. The girls learn some important lessons the hard way. After losing her temper with Amy, Jo learns how much she cares for her sister when Amy falls through the ice. Meg learns the foolishness of pretensions at a high society party. Beth's musical talent helps heal a neighbor's grief. The little women grow up; each eventually establishes a family of her own. Although this novel is rather didactic and sentimental by modern standards, the family values of closeness and sharing make *Little Women* timeless reading.

I Know Why the Caged Bird Sings
by Maya Angelou

This black poet's autobiography recounts Maya's developing years in Stamps, Arkansas during the 1950s. When their parents divorce, Maya and her brother Bailey are sent to live with their grandmother, Momma Henderson. They are visited infrequently by their parents. On one visit to her mother in St. Louis, Maya is raped by her mother's boyfriend. Momma Henderson provides a strong value system for the children. Her discipline is stern, but fair. She illustrates strong religious principles and great courage as she faces mobs of white hooligans who threaten her store. As a child, Maya saw herself as ugly. Her spirit longs to break free of Stamps. After graduating from high school, Maya goes to live with her father in California. She is driven out by her father's girlfriend and is forced to live for a month with a group of hobos in a used car lot. Despite a turbulent childhood, Maya Angelou is a strong woman. She was taught to "sing" in Stamps by the firm teaching and support she received.

My Antonia
by Willa Cather

This novel is set on the prairies of Nebraska at the turn of the twentieth century as Jim Burden recalls his childhood sweetheart, Antonia. When Antonia's family first emigrated from Bohemia, they lived a life of terrible poverty in a sod hut. The stress from this life finally caused Antonia's father to commit suicide. Antonia and Jim, however, found beauty as they explored the plant and animal life of the countryside. As teenagers, Jim and Antonia both boarded in the town of Black Hawk. Jim was being tutored for college, Antonia worked as a housekeeper. Jim's narrative recalls their companions, some of whom remained in Nebraska. Others left forever, like Lena, who became a fashionable dress designer in San Francisco. In the third section of the book, Jim returns after twenty years to visit Antonia. He finds, on the farm with her, an affirmation of the simple values of midwestern life. Jim also knows that anything he achieved was done for his Antonia.

Cheaper by the Dozen
by Frank Gilbreth Jr. and Ernestine Gilbreth Carey

This amusing family memoir recounts the trials of growing up around 1915 in a household with one dozen children. The authors fondly remember their brothers and sisters and their mother, but most of all their father. Father was a blustery extrovert whose word seemed to be law. Mother, however, worked more quietly behind the scenes. An efficiency expert, Father used his children for various experiments, such as teaching lessons by phonograph record and filming their tonsil operations. On trips in "Foolish Carriage," the family automobile, they frequently got lost because Father refused to listen to anyone else's directions. The Gilbreth household is pictured as a place where, in spite of the confusion, each child learned self-respect and a sense of responsibility. Frank and Ernestine remember their childhood with humor and great appreciation for the solid gifts they received from their parents.

Life with Father
by Howard Lindsay and Russel Crouse

Based on the memoirs of Clarence Day, Jr., this play shows how a woman can manage a man. Father's temper is so volcanic that no servants will stay very long. He fights when cousins come to visit because he refuses to spend the money to go out to dinner. Yet, in spite of all his failings, Father deeply loves his wife and sons. The real action of the drama begins when Mother finds out, to her horror, that Father has never been baptized. Meanwhile, sons John and Whitney, who are selling tonic to make money, almost kill their mother when they put some of the stuff into her tea. While Mother is ill, she makes Father promise that he will be baptized. However loudly Mr. Day roars, Mrs. Day always manages to get around him. She feigns ignorance or does things first and tells her husband afterward. This wonderful family comedy provides a humorous look at everyday life in the 1890s.

How Green Was My Valley
by Richard Llewellyn

This novel tells of Huw Morgan's growing up in a mining town in Wales early in the twentieth century. Huw remembers with affection his parents, and he mourns the simple life which has been lost as industry destroys the countryside. Young Huw had his own moment of courage as he risked his own life to save his mother from drowning. After his older brother Ivor is killed in a mine cave-in, Huw looks after his widow Bronwen, the real love of the boy's life. Huw remembers his big brothers, the best colliers in the valley, who were forced to leave when the mine owners would not give them work. Huw's mentor is the village minister, Mr. Gruffydd, who helps the boy get a scholarship to the National School. To get this education, the country boy must learn to defend himself against the taunts of his classmates and the brutality of the masters. Although he graduates with honors, Huw chooses to return to the mines. His father is killed in a great mine disaster. Mr. Gruffydd is driven out when the village gossip tarnishes the character of the minister and Huw's sister, Angharad. Huw finally leaves because everything that he loved is gone. Although the Welch names and words make reading this book a bit difficult, this novel is an excellent account of one boy's passage to manhood.

The Learning Tree
by Gordon Parks

Newt Winger is a young black boy growing up in Cherokee Flats, Kansas in the 1950s. Newt's mother Sarah influences her son's life. She teaches him that honesty matters more than the color of one's skin. Sarah also defends Newt's sister against her drunken husband. When the town refuses to allow the black freshman to enter the high school, Sarah battles the town authorities for educational opportunities for her son. Newt shows this kind of courage as he faces the prejudice of Miss McClintock, a teacher who would keep all black students "in their place." When Newt witnesses the murder of white neighbor Jake Kiner by Negro Booker Savage, Newt is afraid to report what he has seen. Although he fears racial repercussions in the community, Newt finally stands up in court and tells what he has seen. When Newt's mother dies, the boy's childhood ends as he goes to live with his sister. Newt's character has already been formed. Cherokee Flats has been the "learning tree." the young man knows that the most important fruit of people's character is not what they say, but is in the way they live.

A Day No Pigs Would Die
by Robert Newton Peck

Robert's family belongs to a community of Shakers in Vermont. Although Robert does not like school, his father insists that his son have the learning that the father lacks. Robert is wise in the ways of land and animals. His favorite friend is his pet pig, Pinky. The greatest journey of the lad's life was to the Rutland Fair, where Pinky won a blue ribbon. Robert shares the Shakers' close communal identity as he goes with his father to help a neighbor bury a grandchild. The boy's next experience with death comes when Pinky, who refuses to breed, has to be slaughtered. At thirteen, Robert learns that his father is dying. Robert dresses in his father's clothes for the funeral. He must now become the man of the family. The story gains power since it is told from Robert's point of view. Much humor is achieved as Robert misunderstands meanings of words and conversations that he overhears. The book's most moving scene is the closeness between father and son as the pet pig must be killed. The author gives an excellent account of a boy's becoming a man at an early age.

Our Town
by Thornton Wilder

This simple drama is set in Grover's Corners, New Hampshire at the turn of the century. The author's purpose is to call our attention to the basic values of life which people tend to take for granted. George Gibbs and Emily Webb are teenage neighbors who grow up in Act I and are married in Act II. Act III is set in the cemetery. After Emily's death, she desires to return to the past. She views the scenes of one day in her life. This day passed without any real awareness of its importance. Town characters included the town gossip, Mrs. Soames, and Simon Stimson, the choir director who just does not fit in. An omniscient stage manager directs the actors and focuses the audience's attention on the past, the present, and the future. The play has little scenery; the reader's imagination must produce the sets. This optimistic drama affirms the value of everyday life.

The Glass Menagerie
by Tennessee Williams

Narrated by Tom Wingfield, the play is his memory of his mother Amanda and his sister Laura. Amanda's greatest fear is that Laura will be left alone and helpless. Abandoned by Tom's dashing father, Amanda lives in the glamorous past. On one brilliant afternoon, in the best southern tradition, she had entertained seventeen gentleman callers. Laura is a shy, sickly girl who spends her time with a pile of old phonograph records and a menagerie of glass animals. Nagged by his mother, Tom brings Jim, who works with him at the warehouse, home to meet Laura. Jim and Laura find that they had been acquainted in high school, where Laura had worshipped Jim from afar. Jim helps Laura to understand that, in spite of her handicaps, she is special, like the tiny glass unicorn in her menagerie. Amanda is furious with Tom when she finds out that Jim is engaged to someone else. Tom can stand the trap no longer; he leaves to join the Merchant Marine. As narrator, Tom concludes the play by saying that he is still not free because he sees his sister's face everywhere. Williams presents a powerful drama of individuals trapped by circumstances beyond their control. This play is one of the great classics of the American theater.

The Effect of Gamma Rays on Man-in-the-Moon Marigolds
by Paul Zindel

Beatrice is a frustrated woman who desires freedom. She lives in the past and dreams of an impossible future. The play's set, in total clutter and confusion, reflects the state of Beatrice's mind. Her two daughters have opposite personalities. Tillie is quiet, scholarly, and dependable. Ruth, an epileptic, is flighty and extreme like her mother. For the science fair, Tillie is raising marigold seeds which have been exposed to radioactivity. Tillie also has a pet rabbit, which her mother kills in a fit of temper. Nannie, the elderly lady who boards with them, constantly casts a shadow of death over the whole scene. Ruth is proud when Tillie's project wins the science fair. Beatrice continues to dream of the day when she can open a tearoom and make piles of money. Just as Tillie's plants are mutations which have been forced from their natural pattern of growth, Beatrice, Ruth and Tillie have all been psychologically twisted. The play ends on a positive note, however. Tillie, despite her mother's destructive tendencies, is still able to keep her mind alive and believe in human goodness.

NAME _____ DATE _____

A Death in the Family by James Agee

In the numbered blanks at the left, write the letter of the matching person, place, or thing.

_____ 1. Her father's nickname for Mary

_____ 2. Owned a gramophone

_____ 3. Setting of the novel

_____ 4. Was supported in the crisis by her firm religious faith.

_____ 5. Where Jay's body was taken after the accident

_____ 6. Jay's alcoholic brother who could not cope with his responsibilities

_____ 7. Stayed to care for Mary and the children after Jay's death

_____ 8. Elderly relative who looked after Jay's grandmother

_____ 9. Rufus' little sister

_____ 10. Allowed the children to see their father's funeral procession

_____ 11. Negro nurse who looked after the children when they were babies

_____ 12. Used an ear trumpet

_____ 13. Went to bring Jay's body home

_____ 14. Frequently drove too fast

_____ 15. Mary's father

_____ 16. Type of car that Jay drove

_____ 17. Was teased about his name by some older children

_____ 18. The cause of Jay's accident

_____ 19. Jay's epitaph

_____ 20. Priest who did not like children

A. Knoxville, Tennessee
B. Ralph
C. Catherine
D. Victoria
E. Jay
F. Mary
G. Andrew
H. Rufus
I. Aunt Hannah
J. Walter Starr
K. Poll
L. Father Jackson
M. Joel
N. Brannick's Blacksmith Shop
O. Mary's mother
P. "In his strength"
Q. Aunt Sadie
R. Tin Lizzie
S. Cotter pin
T. Mrs. Starr

150 Great Books

NAME _____ DATE _____

A *Death in the Family* by James Agee

Answer each of the following questions in two or three complete sentences.

1. Contrast Jay Follett with his brother Ralph.

   _____

   _____

   _____

   _____

2. On the morning of Jay's departure, how do Mary and Jay show that they love each other deeply?

   _____

   _____

   _____

   _____

3. In the novel's flashbacks, what memories of sight, sound, and smell does Rufus have of his parents?

   _____

   _____

   _____

   _____

4. How does Andrew's attitude toward God contrast with Mary's attitude?

   _____

   _____

   _____

   _____

5. How does Walter Starr show that he understands the real needs of Rufus and little Catherine?

   _____

   _____

   _____

   _____

CHALLENGE

Frequently, children may have a much greater grasp of deep realities than adults ever realize. How does *A Death in the Family* show such a grasp of reality in the ways that Rufus thinks and behaves when his father dies?

NAME _____ DATE _____

Little Women by Louisa May Alcott

Select the letter of the word or phrase which correctly completes each statement.

_____ 1. The book which most influenced the March girls' lives was (A) *Pilgrim's Progress* (B) the *Bible* (C) *Godey's Lady's Book* (D) Hannah Smith's *Advice to Young Girls.*

_____ 2. Mr. March had joined the army as (A) a militia commander (B) a clerk (C) a chaplain (D) a male nurse.

_____ 3. The most musical of the sisters was (A) Meg (B) Jo (C) Amy (D) Beth.

_____ 4. Mr. Brooke (A) was Laurie's tutor (B) married Meg (C) went with Mrs. March to Washington (D) all of the above.

_____ 5. Mr. Laurence gave Beth (A) some books (B) a set of drawing pencils (C) a piano (D) some new dresses.

_____ 6. Jo became very angry with Amy for (A) spilling her paint box (B) lying to her (C) burning her writings (D) spilling ink all over her papers.

_____ 7. Meg learned the foolishness of high society (A) from John (B) from Laurie (C) at the Moffat's party (D) from Aunt March.

_____ 8. Jo worked for a time (A) at the Moffats (B) for Mrs. Kirke (C) for the King family (D) as a newspaper reporter.

_____ 9. The March girls were all fond of (A) cooking (B) sewing (C) playing the piano (D) presenting dramas.

_____ 10. The most serious tragedy of the novel is the death of (A) Aunt March (B) Beth (C) Meg's child (D) Hannah.

_____ 11. Jo had published (A) a novel (B) some poems (C) a series of short stories (D) all of the above.

_____ 12. The first of the March girls to marry was (A) Meg (B) Jo (C) Beth (D) Amy.

_____ 13. Jo lost a chance to travel in Europe because (A) Aunt March didn't like her (B) Jo became ill (C) Jo was too outspoken (D) Jo couldn't leave Beth.

_____ 14. The length of time between the first section of the novel and the second is (A) five years (B) ten years (C) three years (D) six months.

_____ 15. Amy's picnic for her art class was a failure because (A) of the weather (B) no one wanted to come (C) the family wouldn't help (D) Amy got sick.

_____ 16. Jo learned the poor quality of the stories that she had been selling from (A) professor Bhaer (B) Mrs. Kirk (C) Marmee (D) Laurie.

_____ 17. Jo refused Laurie's marriage proposal because (A) Beth had just died (B) Laurie was too poor (C) Jo knew that Amy loved Laurie (D) Jo didn't love Laurie.

_____ 18. Amy and Laurie fell in love (A) in New York (B) in the March's garden (C) in Switzerland (D) in Mr. Laurence's home.

_____ 19. Daisy and Demi were (A) Meg's twins (B) pet Siamese kittens (C) handsome carriage horses (D) Beth's imaginary playmates.

_____ 20. The last of the March girls to marry was (A) Meg (B) Beth (C) Jo (D) Amy.

NAME _____ DATE _____

Little Women by Louisa May Alcott

Answer each of the following questions in two or three complete sentences.

1. How was Laurie important in the lives of the March girls as they grew up?

    _____

    _____

    _____

    _____

2. What important lesson did Jo learn when Amy fell through the ice?

    _____

    _____

    _____

    _____

3. Why did Beth's musical talent greatly help Mr. Laurence?

    _____

    _____

    _____

    _____

4. What advice did Mrs. March give Meg about being a wife and mother?

    _____

    _____

    _____

    _____

5. How did Jo's marriage to Professor Bhaer fulfill many of Jo's dreams?

    _____

    _____

    _____

    _____

CHALLENGE

Write an essay describing the values of family life which are presented by Louisa May Alcott in *Little Women*. How did each member fit into the family, and yet at the same time retain personal independence?

150 Great Books

NAME _____ DATE _____

I Know Why the Caged Bird Sings by Maya Angelou

In the numbered blanks at the left, write the letter of the matching person or place.

_____ 1. White employer who tried to change Maya's name

_____ 2. Negro student whose speech gave his class-mates pride in being black

_____ 3. Maya's full name

_____ 4. Where Maya and her brother lived for a time with their mother's relatives

_____ 5. Glamorous parent who was adored by her son

_____ 6. Grandmother who brought the children up

_____ 7. White dentist who refused to treat a black child

_____ 8. Left his daughter at the mercy of a gang of drunken Mexicans

_____ 9. Stabbed Maya because she was jealous of the child

_____ 10. Married Maya's mother when they lived in San Francisco

_____ 11. Small town in Arkansas where Maya spent her childhood

_____ 12. Her funeral gave Maya her first real awareness of death

_____ 13. Maya's brother and closest companion

_____ 14. Visiting preacher whom the children disliked

_____ 15. Bailey's first girlfriend

_____ 16. Lived for a month in an automobile junkyard

_____ 17. Raped Maya when she was eight years old

_____ 18. Got very emotionally carried away in the church service

_____ 19. Lame man who worked in the general store

_____ 20. Friend who introduced Maya to the beauties of literature

A. Henry Reed
B. Daddy Clidell
C. Big Bailey
D. Mrs. Florida Taylor
E. Joyce
F. Delores
G. Maya
H. Mother Dear
I. Sister Monroe
J. Mrs. Cullinan
K. Mrs. Flowers
L. Dr. Lincoln
M. Mr. Freeman
N. St. Louis
O. Rev. Thomas
P. Uncle Willie
Q. Momma Henderson
R. Bailey
S. Stamps
T. Marguerite

NAME _____ DATE _____

I Know Why the Caged Bird Sings by Maya Angelou

Answer each of the following questions in two or three complete sentences.

1. Why were Maya and her brother sent to their grandmother?

    _____

    _____

    _____

    _____

2. What role did religion play in Maya's childhood?

    _____

    _____

    _____

    _____

3. How did Maya's grandmother show great strength in coping with life?

    _____

    _____

    _____

    _____

4. Why did both children adore their mother?

    _____

    _____

    _____

    _____

5. What experiences in California greatly contributed to Maya's maturing?

    _____

    _____

    _____

    _____

CHALLENGE

Write an essay explaining how Maya Angelou as a child was like a caged bird. What experiences helped her to learn how to sing?

NAME _____ DATE _____

My Antonia by Willa Cather

In the numbered blanks at the left, write the letter of the matching person or place.

_____ 1. Wicked money lender who attacked Jim in the middle of the night

_____ 2. Jim's traveling companion on his first trip from Virginia to Nebraska

_____ 3. Was abandoned by the man that she was supposed to marry

_____ 4. Was greedy for the possessions of her neighbors

_____ 5. Became a great success as a designer of ladies fashions

_____ 6. Antonia's first employer

_____ 7. Antonia's little sister

_____ 8. Grandfather's Austrian hired man

_____ 9. Became head of the family after Antonia's father died

_____ 10. Jim's university friend and tutor

_____ 11. Prairie farmer who still longed for the bright lights of Vienna

_____ 12. Had a terrible fear of wolves

_____ 13. Looked after Antonia when her first child was born

_____ 14. Land from which Antonia's family came

_____ 15. Sent food to help her less fortunate neighbors

_____ 16. Was both a good musician and a good business woman

_____ 17. Became wealthy from a gold claim in the Klondike

_____ 18. Loved the natural beauty of the Nebraska prairies

_____ 19. Had played the violin in the old country

_____ 20. Town where Jim lived as an adolescent

A. Jake Marpole
B. Black Hawk
C. Otto Fuchs
D. Mr. Shimerda
E. Bohemia
F. Antonia
G. Jim Burden
H. Russian Pavel
I. Yulka
J. Mrs. Burden
K. Ambrosch
L. Widow Steavens
M. Lena Lingard
N. Gaston Cleric
O. Tiny Soderball
P. Wick Cutter
Q. Mrs. Harding
R. Francis Harding
S. Cuzak
T. Mrs. Shimerda

402

NAME _____ DATE _____

My Antonia by Willa Cather

Answer each of the following questions in two or three complete sentences.

1. As children, how did Jim and Antonia share the thrills of life on the prairie?

   _____
   _____
   _____
   _____

2. What hardships did Antonia experience as a child?

   _____
   _____
   _____
   _____

3. How did Antonia's life change when she came to work in town?

   _____
   _____
   _____
   _____

4. How did Lena Lingard succeed in getting off the farm?

   _____
   _____
   _____
   _____

5. When Jim returned twenty years later, why did he find peace and contentment in Antonia's home?

   _____
   _____
   _____
   _____

CHALLENGE
Write an essay describing the way that Jim Burden's relationship with Antonia was the shaping force of his whole life.

NAME _____ DATE _____

Cheaper by the Dozen
by Frank B. Gilbreth Jr. and Ernestine Gilbreth Carey

Place a (+) before each statement that is true and a (0) before each statement that is false.

_____ 1. Mr. Gilbreth was a short, slender man.

_____ 2. Dad was fond of playing jokes on his family.

_____ 3. Dad wanted a dozen children, but Mother did not want as many.

_____ 4. Each child in the Gilbreth family was given both discipline and a sense of self-respect.

_____ 5. The Gilbreths had five sons before any of their daughters were born.

_____ 6. All of the Gilbreth children were born at home.

_____ 7. Dad tried to apply all of the efficiency techniques to his family life.

_____ 8. "Foolish Carriage" was pulled by four horses.

_____ 9. Most of the Gilbreth children were dark-complexioned.

_____ 10. On their family trips, Dad frequently got lost because Mother gave him the wrong directions.

_____ 11. Mother usually presided at the family council meetings.

_____ 12. While Father was in the service, Mother took the children to visit her family in Boston.

_____ 13. "The Shoe" was the family's summer home in Nantucket.

_____ 14. Mother taught all of the children how to swim.

_____ 15. Father took most of the family photographs outside so that he could use natural light.

_____ 16. Dad enjoyed musicals, skits, and movies.

_____ 17. The films of the Gilbreth children's tonsil operations were a great success.

_____ 18. Each older child in the family was responsible for caring for some of the younger ones.

_____ 19. When Mr. Gilbreth died, all but two of the children were in college.

_____ 20. After her husband's death, Mrs. Gilbreth carried on his work.

NAME _____ DATE _____

Cheaper by the Dozen
by Frank B. Gilbreth Jr. and Ernestine Gilbreth Carey

Answer each of the following questions in two or three complete sentences.

1. Discuss the methods by which Mr. Gilbreth kept order in such a large family.

   _____

   _____

   _____

   _____

2. What were the basic differences between the father's personality and the mother's personality?

   _____

   _____

   _____

   _____

3. What were some of the special learning techniques that Mr. Gilbreth used with his children?

   _____

   _____

   _____

   _____

4. How did Dad react to the changes of styles and fashions in the 1920s?

   _____

   _____

   _____

   _____

5. How did Mother change after Dad died?

   _____

   _____

   _____

   _____

CHALLENGE
Discuss the aspects of the Gilbreth's home life which helped each of the children grow to become well-adjusted adults.

NAME _____ DATE _____

Life With Father by Howard Lindsay and Russel Crouse

Place a (+) before each statement that is true and a (0) before each statement that is false.

_____ 1. The play opens when the Days are having breakfast.

_____ 2. The family has employed the same maid for fifteen years.

_____ 3. Mrs. Day is very concerned about proper religious upbringing for her sons.

_____ 4. Father is a good host and enjoys having guests in his home.

_____ 5. Clarence and Whitney plan to go into business selling patent medicines.

_____ 6. Mother is better at keeping the household accounts straight than Father is.

_____ 7. Father agrees that Clarence may have one of his old suits altered to fit.

_____ 8. Cousin Cora first learns that Father has never been baptized.

_____ 9. Father willingly agrees to make a large contribution to Dr. Lloyd's church building fund.

_____ 10. Clarence and John accidentally poison their mother.

_____ 11. While Mother is ill, Father promises her that he will be baptized.

_____ 12. Dr. Lloyd agrees to baptize Father.

_____ 13. Clarence is able to pay for his new suit with the money that he has earned selling patent medicines.

_____ 14. Mary never writes to Clarence after she leaves New York.

_____ 15. Father gives Mother the pug China dog as an anniversary gift.

_____ 16. Mary and Cora return to the house on the day that Father is supposed to be baptized.

_____ 17. When he is wearing his own suit, Clarence is able to show his true feelings for Mary.

_____ 18. Father flatly refuses to go with Mother to the church.

_____ 19. Father presents Mother with a diamond ring as a token of his love.

_____ 20. At the end of the play, Father has again given in to Mother's wishes.

NAME _____ DATE _____

Life With Father by Howard Lindsay and Russel Crouse

Answer each of the following questions in two or three complete sentences.

1. How does Father's behavior constantly upset the servants?

   _____

   _____

   _____

   _____

2. What problems does Clarence have while he is wearing Father's suit?

   _____

   _____

   _____

   _____

3. How is Mother almost killed?

   _____

   _____

   _____

   _____

4. Why is Mother so very upset when she finds out that Father has never been baptized?

   _____

   _____

   _____

   _____

5. How does young Clarence finally declare his love for Mary?

   _____

   _____

   _____

   _____

CHALLENGE

Write an essay showing some ways that Mrs. Day shows her skill in the art of managing a husband.

How Green Was My Valley by Richard Llewellyn

In the numbered blanks at the left, write the letter of the matching person, place, or thing.

_____ 1. Stole the Morgans' prize turkeys

_____ 2. The social and religious center of the community

_____ 3. Young wife who went mad after marrying the wrong brother

_____ 4. Taught Huw the art of self-defense

_____ 5. Welsh festival of choral music

_____ 6. Leader of the union movement in the mines

_____ 7. Mine owner

_____ 8. Son who finally settled in Germany

_____ 9. Led the village choir when they sang before Queen Victoria

_____ 10. Spoke to the men who had been speaking against her husband

_____ 11. Schoolteacher who brutalized his students

_____ 12. Huw's first girlfriend

_____ 13. The narrator of the novel

_____ 14. Was dismissed from his post because he was thought to be morally unfit

_____ 15. Married for wealth and position instead of for love

_____ 16. Constantly working on engines and machines

_____ 17. Died in a mine cave-in

_____ 18. The real love of Huw's life

_____ 19. Wealthy heir to a mining fortune

_____ 20. Gossiping housekeeper whose tongue ruined two lives

A. Beth Morgan
B. Bronwen
C. Huw
D. Davy
E. Angharad
F. Marged Evans
G. Owen
H. Mr. Gruffydd
I. Ivor
J. Mr. Elias
K. Mr. Jonas
L. Mr. Evans
M. Dai Bando
N. Ceinwen
O. Gwilym Morgan
P. Eisteddfod
Q. Mrs. Nicholas
R. Ianto
S. Iestyn
T. Chapel

NAME _____ DATE _____

How Green Was My Valley by Richard Llewellyn

Answer each of the following questions in two or three complete sentences.

1. Describe how Huw saves his mother's life.

_____

_____

_____

_____

2. How does Mr. Gruffydd help Huw become a man?

_____

_____

_____

_____

3. Why does Huw find the National School to be a cruel place? What does he learn in this school about survival?

_____

_____

_____

_____

4. How are Mr. Gruffydd and Angharad victims of small-town mentality?

_____

_____

_____

_____

5. What are some of the ways that the families in the valley help and support each other?

_____

_____

_____

_____

CHALLENGE

How Green Was My Valley is a novel about Huw Morgan's growing-up experience. Discuss some of the joys and sorrows which come to Huw in his passage from childhood to manhood.

NAME _____ DATE _____

The Learning Tree by Gordon Parks

Select the letter of the word or phrase which correctly completes each statement.

_____ 1. The setting of the novel is (A) California (B) Kansas (C) Arkansas (D) Mississippi.

_____ 2. Big Mabel saves Newt from a (A) tornado (B) fire (C) blizzard (D) flood.

_____ 3. Clint's wife and children are saved from his drunken rages by (A) Judge Cavanaugh (B) Jack Winger (C) Sarah Winger (D) Sheriff Kirky.

_____ 4. Marcus Savage is sent to reform school for (A) stealing a car (B) stabbing Newt (C) attacking a teacher (D) beating up Jake Kiner.

_____ 5. Newt's interests include (A) music (B) literature (C) science (D) all of the above.

_____ 6. When Newt questions his mother about religion, she (A) tells him that he should not question God (B) is honest about her own doubts (C) sends him to see the minister (D) is angry with him.

_____ 7. The fairest white person in the novel is (A) Judge Cavanaugh (B) Miss McClintock (C) Sheriff Kirky (D) the superintendent of schools.

_____ 8. The father of Arcella's unborn child is (A) Beansey Fuller (B) Newt (C) Chauncey (D) Marcus Savage.

_____ 9. Newt's school guidance counselor advises him to (A) drop out of school (B) get as much education as he can (C) be content to know his place as a black (D) do his homework more faithfully.

_____ 10. Newt's cousin Polly has severe problems because (A) she looks white (B) she is a flirt (C) she is seriously ill (D) she cannot learn.

_____ 11. Newt sees the killing of Jake Kiner (A) from the barn loft (B) through the window (C) from behind the barn door (D) from inside the harness room.

_____ 12. Newt does not report the truth of the killing because (A) he is afraid of race riots (B) he fears Marcus Savage (C) he is afraid that his mother will punish him (D) he is afraid to appear in court.

_____ 13. The weapon used to kill Jake was a (A) gun (B) whip (C) knife (D) crowbar.

_____ 14. Marcus learns that his father killed Jake from (A) the liquor bottles (B) Newt (C) Booker himself (D) the sheriff.

_____ 15. Booker Savage also beat up (A) Newt (B) Silas (C) Mrs. Kiner (D) Jack Winger.

_____ 16. Booker Savage (A) was hanged (B) was shot by the police (C) killed himself (D) got a life prison sentence.

_____ 17. Newt comes to really understand death when he (A) sees Jake die (B) sleeps beside his mother's coffin (C) helps bring up the body of Doc Cheney (D) sees Tuck's body in the embalming room.

_____ 18. Newt has many deep discussions with (A) his uncle Rob (B) his father (C) his brother Pete (D) his science teacher.

_____ 19. Marcus Savage dies by (A) a gun shot (B) a fall into the river (C) a knife wound (D) being lynched.

_____ 20. At the end of the novel, Newt (A) is getting married (B) is killed (C) is going to live with his sister (D) is starting college.

NAME _____ DATE _____

The Learning Tree by Gordon Parks

Answer each of the following questions in two or three complete sentences.

1. What actions of Sarah Winger's show her tremendous strength of character?

   _____

   _____

   _____

   _____

2. Why does getting the black freshmen into the high school represent such a tremendous victory for the blacks?

   _____

   _____

   _____

   _____

3. What does Miss McClintock learn from her confrontation with Newt?

   _____

   _____

   _____

   _____

4. How does Newt show great courage at Silas Newall's trial?

   _____

   _____

   _____

5. How does the death of his mother change Newt's life?

   _____

   _____

   _____

   _____

CHALLENGE

Sarah Winger tells her son that Cherokee Flats is a "learning tree," with both good and bad fruit. Write an essay discussing the most significant lessons that Newt learns as he encounters the various types of "fruit" in the community.

NAME _____ DATE _____

A Day No Pigs Would Die by Robert Newton Peck

Correctly complete each sentence with information from the novel.

1. Robert was severely injured when he tried to _____.

2. The Pecks belonged to the _____ religious group.

3. Pinky was a gift from _____.

4. The story is set in the state of _____.

5. In history class, Robert becomes very confused about the story of Vermont hero

   _____.

6. Aunt Matty tried to tutor Robert in _____.

7. Robert's father earns the main portion of his living by _____.

8. Robert's father believes that the land is important because _____.

9. Tanner's twin bulls were named _____ and _____.

10. When the boys got into her strawberries, Mrs. Bascom _____.

11. Robert went with the Tanners to _____.

12. Two important things that happened at the fair were _____,

    and _____.

13. "To weasel a dog" meant _____.

14. Robert and Tanner tried to mate Pinky with _____.

15. Pinky had to be slaughtered because _____.

16. Robert's father knew that he _____.

17. At the time of his father's death, Robert was _____.

18. Robert found some scraps of paper on which his father _____.

19. At the funeral, Robert is most ashamed of _____.

20. The scene in which Robert is closest to his father is _____.

       150 Great Books

NAME _____ DATE _____

A Day No Pigs Would Die by Robert Newton Peck

Answer each of the following questions in two or three complete sentences.

1. How does Robert show great courage in his encounter with Apron, the cow?

_____

_____

_____

_____

2. Why does Robert's father insist that Robert stay in school?

_____

_____

_____

_____

3. How does this story show the closeness of the Shaker community?

_____

_____

_____

_____

4. Robert frequently misunderstands words or conversations. How do these misunderstandings provide humor in the story?

_____

_____

_____

_____

5. List three episodes when Robert learns about death. How do these episodes foreshadow the death of Robert's father?

_____

_____

_____

_____

CHALLENGE

Discuss the specific experiences which help Robert mature to manhood. How does Robert show this maturity when his father dies?

NAME _____ DATE _____

Our Town by Thornton Wilder

Place a (+) before each statement that is true and a (0) before each statement that is false.

_____ 1. The play begins at daybreak.

_____ 2. *Our Town* has a very elaborate set.

_____ 3. George Gibbs' main interest in school was in football.

_____ 4. Most of the people of Grovers' Corners are very content with small-town life.

_____ 5. Editor Webb narrates the action of the play and presents the author's philosophy to the audience.

_____ 6. George and Emily were childhood sweethearts.

_____ 7. The theme of *Our Town* is to find the importance of the ordinary.

_____ 8. The first act ends with the discussion of a letter that Rebecca had received from her minister.

_____ 9. The second act deals with love and marriage.

_____ 10. Mrs. Soames was Mrs. Webb's next-door neighbor.

_____ 11. Mr. Webb gave George a great deal of helpful advice about married life.

_____ 12. The stage manager assumes the role of the minister at George and Emily's wedding.

_____ 13. George intends to farm for a living.

_____ 14. The stage manager believes that marriage has religious significance.

_____ 15. Ten years elapse between Act I and Act II.

_____ 16. The dead remain very interested in the affairs of the living.

_____ 17. Emily asks to relive her twelfth birthday.

_____ 18. Emily's return is painful as she sees all that she failed to notice before.

_____ 19. George died before Emily did.

_____ 20. Even Emily's death represents a continuation of the life cycle.

NAME _____ DATE _____

Our Town by Thornton Wilder

Answer each of the following questions in two or three complete sentences.

1. What special powers does the stage manager possess?

_____

_____

_____

_____

2. How are the Webb and Gibbs families exactly alike?

_____

_____

_____

_____

3. Why does George change his mind about going to agriculture college?

_____

_____

_____

_____

4. Why is Simon Stimson a misfit in Grover's Corners?

_____

_____

_____

_____

5. What role does Nature play in *Our Town*?

_____

_____

_____

_____

CHALLENGE

In his essay, "A Platform and a Passion or Two," Thornton Wilder wrote that *Our Town* was "an attempt to find a value above all price for the smallest events in our daily life." Discuss some scenes in the play which show how valuable these small events really are.

NAME _____ DATE _____

The Glass Menagerie by Tennessee Williams

Correctly complete each sentence with information from the play.

1. The set of the play is designed to give the audience a feeling of _____.

2. Amanda had once had _____ gentleman callers in a single afternoon.

3. Laura's main problems are her _____ and her _____.

4. Amanda is very upset when she finds out that Laura _____.

5. Tom spends all of his evenings _____.

6. When she was supposed to be in school, Laura spent most of her time _____.

7. Amanda's greatest fear is that Laura _____.

8. Tom's father had _____.

9. To make some extra money, Amanda _____.

10. Amanda knows that Tom plans to leave when she finds a letter from _____.

11. Laura spends most of her time with _____ and _____.

12. Amanda says that one thing Tom's father had was plenty of _____.

13. Music comes to the Wingfield's apartment from _____.

14. The others think that Jim is an ambitious man because he _____.

15. Jim's nickname for Tom is _____ because Tom _____.

16. For Jim's visit, Amanda wears the dress that _____.

17. In high school, Jim had nicknamed Laura _____.

18. In the glass collection, the symbol for Laura herself is _____.

19. Amanda is very angry when she learns _____.

20. Wherever Tom traveled, he was haunted by _____.

NAME _____ DATE _____

The Glass Menagerie by Tennessee Williams

Answer each of the following questions in two or three complete sentences.

1. Why is Amanda so obsessed with the idea of a gentleman caller for Laura?

   _____

   _____

   _____

   _____

2. Why had Laura so admired Jim when they were in high school?

   _____

   _____

   _____

   _____

3. What does Tom mean when he says, "People go to the movies instead of moving."

   _____

   _____

   _____

   _____

4. How does Jim help Laura during his visit?

   _____

   _____

   _____

   _____

5. Why is Amanda so bitter toward her son at the end of the play?

   _____

   _____

   _____

   _____

CHALLENGE

Write an essay explaining how Amanda, Laura, and Tom are each locked in a trap of human desperation. How does each of them seek to escape from that trap?

NAME _____ DATE _____

The Effect of Gamma Rays on
Man-in-the-Moon Marigolds by Paul Zindel

Place a (+) before each statement that is true and a (0) before each statement that is false.

_____ 1. In the preface to the play, the author tells his readers that he has drawn the material for the plot from his own experience.

_____ 2. The set conveys an impression of neatness and order.

_____ 3. Beatrice frequently keeps Ruth home from school to look after Nannie.

_____ 4. Tillie is more physically attractive than Ruth is.

_____ 5. As the play opens, Beatrice is on the phone talking to the principal of Tillie's school.

_____ 6. Tillie's main school interests are in writing and dramatics.

_____ 7. Ruth is an epileptic.

_____ 8. Tillie is deeply offended when the other students laugh at her during the school assembly program.

_____ 9. Beatrice is horrified when she learns that Ruth smokes.

_____ 10. Beatrice constantly dreams of ways that she can make money.

_____ 11. Nannie is Beatrice's grandmother.

_____ 12. The rabbit is part of Tillie's project for the science fair.

_____ 13. Tillie is preparing a study of the effects of radiation on flowers.

_____ 14. Beatrice and Tillie share the repetition of a story about Beatrice's childhood.

_____ 15. Ruth is angry and jealous when Tillie is chosen as a finalist in the science fair.

_____ 16. Janice Vickery is Tillie's main competition in the fair.

_____ 17. Ruth finds out that Beatrice was the most popular girl in her high-school class.

_____ 18. When she plans to go to Tillie's program at the school, Beatrice's chief concern is for herself.

_____ 19. At the end of the play, Beatrice destroys Tillie's marigolds.

_____ 20. Tillie's mother has managed to destroy the child's belief in beauty and mental curiosity about the world.

NAME _____ DATE _____

The Effect of Gamma Rays on
Man-in-the-Moon Marigolds by Paul Zindel

Answer each of the following questions in two or three complete sentences.

1. How does Beatrice's home fit her personality?

_____

_____

_____

_____

2. Contrast the characters of Tillie and Ruth. What is the relationship between the two sisters?

_____

_____

_____

_____

3. What actions and words of Beatrice's show her inability to face reality?

_____

_____

_____

_____

4. What does the figure of Nannie represent?

_____

_____

_____

_____

5. What plans for herself and her daughters does Beatrice have at the end of the play?

_____

_____

_____

_____

CHALLENGE

A mutation is a biological variation produced by the work of specific genetic forces. Beatrice, Ruth, and Tillie are all personality "mutations." Write an essay to discuss the forces which have produced the changes in each of their characters.

ANSWER KEYS

A Death in the Family by James Agee

OBJECTIVE:

1. K	6. B	11. D	16. R
2. T	7. I	12. O	17. H
3. A	8. Q	13. G	18. S
4. F	9. C	14. E	19. P
5. N	10. J	15. M	20. L

SHORT ANSWER:

1. Jay—responsible for his family, happy, easy going. Ralph—unable to face any responsibilities, depressed, alcoholic, cannot handle his father's illness.
2. She gets up to fix his breakfast—he eats more than he really wants.
3. Mother—perfume, the swish of her skirts. Father—smell of shaving lotion and pipe. Both parents coming into his room at night.
4. Mary—passive acceptance of God's will. Andrew—little belief in God, questions the "why" of the accident.
5. Faced the reality of death—he let them see the funeral procession. Took them to hear the phonograph.

CHALLENGE:

Rufus senses the tension of the adults. Instinct to be quiet and to protect his little sister. Absorbs the feelings of the situation without understanding the reason.

Little Women by Louisa May Alcott

OBJECTIVE:

1. A	6. C	11. D	16. A
2. C	7. C	12. A	17. D
3. D	8. B	13. C	18. C
4. D	9. D	14. C	19. A
5. C	10. B	15. A	20. C

SHORT ANSWER:

1. Laurie became the brother that they didn't have.
2. People's lives matter more than things. Holding grudges makes no sense.
3. Her music helped heal his grief for the daughter he had lost.
4. That she had to look after her husband as well as the babies.
5. Real deep, caring love. Sharing of literature. Work together in the home for orphans.

CHALLENGE:

Values of family closeness and sharing. Each person respected for her individuality. Meg learns how empty vanity is. Real love with John Brooke. Jo the writer—Amy the artist—Beth the musician. They share good times, cope with difficulties. Main ingredient that author sees for a happy family is love with the power to cope with whatever comes.

I Know Why the Caged Bird Sings by Maya Angelou

OBJECTIVE:

1. J	6. Q	11. S	16. G
2. A	7. L	12. D	17. M
3. T	8. C	13. R	18. I
4. N	9. F	14. O	19. P
5. H	10. B	15. E	20. K

ANSWER KEYS (continued)

I Know Why the Caged Bird Sings by Maya Angelou (continued)

SHORT ANSWER:

1. Parents divorced. Neither of them wanted the children.
2. Very exciting church services, emotional outlet for black feelings. Humor of these comes through child's perception. Grandmother—very powerful religious faith.
3. Ran the store, stood up to the white trash, stabilizer for the children, figure of leadership in the community.
4. Flashy movie-star personality—gave them an exciting life and luxury unknown in Stamps.
5. Faces the jealousy of her father's girlfriend. Copes on drive down the mountain. Lives as a hobo in a used-car lot.

CHALLENGE:

Maya's spirit yearned to break free. Song in life came from the strength of her grandmother's teachings, relationship with Bailey, Mrs. Flowers' introducing her to poetry and literature.

My Antonia by Willa Cather

OBJECTIVE:

1. P	6. Q	11. S	16. R
2. A	7. I	12. H	17. O
3. F	8. C	13. L	18. G
4. T	9. K	14. E	19. D
5. M	10. N	15. J	20. B

SHORT ANSWER:

1. Love of the beauty of the prairie, exploring trips together, rattlesnake episode.
2. Hunger, lack of warm clothes, hard field work, father's suicide.
3. Better living conditions, easier work, social life with other young people.
4. Became a seamstress and a designer—escaped the farm entirely.
5. Comfortable farm home and children brought back memories of his Nebraska childhood.

CHALLENGE:

She was his ideal. Accomplishments really done for her. As Jim's world became more difficult, Antonia was his link with simplicity and beauty.

Cheaper by the Dozen by Frank B. Gilbreth Jr. and Ernestine Gilbreth Carey

OBJECTIVE:

1. 0	6. 0	11. 0	16. +
2. +	7. +	12. 0	17. 0
3. 0	8. 0	13. +	18. +
4. +	9. 0	14. 0	19. 0
5. 0	10. 0	15. 0	20. +

ANSWER KEYS (continued)

Cheaper by the Dozen by Frank B. Gilbreth Jr.
and Ernestine Gilbreth Carey (continued)

SHORT ANSWER:

1. Family meetings, father as benevolent dictator, emphasis on efficiency with each child having some responsibilities.
2. Father—blustery extrovert. Mother—quiet worker behind the scenes to get things done.
3. Used phonographs for lessons. Practical experiences of swimming, putting on plays and skits.
4. Shocked, as with bobbed hair, but forced to accept the inevitable.
5. Became much more outgoing—went on with Father's work.

CHALLENGE:

Each child given self-respect and responsibility. Learned to laugh and take crisis in stride. All were secure in family love, in spite of frequent confusion.

Life With Father by Howard Lindsay and Russel Crouse

OBJECTIVE:

1. +	6. 0	11. +	16. +
2. 0	7. +	12. 0	17. +
3. +	8. 0	13. 0	18. 0
4. 0	9. 0	14. 0	19. +
5. 0	10. +	15. 0	20. +

SHORT ANSWER:

1. Constantly yelling and throwing things. Very unpredictable.
2. He couldn't do anything that father would not have done.
3. Accidentally gets a large dose of the patent medicine that the boys are selling.
4. He won't go to heaven and they may not even be legally married.
5. He is able to kneel before her when he is wearing his own new suit.

CHALLENGE:

She handles his tantrums, convinces him to entertain Cousin Cora, does things first and tells him afterward. Gets around him by feigning stupidity, especially about money.

How Green Was My Valley by Richard Llewellyn

OBJECTIVE:

1. J	6. D	11. K	16. G
2. T	7. L	12. N	17. O
3. F	8. R	13. C	18. B
4. M	9. I	14. H	19. S
5. P	10. A	15. E	20. Q

ANSWER KEYS (continued)

How Green Was My Valley by Richard Llewellyn (continued)

SHORT ANSWER:

1. By carrying her home in a storm and saving her from drowning.
2. Took him to the mountains to appreciate nature, taught him what faith, love, and real masculine strength were.
3. Beaten and ridiculed for his dress, manners, and language. Learned how to defend himself. Learned the value of education.
4. Gossips said she was involved with Gruffydd. He was driven from his church.
5. Shared what they had when the mines were closed or on strike. Each family shared all joys and sorrows of the others.

CHALLENGE:

Joys—relationship with Mr. Gruffydd, winning scholarship, finding his manhood with Ceinwen. Sorrows—sadness in the deaths of Ivor and his father, leaves the valley after the departure of Gruffydd.

The Learning Tree by Gordon Parks

OBJECTIVE:

1. B	6. B	11. A	16. C
2. A	7. A	12. A	17. B
3. C	8. C	13. D	18. A
4. D	9. C	14. A	19. B
5. D	10. A	15. B	20. C

SHORT ANSWER:

1. Saving her daughter by calming her drunken son-in-law, leading the campaign to get the blacks into high school.
2. Town had to recognize that blacks and whites had equal rights to an education.
3. Realized the nature of her own prejudiced attitudes. Learned that blacks could rise above the stereotype.
4. Told the truth, even though it would affect the whole black community.
5. Childhood has ended. He will go to live with his sister.

CHALLENGE:

Good fruit—positive lessons about life (his mother, his uncle Rob, Jake Kiner, the high school principal). Bad fruit—negative lessons (Chauncy Cavanaugh, Marcus and Booker Savage). Lessons in moral practice learned in lives. Not what is said, but what is done.

A Day No Pigs Would Die by Robert Newton Peck

OBJECTIVE:

1. deliver Apron's calf	7. slaughtering pigs	12. showing the cattle, Pinky's winning a ribbon	16. was dying
2. Shaker	8. it gives a man his identity	13. dog and the weasel fight in a barrel	17. thirteen
3. Tanner	9. Bib and Bob	14. Tanner's boar	18. had been trying to write his name
4. Vermont	10. hit Robert with her broom	15. she couldn't breed	19. his clothes
5. Ethan Allen	11. Rutland Fair		20. the slaughtering of Pinky
6. English			

ANSWER KEYS (continued)

A Day No Pigs Would Die by Robert Newton Peck (continued)

SHORT ANSWER:

1. Helps the calf get born, gets the ball out of the cow's throat, even though he is seriously injured.
2. Education makes a man a first-class citizen.
3. Families help each other—Rob and his father with the burial of Hillman's grandchild. Also gossipy group—everyone knows everyone else's business.
4. Scene with Aunt Mattie—"tutor" and "tooter." At fair, thinks that "pervert" has to do with grammar.
5. The rabbit killed by the vulture, the death of Hillman's grandchild, the slaughter of the pig.

CHALLENGE:

Going to the fair, introduction to the outside world, his love for the pig, but having to give her up. Copes with the death of his father, makes funeral arrangements, prepares to head family.

Our Town by Thornton Wilder

OBJECTIVE:

1. +	6. +	11. 0	16. 0
2. 0	7. +	12. +	17. +
3. 0	8. +	13. +	18. +
4. +	9. +	14. +	19. 0
5. 0	10. 0	15. 0	20. +

SHORT ANSWER:

1. Move back and forth in time, predict the future, direct the actions of the on-stage characters.
2. Ordinary day's activities, concerns of family life and bringing up children.
3. He decides to live on his uncle's farm and marry Emily.
4. Drinks because he can't fit into the small-town value system. Bitter and angry because of failed life.
5. The moving force behind the universe. The great Reality to which all ordinary actions and thoughts are linked.

CHALLENGE:

Family life patterns—the young lovers, mother and daughter relationships. Wedding part of a larger pattern. Jane Crofut's letter linking Grover's Corners with the universe. Death part of the cycle as Emily died having a child. Emily's realization on her "return" of how wonderful life really is.

The Glass Menagerie by Tennessee Williams

OBJECTIVE:

1. being closed in, hazy memory
2. seventeen
3. lameness, shyness
4. has quit business college
5. at the movies
6. at the zoo, in the park
7. will have no one to provide for her
8. abandoned the family
9. sells magazine subscriptions
10. the Merchant Marine
11. glass animals, old phonograph records
12. charm
13. Paradise Dance Hall
14. goes to night school
15. Shakespeare, writes poetry at work
16. she had worn as a girl
17. Blue Roses
18. the unicorn
19. Jim is engaged
20. the image of Laura

424

ANSWER KEYS (continued)

The Glass Menagerie by Tennessee Williams (continued)

SHORT ANSWER:

1. Terrified that Laura will be left alone and helpless.
2. He was an athlete, played the lead in the school operettas.
3. So he can escape from the unpleasant realities of his life.
4. Makes her realize that she is worthwhile and special, brings her out of her shyness for a moment.
5. He runs out on them, just like his father did.

CHALLENGE:

Amanda trapped with no husband and Laura to provide for. Finds escape in her happy girlhood memories. Laura trapped by her own awkwardness—escape to phonograph records and glass animals. Tom—trapped by his need for travel, family responsibilities, and his mother's nagging. Leaves to join the Merchant Marine.

The Effect of Gamma Rays on Man-in-the-Moon Marigolds
by Paul Zindel

OBJECTIVE:

1. +	6. O	11. O	16. +
2. O	7. +	12. O	17. O
3. O	8. O	13. +	18. +
4. O	9. O	14. O	19. O
5. O	10. +	15. O	20. O

SHORT ANSWER:

1. Total clutter and confusion, reflects her life state of perpetual frustration.
2. Tillie—studious, quiet, dependable. Ruth—rebellious and flighty, much more like her mother. Ruth is really very proud of Tillie's accomplishments.
3. Constant escape to repetition of her imaginary childhood memories.
4. Death figure.
5. Open a tearoom, make money, be free.

CHALLENGE:

Beatrice—frustrated desires and repeated failure. Ruth seeming to follow her mother's pattern. Tillie—handicapped by circumstances, hurt by her mother's destructive tendencies, but still able to keep her mind alive and to believe in goodness.

UNIT 10

Moonlight and Roses—
Tales of LOVE and ROMANCE

SYNOPSES

Pride and Prejudice
by Jane Austen

Set in England near the beginning of the nineteenth century, Austen's masterpiece looks humorously at the pretensions of the English middle class. The Bennet family has five daughters and no sons. Silly Mrs. Bennet will stop at nothing to find husbands for her children. Jane, the paragon of goodness, falls in love with Mr. Bingley. Younger daughters Kitty and Lydia chase army officers, until Lydia elopes with the dubious Mr. Wickham. Only Mary, the student, is not interested in men at all. Elizabeth Bennet, the most strong-willed and sensible of the daughters, is the heroine of the story. She meets Mr. Darcy whom she dislikes immediately because of his snobbery. After rejecting the proposal of fawning Mr. Collins, Elizabeth must help Jane cope with Bingley's rejection. In spite of herself, Elizabeth is attracted to Darcy. Darcy saves the family from disgrace by seeing that Lydia and Wickham are provided for. Finally the marriage game is successfully concluded. Jane and Bingley are reunited; Elizabeth and Darcy are happily wed. He has softened his pride. She has gotten over her prejudice against him. Austen's amusing comedy of the manners of a society that she knew well attacks social hypocrisy on all levels.

Wuthering Heights
by Emily Brontë

This romance of passion is set on the windswept English moors. Nellie Dean, the housekeeper, tells Mr. Lockwood, who has recently arrived to rent the Grange and has visited Wuthering Heights, the story of the families who have inhabited the two houses. Catherine Earnshaw, whose father owned Wuthering Heights, loves the wild orphan Heathcliff. Heathcliff runs away when he is mistreated by Catherine's brother Hindley. Heathcliff later returns to take control of the estate. In the meantime, Catherine has married Edgar Linton of the Grange. Heathcliff marries Edgar's sister, Isabella. Still lovers, Catherine and Heathcliff continue to meet on the wild moors. Isabella runs away, taking her son Linton. Catherine dies, leaving Edgar with a daughter, Cathy. When Linton returns to Wuthering Heights, Cathy defies her father and meets Heathcliff's son. Heathcliff wants the two to marry so he can control both estates. The marriage is a disaster, and Cathy remains a prisoner at Wuthering Heights until Heathcliff's death. When Heathcliff dies, he is buried beside Catherine. This complex novel of misdirected passion will be most appreciated by good readers.

Madame Bovary
by Gustave Flaubert

Her imagination fired by a sheltered convent upbringing and a diet of romantic novels, Emma marries mundane physician Charles Bovary. Charles is a good man, but totally fails to satisfy his wife's passionate nature. One night at a grand ball makes Emma further despise her ordinary husband. Emma has two lovers: artistic Léon and aristocratic Rodolphe. Emma and Rodolphe plan to run away, but at the last minute he abandons her. Emma goes deep into debt to finance her secret affair with Léon. They meet once a week, while Emma's husband believes that she is traveling to the city to take music lessons. When she cannot pay the bills she has contracted for, Emma buys arsenic from the village chemist and commits suicide. After Emma's death, Charles finds packets of letters from both her lovers. This great French classic shows a woman in love with the romantic ideals of love, and who cannot be satisfied with what she has.

The Peacock Spring
by Rumer Godden

Set in lush, romantic India in the 1930s, this novel is the romance between a young poet and a British diplomat's daughter. Sir Edward Gwitham brings his two children, Una and Hal, to live with him at the consulate in Delhi. Fifteen-year-old Una meets young Ravi, a handsome poet who is working on the estate as a gardener. As the two share literature and love, Una encourages Ravi to seek the Tagore prize for excellence in poetry. Una's enemy is Alexis Lamont, the Eurasian housekeeper with dark secrets in her past, who wants to marry Sir Edward. Una learns of Alexis' double life and uses the information to blackmail her. Hal, meanwhile, has become involved with Vikram, a dashing young cavalry officer. When Una discovers she is pregnant, she and Ravi decide to elope. Una cannot cope with the realities of the crowds and smells of Indian common life. Sir Edward goes after the couple and brings Una back. After she has a miscarriage, Una realizes that she and Ravi must return to their two totally different worlds. This romance is well-written, combining fine characterizations with excellent descriptions of the land and people of British India.

The Return of the Native
by Thomas Hardy

This romance of Wessex is the ill-fated love story of Clym Yoebright and Eustacia Vye. The action is played against the backdrop of brooding Egdon Heath, which the author almost personifies to become a character in the story. Bored with her rather common lover Damon Wildeve, Eustacia Vye plots to meet handsome Clym Yoebright, the promising native of Egdon, who is expected to return from Paris. Meanwhile, Wildeve is forced into marrying Clym's cousin Thomasin, after Damon had lured the girl away on a pretense of elopement. Eustacia is determined to marry Clym and to escape to the romantic world beyond Egdon. Clym loves the place, and has decided to become a teacher to his people. Seeing that her son is totally captivated by Eustacia's wild beauty, Mrs. Yoebright tries to stop the marriage. The older lady quarrels with her son, and she and Eustacia become enemies. When Clym's eyes fail, shortly after he and Eustacia are married, the bride is trapped on Egdon Heath. Wildeve, now married to Thomasin, again becomes attractive to Eustacia because he has inherited some money. Diggory Venn, the faithful reddleman who loves Thomasin, plots to keep Wildeve from betraying his wife. When Clym's mother dies from heat exhaustion because Eustacia does not open the door, Clym accuses his wife of murder and leaves her. Although Clym relents, his letter proposing a reconciliation is never delivered. As she goes to meet Wildeve on a dark rainy night, Eustacia falls into a weir. She drowns, and Wildeve is drowned trying to save her. Clym alone survives with his grief. Only the grim Egdon Heath remains unchanged, brooding above the actions of insignificant humanity.

Mistress of Mellyn
by Victoria Holt

This novel is another which combines a Cinderella story with a strange mystery. When Martha Leigh goes to Mount Mellyn to become governess to Alvean, Martha is fascinated with the house and its master, Connan. Mysteries surround the place as Martha begins to probe the death of Alice, Connan's first wife. She is also intrigued by the strange child, Gilly, granddaughter of the housekeeper. Peter and Celestine Nansellock, neighbors and family friends, also become involved in the mysteries. Martha believes that Connan intends to marry wealthy Lady Treslyn. She is horrified when she begins to believe that Connan is involved in the death of Lady Treslyn's husband. On a trip to Penzance, Connan declares his love for Martha. That love turns to fear, however, when Martha learns that the body Connan had identified was not his wife's. The novel ends in a hidden passage of the mansion. Celestine, wanting Connan for herself, had killed Alice and attempts to kill Martha. Martha is rescued by Gilly. The couple then can live happily ever after in the best romantic tradition.

Beloved Invader
by Eugenia Price

The novel opens as Anson Dodge goes to St. Simons Island, Georgia. He plans to oversee the family lumber business and to prove to himself that he is not like his father. After he meets Horace Gould and his daughter Anna, Anson is determined to make his home on St. Simons, and to rebuild the church, which had been destroyed by Yankee soldiers. After Anson's beloved wife Ellen dies while they are honeymooning in India, Anson determines to dedicate his life and his church work to Ellen's memory. Horace Gould becomes a second father to the confused young man, and helps Anson to find real faith in God. Some of the islanders resent Anson's work and are determined to destroy him. As time passes, Anson falls in love with Anna Gould and the couple are married. Their lives are again shattered when their only son is killed by a runaway horse. As Anson Dodge comes to terms with his own grief, he can minister to the people of the island with a message that provides real answers for the hard questions of life. The beautiful descriptions of Georgia add greatly to the characterizations and themes of this book.

Ethan Frome
by Edith Wharton

This love story is set in grim Starkfield, Vermont in the late 1800s. A young engineer is fascinated by Ethan Frome's appearance when the taciturn man drives him to the train. The outsider later learns Ethan's story from Mrs. Hale, the young man's landlady. Ethan had married his wife Zenobia because he was lonely after his mother died. Zeena is a stern hypochrondriac. When Mattie Silver, Zeena's cousin, comes to live with the Fromes, Ethan finds in her presence a new dimension of life and love. Ethan and Mattie secretly declare their love for each other in rare stolen moments. Zeena sets a trap for the lovers by leaving them alone overnight. When she returns, Zeena is determined to get rid of Mattie. Ethan shows his weakness of character. He cannot abandon Zeena, and yet he is too weak to openly declare his love for Mattie. Rather than be separated, the lovers decide to make a suicide run into an old elm tree. The attempt fails, leaving the lovers in a living hell. Later, after he has heard Mrs. Hale's story, the young engineer sees for himself the crippled shrew who was once the beautiful Mattie Silver.

NAME _____ DATE _____

Pride and Prejudice by Jane Austen

Correctly complete each sentence with information from the novel.

1. Mrs. Bennet's main objective in life was _____.

2. Elizabeth's closest friend was _____.

3. Because the Bennets had no son, when Mr. Bennet died their property would go to
_____.

4. Kitty and Lydia were primarily interested in _____
_____.

5. Mr. Bingley's estate at which the Bennets were entertained was named _____
_____.

6. When Elizabeth first met Darcy, she found him objectionable because _____
_____.

7. Caroline Bingley wants to marry _____.

8. The person whose real character most totally fools Elizabeth is _____.

9. Darcy's estate in Derbyshire is called _____.

10. After Elizabeth rejects Mr. Collins' proposal, he marries _____.

11. The relatives most helpful to the Bennet girls were _____.

12. Elizabeth learns from _____ that Darcy had been responsible
for Mr. Bingley's leaving Jane.

13. The first time Darcy proposes to Elizabeth, she _____.

14. Darcy writes to Elizabeth to explain _____
and _____.

15. Lady Catherine intends for Darcy to marry _____.

16. Lydia embarrasses her entire family by _____.

17. Wickham's marriage to Lydia is made possible by arrangements made by _____
_____.

18. The relative of Darcy's who is most pleased by his marriage to Elizabeth is _____
_____.

19. The estate of Lady Catherine is named _____.

20. The two sisters who still remain close after they marry are _____
and _____.

NAME _____ DATE _____

Pride and Prejudice by Jane Austen

Answer each of the following questions in two or three complete sentences.

1. What are the strengths and weaknesses of Elizabeth Bennet's personality?

   _____

   _____

   _____

   _____

2. How is Elizabeth different from Jane?

   _____

   _____

   _____

   _____

3. Why is Elizabeth frequently embarrassed by her mother's behavior?

   _____

   _____

   _____

   _____

4. How does the author make fun of the stupidity of Collins and Lady Catherine?

   _____

   _____

   _____

   _____

5. How does Lydia's marriage indirectly aid the marriage prospects of Elizabeth and Jane?

   _____

   _____

   _____

   _____

CHALLENGE

Write an essay describing the change in Elizabeth's attitude toward Mr. Darcy. What are some of the circumstances which cause her to realize her prejudices and to alter her opinions?

150 Great Books

NAME _____ DATE _____

Wuthering Heights by Emily Brontë

Place a (+) before each statement that is true and a (0) before each statement that is false.

_____ 1. Most of the story is narrated by Mrs. Dean.

_____ 2. Mr. Earnshaw adopted Heathcliff because he had no children of his own.

_____ 3. Joseph is the only character who never moves away from Wuthering Heights throughout the entire story.

_____ 4. The entire narrative of the novel spans a period of about twenty years.

_____ 5. Nellie Dean moved from Wuthering Heights to the Grange when Heathcliff and Isabella were married.

_____ 6. Edgar Linton had no idea that his wife was still in love with Heathcliff.

_____ 7. After Hindley Earnshaw's death, Heathcliff treated Hareton as if the boy were his own son.

_____ 8. Catherine died when her daughter was born.

_____ 9. After Catherine's marriage to Edgar, Heathcliff became a frequent visitor at the Grange.

_____ 10. When Isabella ran away from her husband, she left her young son Linton with Edgar.

_____ 11. Cathy seemed to inherit her mother's passionate desire for forbidden love.

_____ 12. Ellen acted as chaperone when Cathy went to visit Linton.

_____ 13. Cathy treated Hareton with exactly the same kind of scorn that her mother had shown toward Heathcliff.

_____ 14. Lockwood and Heathcliff never met.

_____ 15. Nellie was the only witness at the wedding of Cathy and Linton.

_____ 16. Linton outlived his father by two decades.

_____ 17. Edgar Linton refused to allow Heathcliff to be buried beside Catherine.

_____ 18. Heathcliff allowed Cathy and Linton to continue living at Thrushcross Grange after they were married.

_____ 19. Cathy moved to London after Heathcliff's death.

_____ 20. The natives around Wuthering Heights believed that the moors were haunted by the ghosts of Catherine and Heathcliff.

NAME _____ DATE _____

Wuthering Heights by Emily Brontë

Answer each of the following questions in two or three complete sentences.

1. How does the treatment that Heathcliff received when he was a child help to explain his later actions?

   _____

   _____

   _____

   _____

2. In what ways are Catherine and her daughter alike?

   _____

   _____

   _____

   _____

3. Why does Catherine marry Edgar, even though she still loves Heathcliff?

   _____

   _____

   _____

   _____

4. Why is Heathcliff so determined that Cathy and Linton will marry?

   _____

   _____

   _____

   _____

5. Why is Lockwood important to the story?

   _____

   _____

   _____

   _____

CHALLENGE

The destiny of a character is determined in part by the choices that he or she makes. Discuss which choices made by Catherine, Isabella, and Cathy had more influence on their destinies than the force and power of Heathcliff did.

NAME _____ DATE _____

Madame Bovary by Gustave Flaubert

Correctly complete each sentence with information from the novel.

1. Emma was educated in _____.

2. Charles first met Emma when he _____.

3. Emma and Charles attended a grand ball at _____.

4. Emma waltzed at the ball with _____.

5. The town that the Bovarys first lived in was _____.

6. Emma gradually came to despise her husband because _____.

7. Because of Emma's discontent, Bovary moved his practice to _____.

8. Bovary seriously hurt his medical practice when he operated to _____

    _____.

9. The chemist who posed as Bovary's friend while trying to destroy him was _____

    _____.

10. Emma first met Léon Dupuis when he was _____.

11. The coach on which Emma regularly traveled to Rouen was named _____.

12. Emma first met Rodolphe at _____.

13. Emma and Rodolphe made plans to _____.

14. At the last minute, Rodolphe _____.

15. After Rodolphe's departure, Emma _____.

16. Emma and Léon met again at _____.

17. In order to finance her love affair, Emma continually borrowed money from _____

    _____.

18. In desperation, Emma tried to borrow and was refused by _____.

19. When the financial disaster struck, Emma _____.

20. After Emma's death, Charles found _____.

NAME _____ DATE _____

Madame Bovary by Gustave Flaubert

Answer each of the following questions in two or three complete sentences.

1. What experiences in her early life helped to feed Emma's romantic fantasies?

   _____

   _____

   _____

   _____

2. Why did Emma find her marriage to Charles so totally unsatisfactory?

   _____

   _____

   _____

   _____

3. Why did Rodolphe abandon Emma?

   _____

   _____

   _____

   _____

4. How was Emma able to fool Charles while she carried on her love affair with Léon?

   _____

   _____

   _____

   _____

5. How was Emma able to obtain arsenic from the chemist's?

   _____

   _____

   _____

   _____

CHALLENGE

Write an essay discussing whether Emma Bovary was a victim of unhappy and unfortunate circumstances, or a victim of her own foolish nature.

NAME _____ DATE _____

The Peacock Spring by Rumer Godden

In the numbered blanks at the left, write the letter of the matching person, place or thing.

_____ 1. Medical student, Ravi's closest friend

_____ 2. The wise older gardener

_____ 3. Senior diplomat for the United Nations

_____ 4. American friend of Sir Edward, is aware of Alexis' intentions

_____ 5. Does not want her nieces to go to India

_____ 6. Servant falsely accused of stealing liquor

_____ 7. Tells Sir Edward where Ravi and Una have gone

_____ 8. Headmistress at Cerne

_____ 9. Alexis' former lover, Hal's romantic idol

_____ 10. Pretty romantic twelve-year-old

_____ 11. Horse which Una refuses to ride

_____ 12. Exclusive British girls' school

_____ 13. Eurasian woman who wants to marry for security and social status

_____ 14. A constant source of embarrassment to her daughter

_____ 15. Indian writer for whom the poetry prize was named

_____ 16. Sir Edward's chauffeur

_____ 17. Friend of Mrs. Lamont, whom Alexis must keep silent

_____ 18. Setting for the novel

_____ 19. Young poet seeking his identity

_____ 20. Young girl who becomes a woman

A. Ganesh
B. Ravi Bhattacharya
C. Halcyon
D. Mrs. Carrington
E. Cerne
F. Una
G. Aunt Frederica
H. Alexis Lamont
I. Chinaberry
J. Sir Edward Gwithiam
K. Delhi
L. Mrs. Lamont
M. Vikram
N. Mrs. Porter
O. Mouse
P. Hem
Q. Tagore
R. Dino
S. Lobo
T. Srimati Bhattacharya

NAME _____ DATE _____

The Peacock Spring by Rumer Godden

Answer each of the following questions in two or three complete sentences.

1. Why does Sir Edward want his daughters to join him in India? Why do others feel that this is a mistake?

   _____

   _____

   _____

   _____

2. Contrast Hal and Una in appearance and personality.

   _____

   _____

   _____

   _____

3. How does Alexis Lamont lead a double life?

   _____

   _____

   _____

   _____

4. How does Una force Alexis not to tell Sir Edward about Una's relationship with Ravi?

   _____

   _____

   _____

5. How does the author use the physical descriptions and customs of India as background for the account of Ravi and Una's elopement?

   _____

   _____

   _____

   _____

CHALLENGE

Write an essay describing the character maturation of Una Gwithiam. What are some of the major events of the novel which contribute to her transformation from a girl into a young woman?

NAME _____ DATE _____

The Return of the Native by Thomas Hardy

In the numbered blanks at the left, write the letter of the matching person or place.

_____ 1. Weak, vain man who found Eustacia fascinating

_____ 2. Landscape well-suited to humanity's gloomy moods

_____ 3. Character who represents totally unselfish love

_____ 4. Town where Clym planned to set up his school

_____ 5. Let Eustacia take his role in the Christmas play

_____ 6. Needed constant excitement and passionate love

_____ 7. Captain Vye's home

_____ 8. Large, elevated mound of land

_____ 9. Lowest occupation in Egdon society

_____ 10. Lost to Wildeve in a gambling match

_____ 11. Left work as a diamond merchant to become a teacher

_____ 12. Married Wildeve to save her reputation

_____ 13. Reported a dying woman's last words

_____ 14. Clym and Eustacia's home after their wedding

_____ 15. Elderly leader of the common people

_____ 16. Mrs. Yoebright's residence

_____ 17. Failed to deliver Clym's letter to his wife

_____ 18. Tried to practice black magic on Eustacia

_____ 19. Area of England where the story takes place

_____ 20. Died believing that she had been rejected by her son

A. Egdon Heath
B. Johnny Nunsuch
C. Charlie
D. Granfer Cantle
E. Rainbarrow
F. Clym Yoebright
G. Susan Nunsuch
H. Thomasin
I. Diggory Venn
J. Eustacia Vye
K. Wessex
L. Reddleman
M. Blooms-End
N. Mrs. Yoebright
O. Wildeve
P. Captain Vye
Q. Christian Cantle
R. Budmouth
S. Mistover Knap
T. Alderworth

NAME _____ DATE _____

The Return of the Native by Thomas Hardy

Answer each of the following questions in two or three complete sentences.

1. Why does Mrs. Yoebright feel that her son's decision to marry Eustacia is very unwise?

   _____

   _____

   _____

   _____

2. Why does Eustacia find Clym so very attractive?

   _____

   _____

   _____

   _____

3. Why is Clym's blindness so difficult for Eustacia to accept?

   _____

   _____

   _____

   _____

4. Why does Eustacia again turn to Wildeve after she had previously rejected him?

   _____

   _____

   _____

   _____

5. Did Eustacia deliberately jump into the weir, or did she fall in accidentally? Give reasons for your opinion.

   _____

   _____

   _____

   _____

CHALLENGE

The Return of the Native is a novel based on a series of character contrasts. Write a brief contrast of each of the following pairs of characters.

    A. Wildeve and Clym   C. Wildeve and Venn

    B. Thomasin and Eustacia   D. Eustacia and Mrs. Yoebright

                        150 Great Books

NAME _____ DATE _____

Mistress of Mellyn by Victoria Holt

Place a (+) before each statement that is true and a (0) before each statement that is false.

_____ 1. Martha Leigh is an only child.

_____ 2. The story is told by a first-person narrator.

_____ 3. Martha first meets Peter Nansellock on the train.

_____ 4. Connan had been able to clearly identify Alice's body after she was killed in the train wreck.

_____ 5. Mrs. Polgrey is a very pleasant, efficient housekeeper.

_____ 6. Alvean at first is a very difficult pupil for Martha to teach.

_____ 7. Martha is very conscious of her position as a governess in the household.

_____ 8. Alvean learns to ride, primarily to please Miss Leigh.

_____ 9. On the night of the Christmas ball, Martha realizes that she has fallen in love with Connan TreMellyn.

_____ 10. Martha learns the truth about Alvean's birth from Mrs. Polgrey.

_____ 11. The jeweler in the village is able to verify the information that Martha had found in Alice's diary.

_____ 12. Connan blames Martha when Alvean is injured at the horse show.

_____ 13. Martha gladly accepts Peter's gift of the horse, Jacinth.

_____ 14. Martha overhears Connan and Lady Treslyn plotting to murder Lady Treslyn's husband.

_____ 15. Gilly believes that Miss Leigh is Alice TreMellyn.

_____ 16. Miss Jansen was guilty of the theft of Lady Treslyn's bracelet.

_____ 17. Celestine had a thorough knowledge of the architecture of Mount Mellyn.

_____ 18. Lady Treslyn tried to kill Martha.

_____ 19. Gilly saved Martha's life.

_____ 20. Martha is telling this story to us and to her grandchildren when she is an old lady.

NAME _____ DATE _____

Mistress of Mellyn by Victoria Holt

Answer each of the following questions in two or three complete sentences.

1. Why does Martha have very mixed feelings when she first meets Connan TreMellyn?

   _____
   _____
   _____
   _____

2. How do the riding lessons change Martha's relationship with Alvean?

   _____
   _____
   _____
   _____

3. What part do weather and nature description play in building the suspense in the novel?

   _____
   _____
   _____
   _____

4. Why does Martha's happiness change to fear and confusion when she and Connan return home from Penzance?

   _____
   _____
   _____
   _____

5. What was Celestine's motive for killing Alice? Why does she want to kill Martha in the same way?

   _____
   _____
   _____
   _____

CHALLENGE

Mistress of Mellyn is a first-person point-of-view novel. As the protagonist tells her own story, the reader sees the strengths and weaknesses of Martha's character. Write an essay describing her major character strengths. How do these strengths contribute to advancing the plot of the novel?

NAME _____ DATE _____

The Beloved Invader by Eugenia Price

Correctly complete each sentence with information from the novel.

1. Anson's nickname for his mother was _____.

2. The Dodge family business on St. Simons Island was _____.

3. The family member most in favor of Anson's marriage to Ellen was _____.

4. Anson wanted to see his father to _____.

5. Anna saves Procter's life when he _____.

6. Anson and Ellen had gotten acquainted at _____.

7. Anson Dodge Sr. deserted his family and went to _____.

8. _____ became Anson's substitute father.

9. The poet _____ described the beauty of St. Simons marshlands.

10. The church on St. Simons had been destroyed by _____.

11. The name of the Gould home was _____.

12. Before she left on her honeymoon, Ellen gave Anna _____.

13. Ellen died of _____ in _____.

14. The islanders who most resented Anson and his work were _____.

15. Emma Bass tried to _____.

16. Ellen Dodge was buried _____.

17. The name of Anson's assistant pastor was _____.

18. The greatest joy of Anna's life was _____.

19. Anna found answers to her questions about life and death by _____.

20. Anna fulfilled Anson's dream by making their large home a _____.

150 Great Books

NAME _____ DATE _____

Beloved Invader by Eugenia Price

Answer each of the following questions in two or three complete sentences.

1. In what ways was Anson Dodge Jr. just like his father?

_____
_____
_____
_____

2. When did Anson discover the calling that God had given him?

_____
_____
_____
_____

3. What were Anna Gould's feelings about St. Simons Island?

_____
_____
_____
_____

4. What accusations did Emma Bass bring against Anson?

_____
_____
_____
_____

5. How was little Anson killed?

_____
_____
_____
_____

CHALLENGE

Describe the development of Anson Dodge from an impetuous boy into a mature man of courage and faith. What experiences were important steps in this development?

NAME _____ DATE _____

Ethan Frome by Edith Wharton

Select the letter of the word or phrase that correctly completes each statement.

_____ 1. The opening section of the story is narrated by (A) Zeena (B) Mattie (C) Ethan (D) an outsider.

_____ 2. Ethan and the young engineer get acquainted (A) when Ethan drives the young man to the train (B) at Denis Eady's store (C) when Zeena invites the young man to lunch (D) at Mrs. Hale's.

_____ 3. The landscape at Starkfield is (A) sterile (B) cold (C) harsh and rough (D) all of the above.

_____ 4. The engineer goes to Ethan's home (A) to inspect some lumber (B) to get shelter from the storm (C) to collect an overdue bill (D) to meet Zeena.

_____ 5. Ethan's desire for more education had been ended by (A) his father's death (B) lack of money (C) his marriage (D) his lack of intellect.

_____ 6. Ethan goes to the dance (A) to walk Mattie home (B) to escort Zeena (C) to dance with Mattie (D) to discuss business with Mr. Hale.

_____ 7. Mattie gave Ethan (A) warmth (B) color (C) sensitivity (D) all of the above.

_____ 8. Mattie came to live with the Fromes because (A) Zeena was ill (B) Ethan's mother was ill (C) her father's death had left her penniless (D) Ethan's brother asked him to take Mattie in.

_____ 9. The greatest character contrast of the novel is built between (A) Mattie and Ruth (B) Ethan and Dennis (C) Mattie and Zeena (D) Ethan and the engineer.

_____ 10. Ethan's main income came from (A) cattle (B) lumber (C) coal (D) maple sugar.

_____ 11. Zeena goes away overnight (A) to visit her Aunt Martha (B) to do some shopping (C) to consult a new doctor (D) to hire a new maid.

_____ 12. Ethan had married Zeena (A) for her money (B) because he loved her (C) from loneliness (D) because his mother wanted him to.

_____ 13. Ethan did not collect the lumber money from Hale (A) because Hale was stingy (B) because Ethan was proud (C) because Jotham had made a mistake in the bookkeeping (D) because Hale's wife was ill.

_____ 14. Mattie is contrasted to Zeena in (A) light (B) color (C) disposition (D) all of the above.

_____ 15. The symbol of Zeena's presence at the supper table is (A) the cat (B) the pickle dish (C) the rocking chair (D) all of the above.

_____ 16. Zeena uses the new doctor's advice as (A) a way to get more medicine (B) an excuse to blame Ethan for her ill health (C) an excuse to get rid of Mattie (D) a way to make the people in the village pity her.

_____ 17. Ethan's feelings for Mattie may best be described as (A) love (B) protectiveness (C) possessiveness (D) all of the above.

_____ 18. Zeena's fury against Mattie is focused on (A) the broken pickle dish (B) her sloppy mending (C) the missing towels (D) her careless housework.

_____ 19. Ethan cannot run away with Mattie because (A) he cannot abandon Zeena (B) he has no money (C) he is not sure that he could provide for Mattie (D) all of the above.

_____ 20. The real tragedy of Ethan and Mattie's suicide attempt is that (A) both of them survived (B) Mattie is killed (C) Ethan is killed (D) Zeena loses her mind.

NAME _____   DATE _____

Ethan Frome by Edith Wharton

Answer each of the following questions in two or three complete sentences.

1. How is the landscape of Starkfield appropriate to the characters' situations?

_____

_____

_____

_____

2. How does Mattie Silver's arrival change Ethan's life?

_____

_____

_____

3. How is the relationship between Ethan and Mattie contrasted with the relationship between Ned Hale and Ruth Varnum?

_____

_____

_____

_____

4. How is the house different for Ethan on the evening of Zeena's absence?

_____

_____

_____

_____

5. Why do Mattie and Ethan attempt suicide? Why do they fail?

_____

_____

_____

_____

CHALLENGE

Discuss the ways in which Ethan Frome is the victim of fate, and the ways in which he is responsible for his own problems.

150 Great Books

ANSWER KEYS

Pride and Prejudice by Jane Austen

OBJECTIVE:

1. getting her daughters married
2. Charlotte Lucas
3. Mr. Collins
4. army officers
5. Netherfield Park
6. proud, insulting, he refused to dance with anyone
7. Darcy
8. Wickham
9. Pemberly
10. Charlotte
11. Aunt and Uncle Gardner
12. Colonel Fitzwilliam
13. strongly refuses him
14. why he told Bingley not to marry Jane, the truth about Wickham's character
15. her daughter
16. eloping with Wickham
17. Darcy
18. Georgianna
19. Rosins
20. Elizabeth and Jane

SHORT ANSWER:

1. Strengths—forthright, independent spirit, good wit, family loyalty. Weakness—jumps to conclusions, forms opinions based on appearances.
2. Jane—passive, the model of perfection, almost too good. Elizabeth—apt to question and take action, much more a living character.
3. Talks all the time about their lack of money and getting husbands for her daughters—no tact or social graces.
4. Lady Catherine—total upper class boor. Collins—the fawner over the patron who provides his money.
5. Darcy arranges for Wickham's funds, bring Bingley back to Jane. Elizabeth changes her mind when she finds out about Darcy's help.

CHALLENGE:

First meeting—finds Darcy harsh and proud. Change begins with Darcy's letter explaining his side of the situation. Attracted to him at Lady Catherine's and on the visit to his estate. Comes to really care for him when he helps the family by helping Jane and Lydia.

Wuthering Heights by Emily Brontë

OBJECTIVE:

1. +	6. 0	11. +	16. 0
2. 0	7. 0	12. 0	17. 0
3. +	8. +	13. +	18. 0
4. +	9. +	14. 0	19. 0
5. 0	10. 0	15. 0	20. +

SHORT ANSWER:

1. Treated like an animal by Hindley. Desire to get revenge.
2. Both did exactly as they pleased. Defied social conventions and found excitement in forbidden love.
3. Heathcliff had run away. Edgar was attentive and available.
4. So he can own both Wuthering Heights and the Grange.
5. He is the outsider to whom the main plot of the novel is told in flashbacks.

CHALLENGE:

Defiant nature of the personality contributes to the disaster: Catherine with Heathcliff after her marriage, Isabella defied her brother, young Cathy ran away from Nellie to meet with Linton. Each woman chooses the dangerous, not the safe and acceptable.

ANSWER KEYS (continued)

Madame Bovary by Gustave Flaubert

OBJECTIVE:

1. a convent
2. set her father's leg
3. Chateau Vaubyssard
4. a Viscount
5. Tostes
6. he was rough and ordinary
7. Yonville
8. experiment in an operation on a man with a club foot
9. Homais
10. a law clerk
11. Hirondelle
12. an agricultural fair
13. run away together
14. abandoned her
15. had an emotional breakdown
16. the theater
17. Lheureux
18. Rodolphe
19. took poison
20. her love letters from Rodolphe and Léon

SHORT ANSWER:

1. Education in the convent, romantic novels, one evening at the grand ball.
2. He is boring and dull, content with small-town experience. Emma wants something grander.
3. Wants no responsibilities or entangling relationships.
4. Pretends that she is going to the city for piano lessons.
5. Goes to the chemist for rat poison, then eats the arsenic herself.

CHALLENGE:

Emma a victim of her own chronic discontent. Refuses what she has that is good. Money lender leads her into a financial trap by continued temptation with luxury. Finally trapped by her own actions. Neither of her lovers will really satisfy her. Suicide last romantic act of selfishness.

The Peacock Spring by Rumer Godden

OBJECTIVE:

1. P
2. A
3. J
4. N
5. G
6. R
7. T
8. D
9. M
10. C
11. O
12. E
13. H
14. L
15. Q
16. I
17. S
18. K
19. B
20. F

SHORT ANSWER:

1. He wants their company. The girls will be taken away from a structured, organized life and education.
2. Hal—pretty, vivacious. Una—quiet, serious, gentle, more mature.
3. Supported her mother and Lobo secretly. Stole from the embassy supplies and blamed the thefts on the servants.
4. By threatening to destroy Alexis' relationship with Sir Edward through the truth about Alexis' actions.
5. Terrible crowded train conditions, heat, flies, filthy food and water. Mobs along the rivers—worship of sacred animals.

CHALLENGE:

Romance with Ravi springs from their mutual love of poetry and beauty. Ripens into love. Una is pregnant—they elope. Realize that their love cannot compensate for the difference in their worlds. Una has a miscarriage. Returns to rightful life in England. Grieving, but matured by experience.

ANSWER KEYS (continued)

The Return of the Native by Thomas Hardy

OBJECTIVE:

1. O	6. J	11. F	16. M
2. A	7. S	12. H	17. P
3. I	8. E	13. B	18. G
4. R	9. L	14. T	19. K
5. C	10. Q	15. D	20. N

SHORT ANSWER:

1. She is noted for being independent and wild, not an Egdon native.
2. He has come from exotic Paris.
3. She is trapped with no way out. He is reduced to being a common laborer.
4. He now has money and is handsomely dressed—offers her an escape.
5. (Answers will vary.) If she jumped—final act of defiance. If she fell in, the last act of an unjust and irrational Chance.

CHALLENGE:

Wildeve—rogue with no responsibility. Clym—total caring and loyalty. Thomasin—country girl, satisfied with the simple. Eustacia—constant craving for grand excitement and passion. Wildeve and Venn—total faithlessness versus unselfish, sacrificing love. Eustacia and Mrs. Yoebright—used Clym for her own purpose, versus genuine love that is willing to sacrifice.

Mistress of Mellyn by Victoria Holt

OBJECTIVE:

1. 0	6. +	11. +	16. 0
2. 0	7. +	12. 0	17. +
3. +	8. 0	13. 0	18. 0
4. 0	9. +	14. 0	19. +
5. +	10. 0	15. +	20. +

SHORT ANSWER:

1. Finds him mysterious, but fascinating. Is annoyed by his apparent indifference to Alvean.
2. Mutual respect—a secret pact between them as Alvean learns to please her father.
3. Darkness, fog, the sinister presence of the sea.
4. She learns that the body was not Alice. Begins to fear that Connan is a murderer.
5. In both cases Celestine wanted the estate and Connan for herself.

CHALLENGE:

Determination and common sense—keeps her head when Alvean falls. Curiosity about Alice—tracing information in the diary. Tries to be level-headed even when she is in love. Genuine concern for Alvean's welfare and caring for Gilly.

450

ANSWER KEYS (continued)

Beloved Invader by Eugenia Price

OBJECTIVE:

1. Queen Victoria
2. lumbering
3. Rebecca
4. be sure that he was not like his father
5. was bitten by a snake
6. their grandparents' golden wedding party
7. Canada
8. Horace Bunch Gould
9. Lanier
10. Yankee soldiers
11. Black Banks
12. a seagull
13. cholera, India
14. PT and Emma Bass
15. burn the house down
16. under the church altar
17. Rev. Winn
18. her son
19. reading Ellen's letters
20. home for boys

SHORT ANSWER:

1. Headstrong, determined, impulsive.
2. When he sees the ruined church, determines to restore it and minister to its people.
3. Loves every inch of the place.
4. Of trying to attack her when he came on a pastoral call.
5. In a wagon with runaway horses.

CHALLENGE:

Conscious decision to be different from his father. Desire to serve. Marriage to Ellen. Recovery after her death. Horace as a substitute father figure. Marriage to Anna. Strengthening of his own faith so that he in turn could comfort others.

Ethan Frome by Edith Wharton

OBJECTIVE:

1. D
2. A
3. D
4. B
5. A
6. A
7. D
8. C
9. C
10. B
11. C
12. C
13. B
14. D
15. A
16. C
17. D
18. A
19. A
20. A

SHORT ANSWER:

1. Cold, bleak, closed-in.
2. She brought light and color into his dark life.
3. Ethan and Mattie must hide. Ruth's and Ned's love can be out in the open.
4. Mattie has stamped the whole meal with the joy and youthfulness of her personality.
5. They have no other way to keep from being separated forever. Ethan swerves the sled at the last moment.

CHALLENGE:

Forced to cut short his education because of his mother's illness. Trapped into marrying Zeena because he was lonely. Too much of a sense of responsibility to abandon Zeena for his love. Too weak to stand up to Zeena to help Mattie.

ADDITIONAL TITLES
for Student Readings

Designations indicate the unit (1-10) in which each title belongs. A title may fit more than one designation. Letters indicate reading level: (E) Easy, (M) Medium, (D) Difficult.

Author	Title	Level	Unit
Auchincloss, Louis	*The Rector of Justin*	M	7
Bolt, Robert	*A Man for All Seasons*	M	3
Blackmore, R.D.	*Lorna Doone*	M	10, 1
Bradbury, Ray	*The Martian Chronicles*	M	4
Conrad, Joseph	*Lord Jim*	D	1
Cooper, James F.	*The Last of the Mohicans*	D	1
Dana, Richard Henry	*Two Years Before the Mast*	M	1
Delderfield, R.H.	*To Serve Them All My Days*	D	7
Donovan, J.R.	*PT109*	E	1
Doyle, Sir Arthur Conan	*The Hound of the Baskervilles*	M	8
Dumas, Alexander	*The Count of Monte Cristo*	M	1
Faulkner, William	*Intruder in the Dust*	M	5
Golding, William	*The Lord of the Flies*	M	1
	Go Ask Alice	E	5
Head, Anne	*Mr. and Mrs. Bo Jo Jones*	E	10
Heidish, Marcy	*A Woman Called Moses*	M	5
Hemingway, Ernest	*The Sun Also Rises*	M	3
Kaufmann, Belle	*Up the Down Staircase*	E	7
Kennedy, John F.	*Profiles in Courage*	M	7
Kipling, Rudyard	*Captains Courageous*	M	1
Laurents, Arthur	*The Turning Point*	E	7
Michener, James	*The Bridges at Toko-Ri*	E	1, 3
O'Brien, Robert	*Z for Zachariah*	E	2, 4
O'Connor, Frank	*The Last Hurrah*	M	3,7
Peck, Richard	*Something for Joey*	E	6
Rawlings, Marjorie	*The Yearling*	E	2, 9
Richter, Conrad	*The Light in the Forest*	M	2,3
Sayers, Gale	*I Am Third*	E	6, 7
Steinbeck, John	*The Grapes of Wrath*	M	3, 5
Stevenson, Robert Louis	*Kidnapped*	M	1
Uris, Leon	*Mila 18*	D	3, 6
Verne, Jules	*20,000 Leagues Under the Sea*	M	4
Wallace, Lew	*Ben Hur*	D	3
Woodward, R.H. and Bernstein	*All the President's Men*	M	7
Wells, H.G.	*The Time Machine*	M	4

INDEX OF TITLES

The letter designation beside each title indicates the type of literature.

F—Fiction   NF—Non-Fiction   D—Drama

	AUTHOR	TITLE	PAGE
NF	Adamson, Joy	*Born Free*	8
F	Agee, James	*A Death in the Family*	395
F	Alcott, Louisa May	*Little Women*	397
D	Anderson, Maxwell	*Elizabeth the Queen*	101
NF	Angelou, Maya	*I Know Why the Caged Bird Sings*	399
D	Anouilh, Jean	*Becket*	103
D	Archibald, William	*The Innocents*	361
F	Asimov, Isaac	*The Fantastic Voyage*	147
F	Austen, Jane	*Pride and Prejudice*	430
D	Bagnold, Enid	*The Chalk Garden*	363
F	Borland, Hal	*When the Legends Die*	53
F	Bradbury, Ray	*Fahrenheit 451*	149
NF	Braithwaite, E.R.	*To Sir with Love*	185
F	Brontë, Charlotte	*Jane Eyre*	55
F	Brontë, Emily	*Wuthering Heights*	432
F	Buck, Pearl S.	*The Good Earth*	187
F	Cather, Willa	*My Antonia*	401
D	Chase, Mary	*Harvey*	151
F	Christie, Agatha	*And Then There Were None*	367
D	Christie, Agatha	*The Mousetrap*	369
F	Clark, Mary Higgins	*Where Are the Children?*	365
F	Clarke, Arthur C.	*2001: A Space Odyssey*	153
NF	Cleland, Max	*Strong at the Broken Places*	240
F	Cormier, Robert	*I Am the Cheese*	191
F	Cormier, Robert	*The Chocolate War*	189
NF	Cousteau, Jacques-Yves	*Life and Death in a Coral Sea*	299
D	Coward, Noel	*Blithe Spirit*	155
F	Crane, Stephen	*The Red Badge of Courage*	10
F	Craven, Margaret	*I Heard the Owl Call My Name*	242
NF	Creamer, Robert W.	*Babe: The Legend Comes to Life*	301
F	Dickens, Charles	*A Tale of Two Cities*	105
F	Dickens, Charles	*Great Expectations*	57
F	Du Maurier, Daphne	*Jamaica Inn*	371
F	Du Maurier, Daphne	*Rebecca*	373
F	Fast, Howard	*April Morning*	107
NF	Fast, Howard	*Citizen Tom Paine*	303
F	Ferber, Edna	*Cimarron*	109
F	Fitzgerald, F. Scott	*The Great Gatsby*	111
F	Flaubert, Gustave	*Madame Bovary*	434
F	Fleischer, Leonore	*Ice Castles*	244
F	Forbes, Esther	*Johnny Tremain*	113

INDEX OF TITLES (continued)

	AUTHOR	TITLE	PAGE
F	Forester, C.S.	*The African Queen*	1
F	Frank, Pat	*Alas, Babylon*	159
F	Gaines, Ernest J.	*The Autobiography of Miss Jane Pittman*	193
NF	Gibson, Althea	*I Always Wanted to Be Somebody*	305
D	Gibson, William	*The Miracle Worker*	246
NF	Gilbreth, Frank Jr. and Ernestine Gilbreth Carey	*Cheaper by the Dozen*	403
F	Godden, Rumer	*The Peacock Spring*	436
D	Goldman, James	*The Lion in Winter*	115
F	Goudge, Elizabeth	*Green Dolphin Street*	14
F	Greenberg, Joanne	*I Never Promised You a Rose Garden*	248
F	Greene, Bette	*The Summer of My German Soldier*	59
NF	Griffin, John Howard	*Black Like Me*	195
F	Guest, Judith	*Ordinary People*	250
NF	Gunther, John	*Death Be Not Proud*	252
D	Hamilton, Patrick	*Angel Street (Gas Light)*	375
NF	Hampshire, Susan	*Susan's Story*	254
D	Hansbury, Lorraine	*A Raisin in the Sun*	197
F	Hardy, Thomas	*The Return of the Native*	438
F	Hawthorne, Nathaniel	*The House of the Seven Gables*	117
F	Hawthorne, Nathaniel	*The Scarlet Letter*	119
F	Heinlein, Robert	*Stranger in a Strange Land*	159
D	Hellman, Lillian	*The Little Foxes*	199
F	Hemingway, Ernest	*The Old Man and the Sea*	256
NF	Herriot, James	*All Creatures Great and Small*	307
F	Hilton, James	*Lost Horizon*	161
F	Hinton, S.E.	*Tex*	61
F	Holt, Victoria	*Mistress of Mellyn*	440
F	Huxley, Aldous	*Brave New World*	163
F	Jewett, Sarah Orne	*The Country of the Pointed Firs*	121
F	Kafka, Franz	*The Metamorphosis*	63
NF	Keller, Helen	*Teacher: Anne Sullivan Macy*	309
D	Kesselring, Joseph	*Arsenic and Old Lace*	377
F	Keyes, Daniel	*Flowers for Algernon*	258
F	Knowles, John	*A Separate Peace*	65
F	Landorf, Joyce	*Joseph*	311
D	Lawrence, Jerome and Robert E. Lee	*Auntie Mame*	313
D	Lawrence, Jerome and Robert E. Lee	*Inherit the Wind*	201

INDEX OF TITLES (continued)

	AUTHOR	TITLE	PAGE
F	Lee, Harper	*To Kill a Mockingbird*	203
F	Lewis, C.S.	*The Lion, the Witch, and the Wardrobe*	165
F	Lewis, Sinclair	*Main Street*	205
D	Lindsay, Howard and Russel Crouse	*Life with Father*	405
F	Lipsyte, Robert	*The Contender*	315
F	Llewellyn, Richard	*How Green Was My Valley*	407
F	London, Jack	*The Call of the Wild*	16
NF	Lord, Walter H.	*Day of Infamy*	18
NF	Lord, Walter H.	*A Night to Remember*	20
NF	Lund, Doris	*Eric*	260
F	Marshall, Catherine	*Christy*	67
F	McCullers, Carson	*The Heart Is a Lonely Hunter*	69
D	McCullers, Carson	*The Member of the Wedding*	71
NF	Meir, Golda	*My Life*	317
F	Melville, Herman	*Moby Dick*	22
D	Miller, Arthur	*The Crucible*	207
D	Miller, Arthur	*The Death of a Salesman*	319
F	Miller, Walter M.	*A Canticle for Leibowitz*	167
NF	Mowat, Farley	*Never Cry Wolf*	24
F	Orwell, George	*Animal Farm*	209
NF	Oursler, Fulton	*The Greatest Story Ever Told*	321
F	Parks, Gordon	*The Learning Tree*	409
F	Pasternak, Boris	*Doctor Zhivago*	123
F	Paton, Alan	*Cry, the Beloved Country*	211
D	Patrick, John	*The Teahouse of the August Moon*	323
F	Peck, Robert Newton	*A Day No Pigs Would Die*	411
NF	Plimpton, George	*The Paper Lion*	325
F	Potok, Chaim	*The Chosen*	73
F	Potok, Chaim	*My Name Is Asher Lev*	327
F	Price, Eugenia	*The Beloved Invader*	442
NF	Rather, Dan with Mickey Herskowitz	*The Camera Never Blinks*	329
F	Remarque, Erich Maria	*All Quiet on the Western Front*	26
F	Roberts, Kenneth	*Rabble in Arms*	28
D	Rose, Reginald	*Twelve Angry Men*	213
NF	Russell, Bill	*Go Up for Glory*	331
F	Salinger, J.D.	*The Catcher in the Rye*	75
NF	Savitch, Jessica	*Anchorwoman*	333
F	Sayers, Dorothy L.	*Clouds of Witness*	379
F	Schaefer, Jack	*Shane*	77
NF	Schoor, Gene	*Babe Didrikson: The World's Greatest Woman Athlete*	335

INDEX OF TITLES (continued)

	AUTHOR	TITLE	PAGE
F	Scott, Sir Walter	*Ivanhoe*	30
D	Serling, Rod	*Requiem for a Heavyweight*	262
F	Seton, Anya	*The Winthrop Woman*	125
D	Shaw, George Bernard	*Pygmalion*	337
D	Simon, Neil	*The Odd Couple*	79
F	Solzhenitsyn, Alexander	*One Day in the Life of Ivan Denisovich*	264
F	Spark, Muriel	*The Prime of Miss Jean Brodie*	339
D	Spigelgass, Leonard	*A Majority of One*	215
F	Steinbeck, John	*Cannery Row*	266
F	Steinbeck, John	*The Pearl*	268
F	Stevenson, Robert Louis	*Treasure Island*	32
F	Stewart, Mary	*Nine Coaches Waiting*	381
D	Synge, John M.	*The Playboy of the Western World*	341
NF	Ten Boom, Corrie	*The Hiding Place*	217
F	Tolkien, J.R.R.	*The Hobbit*	169
D	Thompson, Ernest	*On Golden Pond*	270
F	Updike, John	*Rabbit, Run*	81
F	Uris, Leon	*Exodus*	127
NF	Valens, E.G.	*The Other Side of the Mountain*	272
F	Villasenor, Edmund	*Macho*	83
F	West, Jessamyn	*The Friendly Persuasion*	129
F	Wharton, Edith	*Ethan Frome*	444
F	Wharton, Edith	*The House of Mirth*	343
F	White, T.H.	*The Once and Future King*	34
F	Wilder, Thornton	*The Bridge of San Luis Rey*	274
D	Wilder, Thornton	*Our Town*	413
D	Wilder, Thornton	*The Skin of our Teeth*	276
D	Williams, Tennessee	*The Glass Menagerie*	415
F	Wister, Owen	*The Virginian*	36
D	Wouk, Herman	*The Caine Mutiny Court-Martial*	131
F	Wright, Richard	*Native Son*	219
D	Zindel, Paul	*The Effects of Gamma Rays on Man-in-the-Moon Marigolds*	417